Selected Readings in
Quantitative Urban Analysis

Selected Readings in Quantitative Urban Analysis

EDITED BY

SAMUEL J. BERNSTEIN

and

W. GILES MELLON

PERGAMON PRESS

OXFORD · NEW YORK · TORONTO · SYDNEY
PARIS · FRANKFURT

U.K.	Pergamon Press Ltd., Headington Hill Hall, Oxford OX3 0BW, England
U.S.A.	Pergamon Press Inc., Maxwell House, Fairview Park, Elmsford, New York 10523, U.S.A.
CANADA	Pergamon of Canada Ltd., 75 The East Mall, Toronto, Ontario, Canada
AUSTRALIA	Pergamon Press (Aust.) Pty. Ltd., 19a Boundary Street, Rushcutters Bay, N.S.W. 2011, Australia
FRANCE	Pergamon Press SARL, 24 rue des Ecoles, 75240 Paris, Cedex 05, France
FEDERAL REPUBLIC OF GERMANY	Pergamon Press GmbH, 6242 Kronberg-Taunus, Pferdstrasse 1, Federal Republic of Germany

First edition 1978

British Library Cataloguing in Publication Data
Selected readings in quantitative urban analysis.
1. Municipal research—Addresses, essays, lectures
I. Bernstein, Samuel Joshua. II. Mellon, W. Giles
301.36   HT110   77-30458
ISBN 0-08-019593-8 (Hard cover)
ISBN 0-08-019592-X (Flexi cover)

Typeset by Cotswold Typesetting Ltd.

Printed in Great Britain by Glevum Press Ltd., Gloucester

Contents

V. Urban Politics and Policy

Preface

One of the most important developments in recent years has been the evolution of quantitative approaches to the solution of the nation's urban problems. The purpose of this volume is to introduce the student of urban problems to this development, and to provide the urban administrator with a review of the most recent advances in urban model building. The literature in this area is by now extensive, and it would have been possible to assemble a traditional book of readings. We have, however, followed an alternative approach. First, an outline of the major areas of urban life, which have been analyzed in a quantitative manner, was laid out. The areas chosen for inclusion were:

Overall urban models.

Urban models dealing with the basic economic factors of urban life—workers and jobs, housing, and transportation.

Urban models dealing with the provision of basic services—education, health care, fire, police, water, and sanitation.

Urban models dealing with the provision of the luxuries of urban life—the theater, ballet, symphony.

Urban models, dealing not with a basic factor in urban life, but with how the decisions to provide these factors are made—the process of policy formulation and the resolution of conflicting priorities.

Following this outline, a number of distinguished economists, political scientists, and operations research specialists were commissioned to write new individual chapters on each topic—chapters which presented the original contributions of each author and/or reviewed the present state of the art in each speciality. With this format, an individuality is inevitable which would not be as prevalent in a book of selected readings. But, by the same token, that individuality imparts a distinctive character which no book of readings could convey. It is our hope that both the beginning student and the experienced urban administrator will, after the completion of this volume, come away with a broad appreciation of where the field of quantitative urban analysis stands in 1975—of what has been done and of what remains to be done.

Acknowledgements

We would like to thank the authors who cooperated in making this book possible. They suffered along with us in many ways including the special requests for rewrites, delays, and other inevitable obstacles related to the production of a multi-authored work. Their patience with us is acknowledged and appreciated. Mr. Deegan, formerly of Pergamon Press, was equally encouraging and always reminded us when the going got rough of our initial objective of producing a first-rate book.

Mr. Harry Starr, President of the Littauer Foundation, stands in a singular position of importance for our endeavors. His support of our quantitative urban research at Baruch College of the City University of New York, of which this volume is a part, helped make this book possible. We are grateful to be associated with the work of this foundation since it supported some of the earliest and finest quantitative applications in the social sciences: the *Statistics of Deadly Quarrels* of the late Professor Lewis Richardson. We hope this volume continues in the tradition of Richardson and makes a significant contribution to understanding the scope of quantitative analysis in urban studies.

Last but not least, we thank our respective wives, Deena and Kate, for their patience, forbearance, and encouragement in the many mutual endeavors which, over the years, have led to many fruitful outcomes.

New York City   SAMUEL J. BERNSTEIN
July 1976   W. GILES MELLON

PART I

Urban Modeling: An Introduction and Critique

1. *Urban Modeling: An Introduction to, and Critique of, Large-scale Models*

SAMUEL J. BERNSTEIN AND W. GILES MELLON

I. Introduction[1]

Only a few years ago the concept of urban modeling—representation of urban reality through systems of mathematical relationships—scarcely existed. Now an explosion has taken place, as quantitatively oriented researchers from such fields as operations research, economics, and public administration have realized that techniques, long used in business or in the military, are applicable to urban problems, and conversely, that the need for efficient techniques to replace traditional means of planning and management in the urban area is critical, given the crisis atmosphere now prevailing in the nation's cities. The purpose of this introductory chapter is twofold: first, to serve as an introduction to the basic topic of model-building; and second, to illustrate the basic principles of urban model-building by reference to a number of particular models. As the chapters which follow deal exclusively with applications to specific aspects of the urban scene, it was thought appropriate that this initial chapter consider only large-scale models of the city as an overall, integrated system.

II. Urban Models: Classification[2]

Urban models may first be classified in terms of the broad functions for which they are designed. In general, we may discriminate between four broad functional purposes for these models, although of course, the same model may serve several purposes. These are:

1. Descriptive-analytical, where the main interest in modeling is to *understand* how the urban system works.
2. Projective, where the main purpose is to be able to *predict* conditions within the urban area at some future date.

---

[1] For general surveys of the field of urban modeling, see: Maurice D. Kilbridge, Robert P. O'Block, and Paul V. Teplitz, *Urban Analysis*, Boston, Graduate School of Business Administration, Harvard University, 1970; Colin Lee, *Models in Planning*, New York, Pergamon Press, 1973; Samuel J. Bernstein, Editor, *Proceedings of an International Seminar on Urban Planning and Management Information Systems*, Jerusalem, Iltam, 1974; Ira S. Lowry, "Seven models of urban development: a structural comparison", Santa Monica, The Rand Corporation, 1967; G. C. Hemmens, Editor, *Urban Development Models*, Highway Research Board, Special Report No. 97 91968; D. B. Lee, Jr., *Models and Techniques for Urban Planning*, Buffalo, Cornell Aeronautical Laboratory, 1968; D. Sweet, *Models of Urban Structure*, New York, Lexington Books, 1972.

[2] Discussion in this section follows the classification scheme developed in: Samuel J. Bernstein, W. Giles Mellon, and Sigmund Handelman, "Regional stabilization: a model for policy decision". *Policy Sciences* 4 (1974). See also Ira S. Lowry, "A short course in model design". *Journal of the American Institute of Planning*, May 1965.

3. Policy oriented, where the main purpose of the model is to be able to *simulate* the effects of alternative policy moves and obtain an accurate read-out of resulting urban conditions.

4. Gaming, where a main purpose is usually to expose the players to the complexities of urban decision-making as a *learning* process.

Secondly within these classes, urban models differ widely in their scope of subjects and their degree of detail. Thus, some models have attempted to deal with the city or its suburbs as a whole, while others have concentrated on one area, such as transportation systems. Within a given scope of subjects, the degree of detail has ranged widely. Some models, for example, have been pitched at an extreme degree of abstraction, describing urban development generally. Others have gone into detail, reaching down as far as block-by-block results for a particular city.

Thirdly, urban models, once a specific function and scope of coverage have been determined, differ widely as to their specific mathematical form. Given, however, that we do not accept anything but a concrete mathematical formulation as being a model, the following broad classes of models have been developed.

1. Classical and modern theories of location. Having its beginning in the classic nineteenth-century economic treatise, *The Isolated State* by Johann von Thunen, location theory is an attempt to explain the physical position of economic activity, depending basically on an analysis of transportation costs. The modern classic in this area is August Losch's, while a comprehensive treatment or location theory is given in the works of Walter Isard.[3]

2. Physical analogy models, which attempt to explain population behavior in terms of Newtonian physics. This approach was pioneered by Princeton physicist John Q. Stewart.[4]

3. Economic-sociological models which attempt to explain location and movement of population and industry in terms of economic and social factors. A good example of this type of approach is given in the Lowry model, where each household or business firm is conceived as having an equation which relates the value of its present location as a function of its own preferences and the attributes of the site. During a decision period, each establishment considers all possible sites, prices them, and bids on them with the highest bidder receiving the location. Owners of sites, on the other hand, may alter the value of their location by a process of investment.[5]

Fourthly, and finally, models which have been developed differ in the specific type of mathematics employed—ranging from the use of systems of linear equations with the coefficients determined by the use of econometric methods[6] to the continuous mathematics utilized in the models developed by J. W. Forrester.[7] Whatever their mathematical form, however, the models developed to this point have been designed for solution through the use of electronic computers. To our knowledge, no models have been set up for solution or demonstration through analog computers.

[3] August Losch, *The Economics of Location*, New Haven: Yale University Press, 1954; Walter Isard, *Location and Space-Economy*, New York: John Wiley, 1956.

[4] John Q. Stewart, "Demographic gravitation: evidence and applications". *Sociometry* (Feb. and May 1948).

[5] Ira S. Lowry, *A Model of Metropolis*, Santa Monica, The Rand Corporation, 1964; also, William Goldner, "The Lowry Model heritage". *Journal of the American Institute of Planners*, (Mar. 1971).

[6] David R. Bradford and Harry H. Kelejian, "An econometric model of the flight to the suburbs", Princeton, Econometric Research Program, *Research Memorandum No. 116* (Oct. 1970).

[7] J. W. Forrester, *Urban Dynamics*, Cambridge: MIT Press, 1969.

III. Urban Models: Some Examples[8]

To give our discussion of overall urban models some concrete form, a number of such models were reviewed. As Fig. 1 illustrates, a wide choice of examples are available. From the available set, five models were chosen to be summarized here: the choice was made in a manner which would illustrate the current state of the art.

Name of model or author	Development year	Area of application
1. Lowry	1963	Pittsburgh Community renewal project (CRP)
2. TOMM (time oriented metropolitan model)	1964	Pittsburgh CRP
3. Bass I, II, III	1965–1968	Bay Area Simulation Study
4. PLUM (Projective Land use model)	1968	Bay Area Transportation Study Commission
5. Garin–Lowry	1966	Theoretical extension of Lowry
6. CLUG (Cornell land use game)	1966	Gaming simulation model for educational purposes
7. TOMM II	1968	Extension of TOMM
8. Wilson	1968	Theoretical extension of Lowry
9. Cripps and Foot	1969	Bedford, Reading
10. Batty	1969–1970	Nottingham–Derby, Lancaster
11. SCANCAP	1965–1967	New Haven
12. SCANPED	1968–1969	Denver
13. NUCOMS (New community simulator)	1971–1972	Dept. of Housing & Urban Development, Park Forest South, Stansbury Park
14. PROMUS	1970–1972	Toronto
15. Nottinghamshire model	1971–1972	City of Nottingham and County of Nottinghamshire

Fig. 1. List of Urban Models

Taken from Dilip R. Limaye and Donald F. Blumberg, "Systems for urban planning and management", *8th Annual Urban Symposium*, Association for Computing Machinery, New York, 1972.

1. *The Lowry Model*—developed by the Rand Corporation.
2. *The Detroit Model*—being developed by the National Bureau of Economic Research.
3. *The Urban Performance Model*.
4. *The Regional Stabilization Model*—Bernstein and Mellon for the City of Newark.
5. *The Promus Model*—for the City of Toronto.

1. THE LOWRY MODEL[9]

A. *General description*

The Lowry model focuses on three interrelated urban systems: (1) Employment, (2) Population, and (3) Transportation, which interconnects the previous two. Employment is segmented into (a) a basic sector corresponding to production industries in the Central

---

[8] Material in this section follows that developed in Bernstein, *op. cit.*, note 1.
[9] Cf. works cited, note 5.

Business District; (b) a service sector corresponding to retail shopping in various neighborhood subareas. Population is considered as an aggregated sector constituted by household units with one breadwinner per household. The distribution of households in subareas is carried out by a distribution function based on a gravity model. The transportation network is similarly homogeneous. Only cost and distance factors are considered as affecting transport decisions.

B. *Listing of variables*

   Exogenous:

1. Subarea distribution of employment used by the export industry.
2. Amount of usable land in each subarea.
3. Space occupied by export industry in each subarea.
4. Retail production functions: fixed amounts of space and labor required per customer in each retail line.
5. Air distances between subareas.
6. Labor force participation rates.

   Endogenous:

7. Population by subareas.
8. Subarea total employment.

C. *Constraints*

1. Minimum size required for each retail cluster.
2. Minimum market size for subareas which justify a retail operation.
3. Maximum population densities, in subareas.

D. *Procedure*

1. The export employment is determined at the subarea level.
2. Labor force participation rates are employed to yield the number of households needed to produce the employment in export industries.
3. Work–home trip distribution function is used to distribute these households. This is based on the distances between subareas and subject to the population density constraint.
4. Number of households in each subarea determines whether retail services will be opened in that area. If the minimum market size constraint is not met, these households are reallocated to other places.
5. Production functions of retail services are used to determine space and labor required for the retail clusters in each subarea.
6. The number of households needed for retail labor is determined by using a similar procedure to the one described in step 2 above.
7. A work trip distribution function is used again for distributing the households of retail related employees.

The iterative procedure begins with step 1 and proceeds through step 7. This is repeated until sums of retail employment and population per subarea converge to the known totals for the region or the increments become statistically negligible.

A flow chart of model's procedures is shown in Fig. 2.

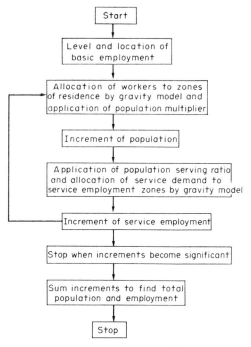

Fig. 2. Lowry model.[10]

E. *Evaluation*

1. The Lowry model is a highly theoretical and abstract formulation, and the prototype for many subsequent urban models. The model tries to explain city development: it is not primarily designed for policy analysis.

2. Various externalities are ignored in this model, which seem essential for policy analysis. For example:

    (a) Race.
    (b) Income.
    (c) Family size.

3. Similarly, significant variables are ignored in this large-scale formulation.

(a) Unemployment.	(f) Changes in basic industries.
(b) Property values.	(g) Access to recreational centers.
(c) Neighborhood amenities.	(h) Government policies.
(d) Job discrimination.	(i) Political interaction groups.
(e) Social discrimination.	(j) Services (baby sitters, gardening, etc.).

[10] Taken from Colin Lee, *Models in planning, op. cit.*, note 1.

(k) Housing availability.
(l) Migration of workers.
(m) More than one employee per house-
     hold.
(n) Congestion.
(o) Pollution.
(p) Rents.

(q) Tendency for social clustering in
     neighborhoods.
(r) Access to cultural centers and activities.
(s) Crime rates.
(t) Municipal services.
(u) Taxes.
(v) Zonal restrictions.

4. Long-range equilibrium of the urban area is the underlying goal. Consequently, the variables in the model begin in equilibrium; for example, the allocation of households and retail businesses to various subareas are made without regard to existing stocks at time t_0. Similarly, small marginal effects are omitted as being irrelevant to the overall equilibrium.

5. The present supply of houses and services is therefore assumed to satisfy the residential and employment service submodels.

6. The model is static in that time is not a dimension.

7. Industry and commerce are treated as homogeneous factors and their production functions are too simplistic.

8. Housing market is represented only as a function of distance and travel cost and consumer preferences are not considered.

9. Allocation of households to subareas is based on a gravity model distribution function which is primarily transport oriented. The gravity model is a physical model, borrowed from the natural sciences. Its application to behavioral phenomena, however, is inadequate in our opinion, because it ignores the psychological components in choosing a family living site. A maximum density constraint is built into the Lowry formulation because the gravity model does not consider population densities.

10. Industry is considered an exogenous factor to the model whereas in reality it may be endogenous. A city may change basic industry preferences by direct intervention through taxation or indirect intervention via investments in infrastructure. This leads to a further inadequacy; that municipal government plays no role.

11. The household has not budget constraint.

12. The objective function of the household is merely to minimize transport costs.

13. Retail businesses are placed within subareas based upon a minimum market size constraint. The model assumes that this represents the profit maximization goal of business. However, these businesses must maximize sales (supplied by the minimum size constraints) as well as minimize costs. The cost minimization aspect is not considered.

14. The Lowry model produces cross hauling of workers. Identical workers from the same industry are placed within entirely different areas. Some workers are allocated to high-density areas, far from their work. Others are allocated to low-density areas, close to their work place.

F. *Extensions*

Extensions of the basic Lowry model are summarized in Table 1. The table presents chronological data as well as some characterization of the various models and their extensions. The table is based on Goldner's article "The Lowry Model Heritage".[11]

----
[11] *Op. cit.*, note 5.

Table 1. Extension of the Lowry model

Author and model	Year	Disaggregation						Area studied							
		Operational	Conceptual	Work(1)	Residence(2)	Zone(3)	Popul.(4) Serving	Town	Subregion	Census Tract	Group Tract	Grid	Time(5)	Calibra.(6) Eval.	Develop.(7) Constraints
Consad Research Corp., *TOMM-I* (Time-oriented Metropolitan model)	1964		X		X					X			X		
Goldner and Graybeal, *BASS I* (Bay Area Simulation Study)	1965		X			X									X
Grain and Rogers, *Extension of BASS I*	1966		X		X	X							X		X
Cornell University, *CLUG* (Cornell Land Use Game)	1966		X	X	X	X									
Crecine, *TOMM-II*	1968		X	X											
Goldner, *PLUM* (Projective Land Use Model)	1968		X			X	X				X		X		X
Echnique *et al.*, *A Model of a Town*	1968	X						X				X			X
Cripps and Foot, *Subregional Model*	1968	X			X		X		X		X			X	X
Wilson, A. G., *Enlarged Conceptual Framework*	1969		X	X	X								X		X
Cripps and Foot, *Expanded Subregional Model*	1969	X			X		X		X		X			X	X
Batty, *Northwest England*	1969	X					X		X					X	
Batty, *Nottingham–Derby*	1969	X					X		X					X	
Cripps and Foot, *A Third London Airport*	1970	X			X		X		X		X			X	X
Stubbs and Barber, *Ljubliana Model*	1970	X								X					

1. *Work* Disaggregation includes breakdowns by wage stratification (Wilson) or blue/white collar segments (TOMM-II).

2. *Residence* disaggregation includes using different income levels or household types.

3. *Zone* disaggregation tries to incorporate a spatial stratification which implicitly acknowledges varying historical differences of different zones within the region.

4. *Population Serving* Centers along with the minimum size required by Lowry are abandoned in favor of single homogeneous categories.

5. *Time* is handled differently by some of these models. They try to break the long-run static equilibrium and introduce dynamic elements.

6. *Calibration and evaluation.* Experimenting with optimizing models (Cripps and Foot, Batty) as well as adding and testing a spectrum of evaluative indices is a new dimension.

7. *Developmental constraints.* Using lower and upper bound constraints to keep the models within control.

2. THE DETROIT MODEL[12]

A. *General*

The NBER model is a composite of seven submodels of the urban scene: (1) Movers, (2) Employment, (3) Demand for housing, (4) Vacancy, (5) Filtering, (6) Supply, (7) Allocation.

The movers' submodel multipliers demographically determined (72) moving rates by the numbers of households/type/work zone; this results in the number of movers per period. The employment submodel generates the exogenous net changes in employment plus net changes in movers to yield the number of houses released by these changes, and the new demanders. The third submodel allocates demand for houses (regardless of location) based on prices of houses and cost of travel.

Vacancies from previous periods plus vacancies from present period movers are added by the vacancies submodel. The filtering submodel changes the quantities of the vacant stock based on a response function to three different prices (qualities) and upgrading costs. The supply submodel changes the stock supply of the nine types by adding new construction and the changes from one type to another. The final submodel allocates workers into houses by solving twenty-seven L-P equations seeking to minimize commuting costs.

This model focuses on the housing market. It tries to incorporate heterogeneity of structures with the dynamics of moving and maintenance/improvement investments. In this respect, the NBER model is unique.

B. *Listing of variables*

Exogenous:

1. Initial prices of twenty-nine housing types, comprised of nine different structures, and three possible quality levels.

2. Initial stocks of house types in the city's forty-four residential areas.

3. Initial prices and amounts of land available for residential use per subareas.

4. Initial distribution of employment in the city's nineteen work zones. (The nineteen zones are arbitrary aggregations of the forty-four residential zones.)

5. Changes in the level and location of employment.

6. Labor force participation rates.

7. Demographic characteristics of workers by each of eleven industries.

8. Demographically determined moving or mobility rates which indicate the percentage of households entering the housing market each year (seventy-two classes of households and four income groups).

9. Monetary and time costs of travel by bus/car between residential and work zones.

10. Cost of transforming a unit of housing from one type to the next.

11. Cost of raising the quality level of a given structure.

---

[12] Cf. Gregory K. Ingram, John P. Kain, and J. Royce Ginn, *The Detroit Prototype of the NBER Urban Simulation Model*, New York, National Bureau of Economic Research, 1972.

Endogenous:

1. Stocks and prices of each house type.
2. Value of land in each residential area.
3. Travel patterns.

C. *Constraints*

Supply submodel

1. Conversion of housing to an improved level is limited by the number of vacant units at each period.

2. Changes in housing stock must not create an excess supply for any type of housing.

3. New supply is arbitrarily limited to 10 percent of the vacant land in residential zones.

Allocation submodel

1. All households demanding a given type of housing must get it. (If there is excess demand for a given house type, a forty-fifth residential area is created, which is assumed to have enough of every type of housing. Transport costs are 5 percent higher than those to other zones.)

2. The number of demanders assigned to a residential zone must not exceed the stock available.

D. *Procedure*

The simulation starts by determining the number of demanders of each family type in each work zone. The movers' subroutine enters at this point to determine the number of movers. The employment subroutine then converts exogenous changes in employment to changes in the number of households of different types in each work zone. The number of demanders of each family type is the sum of movers plus net employment increases. Net increase is the mover plus employment increase minus decreases in employment. After demanders are known by work zone and income, they are allocated to the housing stock— regardless of housing location—via the gross price. Gross prices include the price of the house type and condition as well as the cost of travel to work. The above is accomplished by the demand sub-routine.

Changes in housing stocks are carried by the supply, filtering, and vacancy submodels. Houses vacant from last period are combined with newly vacated houses by the vacancy submodel. Only vacant houses can be changed in quality. The filtering submodel accomplishes this by a response function to (1) price differentials of equal structure with different quality, (2) upgrading cost. The supply changes due to upgradings is taken care of by the supply submodel, subject to some constraints. The allocation of households to house types is then computed based on linear programming equations. Their objectives are to minimize commuting costs.

A block diagram and a diagram of the submodels' sequence follows (Fig. 3).

FLOW CHARTING

Block Diagram of Submodels as Encountered in the Model

EMPLOYMENT LOCATION SUBMODEL
Revise level and composition of employment at each workplace and by each of nine industry types.
Translate employment changes by industry to changes in employee characteristics.

MOVERS' SUBMODEL
Generate households vacating housing units, and modify them to produce households seeking
housing this period.

VACANCY SUBMODEL
Generate vacancies in housing stock created by intermetropolitan moves, outmigration, and
household dissolution by residence zone and house type.

DEMAND ALLOCATION SUBMODEL
Combine transportation costs from work zones to residence zones with expected housing prices to
form gross housing prices. Form expected gross housing prices by workplace for each housing
type. Allocate households to housing types with demand equations and expected gross prices.

FILTERING SUBMODEL
Change quality classification of available housing stock according to quality premiums derived
from expected prices and exogenous maintenance costs.

SUPPLY SUBMODEL
Calculate profitability of construction and transformation activities from expected prices and
exogenous building costs. Perform stock transformation according to profit levels and several
constraints.

MARKET-CLEARING SUBMODEL
Match moving households to available units of the type chosen by households in the demand
allocation submodel. Each house type or submarket is solved separately. Shadow prices are used
to generate prices for the next time period. Work trip patterns are updated.

(a)

Fig. 3(a,b) Detroit Model [13]

E. *Evaluation*

1. As in the Lowry model approach, various variables are ignored.

(a) unemployment	(k) political groups
(b) income	(l) location of business
(c) neighborhood amenities	(m) no more than one breadwinner
(d) job discrimination	(n) pollution
(e) housing discrimination	(o) congestion
(f) access to shopping	(p) crime
(g) access to recreation facilities	(q) zonal restrictions
(h) quality of schools	(r) tendencies for social clustering
(i) municipal services	(s) taxes
(j) federal government policies	

[13] *Op. cit.*, note 12, pp. 28–9.

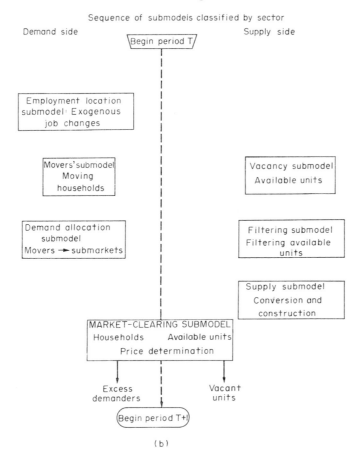

(b)

2. However, unlike the Lowry formulation the urban system variables selected for inclusion in NBER model at time t_{-5} or t_0 or t_{+5} are not necessarily in equilibrium. That is, stocks of housing facilities, for example, may not equal the demand for the same.

3. Although little explanation for the growth of decline of cities is offered and the questions of stability and equilibrium in urban areas is not approached, the model permits the evaluation of different housing policies.

4. Households are assigned to house types first and then to residential areas. Because there are no budgetary constraints, the household may go into debt indefinitely.

5. In the model, house types bid for land use and determine price. Outside influences on land use/or prices, like the relationship of business to residential location, are not considered.

6. The model tends to produce inverse relations between family income and traveling distance to work: that is, the higher the income, the closer to work. Although this relationship may hold true for European cities it is clearly not true for American cities.

7. The discussion of how businesses choose their place of business is perfunctory. Cost and local available labor considerations, for example, are ignored as determinants of business locations.

8. Industry is considered a homogeneous and exogenous variable. The segmentation of Lowry into Basic and Commerce components is not undertaken.

9. Workplaces are determined before housing. Only household with employed heads are included.

3. THE URBAN PERFORMANCE MODEL[14]

A. *General*

The Urban Performance Model consists of six basic submodels: (1) the travel habits submodel; (2) the opportunity and quality of life submodel calibrated to neighborhood cells; (3) a matrix model of land uses which analytically corresponds with quality and opportunity measures; (4) a regional forecasting submodel; (5) three allocation-constraint submodels, and (6) an allocation submodel.

(1) The travel submodel uses interview data on travel habits to calculate regressions for determining transport needs.

(2) The second submodel calculates opportunity and quality measures per cell. According to UPM, urban residents seek to: (a) increase freedom of choice in significant aspects of life—called "Opportunity" = "P"; (b) increase quality of immediate neighborhood—called "Quality" = "Q". Opportunity consists of (A) attractions for jobs, schools, shopping, recreation, etc., in a particular neighborhood area or cell and (B) income to be able to consume these attractions.

Quality consists of satisfaction in different areas, i.e. job, school, shopping, and recreation variables dimensioning P. For example, the number of rooms per family member may be used as an indicator of quality. This submodel can have a matrix of upward $1000\,p + Q$ cells with six population groupings.

(3) The land matrix submodel distributes land uses and activities on the PQ matrix for which an absorption factor is calculated. This factor is used to determine the utilization of land areas in a given cell taken up by increments of activity. This information then serves as basic inputs for the allocation submodels.

(4) The regional forecast subroutine calculates employment and population projections by cell and the relationship between these to the total growth forecasts.

(5) and (6) The allocation and constraint submodels ensure that: (a) the various PQ cells cannot have negative land use activities; (b) in any given period only a designated rate of activity may be removed from a cell; (c) an activity may be removed only from the portfolio of existent activities in the cell at time t_0; (d) there is an exogenous maximum limit on the activity in an area. The allocation submodel then distributes new land use activity to the various PQ cells, in accordance with the following considerations: the existing utility in the cell be positive and that the added marginal utility also be positive.

B. *Listing of variables*

Exogenous:

1. Population growth increments.

[14] Research Systems Associates, *UPM-Users' Manual*, Tel-Aviv, Jan. 1972.

2. Distribution of income groups.
3. Labor force forecasts.
4. Rate of motorization and model split.
5. Changes in housing standards.
6. Population by income groups.
7. Employment (represents economic activity) by area (per predefined cell).
8. Travel matrices by model of travel for the urban area.

Endogenous:

1. Relative attraction values for land uses to resident population groups for work and non-work. (This calculated from travel habits and other related data.)
2. Opportunity and quality are calculated after each iteration.

C. *Constraints*

1. Removal of activity whose holding capacity has been overreached.
2. Removal of activity from cells when negative increments of activity are forecast.
3. Removal of residential activity for cells in which internal migration is expected.

D. *Procedure* (Fig. 4)

The UPM has basically two phases: (1) descriptive and (2) projective. The descriptive phase begins by reading the input data. This includes information or attractions to cells in terms of average income, education and or number of rooms per household members, etc. Travel habits and cost data are also incorporated here through the transportation sub-model. The opportunity and quality measures are then computed on the basis of this data for the entire urban study area involved, resulting in a PQ print-out of measures for each predetermined cell. A corresponding matrix of land activities in terms of the P and Q values is constructed and printed, bringing to an end the descriptive phase of the UPM model. The projective phase begins with the successive iterations of the above procedures into future time periods. These incorporate two additional elements: (1) forecasts, (2) allocation and constraints. The forecasts use general exogenous data about growth to predict growth changes in the cells. The allocation of activities and the constraints to cells determines which new business activities are placed in the various PQ matrix cells. (These constraints are noted in Section I, paragraphs 5 and 6.) The iteration procedure may be repeated as many times as necessary to reach desired equilibria.

E. *Evaluation*

1. While the model considers many factors affecting demand which previous models did not, it requires masses of data. The more comprehensive the data used the less feasible, however, the model becomes. The size of the cells is determined by the data availability. The smaller the cells the better the approximation of reality. However, this renders the cost effort of updating the base year inventory data prohibitive.

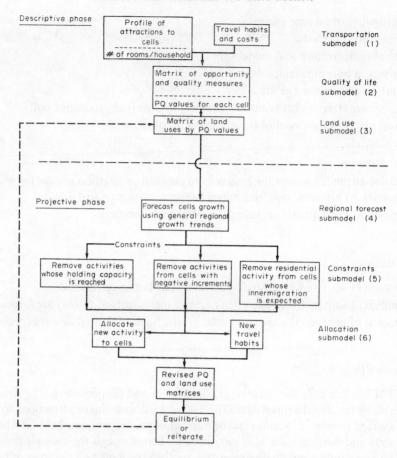

FIG. 4. Schematic flowchart of UPM program.

2. The model assumes that present modes will continue into the future indefinitely. For example, transportation habits may change drastically because of a new highway, a larger escape to suburbs, etc. A forecast which does not take into account such qualitative changes may be misleading.

3. The model ignores:

    (a) Government
    (b) Racial problems
    (c) Job discrimination
    (d) Political groups
    (e) Pollution
    (f) Congestion
    (g) Crime
    (h) Taxes
    (i) Housing availability

4. The model takes into partial consideration various variables. However, it is left to the quality of data collected to determine how well these variables are represented:

(a) Income (use of a mean income per household).
(b) Housing (use of a number of rooms per person).
(c) Education (use of a mean figure).
(d) Access to recreational facilities.
(e) Access to shopping.
(f) Access to school, and its quality.
(g) Municipal services.

The above are examples of variables which the model treats by calculating a mean measure of quality. This may lead to distortions in PQ values for particular cells. For example, young families may be artificially ascribed lower incomes due to children in the family.

5. The model assumes homogenous cells which can be described in identical P's and Q's. It is conceivable that families living in the same apartment house will have different real opportunities. They may perceive the quality of the area differently. Elderly and young couples attach different values to entertainment centers, for example.

6. UPM is not dynamic. It arrives at static equilibrium states. Comparing the difference between these steps gives the model its dynamic appearance.

7. Negative increments within cells are not permitted. Inner migration between cells, without growth in the system as a whole, cannot be considered in this model.

8. No appropriation is made for creating new cells, over time. The original cells change QP levels. This is allowed until the optimum level of PQ per cell is reached. After the optimum has been reached, the constraints are relaxed.

4. THE REGIONAL STABILIZATION MODEL[15]

A. *General*

A model with the main purpose of simulating the effects of alternative policy moves and obtaining an accurate read-out of resulting urban–suburban conditions, the Bernstein–Mellon formulation deals with the movement of various population groups and the resulting effects on some very broad indicators of city–suburban life, rather than with particular topics like transportation, land use, and the like. The level of abstraction is thus intermediate and is arrived at providing practical policy suggestions for a particular city—Newark—for which the model is calibrated. The model, however, is designed to be general enough in nature so that it can be applied to other urban–suburban complexes and, therefore, the policy suggestions are made on a fairly broad basis.

B. *Listing of variables*

Exogenous:

Residence-determining Variables

A. The Social Dimension = Index of Social Conditions, I_s

s_1 crime rate

---

[15] *Op. cit.*, note 2.

s_2 drug addiction rate
s_3 ratio of welfare to total population
s_4 index cost of housing

B. The Education Dimension = Index of Education Conditions, I_{Ed}
   e_1 educational achievement index
   e_2 teacher/student ratio
   e_3 index of mean cost of school per pupil per year

C. The Economic Dimension = Indexing Economic Conditions, I_{Ec}
   ec_1 income distribution index
   ec_2 unemployment index
   ec_3 rate of investment in new building construction and renovation
   ec_4 ratio of private to public housing

D. The Environmental Dimension = Indexing of Environmental Conditions I_{En}
   en_1 population density
   en_2 ratio of park space to total residential space
   en_3 number of reported fires per year
   en_4 mean age and condition of dwelling units
   en_5 mean number of rooms per family units

E. The Demographic Dimension = Index of Demographic Conditions I_D
   d_1 ratio of blacks to whites
   d_2 mean community age
   d_3 family types
   d_4 family size

F. The Community Service Dimension = Index of Community Services, I_C
   c_1 accessibility to health centers as measured by the mean time to reach a hospital
            emergency room in a given community
   c_2 sanitation pick-ups per week
   c_3 police facilities (manpower × equipment × mean response time)
   c_4 accessibility to recreational facilities as measured by the mean access time

Endogenous:

G. The Population as Distinguished by Income and Race = P_i, where i = 1 thru 4
   p_1 = middle class white ⎫
   p_2 = middle class black ⎬ with incomes above \$10,000 per annum in community 1
   p_3 = lower class white ⎫
   p_4 = lower class black ⎬ with incomes below \$10,000 per annum in community 2
Employment by location of job.

C. *Constraints*

   Budgetary allotments.
   Underlying trends in each of the exogenous variables.

D. *Procedure*

The model consists of a series of ten simultaneous econometric equations, five each for the city and its suburbs which interrelate the community condition variables with the population variables. The city equations, for example, consist of an equation for each of four population groups: whites with family incomes below $10,000 a year, whites with incomes above $10,000, and two similar equations for minority group members; plus a single equation for location of jobs with the city. These equations repeat for the suburbs.

Looking at an individual equation, for example, that for middle-class whites living in the city, equation 1, the model states that the *change* in the number of such persons in any given year is a function of changes in the current and recent past years of the community conditions which are hypothesized as controlling residential location: for example, social conditions as measured by an index of crime rate, environmental conditions as measured by density and number of apartment rooms per family, available employment, and any feelings of discrimination toward minority group members in the area. Worsening of these or other indicators will cause members of this group to move to the suburbs. The equations are linear econometric ones, similar to those developed for GNP models, but which show how many thousand persons will move in response to any given percentage change in one of the locational factors, rather than a response in GNP to such factors as monetary policy. In the case of the employment location indicators, a decline in social conditions within the city and/or increases in taxes will cause employers to move their operations to the suburbs. (Tax rates on individuals enter the model in the form of real estate taxes which alter the value of the public's housing stock.)

Looking now at the derivation of the condition indexes which determine population movements we may take educational conditions as an example. The various population groups are assumed to have varying responses to changing educational conditions, as measured by some index of test scores, student/teacher ratios, conditions of school plant, and so on. These indexes are affected in turn by the following types of "feedback" factors. The model assumes an initial stock of school plant in some given physical condition. This plant decays at a given rate, while maintenance costs rise at an estimated rate, based on past inflation. Thus, to even hold the plant at its current physical state, the city must spend an ever-increasing amount of its revenues, or obtain Federal or State grants. But city revenues are, in turn, a function of its tax base, so that if middle-class citizens leave the city this erodes the tax base so that less can be spent on the schools, which causes their condition to worsen, which causes still more middle class to flee to the suburbs, and so on. Population trends also enter into the dynamics of the situation in that a rising school population automatically increases pupil/teacher ratios unless offset by increased faculty. A similar analysis can be made of each of the other locational determining factors.

In summary, what we have is a dynamic model which consists of four basic parts:

** a set of equations describing the locational tendencies of individuals and businesses as a function of social, economic environmental, demographic, and community service conditions;

** a set of equations which describe present economic and social conditions as a function of the population density and composition, and of spending for governmental services;

20   *Samuel J. Bernstein and W. Giles Mellon*

** underlying trends in: costs of city services, decay of physical facilities, growth of
income, and population birth rates for the various population groups;

** a set of equation budgets which give the distribution of spending by type of governmental services by City and suburban areas; and which constrain such spending to
the sum of revenues, borrowing, and Federal and State grants, with revenues as a
linear function of the income of residents and businesses.

E. *Evaluation*

1. The outputs of the model include:

   (a) the number of persons in each population category for city and suburb,
   (b) the available employment in each,
   (c) the state of quality of life based on six conditions making a total of eighteen
   separate outputs.

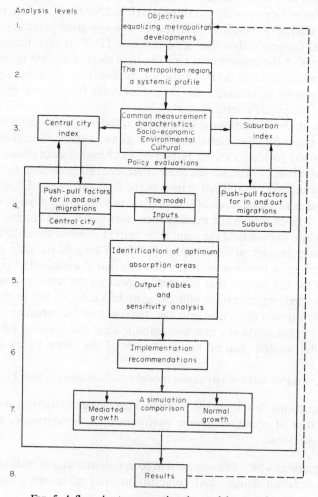

FIG. 5. A flow chart representing the models operation.

2. The model is concerned with filling the gap left by Forrester's *Urban Dynamics*, in that, the city and suburban areas are dynamically interrelated.

3. Consumer behavior tendencies are incorporated as a factor to be concerned with in evaluating the impact of urban policies which other policy models ignore.

4. Time discounting and uncertainty characteristics, however, are not included in the model although the model does project into the future.

5. Budget allocations may be varied.

6. Estimates of the locational indicators are still only rough approximations.

7. The model does not permit the consideration of important discrete events as determinants of residential behavior, for example, the Newark riots.

8. The model does provide a comprehensive middle-range framework for contemporary urban–suburban relationships.

5. THE PROMUS MODEL[16]

A. *General*

The PROMUS model, unlike the previous formulations, attempts to formally interconnect the governmental with neighborhood community subsystems of any city. The governmental subsystem is represented by a financial policy-planning model. The neighborhood subsystems are represented by a community model system. The community system has three submodels: (1) a small area model, (2) neighborhood model, (3) population and income submodels. The financial policy planning has six submodels: (1) policy implementation, (2) budgetary expenses, (3) program performance, (4) cash flow, (5) revenue forecast, (6) policy decisions.

The unique feature of PROMUS is the financial policy-planning model which is designed to:

1. Provide a framework for citywide budgeting, incorporating levels of desired service and a range of alternatives (levels of revenues + expenses).

2. Allow rapid evaluations of different mixes of the above.

3. Relate changes in budgets to changes in community characteristics.

4. Produce projections of expenditures for the city as well as for each department.

5. Provide forecasts of required changes in expenditures and revenues over time as a function of alternative programs and anticipated community developments.

6. Allow sensitivity analysis of the above.

The interface between the community and financial subsystems is described in terms of:

1. Computing revenues to the community based on changing real property and population bases.

2. Computing expenditures due to changing needs.

3. Computing impacts of the policy action on the community.

---

[16] Cf. Dilip R. Limaye and Donald F. Blumberg, *Systems for Urban Planning and Management*, Decision Sciences Corporation, 1972.

B. *Listing of variables*

   Exogenous:

1. Basic employment.
2. Distances between residential and industrial sectors.
3. Demand for labor.
4. Household characteristics.
5. Department program matrices.
   (a) Activities.
   (b) Service levels.
   (c) Inputs (controllable and exogenous).
   (d) Output.
6. Policy statements.
7. Community characteristics (exogenous for financial system, but endogenous for the model).

   Endogenous:

1. Housing (neighborhood submodel)
2. Employment (neighborhood submodel)
3. Education (neighborhood submodel)
4. Health (neighborhood submodel)
5. Welfare (neighborhood submodel)

These are exogenous to the neighborhood submodel but endogenous to the model as a whole

C. *Constraints*

1. Budgetary allotments.

D. *Procedures*

   The operation of the model is graphically shown in the following flow charts (Figs. 6–8), taken from Limaye and Blumberg.[17]

E. *Evaluation*

   1. Of all the models presented PROMUS is the least theoretically grounded; however, it has been applied experimentally to the City of Toronto as a policy evaluation and budget-control apparatus. Whether it has actually improved governmental performance is not yet clear.

   2. Because of its pragmatic bent the model is more data processing oriented than analytically oriented which may be its biggest asset. For example, PROMUS begins with the consideration of department budgets and agency programs as a basic input to the model. It is these that interconnect the community with the government: a realistic representation.

[17] Limaye and Blumberg, *op. cit.*

3. The basic handicap with the model is its generality. From this derives the basic difficulty of evaluating the benefit and costs of policies in cities. That is, the model reports on policy performances in terms of community system variables but provides few, if any, objective indicators which permits comparison as to goodness.

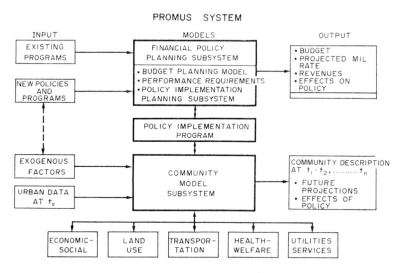

FIG. 6. Flow chart, general.

Summary: The Models as a Group

1. Although the models reviewed attempt to structure urban reality in single comprehensive analytical format, they tend to incorporate too many variables without specifying all their interrelations. For example: (a) potential externalities resulting from interrelationships between variables tend to be ignored; (b) the effect of time as a variable feeding back on other variables is not considered.

2. Relations between variables other than those specified in the descriptions of the model are implicit in these models and hard to perceive. For example:

(a) Lowry, NBER, PROMUS have trip distributions functions which are fitted to different household types. While validated on the metropolitan level these are not validated on the neighborhood or subarea level.

(b) Modes of transit utilization at t_{-5} through t_0 are used to forecast transit utilization at t_5 through t_{10}. Qualitative changes such as building a new beltway or, the increased utilization of private cars as in Israel from 1967 to the present or, an impending decrease in private cars due to the energy crisis in the United States are not included in these models.

(c) The constraints in each of the models are easily glossed over and no mention is made on how to treat unexpected or unintended constraints in the frameworks of each model.

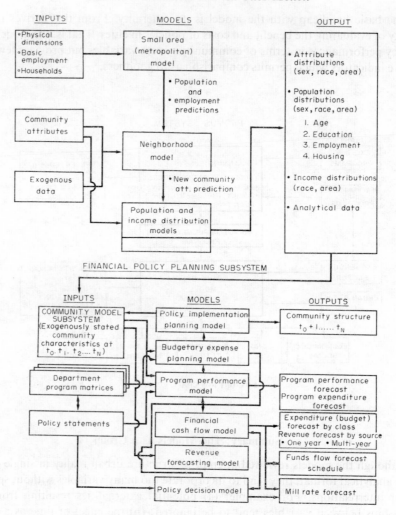

FIG. 7. Flow charts, detailed. Community model system.

3. The data requirement of all the models are fairly large and getting the models to run with a regular policy/planning framework is a complicated task. In this sense the models are more research oriented. Converting the simulations to interactive modes would greatly enhance the policy-analysis utilities of these models.

4. The models are expensive.

5. Nevertheless, it may be said that the analytical scope of the models are extensive and may aid in the following areas of planning and policy making: understanding how the urban system works; predicting conditions within the urban area at some future date; on educational program for learning the complexities of urban decision-making; and evaluating specific impacts of policy intervention by governments.

Table 2 provides a concise summary of the basic features of the five models considered in this section.

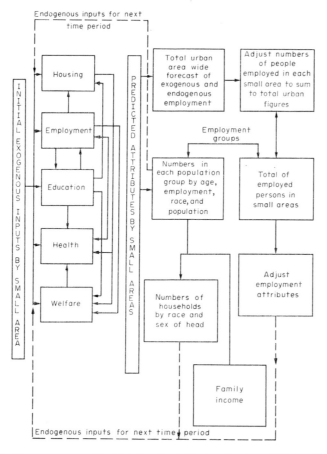

FIG. 8. Flow chart, specific. Details of neighborhood submodel interaction in community model subsystem.

IV. Problems and Pitfalls in Urban Model Building[18]

In the development of overall urban models—of whatever form and whatever purpose—problems and pitfalls inevitably are encountered. These can be considered as falling into one of three categories: conceptual/technical, administrative, and societal. Within the first two classifications the problems may be further classified as either analytical or decisional in nature.

Analytical problems are those associated with the description and definition of an urban reality under investigation. These involve questions of concept formation, measurement, and the format or relationships between concepts in models. Definition and description are significant endeavors in quantitative urban analysis because they result in a base profile of conditions from which to calculate changes resulting from various policy inputs. Decision problems refer to policy design and the related measurement questions of indicating the

[18] The material in this section is taken from: Samuel J. Bernstein, Roman Ferber, and A. Isaac Bernstein, "The problems and pitfalls of quantitative methods in urban analysis". *Policy Sciences*, **4** (1973).

Samuel J. Bernstein and W. Giles Mellon

TABLE 2

Subject	Lowry	NBER	UPM	PROMUS	Bernstein
Industrial employment	+	+	*	−	−
Commercial employment	+	+	*	−	−
Unemployment	−	−	*	−	*
Income of household	−	*	*	+	+
Race	−	−	−	−	*
Family size	−	+	*	*	
Property value	−	*	*	−	+
Neighborhood amenities	−	−	+	−	+
Job discrimination	−	−	−	−	*
Housing discrimination	−	...	−	−	*
Access to shopping	−	--	+	−	−
Access to entertainment and recreation	−	−	+	−	−
Quality of schools	−	−	+	−	+
Local government (tax)	−	−	−	−	+
Housing availability	−	*	−	−	−
Political groups	−	−	−	−	−
Migration of workers	−	+	−	−	+
Traffic congestion	−	−	−	−	−
Municipal services	−	−	−	−	+
Location of business	−	−	+	+	−
One employee per household	+	+	−	*	−
Pollution	−	−	−	−	+
Crime	−	−	−	−	+
Expensive	+	+	+	+	+
Huge data requirements	+	+	+	+	+
Not dynamic models	+	*	+	*	*
Too general for policy	Allocation[1]	Housing[2]	Traffic[3]	Finance[4]	Tax base + immigration[5]

[1] Lowry model though limited may be used by government to analyze tax inducement to external industries.
[2] Changes in housing subsidies and residential consequences (urban renewal).
[3] Changes in traffic modes and future needs vs. opportunity and attractions (ADL model even better).
[4] Changes in budgets and their impacts.
[5] Changes in migration and tax policies.
(−) No. (+) Yes. (*) Partially.

impacts of various improvement policies in terms of changing the conditions of the base profile.

A table of the problems and pitfalls in the sequential order confronting the urban analyst, policy-maker, and administrator is presented here (Table 3) at the outset to guide the discussion which follows.

A. CONCEPTUAL/TECHNICAL PROBLEMS

1. *Parameter selection*

Whenever quantitative analysis techniques are employed in the explanation of a social reality, the first glaring problem is almost always: What are the parameters of the problem

TABLE 3. A SUMMARY OF PROBLEMS AND PITFALLS IN QUANTITATIVE
URBAN ANALYSIS

Problems	Analytical	Decision
Technical		
1. Parameter selection	×	×
2. Parameter estimation and data availability	×	
3. Social momentum and time lags	×	
4. Time series and their meaning	×	
5. Time discount and uncertainty		×
6. Social costs		×
Administrative		
1. Finding meaningful solutions	×	
2. Selecting pilot programs		×
3. Immediate commitment and program flexibility		×
4. Political realities	×	×
Societal		
1. Implication of the *status quo*	—	—
2. The local community	—	—
3. "Fads and foibles"	—	—

to be included in the model? At the heart of the issue is the trade-off between comprehensiveness and analytical elegance or simplicity. Turning to urban analysis the question
becomes: Is the urban model to be a complete representation of reality as in a large-scale
computer simulation which is analytically almost insoluble, or is the urban model to be an
abstraction of what seem to be the essential factors for determining urban changes and is
analytically soluble? By way of example, consider the differences in scope between the
comprehensiveness of the Forrester general urban dynamics model and the various more
limited urban transportation and administration models among others. A general guide-
line in this regard—although by no means binding upon the analyst—may be stated as
follows: If the model is to be used for heuristic purposes, then analytical simplicity and
thus illustration of social dynamics ought to be emphasized. If, however, the model is to
be used for planning and policy analysis, comprehensiveness ought to be emphasized,
time and resources permitting.

2. *Parameter estimation and data availability*

These two problems combine to form the next hurdle facing the urban analyst. That is,
how to measure the variables included in a model and where to find the data. They are said
to be combined because the latter data availability determines the nature of the former
estimation procedures. For example, to measure the quality of urban housing one has to
consider at least three dimensions for which directly available information is lacking.
These are structural quality, crowdedness, and environmental conditions adjacent to
housing. To derive a single numeric indication of the multi-dimensional nature of housing
quality, therefore, requires the construction of a weighted index and a rating system for
ordering the different levels of quality. Index construction is always difficult in so far as the

methods of combination are open to question. Additionally, however, the lack of directly available data in the form required by the index further limits application; because invariably each link in the estimation phases of converting the necessary raw data into the informational format of the index magnifies the error potential of producing information output of questionable significance for decision and policy purposes. And to these problems must be added the standard estimation problems of econometric analysis. The NBER, for example, in describing the estimation results obtained for its massive Detroit model in its 1974 *Annual Report* found them far from satisfactory and needing a great deal of further work.

3. *Social momentum and time lags*

Urban phenomena share in common with other socio-economic phenomena the problem of time-oriented effects. Changes induced by external and even internal stimuli, thus, do not become directly observable as with physical phenomena in a direct "S-R" form, but rather becomes apparent only after intervening lags or lapses of time. The momentum of the social factors accounting for present conditions is in part responsible for this because it simply cannot be turned off like a water faucet. Accounting for time effects is thus an essential endeavor in urban analysis. It is the basis for establishing valid representations of reality and deriving effective improvement policies. Such is generally accomplished in the urban model by time-lagging the variables and testing to determine which intervening time intervals approximate real world conditions. The impact of improperly valued time lags is frequently seen in urban population migration models where incorrectly estimated time factors result in a model predicting highly unrealistic white and black middle-class population flows.

4. *Time series data and their meaning*

In light of social momentum and time-lag factors the importance of historical data for effective representations of urban dynamics becomes self-evident. Two methodological concerns confront the urban analyst here.

(1) The determination of a meaningful starting date from which to begin collecting time series data. A minimum 5-year data base may be necessary in this regard for a study of changing urban conditions which commences on the sixth year. This base period is required for marking trends, identifying interrelationships of variables accounting for the social momentum determining present urban conditions, and indicating guide posts for policy formulation and analysis.

(2) The multi-colinearity of time series data and the derivative danger of ascribing causation of change in urban conditions to one variable from a set of time series data where, in reality, that variable's change is interwoven and occurring simultaneously with the remaining set. Although specific statistical tests for multi-colinearity exist, the problem is always present for the urban analyst.

The discussion of the first four conceptual problems focused on the analytical or representational problems in building an effective urban analysis framework. They fall therefore into the first stage of the quantitative urban analysis model: defining initial conditions. The following two problems involve policy design and related impact questions. They are set within the second and third stages of the generalized quantitative urban analysis model of explaining urban reality and gauging impact of changes induced by improvement policies.

5. *Time discount and allowance for uncertainty*

Once the representational components of an urban model have been decided on, the urban analyst and decision-maker are confronted with the first set of major decision questions: (a) How to calculate social discount rates for indicating the added value of presently implementing particular urban-improvement policies or programs; and (b) How to include in the policy analysis a probability of success or risk discount for particular programs.

(a) A constant social discount rate for policy analysis similar to prevailing private interest rates cannot simply be adopted *ipso facto* because improvement projects' value are a function of the priorities attached to that project by different people and groups in urban society. Ghetto priorities may be said to differ in this regard from suburban priorities. The marginal gain accomplished by a public dollar spent in the ghetto as opposed to one spent in suburbia, furthermore, may not be assumed to be equal. Consequently, as these priorities vary so does the social discount rate for different improvement policies and programs. Further, simply setting the social discount rate below the private interest rate consistently makes an improvement policy or program appear more desirable. Similarly, if the discount rate is set higher than the private interest rate, improvement policies and programs will seem less attractive—damaging overall urban improvement possibilities. Complicating this issue even further is the source of resources for urban improvement. That is, are the resources for planned improvement presently unemployed or must they be siphoned off from other programs which may in part have to be discontinued?

(b) The allowance for risk or the probability of success in urban-improvement policies is the second decision question to be addressed by the urban analyst. First, it may be questioned whether the stream of future returns projected for urban projects is normally realistic, because there is a tendency by government experts to overstate expected benefits from improvement programs. Studies showing overstatement of benefits from urban improvement programs have recently confirmed this. But even assuming that the mean value of expected benefits is accurately stated, the question still remains as to how some further allowance should be made for possible variation in payoff around these mean values because of the obvious existence of widespread uncertainty with respect to payoffs from urban-improvement policies programs. This does not of necessity mean that a high discount for risk must be applied to each individual project. For as several authors have pointed out, when various programs are combined in an overall development policy the "law of large numbers" serves to sharply reduce—if not eliminate—any variation around the expected average return for an entire set of many urban-development projects. The general validity of this point, in theory, seems evident. The empirical implications for a smaller city undertaking a very limited number of projects, or where a single massive project takes up a very substantial portion of the overall urban-development budget have not, however, been fully investigated. Thus, at this point the question as to the correct method for allowing for uncertainty in the evaluation of urban-development policies and projects is in a highly unsettled state for urban analyst and decision-maker.

6. *Social costs and benefits*

Urban as well as other social-improvement policies and programs incur fiscal and social costs. These latter costs are generally indicated by the term "externalities" and include things like the cost of family relocation and community break-up.

Confronting the urban analyst head-on is the question of units of analysis. There are few, if any standardized measures of social costs or benefits resulting from changed conditions induced by urban improvement programs and policies. Estimates of social costs and benefits thus become vulnerable to various legitimate and even illegitimate manipulations. In order to minimize these manipulations, guidelines for social cost calculations should be drawn early in project planning. Violations of the guidelines invariably come at the end of a project's life span, and at that point they may be easily identified because the rules become institutionalized as part of the project's life.

B. ADMINISTRATIVE PROBLEMS

Technically competent and generally experienced personnel confront the problems discussed in the previous section. The problems to be discussed in the present section, in contrast, primarily confront administrative personnel whose competence and experience from the perspective of quantitative analysis is marginally less than required or at least desirable. Four problem areas are indicated here. They primarily come in the second and third stages of quantitative urban analysis framework of explaining urban reality and calculating the impact of change on initial conditions induced by policy.

1. *Finding meaningful solutions*

The most basic problem facing the urban administrator dealing with specific quantitative applications is: What do the results mean? Clearly, to the "uninitiated" the reams of computer print-out—in both massive tabular row and column and graphic formats showing changed conditions resulting from policy inputs—seem impressive. However, suppose the print-out does not provide the singular answers which are expected of it? This leads to the further question: What is it then all needed for? The rebuttals are manifold: time and money savings, rapid information retrieval, better planning, greater managerial control, etc. No doubt these are true and are in part the reasons for computerizing the "data-bases and operations" of large-scale governmental operations. They do not talk, however, to the policy questions of finding meaningful solutions.

Quantitative urban analysis in this regard may be said to provide the urban administrator with a bird's-eye view of the reality he is confronted with. This is accomplished by reflecting in miniature format the simultaneous and interrelated dynamics of changing populations—decreasing property values, diminishing tax bases, fewer urban services, commuting problems—among other characteristics of the present urban condition. With this background the information format is thus set for developing and evaluating more specific urban improvement policies and programs in terms of their direct and indirect marginal impacts on present conditions.

2. *Selecting pilot programs*

Following in importance to the urban administrator is the question of how to construct a pilot test through quantitative application. That is, how to specify the essential elements of a pilot program for adequately testing experimentally derived policy recommendations in a real world context. Urban analysis is seemingly hampered in this regard, for "real world" urban test cases require massive undertakings. A recent simulation study of Newark, New Jersey, for example, suggested that only a massive federal financial undertaking to improve city facilities would suffice to diminish the rate of the middle-class black—no less remaining white population—outflows from the city. Clearly any pilot program short of a massive infusion of federal funds would be of little avail in showing appreciable improvements in meeting policy priorities.

3. *Determining between need for immediate commitment and flexibility*

Assuming the formulation of an improvement-policy package, the optimal design for public investment in urban facilities (i.e. education, housing, health, or recreation) in terms of what facilities to invest in and in what time frame becomes the next major issue facing urban policy-makers and administrators. The generally macro-level of the quantitative urban model does not confront this issue, because it is seldom geared to produce specific micro-level resource allocation-type decisions within tightly set tolerance levels or bounds. Results are therefore rounded estimates which take on the character of "ballpark figures". In the alternative it may be argued, however, that expending greater effort in estimating the variables for determining urban quality of life would not result in significantly improved policy decisions because of the data-availability problem.

A fruitful avenue for improving administrative capability in this regard may involve the greater utilization of programming and other maximizing techniques in urban-investment problems which have become highly developed for solving private-investment problems.

4. *Political realities*

While quantitative applications dictate policy solutions, these may differ from the solutions suggested by the urban political structure. In fact, solutions from quantitative analysis seem invariably to differ from political solutions. Pressures of vested interests account for this in large measure, for they are factored into political but not quantitative solutions—as clearly indicated by the Forest-Hills Housing controversy in New York City. Political solutions consequently tend to emphasize minimum incremental changes in the *status quo*. Successful quantitative analysis must contend with political reality as one component of uncertainty to be reckoned with. Probability models which attempt to indicate the potential of different improvement policies and programs being accepted by relevant political factors used in conjunction with the urban model must be thus developed, if the results of urban models are to be more readily accepted and implemented by urban administrations.

C. SOCIETAL PROBLEMS

The conducting set of problems speak to the broader issues affecting the utilization of quantitative applications in urban analysis. They address society and its desire to follow "non-apparent" and sometimes "non-common sense" solutions derived from quantitative applications.

1. *Implication of the* status quo

Quantitative representations of urban reality are based on assumptions which determine how realistic a particular model will be. Generally, the more constraining the assumptions the more simple the model. To be an effective policy tool the urban model must not vary too widely in its analytical representation of urban conditions. Realism in the model, however, opens the door to criticisms by local planning groups and other interested parties that the model legitimates and even attempts to preserve the status quo by neglecting to consider bold new and qualitatively different alternative improvement policies. If realistic description of present urban conditions is an essential element in the urban modeling enterprise for deriving effective improvement policies and gauging their impact in terms of changing present conditions, then the *status quo* limitation must be accepted as part of the *modus operandi* of quantitative applications.

2. *The local community*

Local community demands for greater decentralization of power in conjunction with their suspicion of "uptown" city hall proposals for improvements tend to further confound both the utilization of quantitative urban analytical techniques and the implementation of their results. First, local power brokers and politically relevant actors perceive "the numbers" in quantitative urban analysis as the means for confusing basic community issues and for gaining submission to "uptown" city hall programs because of the lack of necessary expertise. Moreover, local community groups—particularly urban ghetto residents—see themselves as closer to their own problems and therefore better suited and indeed more qualified to accomplish the necessary improvements in the quality of life if they were provided with the necessary funds.

3. *Fads and foibles*

Lastly, it may be said that there is an underlying tendency to consider all quantitative approaches in social science—not merely in urban analysis—as part of passing academic "fads and foibles". In the past some of these academic endeavors have been shown to be without much substance and merit. This feeling casts a heavy shadow today on the utilization of quantitative methods in urban analysis.

Set against these problems are the very real gains which a well-formulated model may yield. These include:

1. *Formalization of planning and control*

Urban analysis proceeds by setting a consistent framework in the form of a model for bringing together knowledge on the physical and socio-economic characteristics of urban systems in order to increase our understanding of present urban conditions and for evaluating impacts of alternative improvement policies against priorities.

2. *Increased richness of analysis*

Quantitative methods through formal models set the base for computer applications to simultaneously handle large numbers of variables which human evaluators feel are relevant to urban policy-making yet are beyond the capacity of the human brain to handle at any one time.

3. *Consistency of input and output*

Once the formal urban model has been established, it tends to set guidelines for consistency in results, even though various groups of decision-makers may be involved in the policy formulation, implementation, and evaluation processes. Consistency in results is accomplished by rigorous definition of the concepts being employed, formalization of measures and specification of the format of relationships in quantitative applications.

4. *Reduced costs and time*

Quantitative methods seek to standardize and generalize informational requirements for computer applications which may streamline urban governmental activities. These can substantially reduce the costs and increase the speed as well as the quality of taking policy decisions in contrast to individual consideration for each decision.

5. *Continuous monitoring allowing for flexibility*

The utilization of models in conjunction with computer applications provides the potential for continuous monitoring of changes resulting from improvement policies and programs, by allowing for rapid recalculations in parameters dimensioning urban reality. In the event of sudden and non-expected major changes, this capacity provides policy-makers with the added flexibility of responding immediately and adopting alternative courses of action.

No model can ever be expected to possibly mirror the total complexity of urban conditions and trace their changes. Nor can a model ever provide exact numerical answers for urban policy-making given the analytical and decisional described problems above. Nevertheless the utility of quantitative urban analysis may be summarized as follows: (1) providing a consistent means for gaining understanding of urban conditions and problems through clearly defined and rigorous steps of intellectual immersion; and (2) evolving a mechanism for improved policy formulation, implementation, and evaluation.

Turning from the abstract to the concrete, is it possible to come to any basic conclusion as to whether the benefits of overall urban models have repaid the effort and expense which has been pound into them? In the minds of many, the answer is clearly "No". An especially lucid statement of this position is given in a recent article by Douglas Lee.[19] We find ourselves in sympathy with many of Lee's comments about over-elaborate models and their lack of usefulness, as given for urban policy and, indeed, this field of large-scale urban models runs a great risk of making the same mistakes which were made in developing massive GNP models, whose predictive accuracy remain highly questionable. However, if the models are kept general and simple enough, it is still not clear that they may not prove of significant use to planners as *general guides* for urban policy. Here, we feel that the final verdict on large-scale urban models is still not in. For the usefulness of models which deal with specific urban problems rather than overall formulations, the reader must now turn to the chapters which follow.

[19] "Requiem for large-scale models", *Journal of the American Institute of Planners*, May 1973.

PART II

The Economic Base of Urban Life

2. *Urban Labor Markets and Labor Force**

ELCHANAN COHN, C. GLYN WILLIAMS, AND RICHARD M. WALLACE
WITH JANET C. HUNT

I. Introduction

"America the melting pot" has long been one of the cherished traditions of the United States. The notion held that wave after wave of varying nationalities and races could come to this land and with relatively little delay and discomfort be assimilated into the rest of the population. And the notion seemed to hold true through most of the nation's history, with the large city acting as the catalyst which forged the process.

For two centuries they came, the Scots, the Germans, the Irish, the Jews, the Italians, and other Europeans, largely from agrarian backgrounds and speaking little English. On arriving, they settled largely in the great cities of the Eastern seaboard, New York, Boston, Philadelphia, and Baltimore, where they learned the language, the customs, and the discipline demanded in the industrial setting. And for two centuries or more the process seemed to work well, albeit not as painlessly as some might choose to believe. The immigrants worked and learned and after a generation or two moved on to make room for the next wave.

In the years following World War II the city appeared no longer able to fulfill its traditional catalytic function in the assimilation process. Rather than being the gateway to opportunity, the city appeared to have become the agent of radial isolation and economic repression. The last great wave of immigrants arrived to find the jobs not available to them and the opportunity for mobility and assimilation lacking. The changes taking place in the urban areas were driven home to the rest of the nation by the great urban riots of the middle and late 1960s. Although some writers, such as Edward Banfield (1968), dismissed the phenomenon as being of little relevance, many others were not content to dismiss the problem so lightly, and attention was focused on the high rates of unemployment, low wages, and low labor force participation rates found in a number of urban poverty areas.

Ever since separate census data on blacks were first kept in 1880, each decennial census has shown a movement of blacks into urban areas, and particularly from the rural South to the industrial centers of the Northeast (Taeuber, 1974). The immigration did not begin in earnest, however, until World War I, and prior to that time even Harlem, the nation's oldest black ghetto, was predominantly white (Edwards, 1968). During the War, manpower shortages opened many employment opportunities to blacks in the factories of the Northern industrial states.

The new employment opportunities, combined with a long-term trend in the displacement of agricultural workers through mechanization, initiated the first great wave of black migration to the cities which continued unabated throughout the twenties.

* We would like to thank without implicating our colleagues G. E. Breger, C. R. Hill and R. C. Martin for extensive comments on a previous draft of this chapter.

World War II again brought manpower shortages, and manufacturing job opportunities were available to blacks in large numbers. With employment in agriculture still declining, the second great wave of immigration began, and has continued up to the present time. The magnitude of these waves of immigration has been such that the Black American is now far more urbanized than his white counterpart (Taeuber, 1974).

Traditionally the well-paying jobs available to the unskilled or semiskilled in the city have been manufacturing jobs, and it was primarily such jobs that represented opportunities for training and advancement. However, throughout this century, two trends have operated which eventually had far-reaching effects on employment opportunities for inner city residents. The first of these was the relative decline in the importance of manufacturing in the economy, along with an absolute drop in manufacturing employment due to automation. Furthermore, the growing service sector was experiencing most of its increment in skilled service areas. The second trend has been the movement of manufacturing jobs away from the inner cities to suburban areas. This process became very evident immediately following World War II when a great deal of new plant construction occurred, nearly all of it on extensive land sites often located many miles from the center of the city.

Thus the situation faced by the unskilled inner city resident in the post-war years was one of rapidly declining manufacturing job opportunities. The manufacturing jobs that were left were in the oldest and least productive plants, and had little scope for skill advancement. The service jobs in the inner city were becoming more skilled, and race might have constituted a greater barrier to entry than in manufacturing. The manufacturing jobs in newer, more productive plants were located far away. Being unable to afford a private automobile or the higher priced suburban housing, with a public transportation system incapable of delivering inner city residents to the highly dispersed plant sites in the suburbs, the new immigrants were effectively cut off from any but low-paying, dead-end jobs.

During the same time period agricultural employment has continued to decline, so the process of migration has continued long after one would have expected the limited opportunities of the city to have reversed it. One might better speak of blacks being driven from the rural areas by the absolute lack of any opportunity than to speak of their being drawn to the increasingly narrow opportunities of the city. At least there is some opportunity for employment and advancement there. This same factor has brought large numbers of Southern blacks, Puerto Ricans and Mexican-Americans into a number of large cities further confounding the situation.

Additional evidence by Knight (1973) indicates that the nature of industrial production and employment in metropolitan areas has been undergoing significant change during the last 30 years. Firms have found it attractive to locate in urban areas in response to growth in the urban labor markets which, in turn, caused labor to become more heterogenous. However, as metropolitan industries have shifted from export-oriented (i.e. exports to other areas, not necessarily other countries) to local-oriented productions, "metropolitan labor markets [have] continuously [been] upgraded" with firms demanding low-level skills (such as apparel and textiles) moving outside the metropolitan areas to tap available surpluses of unskilled labor (Knight, 1973, p 101). Such labor market dynamics have created a rising demand for highly skilled workers along with a decline in the demand for low-skilled workers. To the extent that migration of low-skill labor into metropolitan areas continues unabated despite the changes just described, urban labor-market imbalances are likely to be exacerbated (Knight, 1973, pp. 107–8).

The focus of this chapter is on "urban" as distinct from "rural" labor markets. However, if the term "urban" is broadly defined, and if account is taken of the extra urban fringe which combines urban work with rural residence, then the term "urban labor market" covers most of the nation's labor force. This has been true for some time. However, until recently, discussion of urban labor markets tended to center on the inner city. This practice highlighted the phenomena which were important for manpower policy but unduly narrowed the framework for inquiry. More recently interest has grown in urban labor market segments other than the inner city. Thomas Stanback's (1974) discussion of suburban labor markets is an excellent overview of research on this important part of the urban structure.

THE PLAN OF THIS CHAPTER

Before discussing labor market theory and characteristics, it is necessary to ask: Just what is an urban labor market? Section II will be addressed to that question, followed in Section III by a brief discussion of the various theories of the labor market. Section IV provides some data and discussion concerning labor market characteristics, followed by an examination of problem areas in urban labor markets in Section V. In Section VI we provide a brief outline of various measures adopted or proposed to reduce unemployment and underemployment and increase labor force participation and wages for the urban (mainly inner-city) workforce. Some concluding comments appear in the final section.

II. Delineating Urban Labor Markets

It is easier to analyze the labor market as a theoretical construct than as a spatial administrative entity. Theoretically, a geographic area may contain as many labor markets as there are individuals and firms. For some workers their labor markets extend discontinuously far beyond their commuting range. For other (probably most) workers, the commuting range defines their effective labor market. Similarly firms in close proximity with one another might draw on labor markets differing greatly in areal characteristics, depending on their labor force size, job content, wages, and other factors. What might therefore be termed as an urban labor market would be composed of a vast assemblage of submarkets delineated by various characteristics and linked by labor mobility.

Clearly, labor market delineation is important for administrative and policy purposes. However, the administrative areas may not be based solely on labor market considerations, and the labor market may itself be partly determined by the location of political and administrative boundaries. Residential and plant location decisions are, at least in part, determined by zoning, municipal tax structures, and by public services in the form of education, transportation, and medical facilities.

STANDARD METROPOLITAN STATISTICAL AREAS (SMSAs) AND BEA's ECONOMIC AREA

The ties between labor market and administrative areas have led many government agencies and urban or regional analysts to formulate planning areas in terms of labor market divisions. The standard metropolitan statistical area (SMSA) used by the Bureau of the Census has strong labor market ties, SMSA being so defined as to include areas in which a high proportion of the workers is employed in the central city. The Economic Areas designed by the Bureau of Economic Analysis (BEA) are likewise functionally integrated areas. As described by the BEA, each area is a nodal entity having an export sector, a residentiary sector and, as nearly as possible, a self-contained labor force so that inter-area commutation is minimized.

FUNCTIONAL ECONOMIC AREAS (FEAs)

An alternative approach by Karl Fox has among its objectives the incorporation of urban centers excluded from coverage by the SMSA concept. Fox defines a "functional economic area" as an area whose residents can "purchase within its boundaries a complete or nearly complete line of consumer goods and (can) enjoy a full range of local government services. Relatively few people living in one FEA would work or shop . . . in another. Each FEA is envisaged as a relatively self-contained labor market in the short run" (Fox, 1974, pp. 137–8).

In a discussion of urban labor markets, the FEAs provide a more comprehensive frame-work than do the SMSAs. Being based largely on home-to-work commuting patterns and having the characteristic of nodality, the FEA are so constructed that employment and residential income have the same boundaries. Moreover, a large part of the income produced in the FEA comes from the production of goods and services consumed by residents of the FEA, the remainder of course, being the exports of the area.

It is obvious though not meaningless to say that urban areas are centers of attraction for firms seeking labor and for labor seeking jobs. Both firms and labor have many different kinds of wants met by location in an urban area. For firms the attractiveness of location near other firms stems from advantages of supplemental services and suppliers that accrue to groupings of firms and more efficient informational services that arise from the proximity of many firms. These localization economies are apart from the pool of labor that a centralized group provides. This is not an explanation of why the groupings occur where they do, but it does explain why the process of grouping has its own dynamics once it is begun. However, the forces are separate and those that dominate under one set of conditions such as a state of technology may become subordinate to others when conditions change. Thus, for example, the lengthening of residence-work radii was strongly tied to developments in commuter transportation over the years, until finally the implicit residential suburbanization process, combined with other factors, such as low land and tax costs, created strong inducements to firms also to suburbanize.

For labor, the urbanization process has many advantages and disadvantages quite apart from those associated with jobs. But the labor market net advantages are powerful and have resulted in a persistent urbanization trend. This is illustrated by the fact that between 1900 and 1960 the percentage of the population residing in urban places (of 2500 or more people, and having certain political features) increased from 39.7 to 63.0. In 1970, on a wider definition, namely that of the metropolitanized area which includes all the suburbs and fringe areas from which workers regularly commute into SMSA central cities, 87 percent of the United States population was urban (Olmstead and Smolensky, 1973, pp. 19–20).

LABOR SHEDS AND EMPLOYMENT FIELDS

Urban labor markets may be thought of in terms of labor sheds, as they relate to firms, and of employment fields, as they relate to workers. A labor shed may be defined as the area from which a plant or firm draws its workers. Frequently cited as a radius extending from a central zone implying a centralized industrial area, a labor shed will in practice display more complex features than symbolized by a radial system. An employment field, in turn, is the area in which the residents from a particular "zone of dispersion" work (Vance, 1960, p. 200). This again is frequently described by a radial system, even though this, too, oversimplifies what is obviously a complex network of job opportunities and commutation patterns.

If labor markets are envisaged as being composed of labor sheds and employment fields, then clearly the boundaries of these markets shift as economic circumstances vary periodically and as economic parameters change over time. During a period of boom, workers may restrict their job preferences to narrower areal boundaries because they can get a satisfactory job nearer home. Firms, on the other hand, in a boom have to go further afield for workers of satisfactory quality, or compromise through higher wages or lower hiring standards to fill their vacancy needs.

Secularly, parameters based on legal, cultural, economic, sociological, and technological factors will also change boundaries which could well be constant in the short-run. Higher incomes might change the labor-supply propensies of families, role changes among husbands and wives might alter the labor force participation rates by sex, and legal changes might alter employment practices and affect the boundaries within which firms can get the labor they desire.

Technology would change in the long run with an effect on the ease and speed of commutation, on the qualitative content of jobs in terms of labor attributes of different kinds (strength, skill, emotional empathy, educational attainment) and on the optimum size of plants. In the long run, moreover, new firms emerge and existing firms expand or contract thereby affecting the intensity of use within a given labor shed and shifting its boundaries.

If such parameters are assumed to be given in the short run, then the determinants of a plant's labor shed will be the size of its required force, its indulgence in non-wage recruitment costs, the wage rate it will pay to fill a given vacancy, and the occupational status level of its labor needs. These are not independent determinants. Given a firm's wage policy and occupational standards, the bigger a firm's labor demands the more extensive will its labor shed boundaries be. Similarly, given a firm's wage policy and labor force size, the higher the occupational status of its labor force the more extensive will its labor shed boundaries be. Or again, the quality and size of the labor force that it can get from a given set of labor shed boundaries will tend to vary directly with the level of its wages relative to the wages of other firms drawing on the same area.

The employment field of an individual will also have variable determinant elements in the shor run. It will be more extensive the greater the willingness to incur search, commutation, or migration costs and to intensify commitment to the labor force, and the more stringent the worker's employment specifications.

Urban studies appear to substantiate the operation of these principles of labor market delineation. Goldner (1955, pp. 121–2) cites a study of journey to work in Chicago which shows that "the degree of work–residence separation increases as the level of occupation rises". This is consistent with the principle that the degree of labor scarcity varies positively with the occupational level so that employers have to search further afield for higher-grade labor. But it is also consistent with the idea that high occupation labor is better informed and able to take advantage of job opportunities over a wider area; that employers may defray the tangible costs of movement for high-skill personnel; and that the higher occupation commands higher earnings which lessen the significance of a given commuting cost (Burtt, 1958, p. 15). Lester (1967, p. 66) concludes that a substantial positive relationship holds between wages and plant size, reflecting the fact that plant size is a determinant of the area from which the firm must draw its labor.

Goodman (1970, p. 190) cites studies showing positive correlations between distance and time spent in travelling to work and pay received. Rees and Schultz (1970, pp. 173–4), in their study of the Chicago labor market, show that additional earnings are associated with travelling 10 miles to work compared with travelling only one block. The association between earnings and distance is positive for all occupations (though varying absolutely and in percentage terms). Although they find that not all the occupational earnings differences by distance to work cover the direct costs of commuting, they point out that only part of the compensation for commuting may be in earnings since some may be in lower housing costs and non-pecuniary income associated with preferred residential locations.

Labor sheds and employment fields may vary for other general reasons besides those discussed above. The employment fields of secondary earners tend to be more limited than those of primary earners. However, since secondary earners are more likely to be female than male, to be less skilled, to be of other than prime age, and to be lower paid than primary labor, it becomes difficult to isolate each of these elements as a determinant of secondary earners' employment fields. Yet it appears that suburban shopping centers depend heavily on such labor, and that the increased labor force participation rates among suburban married women have been an inducement to the suburbanization of light manufacturing industry (Fox, 1974; Olmstead and Smolensky, 1973).

Race is also a complex determinant of employment fields. Race is associated with many variables which, in turn, are associated with limited employment fields. Lower occupational status, educational attainment in years and quality of schooling, lower wage rates in given occupational strata, less mobility because of a lower rate of automobile ownership, also imply limitations on the employment field. Residential and job discrimination, on the other hand, imply more distant travel for work. It is easy to see then that discontinuities can arise in the job-search process, and that urban labor markets may develop segments of poverty, limited opportunity and occupational stratification in which race is a determining factor. This is not at all inconsistent with Taylor's findings in a study of the Chicago labor market that, among other things, blacks travel further to their jobs than whites, notwithstanding that in like jobs they receive lower wages than whites (Taylor, 1968, p. 376). It is these discontinuities that have caused analysts to discuss urban labor markets by segment, and to separate the inner city (or poverty area or ghettoes) from the more affluent suburban areas.

In this section we have identified some determinants of labor sheds and employment fields. We have seen how studies bear out intuitively derived relationships among such variables as commuting distance, firm size, wage rates, worker characteristics, and market discrimination by race and sex. This is not to suggest that these areas are determined by economic factors alone. Rather it is that urban labor markets should be viewed as a complex but systematic network of interdependent labor sheds and employment fields. However, the studies do not rule out discontinuities and it is to these that we now need to address ourselves.

III. Theories of the Urban Labor Market

Efficient though the urban labor market may have been over the years as a clearing mechanism for successive waves of migrants from rural America and from foreign countries, its efficiency is today under heavy attack. Its failings were vividly dramatized by civil disorders in the ghetto areas of many of our large cities in 1966 and 1967. Surveys have shown continuing high rates of poverty, unemployment, underemployment through involuntary labor force non-participation and involuntary part-time work, and even full-time earnings that fall short of poverty standards set by governmental agencies.

Recent writings have examined the labor market discontinuities implicit in the reality of the urban ghetto. They have emphasized the seemingly permanent nature of the barriers to the free flow of labor in the urban community. The labor markets delineated by these barriers have been characterized by theories ranging from those which suggest that the barriers to mobility are imperfections in an otherwise fluid system, to those which hypothesize the existence of the ghettoes as separate and self-sustaining labor markets, to those which view the structures of labor demands and supplies to be institutionally determined in the interests of employers as a social and economic class.

THE NEOCLASSICAL ("ORTHODOX") MODEL

The requirements of a unified labor market in which there are no institutional restraints on mobility are familiar from most elementary textbooks. In the simplest case, labor is assumed homogeneous, information is complete, mobility of both labor and capital is costless, and atomistic competition prevails between large numbers of buyers and sellers (King, 1972, p. 13). The market is characterized by a single wage rate with employers adapting to it according to the constraints imposed by their production functions and workers adapting to it according to their preferences between income and leisure. In more complex markets, in which both jobs and labor are heterogeneous, the resultant wage structure will reflect the relative demands and supplies of jobs and workers. If jobs vary solely in their skill content and the skill can be acquired by education, the wage rates for jobs will reflect the cost of the education needed to enter them. Or again, if laborers are homogeneous in skill but vary in preferences and jobs vary only in their nonpecuniary advantages, the wage structure will reflect the relative supplies of various jobs and demands of workers for these various jobs.

The real world is a far cry from this simple model. Workers vary in many economically meaningful ways, by age, race, sex, marital status, occupational experience, innate abilities and motivations, education and training, and so on. Jobs, too, vary in skill content, wage, location, and so on. Institutional practices in job search by workers and in worker recruitment by employers, institutional wage-determination practices, and the roles of time, uncertainty and imperfect information all serve to make the real world far more complex than that portrayed in simple unified labor market models.

However, many labor theorists find it analytically useful and relevant to view the complex system in a general competitive labor market framework. Reder (1955) and Oi (1962) explain cyclical changes in wage differentials as a response to cyclical changes in relative supplies and demands, respectively, of skilled and unskilled labor. Studies of the household as a resource supplying and utility consuming unit either use or do not rule out continuous functions among household members to arrive at the division of responsibilities and rewards in a family context (Heckman, 1974; Gronau, 1973; Gramm, 1975). Theorists interested in decision-making under conditions of imperfect information and uncertainty (Phelps *et al.*, 1970) find it useful to segment the labor force within a competitive framework. Holt (1974) uses a segmented model to simulate the labor market activity of workers and employers in a total market system.

Thus, it is not the case that the competitive labor market framework has no analytic relevance. But many writers claim that it has little meaning in analyzing the ghetto labor market. These ideas have been embodied in what have become known as the dual and radical labor market models.

Even Albert Rees, a learned analyst in the traditional mode, recognizes the bases of dual and radical ideas which are discussed below. He describes (1968, p. 11) the Chicago labor market as being, in one sense, a single labor market because it is linked together by commutation flows and by some area-wide collective bargaining agreements. But it has a number of geographic submarkets within it—marked by wage differences related to patterns of residential and non-residential areas, concentrations of particular kinds of industry, and concentrations of non-white population. He is not persuaded, though, that a depressed secondary labor market is an inevitable feature of America's capitalism, believing instead that a free enterprise economy with full employment and without discrimination in employment "could perhaps wipe out much of the present low-wage, dead-end job syndrome" (Rees, 1974, p. 143).

Some criticisms of the neoclassical model. The dual labor market and radical theorists point to many characteristics of ghetto labor and labor markets that cast doubt on the efficacy of the competitive model.[1] Among the features that distinguish the ghetto labor markets from those of the suburbs are the persistence of wide differentials in earnings, unemployment, in voluntary part-time work, job instability as reflected in frequent short spells of unemployment, and the incidence of poverty, which in the ghettoes often coincides with full-time work. Also, the national experience in which investment in human capital through education and training of various kinds leads to higher earnings and less unemployment is found by observers to be untrue in the ghetto. The range of jobs tends to be the same irrespective of worker qualifications. Work as a source of income alternates with other sources such as welfare, participation in a government-sponsored training program, and illegal activities. Workers move from one training program to another, but the new jobs they get are no higher in status than those which they held prior to entering the initial program.

THE DUAL LABOR MARKET

The dual labor market model has been described by Piore (1972, p. 2). In his words*:

> The basic hypothesis of the dual labor market was that the labor market is divided into two essentially distinct sectors, termed the primary and the secondary sectors. The former offers jobs with relatively high wages, good working conditions, chances of advancement, equity and due process in the administration of work rules and, above all, employment stability. Jobs in the secondary sector, by contrast, tend to be low paying, with poorer working conditions and little chance of advancement; a

[1] See especially Piore, 1971; Doeringer and Piore, 1975; Piore, 1974; Vietorisz and Harrison, 1972; Reich *et al.*, 1973.
* Reprinted by permission.

highly personalized relationship between workers and supervisors which leaves wide latitude for favoritism and is conducive to harsh and capricious work discipline; and with considerable instability in jobs and a high turnover among the labor force. The hypothesis was designed to explain the problems of the disadvantaged, particularly black workers in urban areas, which had previously been diagnosed as one of unemployment.

Most jobs in the secondary sector are dead-end and unstable jobs so that the workers are on frequent layoff. The jobs tend to be self-terminating, give little return to experience and seniority, and thus generate high voluntary turnover. The jobs are plentiful so that unemployment in the sector is not associated with waiting for a good job so much as waiting to take on a similar low-paying and undesirable job.

The dual labor market model was not intended to portray urban labor markets in their entirety, with the primary sector relating to the suburbs and the secondary sector to the inner city. Piore asserts, however, that the secondary sector portrays convincingly the realistic condition of black urban ghetto labor markets (Piore, 1971, p. 94). Segmented by kinds of job and by a complementary structure of kinds of workers, the urban ghetto labor market is set apart from the urban labor market in general. It has its own self-perpetuating mechanism which can be influenced only by direct interference through manpower policies to break the cycle of poverty and underemployment.

THE RADICAL THEORY

The radical theory as it might be applied to urban labor markets goes beyond the dual labor market model. It accepts the division of the labor market into primary and secondary sectors, and that division's implicit segmentation of workers. The ruling capitalist employing class makes use of natural differences in workers (in terms of race, age, sex, or other attributes) to emphasize divisions among the labor class. Cultural and institutional differences also provide divisions among which employers as a class effect coalitions designed to further employer class interests. It is an interpretation of history and current affairs into which the alleged exploitation of workers generally, and more specifically the alleged discrimination by race, sex and age fits neatly. But its validity is hard to prove. Improvements in the economic status of any working-class segment result only from the coincident interest of employers in improvements. Moreover, classes are difficult to define, and apart from the very general coalitions that express themselves on general issues through political process even coalitions are difficult to organize particularly on an ever changing basis to meet changing needs.

THE THREE MODELS: A DISCUSSION

All three models of the ghetto labor market have elements of truth. This is evident from studies clarifying and comparing the ideas of the main protagonists.[2] The neoclassical model explains much of the ghetto poverty unemployment and underemployment in terms of productivity differences. These differences stem from human capital variations in education, training, health, and the other components of motivation and aptitudes that fit workers for competition for work. But many facts about the ghetto remain unsolved in the neoclassical framework. Among these are the persistent inequality in the distribution of

[2] See Cain, 1976; Wachter, 1974; Flanagan, 1973; and Rosen, 1974.

income, continuing inequality in the earnings of black and white male full-time, year-around workers, and the failure of education and training programs to improve in any statistically significant way the work experience of the urban poor. Moreover, the neo-classical model is not able to explain the persistence of discrimination and apparent inefficient use of black labor resources which characterize the urban ghetto. Important also is the need to accept racial discrimination as an exogenous factor in explaining income variations in human capital terms. However, whether the last objection is sufficient grounds for rejecting the neoclassical theory and substituting the radical theory is clearly another matter.

The dual labor market model also contains valid elements. There are good jobs and poor jobs having the characterstics that Piore and others ascribe to them (Doeringer and Piore, 1971 and 1975; Reich, Gordon and Edwards, 1973). Moreover, they may well have the self-sustaining dynamics that some of the dual theorists ascribe to them (Vietorisz and Harrison, 1972). They may be particularly identifiable in the context of the general urban labor market structure, with its characteristic division into suburban and inner city segments. But as Rees (1974, pp. 131–4) points out it is difficult to establish the comprehensiveness of the classification. There are low-wage jobs with good promotion ladders, high-wage jobs which are unstable and high-wage jobs which are dead-end. Poor jobs merge into good jobs along many lines, and there is no single spectrum on which jobs can be intuitively ranked.

The documentation of these differences lies outside the discussion at this point. However, a group of writers (Spring *et al.*, 1972) describe the problem of underemployment as revealed by the Census Employment Survey (CES) of 1970. The survey covered central-city areas which included city poverty areas but were not restricted to them. The authors show that in 1970 when nationwide unemployment amounted to 4.9 percent of the labor force, unemployment in the CES central city survey areas was 9.6 percent. Distinguishing workers who wanted to work but were not in the labor force added 2.9 percentage points (the New York City figure only) to the unemployment figure. Adding again the percentage of persons working part-time who wanted full-time work added another 2.3 percentage points (again for New York City) to the index of underemployment. Accepting a poverty cut-off wage rate of $3.50 an hour, the number receiving less than that figure swells the underemployed to 61.2 percent for the survey areas. Setting the poverty wage rate at $2 puts the 51-city average underemployment rate at 30.5 percent.

Whether or not the segmentation is permanent only time will tell. Over time the barriers to mobility may be undermined by competitive forces, by reductions in institutional racism because of cultural or legal developments; by the active involvement of government in human capital augmenting programs or in activities to break the cycle of poverty and underemployment. Till then it would seem that all three theories can contribute to understanding the urban labor market and to forming appropriate government policies to meet its obvious failings.

IV. Characteristics of the Urban Labor Market

This section includes a brief discussion of both historical developments and current (as of 1970) labor market characteristics. Additional discussion of urban labor market characteristics is provided in the next section (Problems in Urban Labor Markets).

The variables that are commonly discussed in the present context include wages, unemployment rates, and rates of male and female labor force participation. Of particular interest is the variation in such variables (1) between urban and rural places; (2) between small and large cities; (3) between center cities and their suburban fringe; and (4) between poverty and nonpoverty sections of metropolitan areas.

A number of studies bearing on our investigation have appeared in recent years. In a National Bureau of Economic Research (NBER) study, Fuchs (1967) found that wages (for the same type of job) vary directly with city size, the results taking into account adjustments for race, age, and other pertinent factors that might otherwise cloud the city-size wage relation.

Studies do not, however, show a consistent relationship between city size and unemployment rates. In one British study, Vipond (1974) found that unemployment increases with city size over most of the range (for size), but decreased for the largest city, London (suggesting an inverted U curve). Data for the United States, in contrast, indicate a positive relationship between city size and unemployment, but the results are not statistically significant. A reasonable explanation for such results is that larger urban areas in the U.S. have attracted large populations of low-skill, specifically black workers. Thus, although one would expect lower unemployment rates to be associated with increased city size, other things being the same, it appears that other things are not equal, and the existence of large, perhaps self-contained, urban slums with a concentration of minorities and other poverty neighborhoods contribute to the positive relationship between city size and unemployment.

In an effort to isolate the characteristics of the center city labor market from the suburban fringe, attempts were made by Kain (1968) and Stanback (1974) to divide the labor market areas. Over the post-war period both authors found a decline in employment for center cities in manufacturing, wholesaling, and retailing. In contrast, the suburban ring showed increases in employment in all three sectors, the growth in suburban employment exceeding the loss of jobs in the center city. The only sector in which employment gains were made for the center city was services, where the suburban ring made about the same gains.

Stanback (1974), examining ten metropolitan areas, obtained results similar to Kain's. His study provides not only support for Kain's empirical analysis, but also provides the clearest analysis to date of the urban–suburban distinction as far as labor markets are concerned.

When such studies are viewed in perspective, a pattern emerges of a center city characterized by older firms in manufacturing, wholesaling, and retailing, with new jobs occurring mainly in services, usually requiring high skills. The suburbs, in contrast, are characterized by newer firms, offering generally higher-paying jobs in all sectors with the exception of services in which the wage and skill content is likely to be lower than that found in the center city.

Stanback (1974) points out that the employment structure of the suburbs is determined largely by the structure of the center city. For example, metropolitan areas in which the central city had (historically) been characterized by heavy concentration of manufacturing are likely to have manufacturing represented in the suburbs, while those historically dominated by commerce are likely to have suburbs with a heavy representation of wholesaling and retailing.

DATA FROM THE 1970 CENSUS

Recent Census data shed additional light on the characteristics of urban labor markets. In Table 1, various population and labor-market characteristics are examined for the

TABLE 1. AVERAGE POPULATION AND LABOR-MARKET CHARACTERISTICS OF FIFTY LARGEST CITIES: U.S., 1970

Characteristic	Total (1)	Low-income areas[a] (2)	Higher-income areas[b] (3)
Percent black	24.5	58.1	12.5
Percent Spanish surname	9.3	16.4	6.8
Percent under 18 years old	31.7	37.5	29.7
Percent over 65 years old	10.6	9.4	11.1
Percent high school graduates over 25 years of age	49.9	31.4	55.6
Percent high school graduates of 16–18 years old persons not in school	59.9	46.0	67.1
Percent of female family heads	16.5	29.1	12.7
Percent males over 16 years of age in labor force	79.6	69.2	79.3
Percent males 16–24 years of age in labor force	64.4	58.8	66.6
Percent females over 16 years of age in labor force	45.2	41.6	46.4
Percent females in labor force with children under 6 years of age	32.6	34.5	31.8
Percentage males unemployed	4.6	7.3	3.8
Percent females unemployed	5.0	7.2	4.3
Percent males holding white-collar jobs	43.2	25.2	48.0
Percent females holding white-collar jobs	65.5	44.8	71.4
Percent with income below poverty level	11.3	26.8	6.6
Percent with income over $10,000 per year	47.4	22.4	55.1
Median income	$9607.0	$6099.0	$10,744.0

Source: Bureau of the Census (1973), Tables S1 and S2.
ª Includes areas where at least 20 percent of households have income below the poverty level.
ᵇ Includes all areas not in column 2.

largest fifty cities. The focus here is on the substantial differences found between poverty (low-income) and non-poverty (not low-income) areas. For instance, the rate of male labor force participation is 10 percentage points lower in the poverty areas, while male unemployment in poverty areas is almost twice that in the non-poverty areas. We also find a large difference in the percent of white-collar workers, both male and female, and substantial differences in median income.

Some of the results in Table 1 may be contrasted with the national averages for some of the labor-market characteristics. For example, the percent of family heads who are female is 10.8 nationwide in contrast with 16.5 in Table 1. This indicates a much lower incidence of female family heads in small cities and rural areas. Also, the poverty rate (percent of families with income less than $3000) is somewhat smaller nationwide (10.3) than in the fifty largest cities (11.3). Also noteworthy is the fact that the cities contain, on the average, a larger percent of persons over 65 years of age (10.6 percent compared to 9.9 percent nationwide). Finally, we find a nationwide median-income level for whites lower than the reported average in the non-poverty areas ($9957 compared to $10,744), yet the nationwide median income for blacks ($6063) is almost identical to the figure found for the low-income areas ($6099).

Further insights may be gleaned from Table 2, in which data for the U.S. as a whole are contrasted with data for SMSA's and urbanized areas (including only the urban portion of the SMSA's, which also contain some rural areas adjacent to cities). In some instances, the lack of substantial differences between the three categories is quite striking. For

TABLE 2. LABOR FORCE AND POPULATION CHARACTERISTICS: TOTAL U.S., SMSA'S AND URBANIZED AREAS, 1970

Characteristic	Total U.S.	SMSA's	Urbanized areas
Percent urbanized	73.5	88.2	100.0
Percent of total population	100.0	68.6	58.2
Percent white	87.6	86.7	85.2
Percent black	11.1	12.0	13.2
Percent foreign stock	16.5	20.0	21.6
Percent Spanish origin	4.6	5.5	6.5
Percent with less than 12 years education	52.3	55.3	55.9
Rate of unemployment (percent)	4.4	4.3	4.3
Type of employment (*percent*)			
Manufacturing	25.9	25.8	25.5
Wholesale–Retail	20.1	20.7	21.1
Services	7.7	8.0	8.2
Education	8.0	7.8	7.8
Government	16.1	16.0	16.0
Construction	6.0	5.6	5.3
Percent of families with female heads	10.8	11.5	12.3
Family income (*percent*)			
Less than $3,000	10.3	8.1	7.9
$3,000–$4,999	10.0	8.4	8.2
$5,000–$6,999	11.9	10.4	10.2
$7,000–$9,999	20.6	19.9	19.5
$10,000–$14,999	26.6	28.7	28.7
$15,000–$24,999	16.0	18.9	19.4
$25,000 and up	4.6	5.6	5.9
Median income	$9586	$10,469	N.A.
Median income—whites	$9957	$10,885	N.A.
Median income—blacks	$6063	$6,828	N.A.

N.A. = not available.
Source: U.S. Department of Commerce, *1970 Census of Population: City and County Data Book*, Washington, D.C.: Government Printing Office, 1973, Tables 1, 3, and 4.

example, the distribution of employment by type of industry reveals only slight differences between urbanized areas and the U.S. as a whole, although we do see a pattern suggesting a greater weight of service jobs in urbanized areas. We also find little differences in the unemployment rates among the three categories, though we have already noted the substantial variation found between the poor and non-poor sections *within* cities.

We do find, however, substantial variations between urbanized areas and the U.S. data in such population characteristics as percent black, percent foreign stock, percent Spanish origin, education levels, the percent of families with female heads, and family income distribution.

What the results presented here suggest is that urban labor markets are distinguishable from other labor markets in a few characteristics, such as percent black in population, percent female heads, and median income. The most pervasive distinction of urban labor markets, however, lies not in comparison to total labor markets but rather in the existence of diverse submarkets within metropolitan areas. The data in Table 1, and other data discussed elsewhere in the chapter, clearly demonstrate the substantial differences between the so-called ghetto urban areas and other non-poverty (typically white) portions of the urban labor market.

V. Problem Areas

This section attempts to identify problems in urban labor markets. A study of this kind must necessarily focus on the central city poverty areas as it is here that the mechanisms enabling a smooth flow of labor into jobs fail to work, and problems manifested in this area are of a uniquely urban character. Historically the urban environment has efficiently attracted and dispersed immigrant labor. However, today transportation problems and minority concentration and isolation have established these core centers as areas of high unemployment and underemployment. Center cities lack steady job availability and information concerning employment as well as opportunity for their residents to acquire skills needed in the labor market.

Students of labor economics are usually introduced to three types of unemployment: frictional, demand-deficient (cyclical), and structural. Frictional unemployment is due to job turnover, taking place between the time a worker leaves one job and the time he accepts another. It reflects the lack of perfectly smooth adjustments from one employment to the next, due (in part) to lack of perfect knowledge both by workers and employers, and to the lag that inevitably occurs between the time a worker leaves one job and enters another. Demand-deficient unemployment occurs when not enough jobs are available for those seeking work due to insufficient aggregate demand (either nationally or in some regions). In this case, better information systems (such as a job bank) or training and retraining programs would not alleviate unemployment. Structural unemployment refers to an imbalance between the skills demanded by employers and the skills workers seeking employment possess. Thus, unemployment would occur alongside with job vacancies. It is the structural-type of unemployment that is most frequently cited as the main cause of problems in urban labor markets.

Structural unemployment has been linked to automation. Its impact has been described dramatically by Seligman (1966)*:

> ... [T]he economy tends to create a frozen, unusable industrial reserve army with no palpable relation to the affluent, functioning segment of the society. One may estimate the hard-core unemployment attributable to such structural change, that is, stemming from alterations in production functions or capital–labor coefficients, or whatever it is the theoretical economist wishes to call them—changes that are inherent in technology—at approximately 1.3 million persons. But this is merely the visible portion of technology's toll. To these souls one must add, as does Leon Keyserling, a million or more workers who have dropped out of the labor force because they got tired of looking for jobs and are therefore not counted in the official census, and a million in fulltime equivalents for those working part-time. (p. 9.)

Underemployment is also an issue in the inner-city labor markets. Harrison notes that a greater proportion of poverty neighborhood residents work part time and work less overtime than the national average (Harrison, 1972, p. 45). Also jobs tend to be of a lower occupational status and earnings are less (Harrison, 1972, pp. 45–50). In 1968 both white and nonwhite laborers in poverty areas worked slightly fewer hours per week than their non-poverty area counterparts—38.2 against 39.1 hours (Ryscavage, p. 53). In almost all areas non-whites suffer greater underemployment than their white neighbors and benefit less from acquiring skills that should make them more marketable.

The physical location of slum areas is another negative factor in employment. As noted earlier, jobs for the unskilled and semiskilled within cities have long been replaced by those of a highly technical nature. Manufacturing initially moved to the suburbs, but the greatest

---

* Reprinted with permission.

gains in suburban employment today are in retailing, wholesaling, and other service occupations. Access to jobs is of key importance. Public transportation primarily serves to move suburban residents into the cities. Thus the only feasible solution to get inner-city workers to jobs which are widely dispersed throughout the suburbs is the automobile, and ownership and operation is especially costly for city residents.

Demographic factors also affect the employment status of inner-city residents. Minorities, who comprise the majority of central city occupants, are discriminated against in the job market. Empirical evidence supports the hypothesis that blacks are "last hired, first fired" during periods of varying economic activity (Harrison, 1972, p. 45). In 1971 when unemployment on the whole climbed to 5.9 percent, it was estimated that non-white unemployment reached 9.4 percent (Friedlander, 1972, p. 209).[3]

Sex discrimination, too, should not be overlooked if one considers the higher incidence of female family heads and labor force participation rates among black females. With unemployment of female family heads at 9.3 percent in 1973, this surely contributed to the poor status of urban-core families. The younger age structure of minorities relative to whites has been cited as a possible factor in these higher unemployment rates. Notice that unemployment among inner-city teenagers has been twice the national rate in recent years (Harrison, 1972, p. 45).

A related problem is that of the discouraged worker. Because of the greater difficulty for ghetto workers to obtain jobs, whether because of availability, discrimination, or low investments in human capital, we would expect the discouraged worker effect to be higher than normal.[4] Thus disguised unemployment exists in the sense that those who have dropped out of the labor force are not included in statistical counts of unemployment.

The labor force participation rate (LFPR) for the urban poor was lower than for urban non-poverty area residents: 56.5 percent compared to 60.5 percent of population 16 and over in 1968 (Ryscavage, 1969, p. 54). Here, lack of motivation appears to be a problem which conceivably might be compounded by availability of public assistance. Empirically we find a higher incidence of inner-city population receiving government aid than elsewhere, but caution must be used in associating this with negative work incentives. Results of different studies are contradictory. For example, the labor supply was found to be only slightly reduced when families received financial assistance in the New Jersey–Pennsylvania experiment.[5]

---

[3] It should be pointed out, however, that these phenomena might be attributable to lower productivity levels of backs and not to racial discrimination as such. See Gilman (1965).

[4] The discouraged worker phenomenon refers to the situation where workers who have despaired of finding suitable jobs leave the labor force (which includes both those working and those seeking work) altogether. Related to this phenomenon is the "discouraged worker hypothesis" which states that in times of declining aggregate demand more persons will be leaving the labor force; and vice versa in times of increasing aggregate demand. Mention could also be made of the "additional workers hypothesis", arguing that in times of declining aggregate demand, "the rising levels of unemployment bring additional or secondary workers *pari passu* into the labor market. As unemployment contract . . . these additional workers will leave the labor force" (Barth, 1968, p. 375). See also Strand and Dernburg (1964).

[5] The issue of the work incentives effects of government welfare programs has received considerable attention in recent years. While the results are conflicting, the majority of studies conclude that labor-supply effects of welfare payments are negligible for the entire population. There are, though, some findings that support the contention that workers with very low incomes might be affected more severely by such programs. See, for example, Brehm and Saving (1964), Stein and Albin (1967), Kasper (1968), and Leuthold (1968). Findings of the New Jersey–Pennsylvania negative income-tax experiment (conducted jointly by Wisconsin's Institute for Research on Poverty and Mathematica, Inc.) are summarized in Pechman and Timpane (1975) and Cain (1974). For a fuller account see Watts and Rees (1973).

The social costs of underutilization of inner-city labor involves more than loss of a production base. Poverty induces atypical behavior as a rational reaction to intolerable circumstances. The high rate of crimes and the rioting of the sixties support this belief. Studies have shown that the greater the opportunity for illegal activity, the lower the reported unemployment rate among non-whites and slumdwellers (Friedlander, 1972, p. 207). Also heroin addiction is negatively related to unemployment. Under these conditions an alternate labor system develops whose members are engaged in gambling, stealing, prostitution, and the like. This results in lower labor force participation among those whose income is from illegal means (Friedlander, p. 208). The social consequences of economic insecurity tend to perpetuate illegality and alienation. In addition, external effects of poverty, in the form of crime spreading outside the poverty neighborhoods, are shown to exist, so that losses from crime and the additional police protection required to stem the tide of crime accrue to the entire metropolitan area (Wolfgang, 1968, p. 251).

VI. Manpower Programs and Policies

Since many of the poor and the disadvantaged are concentrated in poverty areas of large cities, any manpower program of national scope may be expected to have an impact on cities, and particularly on urban poverty areas. Major programs which have been proposed or implemented will be described, and empirical evidence on the effectiveness of programs will be discussed where such studies have been made. We will attempt to relate each program to its actual or expected impact on urban poverty areas. The analysis will focus on programs designed to reduce frictional and structural unemployment or underemployment.

THE AREA REDEVELOPMENT ACT

The first serious attempt by the Federal government to reduce the impact of structural unemployment culminated with the passage of the Area Redevelopment Act (ARA) in 1961. The ARA program has later been replaced by such programs as the Manpower Development and Training Act (MDTA) and various Economic Opportunity Act programs that will be discussed below. We note, however, that the ARA excluded the large urban areas, being focused upon depressed, rural areas.

An examination of a sample study of the ARA program in West Virginia by Stromsdorfer (1968) indicates that the program was successful in increasing employment and before-tax earnings. Moreover, Stromsdorfer concludes that the "average monetary benefits exceeded average monetary costs during the 18-month post-training period" (p. 139). Although he cautions against generalizing the conclusions, it seems that the program clearly had substantial potential for alleviating structural unemployment.

THE MDTA

The first program open to urban residents, the MDTA combined both institutional and on-the-job training. Enacted in 1962, the program drew its enrollees from heterogeneous backgrounds, and of the major manpower programs that followed it was the only one designed for all age groups.

Because of the length of time the program has run and the large numbers of people it has enrolled, the MDTA has been the most extensively studied of all manpower programs. The empirical studies have yielded a wide range of estimates which can be discerned in most of the studies. Enrollees in the MDTA generally display higher wage rates and lower rates of unemployment after completing the program than do peer groups who received no training. The on-the-job training programs were found to be more effective than were the institutional programs, both in increasing wages and in reducing unemployment. Although the disadvantaged did not profit as much as others from the institutional programs, the differentials in on-the-job training programs were found to be much narrower (Goldstein, 1972).

THE JOB CORPS

Two additional manpower programs—the Job Corps and Neighborhood Youth Corps —were implemented in 1965 and were directed at youth (defined as those between 16 and 21 years of age), in contrast to the general scope of the MDTA. The Job Corps employed an institutional framework in which volunteers were sent to Job Corps Centers where they spent half the time in classes and the other half working on projects operated by the Center. Depending on the particular Center, there was some flexibility in the program, with older enrollees being permitted to work outside the Center, or with the 50 percent academic load being reduced or even eliminated. The research on the effectiveness of the Job Corps is neither as extensive nor as reliable as that for the MDTA, but the results of studies are uniformly discouraging, largely because of the programs' high cost per enrollee balanced against modest initial increases in earnings of only $203 per year (Cain, 1968). Further studies revealed that even those small earnings increments did not persist long, and after a year had fallen to a level where even if persisted forever would not cover the costs of the program.

It should be noted, in fairness to the program, that the studies were made in the early phase of the Job Corps Program, at a time when it was plagued by administrative problems and uncertainty as to direction. There was also considerable variation in the quality of Centers, and the selection of the sample could have biased the study. Furthermore, a large number of the enrollees in the program were there involuntarily, having, in effect, been "sentenced" to the program by juvenile courts in lieu of jail (Public Law 88–452, Section 111).

NEIGHBORHOOD YOUTH CORPS

Of all the manpower programs, the Neighborhood Youth Corps (NYC) was directed most specifically at urban poverty areas. Although the program contained both public employment and manpower aspects, its principal thrust was to increase skill levels and formal education among disadvantaged youth. The Economic Opportunity Act of 1964 stated the purpose of the Neighborhood Youth Corps as being: "... to provide useful work experience opportunities for unemployed young men and young women, through participation in State and community work-training programs, so their employability may be increased or their education resumed or continued . . ." (Fechter, 1975, p. 22).

In order to achieve the goals stated in the Act, three separate programs were established: (1) the Neighborhood Youth Corps In-School Program was designed to reduce the number of school dropouts by providing public employment after school and on weekends; (2) the Summer program provided summer employment for youths, principally those still in school or who had just graduated; and (3) the Neighborhood Youth Corps Out-of-School Program provided jobs for dropouts in order to increase their skill levels and to encourage them to resume their formal education. Between the time it began to function in 1965 and the elimination of the program by the Comprehensive Employment and Training Act of 1973, over 800,000 participated in the In-School Program, over 2,000,000 in the Summer Program and over 700,000 in the Out-of-School Program. Because of its 8 years of existence and the magnitude of the program, the Neighborhood Youth Corps has been the subject of a number of empirical studies, the findings of which will be described as they relate to the major goals of the program.

One of the major goals of the Neighborhood Youth Corps, particularly of the In-School Program, was the continuation of education. In the most comprehensive study of the program, Somers and Stromsdorfer (1970, pp. 251–2) found that participation in the program had no significant effect on the probability of graduation from high school or on the number of school years completed. They did, however, report a significant effect on the probability of attending college and on the probability of participation in post-high school training.

Two other studies yielded results similar to those of Somers and Stromsdorfer, although with some differences. Gerald Robins (1969), using data on the Neighborhood Youth Corps in Detroit and Cincinnati, found no reduction in the school dropout rate and no increase in levels of educational aspiration or scholastic achievement on the part of enrollees in the program. George F. Brown (1972), using the same data base as Somers and Stromsdorfer, found no improvement in school dropout rates or in the probability of post-high school training that could be attributed to participation in the program.[6]

The second major objective of the Neighborhood Youth Corps was to improve employability and implicitly to improve earnings of the disadvantaged youth. Somers and Stromsdorfer (1970, Table 39) found that having participated in the program yielded increased annual earnings of $830, with blacks receiving more advantage than whites, and women receiving practically no advantage. About half the earnings increment resulted from lower unemployment rates among those who had completed the program. The high rates of return reported by Somers and Stromsdorfer have been challenged, particularly on the grounds that length of participation in the program was not a significant determinant of added earning power, and, thus, participation in the program was actually a proxy for other factors, such as ambition.

THE CONCENTRATED EMPLOYMENT PROGRAM (CEP)

During the late 1960s another program was inaugurated specifically addressed to alleviate unemployment among the urban hard-core. Known as the Concentrated Employment Program (CEP), it was distinguished from other programs in two main characteristics. First, it provided a variety of services to participants, including a 2-week orientation program, testing, counseling, job training (through any one of the federal programs

---

[6] A critical evaluation of the Robins and Brown studies is contained in Pitcher (1973), p. 59.

available at the time), and job referral. Second, efforts were made to recruit persons who might be eligible for the program. By centralizing all such services within one program the CEP was supposed to avoid the bureaucratic runaround that often causes its potential clients to fail to secure the help they need. And by seeking out potential enrollees the program attempted to close an informational gap and reduce suspicion of and hostility toward government programs.

Although substantial sums were expanded on the program, it is not clear that the long-run effects were favorable. Two studies of the CEP—one for Columbus, Ohio (Lewis *et al.*, 1971; and Lewis and Cohn, 1973), and the other for Cleveland, Ohio (Allerand *et al.*, 1969)—indicate that orientation, training, job referral, and other services provided to the hard-core will not materially increase their propensity to hold jobs unless, at the same time, attractive jobs are opened to them. Most of the unemployed youth in Columbus, for instance, were aware of the existence of vacancies in low-skill, low-paying jobs. They simply did not care to work in such jobs, and there is no reason to believe that any amount of coaching, job guidance, or orientation programs could convince them that they should take them (Lewis *et al.*, 1971, p. 2).

OTHER PROGRAMS

In addition to purely public programs, such as Job Corps, Neighborhood Youth Corps, and Manpower Development and Training Act Programs, others have been implemented which attempt to achieve on-the-job training for the disadvantaged through private businesses. Among such programs is the Work Incentive Program (WIN, not to be confused with the buttons which appeared briefly in the latter part of 1974). WIN largely represents an effort to "get people off the welfare rolls", but is also intended as a manpower training program. Directed at recipients of Aid to Dependent Children (ADC), the program offers employers a subsidy of 20 percent of the salary for hiring ADC recipients, while providing penalties if the recipients failed to accept employment under the program. Unfortunately, deficiencies in data have made any analysis of the program impossible. There are certain disincentives which make its success doubtful, however. Any earnings over $30 a month are taxed at a two-thirds rate, and males who work over 100 hours per month are ineligible for any assistance under ADC.

Another program similar to WIN is the National Alliance of Businessmen—Jobs in the Business Sector (NAB-JOBS) program, a cooperative effort of the NAB and the United States Department of Labor. Under the JOBS program, employers voluntarily pledge to give a certain number of jobs to disadvantaged workers, and to provide on-the-job training for them. Criticism has been leveled at the programs' optimistic claims of success, particularly in a General Accounting Office (1971) report which contended that most of the jobs pledged under the program were low-skilled ones with traditionally high turnover rates. In addition to JOBS and WIN, proposals have been made to require government contractors to employ a fixed proportion of disadvantaged as trainees (Meyers, 1968) and to subsidize private industry to locate in poverty areas and employ disadvantaged workers (Levitan *et al.*, 1970). Criticism of both types of proposals have centered on the fact that they would merely reinforce existing tendencies by bringing more unskilled workers into the poverty areas (Feldstein, 1973).

Another class of manpower programs is public employment programs which have manpower aspects. The first major public employment programs were implemented in the

United States during the 1930s with the creation of the Works Progress Administration and the Public Works Administration, but with the end of the Great Depression, those programs were not seriously considered for over a quarter of a century.

In 1965 an amendment to the Economic Opportunity Act established "Operation Mainstream", a relatively small-scale program to provide work on conservation projects for the unemployed and underemployed. A larger-scale program was implemented when the Emergency Employment Act of 1971 created the Public Employment Program (PFP), which was the largest public employment program since the 1930s and was designed to provide approximately 160,000 jobs in the public sector. The jobs were to be of a temporary nature and were to be administered by the state and local governments, being made available whenever the overall unemployment rate exceeded 4.5 percent.

The PEP expired in 1973, a period of relatively high employment, and was replaced by a more modest public employment program under the Comprehensive Employment and Training Act (CETA). The fall of 1974, however, saw the beginning of a sharp rise in unemployment which reached nearly 10 percent in 1975, so several increases in funding have been made to provide public service jobs for those unemployed workers whose benefits have been exhausted. Proponents of PEP, CETA, and other public employment programs contend that the benefits of such programs are: (1) they relieve cyclical unemployment; (2) they reduce structural unemployment by teaching job skills to the disadvantaged; and (3) they increase the levels of public services (Davidson, 1972, p. 31).

Opponents of PEP and CETA contend that the programs merely displace other public employment. Both programs provide federal funds for the creation of new employment at the state, county, and municipal levels, with the bulk of employment actually being at the municipal level. Evidence has been presented that demonstrates that the programs merely displace employment in local governments which would have occurred in any case, and thus the effects of the programs might not be significant (IRRA, 1974, and Fechter, 1975, pp. 12–20).

In order to reduce urban poverty, any of the manpower programs discussed must aim primarily at the young members of minority groups, particularly blacks and those of Spanish heritage, and toward women who are heads of household. It is those groups who constitute the bulk of the problem of unemployment and underemployment. There are, however, certain inherent weaknesses in any manpower solution to the problem.

Perhaps the greatest weakness is the absence of jobs for which manpower programs qualify the urban poor (Lewis and Cohn, 1973, p. 850). The perception of job opportunities must be expected to have an important effect on the willingness of people to make the investment in time and effort required by the program. The fact is that even after completing the training, the disadvantaged worker often finds good jobs inaccessible. This problem is particularly acute for minority groups who are faced with barriers to employment and housing, isolating them from many of the better-paying jobs in the suburbs.

It is obvious that manpower training alone cannot have the desired effect of eliminating urban poverty areas. Any such programs must be accompanied with programs to make jobs available, either through encouraging industries to locate in the inner city, or by giving residents of the inner-city access to jobs in the suburbs. The access to suburban jobs can be accomplished either through transportation policy, or through housing programs. In addition, a two-tier minimum wage system, offering a lower minimum wage to youth and possible other hard-core groups, might reduce the reluctance of employers to provide on-the-job training (Feldstein, 1973).

VII. Conclusions

It is clear by now that our focus has been placed on identification of imbalances in urban labor markets and search for government policies that could resolve them. But first, we had to distinguish urban labor markets from other labor markets and discuss the framework(s) within which labor imbalances are assumed to occur (that is, what theory of the labor market one assumes to hold). An examination of labor market characteristics indicates that labor problems are typically associated with low-income residence, hence programs which attempt to reduce labor market deficiencies (in wages, unemployment, or under-employment) must be directed mainly at the "hard-core" population who typically reside in the black ghettos of America's large cities. Our examination of the various man-power programs dating back to 1961 indicates both successes and failures, with the latter occurring far more frequently in those programs designed to help those with whom most of the labor market problems are said to be associated.

AREAS FOR FURTHER RESEARCH

There is room aplenty for those who wish to pursue research in this area. First, we are not totally satisfied with the delineation of urban labor markets, as discussed in Section II, nor do we have sufficient information to study the inner-city–suburban segmentation hypothesis. Although census data provide detailed information by census tract, the latter is not necessarily identical with labor market areas, and additional investigation in both original data collection and further analysis of existing data should be extremely helpful.

There are many who are not convinced of the accuracy of the dual labor market hypo-thesis. Is the phenomenon of segmentation transitory? Is it possible that the dynamics of the labor market, through the infusion of additional human capital into the urban poverty areas, would in time reduce black-white differentials in income, employment, and social status? Such questions require not only additional data but a refinement of available methodology to deal with labor market dynamics.

Students of both labor economics and poverty would be delighted to know more about the characteristics of urban labor markets. For example, what is the *net* relationship between city size and wages, unemployment, and labor force participation rates (when other things are held constant)? What is the relationship between the nature of urban environment (including such considerations as type of employment, general characteristics of the areas in terms of the availability of municipal services, recreation, etc., geographic location, and other factors) and labor market characteristics? How do workers, especially in poverty areas, respond to welfare and other government programs? What are the short- and long-run consequences of various manpower programs? Such questions are obviously begging suitable answers.

In summary, we need further evidence on the nature, magnitude, and causes of labor imbalances in urban areas, and on methods that would effectively reduce them.

References

Allerand, M. E. *et al.* (1969) *A Study of Impact and Effectiveness of the Comprehensive Manpower Pro-gram of Cleveland, AIM-JOBS*, Vol. 2, Cleveland, Ohio: AIM Research Project, Case Western Uni-versity.
Banfield, E. C. "Rioting mainly for fun and profit." In Wilson (1968), pp. 311–34.

Barth, P. S. (1968) "Unemployment and labor force participation." *Southern Economic Journal*, **34**, 375–82.
Brehm, C. T. and Saving, T. R. (1964) "The demand for general assistance payments." *American Economic Review*, **54**, 1002–18.
Brown, G. F. *et al.* (1972) *Analysis of the Neighborhood Youth Corps Program*, Arlington, VA: Center for Naval Analysis.
Bureau of the Census (1973) *Census in Population: 1970, Subject Reports, Final Report PC (2)—9B—Low Income Areas of Large Cities*, Washington. D.C.: U.S. Government Printing Office.
Burtt, E. (1958) *Labor Supply Characteristics of Route 128 Firms*, Research Report Number 1, 1958. Boston: Federal Reserve Bank of Boston.
Cain, G. G. (1968) *Benefit/Cost Estimates for Job Corps*, Madison, Wisconsin: Institute for Research on Poverty, University of Wisconsin.
Cain, G. G. (ed.) (1974) "Symposium on the graduated work incentive experiment." *Journal of Human Resources*, **9** (Spring), 156–278.
Cain, G. G. (1975) *The Challenge of Dual and Radical Theories of the Labor Market to Orthodox Theory*, Discussion Papers 255–75. Madison, Wisconsin: Institute for Research on Poverty, University of Wisconsin.
Cain, G. G. (1976) "The Challenge of Segmented Labor Market Theories to Orthodox Theory: A Survey." *Journal of Economic Literature*, **14** (Dec.), 1215–57.
Davidson, R. H. (1972) *The Politics of Comprehensive Manpower Legislation*, Baltimore: The Johns Hopkins Press.
Doeringer, P. B. and Piore, M. J. (1971) *Internal Labor Markets and Manpower Analysis*, Lexington, Mass.: D. C. Heath & Co.
Doeringer, P. B. and Piore, M. J. (1975) "Unemployment and the 'dual labor market'." *The Public Interest*, **38** (Winter), 67–79.
Edwards, F. E. (ed.) (1968) *Franklin Frazier of Race Relations*, Chicago: University of Chicago Press.
Fechter, A. (1975) *Public Employment Programs*, Washington, D.C.: American Enterprise Institute for Public Policy Research, Evaluative Studies No. 20.
Feldstein, M. S. (1973) *Lowering the Permanent Rate of Unemployment*, A Study for the Joint Economic Committee, U.S. Congress. Washington, D.C.: Government Printing Office.
Flanagan, R. Y. (1973) "Segmented market theories and racial discrimination." *Industrial Relations*, **12** (Oct.), 253–73.
Fox, K. A. (1974) *Social Indicators and Social Theory*, New York: John Wiley & Sons.
Friedlander, S. L. (1972) *Unemployment in the Urban Core*, New York: Praeger Publishers.
Fuchs, V. R. (1967) *Differentials in Hourly Earnings by Region and City Size, 1959*, Occasional Paper no. 101. New York: National Bureau of Economic Research.
General Accounting Office, Comptroller General of the United States (1971) *Evaluation of Results and Administration of the Job Opportunities in the Business Sector (JOBS) Program in Five Cities*, Washington, D.C.: Government Printing Office.
Gilman, H. J. (1965) "Economic discrimination and unemployment." *American Economic Review*, **55** (Dec.), 1077–96.
Ginzberg, E. (ed.) (1974) *The Future of the Metropolis: People, Jobs, and Income*, Salt Lake City: Olympus Press.
Goldner, W. (1955) "Spatial and locational aspects of metropolitan labor markets." *American Economic Review*, **45** (March), 113–28.
Goldstein, J. H. (1972) "The Effectiveness of Manpower Training Programs: A Review of Research on the Impact on the Poor", a staff study prepared for the use of the Subcommittee on Fiscal Policy of the Joint Economic Committee, 92nd Congress, 2nd Session. Washington, D.C.: U.S. Government Printing Office.
Goodman, Y. F. B. (1970) "The definition and analysis of local labour markets: some empirical problems." *British Journal of Industrial Relations*, **8** (July), 179–96.
Gramm, W. L. (1975) "Household utility maximization and the working wife." *American Economic Review*, **65** (Mar.), 90–100.
Gronau, R. (1973) "The intrafamily allocation of time: the value of the housewives time." *American Economic Review*, **63** (Sept.), 634–51.
Harrison, B. (1972) *Education, Training, and the Urban Ghetto*, Baltimore: The Johns Hopkins University Press.
Heckman, Y. (1974) "Shadow prices, market wages and labor supply." *Econometrica*, **42** (July), 679–94.
Holt, C. C. (1974) *Modeling a Segmented Labor Market*, Working Paper Number 350–63. Washington, D.C.: The Urban Institute,.
IRRA (1974) "Employment and training: CETA's first year", Four Articles. *Proceedings*, Section VII. Madison: Industrial Relations Research Association.
Kain, J. F. (1968) "The distribution and movement of jobs and industry." In Wilson (1968).

Kasper, H. (1968) "Welfare payments and work incentives: some determinants of the rates of general assistance payments." *Journal of Human Resources*, 3, 86–110.

King, Y. E. (1972) *Labour Economics*, London: The Macmillan Press.

Knight, R. V. (1973) *Employment Expansion and Metropolitan Trade*, New York: Praeger Publishers.

Lester, R. A. (1967) "Pay differentials by size of establishment." *Industrial Relations*, 7 (Oct.), 57–67.

Levitan, S. A., Mangum, G. L., and Taggart, R. III (1970) *Economic Opportunity in the Ghetto: The Partnership of Government and Business*, Baltimore: The Johns Hopkins Press.

Leuthold, J. J. (1968) "An empirical study of formula income transfers and the work decisions of the poor." *Journal of Human Resources*, 3, 312–23.

Lewis, M. V. and Cohn, E. (1973) "Recruiting and retaining participants in a manpower program." *Industrial and Labor Relations Review*, 26 (Jan.), 842–50.

Lewis, M. V., Cohn, E., and Hughes, D. N. (1971) *Recruiting, Placing, and Retaining the Hard-to-Employ*, University Park, PA: Institute for Research on Human Resources, The Pennsylvania State University.

Meyers, F. (1968) "Jobs and housing: a program." Los Angeles: University of California, Institute of Industrial Relations, Reprint No. 183.

Oi, W. (1962) "Labor as a quasi-fixed factor." *Journal of Political Economy*, 70 (Dec.), 538–55.

Olmstead, A. and Smolensky, E. (1973) *The Urbanization of the United States*, Morristown, New Jersey: General Learning Corporation.

Pechman, J. A. and Timpane, P. M. (eds.) (1975) *Work Incentives and Income Guarantees: The New Jersey Negative Income Tax Experiment*, Washington, D.C.: The Brookings Institution.

Phelps, E. S. *et al.* (1970) *Microeconomic Foundations of Employment and Inflation Theory*, New York: Norton.

Piore, M. J. (1971) "The dual labor market: theory and implications." In *Problems in Political Economy: An Urban Perspective*, D. M. Gordon (ed.), Lexington, Mass.: D. C. Heath & Co.

Piore, M. J. (1972) "Notes for a theory of labor market stratification." Working Paper Number 95. Cambridge, Mass.: MIT Department of Economics, October.

Piore, M. J. (1974) "The 'New Immigration' and the presumption of social policy." Industrial Relations Research Association, *Proceedings of the 27th Annual Meeting*.

Pitcher, H. H. (1973) *The Neighborhood Youth Corps, an Impact Evaluation*, Washington, D.C.: U.S. Department of Labor, Technical Paper No. 9 (Sept.).

Reder, M. W. (1955) "The theory of occupational wage differentials." *American Economic Review*, 44 (Dec.), 833–52.

Rees, A. (1968) "Spatial wage differentials in a large city labor market." Industrial Relations Research Association, *Proceedings of the Twenty-first Annual Meeting*, pp. 1–11.

Rees, A. "Low-wage workers in metropolitan labor markets." In Ginzberg (1974), pp. 131–43.

Rees, A. and Schultz, G. P. *et al.* (1970) *Workers and Wages in an Urban Labor Market*, Chicago: The University of Chicago Press.

Reich, M., Gordon, D. M., and Edwards, R. C. (1973) "Dual labor markets, a theory of labor market segmentation." *American Economic Review* (Proceedings), 50 (May), 359–65.

Robins, G. D. (1969) *An Assessment of the In-School Neighborhood Youth Corps Project in Cincinnati and Detroit with Special Reference to Summer-Only and Year-Round Enrollees*, Philadelphia: National Analysis.

Rosen, S. (1974) "Theories of poverty and unemployment", by David M. Gordon (book review). *Journal of Political Economy*, 82 (Mar.–Apr.), 437–9.

Ryscavage, P. M. (1969) *Employment in Urban Poverty Neighborhoods*, Washington, D.C.: Bureau of Labor Statistics, U.S. Department of Labor, Special Labor Force Report No. 109, June.

Seligman, B. B. (1966) "Introduction." In B. B. Seligman (ed.), *Poverty as a Public Issue*, New York: The Free Press.

Somers, G. G. and Stromsdorfer, E. W. (1970) *A Cost-Effectiveness Study of the In-School and Summer Neighborhood Youth Corps*, Madison, Wisconsin: Industrial Relations Research Institute.

Spring, W., Harrison, B., and Vietorisz, T. (1972) "Crisis of the underemployed." *New York Times Magazine*, Nov. 5.

Stanback, T. M. "Suburban labor markets." In Ginzberg (1974), pp. 51–69.

Stein, B. and Albin, P. S. (1967) "The demand for general assistance payments: comment." *American Economic Review*, 57, 575–84.

Strand, K., and Dernburg, T. (1964) "Cyclical variations in civilian labor force participation." *Review of Economics and Statistics*, 46, 378–91.

Stromsdorfer, E. W. (1968) "Determinants of economic success in retraining the unemployed: the West Virginia Experience." *Journal of Human Resources*, 3 (Spring), 139–58.

Taeuber, K. E. "Social and demographic trends: focus on race." In Ginzberg (1974), pp. 31–50.

Taylor, D. P. (1968) "Discrimination and occupational wage differential in the market for unskilled labor." *Industrial and Labor Relations Review*, 21 (Apr.), 375–90.

Thompson, W. R. (1965) *A Preface to Urban Economics*, Baltimore: The Johns Hopkins University Press.
Vance, Y. E. Jr. (1960) "Labor-shed, employment field, and dynamic analysis in urban geography." *Economic Geography*, **36** (July), 189–220.
Vietorisz, T. and Harrison, B. (1972) "Labor market segmentation: the endogeneous origin of barriers to mobility." Industrial Relations Research Association, *Proceedings of the 25th Annual Meeting*, pp. 277–85.
Vipond, J. (1974) "City size and unemployment." *Urban Studies*, **11**, 39–46.
Wachter, M. L. (1974) "Primary and secondary labor markets: a critique of the dual approach." *Brookings Paper on Economic Activity*, **3**, 637–93.
Watts, H. W. and Rees, A. (eds.) (1973) *Final Report of the New Jersey Graduated Work Incentive Experiment*, Vols. 1, 2, and 3, Madison: University of Wisconsin, Institute for Research on Poverty.
Wilson, J. Q. (ed.) (1968) *The Metropolitan Enigma*, Cambridge, Mass.: Harvard University Press.
Wolfgang, M. E. "Urban crime." In Wilson (1968).

Further Readings

(*Note:* Although some of the items listed here are also contained in the list of Literature Cited, the present list provides a selection of basic works providing a general discussion of the issues outlined in the chapter.)

Aronson, R. L. *The Localization of Federal Manpower Planning*, Ithaca, New York: State School of Industrial and Labor Relations, Cornell University, 1973.
Ashenfelter, O. and Rees, A. *Discrimination in Labor Markets*, Princeton, New Jersey: Princeton University Press, 1973.
Cain, G. G. "Symposium on the graduated work incentive experiment." *The Journal of Human Resources*, Vol. IX, No. 2 (Spring 1974).
Cain, G. G. *The Challenge of Dual and Radical Theories of the Labor Market to Orthodox Theory*, Discussion Papers 255–75, Madison, Wisconsin: Institute for Research on Poverty, University of Wisconsin, 1975.
Cain, G. G. (1976) "The Challenge of Segmented Labor Market Theories to Orthodox Theory: A Survey." *Journal of Economic Literature*, **14** (Dec.), 1215–57.
Chinitz, B. *City and Suburbs*, Englewood, New Jersey: Prentice-Hall, Inc., 1964.
Durbin, E. F. *Welfare Income and Employment*, Praeger Special Studies in U.S. Economic and Social Development. New York: Praeger Publishers, 1969.
Friedlander, S. L. *Unemployment in the Urban Core*, New York: Praeger Publishers, 1972.
Ginzberg, E. (ed.) *Manpower Strategy for a Metropolis*, New York: Praeger, 1970. [Especially "Education and work", by Ivar Berg.]
Ginzberg, E. (ed.) *The Future of the Metropolis: People, Jobs, Income*, Salt Lake City: Olympus Press, 1974.
Gordon, E. M. *Theories of Poverty and Underemployment*, Lexington, Mass.: D. C. Heath, Lexington Books, 1972.
Hall, R. "Why is the unemployment rate so high at full employment?" *Brookings Papers on Economic Activity*, **3** (1970), 369–410.
Hammermesh, D. S. *Economic Aspects of Manpower Assuming Programs*, Lexington, Mass.: Heath Lexington Books, 1971.
Hansen, N. M. (ed.) *Growth Centers in Regional Economic Development*, New York: The Free Press, 1972.
Harrison, B. "Ghetto economic development." *Journal of Economic Literature*, **12** (Mar. 1974), 1–37.
Hirsch, W. Z. *Urban Economic Analysis*, New York: McGraw-Hill Book Co., 1973.
Holt, C. C. *Modeling a Segmented Labor Market*, Working Paper Number 350–63, Washington, D.C.: The Urban Institute, 1974.
Kerner, Otto. *Report of the National Advisory Commission on Civil Disorders*, New York: Bantam Books, 1968.
Knight, R. V. *Employment Expansion and Metropolitan Trade*, New York: Praeger Publishers, 1973.
Leven, C. L., Legler, Y. B., and Shapiro, P. *An Analytical Framework for Regional Development Policy*, Cambridge, Mass.: The MIT Press, 1970.
Levitan, S. A., Mangum, G. L., and Marshall, R. *Human Resources and Labor Markets*, New York: Harper & Row, 1972.
McLennan, K. and Seidenstat, P. *New Business and Urban Employment Opportunities*, Lexington, Mass.: D. C. Heath & Co., 1972.
Mangum, G. L. "Manpower research and manpower policy." In Somers, G. G. (ed.), *A Review of Industrial Relations Research*, Madison, Wisconsin: Industrial Relations Research Association Series, Vol. II, 1971.

Marshall, R. "The economics of racial discrimination." *Journal of Economic Literature*, **12** (Sept. 1974), 849–71.

Olmstead, A. and Smolensky, E. *The Urbanization of the United States*, Morristown, New Jersey: General Learning Corporation, 1973.

Pascal, A. H. (ed.) *Racial Discrimination in Economic Life*, Lexington, Mass.: Heath Lexington Books, 1972.

Rees, A. and Schultz, G. P., *et al. Workers and Wages in an Urban Labor Market*, Chicago: The University of Chicago Press, 1970.

Segal, M. *Wages in the Metropolis*, Cambridge, Mass.: Harvard University Press, 1960.

Stanback, T. M. and Knight, R. V. Suburbanization and the City, unpublished manuscript. New York: Columbia University, 1975.

Thompson, W. R. *A Preface to Urban Economics*, Baltimore: The Johns Hopkins Press, 1969.

Ulman, L. (ed.). *Manpower Programs in the Policy Mix*, Baltimore, Md.: Johns Hopkins University Press, 1973.

Wachter, M. L. "Primary and secondary labor markets: a critique of the dual approach." *Brookings Papers on Economic Activity*, **3** (1974), 637–93.

Wilson, J. Q. (ed.) *The Metropolitan Enigma*, Cambridge, Mass.: Harvard University Press, 1968.

Yavitz, B., Morse, D. W., and Dutka, A. B. *The Labor Market: An Information System*, New York: Praeger Publishers, 1973.

3. *Urban Housing Markets and Housing Policy*

JEROME ROTHENBERG

I. Introduction

This chapter will discuss the question of housing policy. I state this as "the question of housing policy", rather than housing policy itself, because I shall not be undertaking a systematic examination of the variety of possible housing policies and their consequences. Rather, I shall be considering what has to be understood about urban housing markets in order to be able to predict the consequences of different types of housing policy.

I shall begin in Section II by discussing what appear to be the major characteristics which distinguish urban housing markets from other types of commodity markets. This will suggest the kinds of variables and relationships that have to be delineated in analytic models. Following this, I shall present in Section III a comparative static model of the market which captures some salient aspects of the phenomena described earlier, and which contains novel features relative to existing literature. I shall then indicate in Section IV how the insights drawn from such a model can be used to evaluate housing policy by applying the model to the analysis of a rent-control program. Finally, since Section II will argue that a number of the truly characteristic features of urban housing markets are expressly dynamic phenomena, I shall sketch out in Section V the requirements for an effective dynamic model, as well as additional questions for future research in the field.

II. Distinctive Characteristics of Urban Housing Markets

A. STRUCTURAL FEATURES

Urban housing markets are not a good representative of the abstract general market of conventional economic theory. They possess a number of distinctive features that are, at one and the same time, integral to urban housing and difficult to integrate within conventional market theory. Inclusion of these features does considerably complicate the analytic, and even more the econometric, treatment of the field; but omission in the interests of tractability may seriously misrepresent the phenomena being modeled. The purpose of this essay is to bring to attention some of these distinctive features, and to delineate a theoretical approach which attempts to grapple with them in a constructive manner. The approach underlies a particular set of currently ongoing econometric studies in which the author is involved, but is compatible with a broader family of empirical efforts.

The two most important features of urban housing are the localization in consuming housing services and durability of housing capital.

1. *Localization*

Housing is a consumption activity that for an overwhelming proportion of households occurs at a single spatial location during each conventional economic period (say one year). Most commodities are produced in a great variety of places and are transported to—or by—consumers for consumption at one or more places, or consumers selectively travel to various sites where different instances of consumption may occur. Housing does not possess either the portability of the typical commodity or the variety of sites at which sequences of consumption may take place. For most households consumption of housing services takes place at a single site, where the selected combination of components of the housing package exists. Housing therefore serves as an anchoring function, "placing" a household at a particular spatial location which, because of the real costs in overcoming distance, becomes a base for a variety of other forms of consumption involving both private and public goods. It is this localization that creates the concept of residential neighborhood and household accessibility, and hence deeply links the economic dimension of urban activities with the sociological and political dimensions.

2. *Durability*

Housing capital is by far the most durable capital incorporated in consumer goods. Indeed, it is much more durable than any form of business capital as well, if the longevity of housing units in older countries like Europe is considered—units at every quality level which are up to 400 and 500 years old!

Durability means more than simply the continued physical existence of a structure. It means that a structure does not ineradicably lose its current marketability just because of growing age. An older unit remains a good substitute in the market for units just built, even at advanced age. This continued relative serviceability is due partly to the fact that technological change in residential construction has not so much changed the nature of housing services as the materials used to produce them. The more fundamental changes in the nature (or quality) of the services have generally been associated with capacities instalable in older units at modest cost or with equipment obtainable independently of the housing unit proper.

Not only does economic viability remain with age, it is not marginal. While depreciation does occur with time and usage, maintenance, repair, and larger improvements can enable high-quality units to continue to offer high-quality services through advancing age. Thus, old houses are not necessarily poor houses. They can exist throughout the spectrum of quality. Advancing age does influence the cost at which any given quality can be maintained: it becomes more expensive with time. Thus, older houses are often observed to be of low quality (or in poor condition) due to *economic* calculation, not by physical necessity; but in other market circumstances the higher maintenance costs are worth making, and units are observed at higher qualities (and better condition).

We have stressed the persistence of economic viability in terms of the services that older units render. But there is another side to durability. Housing structures are very expensive to do away with. Even where age makes serviceability disappear it does not make the structure disappear. Units which are desired to be retired may simply be allowed to crumble. But the site occupied by them cannot be reclaimed for re-use unless the structures are physically demolished. This demolition is very expensive, amounting to a not inconsiderable proportion of the original cost of the structure itself (at constant prices). Thus, even when not wanted, old structures tend to remain in existence and, under many circumstances, this continued existence makes it economically worthwhile to continue to use them for housing.[1]

3. *Multi-dimensional heterogeneity*

Housing units in an urban area are heterogeneous, not homogeneous. They differ markedly in a number of dimensions. Differences in the physical units themselves are well known, embracing size, number of rooms, architectural layout and style, structural amenities, and condition, among others. But a housing unit comprises more than simply the structure, because of the localization function referred to above. It is a package, consisting of the structure, the land lot, the neighborhood and the configuration of accessibility to different desirable destinations within the urban area and outside. Each of these other dimensions displays wide differences as well. Lots differ in size, topography, view, placement on the block, etc. Neighborhoods differ in demographic character, assortment of private goods available, quality and variety of public goods provided (and their effective tax rates), density and land-use mix. Locations differ greatly in the real cost involved in reaching different desirable destinations because of distance, and availability and quality of different transportation modes.

Most commodities can be shown to be packages of several components, and some or all of these components can be shown to differ for different brands or sellers. But heterogeneity has some special features for urban housing.

First, households differ substantially in their tastes for housing. They differ in the importance they ascribe to alternatives on each dimension of the package, and in the relative importance of the different dimensions, i.e. the preference tradeoffs within each component, and across components. This means that the differences to be observed in actual units matter in the market and are thus likely not to be accidental but at least to a degree intended. Second, households behave as though these differences matter a great deal. They engage in very substantial (and thus costly) search in order to find an especially appropriate package. Also, they show a willingness to pay very high premiums for notably attractive combinations. Price differences in the market are considerable for packages that seem to differ only slightly. Third, while for most commodities the multiple dimensions that matter to consumers are subject to the control of producers and sellers, this is significantly untrue for urban housing. A producer/owner of a housing unit can substantially control the structure characteristics of the unit over time and, to a lesser extent, the land component. But the neighborhood and accessibility components are at most *selected* by the producer/owner at the outset (and even this selection is likely to be severely constrained) and all subsequent changes are outside his control. Since such subsequent changes can have large effects on the overall desirability of the package, and since they occur without the direct mediation of market transactions between the owner and those responsible for the changes, their existence amounts to a serious potential for pervasive externalities within urban housing markets.

[1] The recent substantial growth in abandonments shows an opposite configuration. Rapid neighborhood decline due to demographic factors, tax considerations, public regulations like rent control, make for a sudden collapse of profitability not associated with age. These units are withdrawn from the housing markets despite basic structural integrity.

4. *Convertibility of existing units*

Housing units are highly durable. But their durability is not independent of human action during the aging process. Continued viability in the market requires continued maintenance and repair. Indeed, human intervention during the lifetime of a housing unit can have more radical impact than ensuring its sheer economic survival. A unit constructed to render services at a certain quality level can be converted during its lifetime to render services at either a higher or lower level. Upward conversion is accomplished by making additions to a unit, or improvement of plumbing or electricity, or upkeep, or making architectural changes, or consolidating two or more originally separate units into a single larger unit. In most of these, real resources are being invested to create an improvement.

Downward conversion has two main forms. One is like upward conversion, involving an investment of real resources to decrease the quality of individual units. This occurs where one unit is split into two or more units, each one containing less space and probably fewer rooms than its predecessor. Investment is required here to put up additional partitions and provide the utilities to make each unit complete. The second involves decreasing the level of maintenance and repair so that usage and time will gradually worsen the conditions of the unit.

5. *Capital and current transactions: the capital market*

In Urban America, given conventional standards of living and their translation into technology, a housing unit is a very expensive commodity. Most people occupy units whose market value is at least three times as great as their annual income and greater than their total portfolio of assets. The durability of housing makes it possible to accommodate to the budget and wealth position of households by two means: (1) high mortgages on owner-ship claims; (2) a very important rental market. Probably a larger proportion of housing uses are rented than for any other consumer good. Both of these market patterns lead the housing sector to make very heavy demands on loanable funds, especially long-term funds. Housing is one of the largest clients of the national capital market.

6. *Moving costs*

To a much greater extent than with other types of consumer goods, a change in consumption of housing is costly. First, since heterogeneity in the available stock of housing is considerable, and tastes regarding these differences quite important, substantial search may be required for a household to assure itself of a satisfactory change. Second, even after search is ended, the transaction itself may be costly, because substantial legal and other specialized services are required when a sales transaction occurs, and may even be necessary when long-term lease agreements are involved. The situation is especially complicated when an owner-occupier household wishes to buy a different house, because then the household must not only incur the costs of finding and buying, but must also sell its present unit. Third, move to a new dwelling entails the cost of physically moving a household's possessions, an expensive and often time-consuming process.

One last aspect of moving costs stems from the localization function performed by housing. A household will often embue its present neighborhood with an emotional aura because of the presence there of close friends and relatives, and because of past associations.

This is lost to a greater or lesser extent when moving, depending on what move is involved. For some families this can be an extremely heavy cost. It is not so invariably, however, since families differ in their attitudes toward their neighborhoods. Some actually dislike theirs, and it is in fact the desire to move out of the neighborhood that induces them to change housing. Despite differences, the disruption of a particular style of life anchored around housing is a potentially important element in considering the cost of changing housing.

The above items all refer to a change in consumption brought about by physically changing the site of housing consumptions. But an alternative way to change without moving is to convert a household's present residence to provide the desired changes in housing services. This is generally not possible with rental occupancies, and even with ownership occupancies it is sometimes constrained by the existing lot and perhaps even by zoning. Moreover, it applies only to structure services, and not to other aspects of the housing package. It is, however, a substitute of variable attractiveness for physical moves that avoids the substantial costs of moving.

7. Public constraints

Because of the localization function, and the close association of physical housing conditions on health and safety, housing has been the target of a variety of public interventions, including zoning regulations, health and building codes, and rent control, among others. These can exercise substantial constraints on the actions of suppliers and demanders in the market, and on the working of the market itself. The housing market is not a perfectly free market.

B. SOME OPERATIONAL CONSEQUENCES

1. Pre-existing stock and new units

Because of the durability of housing, units of many ages will offer services at any time. Indeed, in any year all but a minute percentage of all units offering services will have been built before the beginning of the year. The pre-existing stock is the paramount component in the supply of housing in any period. Newly produced units are a small part of the story, although they may have influence disproportionate to their numbers in some respects.

The pre-existing stock is not, however, a passive component of the supply of housing. Because of convertibility, owners of existing units can modify them in directions suggested by changing market opportunities. Thus there are two forms of actual supply response to market forces: the building of new units and the conversion of older units. While the two have similarities, they have differences as well. The sheer magnitude of the pre-existing stock makes the conversion form of supply eminently deserving of understanding.

2. Information

The great variety of housing packages and the importance of tastes regarding differences in those packages lends corresponding importance to information. Active participants in the market must be adequately informed about alternatives to avoid large opportunity losses. Households looking for a unit can expect a wide variety to be available. Substantial search is called for, often lengthy face-to-face search because of the multiple dimensions to be examined.

Costly information is important to sellers as well. The very same diversity in the market makes it difficult for a prospective seller to know the most favorable terms he can realize for his particular unit. He knows that prospective buyers will differ in tastes and information, and therefore in what they are willing to offer for his unit. He must therefore "search" among prospective buyers for the most suitable. His "search" consists in deciding on asking prices, willingness to bargain, length of time to wait before bargaining, etc. This search, no less than buyers search, involves costs—opportunity costs here, as against the combination of opportunity cost and active search costs for buyers.

3. *Market segmentation*

The great diversity of housing packages in the market means that they are not all perfect or even near-perfect substitutes for one another. They are likely to exhibit a whole spectrum of substitutive relationships, from very close to nearly non-existent. It is even possible that various irregularities may exist, e.g. where households differ markedly in the degree of substitutability they accord within a given set of units.

The presence of this spectrum of substitutability means that "the" urban housing market is not *one* market but a complex of differentially related submarkets. Each submarket is a cluster of units widely considered as close substitutes and related to other clusters in terms of the differing degrees of substitutability with them.

This kind of segmentation of the market is abetted by the high cost of adequate information for participants. Participants cannot afford to scan all or even a major part of the market. They delimit their search to the most "relevant" portion of the market, a demarcation probably based on various rules of thumb that reflect prevailing knowledge about highly substitutive clusters. The deliberate decision to avoid being well informed outside modest portions of the market would tend to consolidate both the inequality of substitutability and the unevenness in the distribution of degree.

One consequence of this segmentation is that the different submarkets can experience an independent margin of variation relative to one another: one can have high excess demand, another excess supply, another be well balanced. So housing prices may move disparately among them. Another consequence is that variation initiated within one subsector will have very uneven repercussions on the other subsectors: in general, the closer the relatedness the more nearly parallel the repercussion in direction and intensity.

4. *Transactional friction*

The high costs of active participation in the market—search, transactions, and moving costs—imply that the prospective gains from becoming an active participant (i.e. seeking to make a change) may have to be quite substantial to warrant such participation. Prospective gains arise from changes within the household that affect its housing preferences (among different combinations of the components of the housing package and between housing and non-housing commodities) and from changes in the character and prices of different packages available on the market. Both of these are likely to occur gradually most of the time, although some sudden changes in both do happen.

This suggests that a household that has just made a change is not likely to make another change very soon because of the high participation costs. So active participation is not likely to be continuous for most households but sporadic, with long periods of non-participation not uncommon. This in turn implies that in each period the particular lineup of units available for sale or rental and households seeking units is very important in determining the outcomes of current transactions. Some adaptive self-selection may be involved in determining this lineup, but chance factors are likely to be present as well. The upshot of this raises real questions about the overall efficiency of the market in pairing wants with availabilities, both at any one time and when adaptive responses are made over time by both demanders and suppliers (in the latter because they are adapting to signals that are distorted).

5. *Neighborhood externalities*

The localization function of housing makes the neighborhood component of the housing package important. Since third party changes in neighborhood can affect the desirability of a housing unit independently of the actions of its owner or taste changes by its user, external effects in the housing market can be strong and pervasive. The usual market distortions resulting from externalities are likely to result. In addition, less usual forms of resource immobility can result. For example, adaptation to new market opportunities might be optimal if a group undertook it, yet no one member of the group finds it worthwhile to undertake without the expectation that the others will do so too. Decentralized behavior fails to secure such an expectation and so results in inappropriate individual—and hence aggregate—market performance.

6. *Vulnerability to capital market*

The heavy dependence on the national capital market gives the housing sector a special vulnerability. Aggregate forces can impinge on the capital market for reasons that have little to do with the worthwhileness of housing versus other production or consumption sectors; yet these may have a powerful positive or negative net impact on housing. Macroeconomic conditions may call for heavy use of monetary policy. This will have effects on housing far greater than on other production and consumption sectors, yet unmotivated by any real change in relative national priorities among the sectors.

Thus, vulnerability to the national capital market makes for rather special features in housing.

7. *Dynamics*

Most of the foregoing suggests that actual sequences and timings of actions by participants matter. Disequilibria maintained through frictions and uninformedness and immobilities, and substantial adjustment lags, make it important to understand ongoing processes even more, perhaps, than hypothetical equilibrium destinations. Indeed, they even raise the question whether equilibrium is ever to be observed under any but very special circumstances. The housing market's most distinctive features may well be dynamic, and so efforts to understand it theoretically may have to have much the character of dynamic models.

III. Modeling of Urban Housing

A. A BRIEF BIBLIOGRAPHIC NOTE

Recent years have seen a substantial increase in studies of housing. These have reflected a variety of emphases and styles. One has brought housing use as a consumption activity into close association with mainstream consumption theory. An important work in this direction is Margaret Reid's *Income and Housing*.[2] In this she distinguishes between housing as a capital stock and as a flow of services. She treats the latter as the counterpart of conventional consumer goods, and relates that as the dependent variable to be explained by household demographic and economic circumstances. But housing is treated as a homogeneous commodity available in different quantities and urban market areas are not treated as intrinsic units of analysis. Household permanent income is the critical explanatory variable.

Muth's early paper, "The Demand for Non-farm Housing",[3] goes beyond this in elaborating the relationship between housing as durable capital and as a flow of services. But only a single quantitative dimension—size or amount—is dealt with, and non-structure characteristics are not treated. The supply side is treated as a conventional Cobb–Douglas competitive industry in long-run equilibrium.

The localization dimension of housing has been dealt with heavily mostly in the context of the intra-urban location of residential activity. Indeed, in the early and highly influential treatments of Alonso[4] and Wingo[5] it is not really housing but only residential land use that is studied. The residential function is implicitly assumed to be determined by workings of the land market—so that residential location and quantity of residential land patterns are derived without reference to housing structures at all. The chief issues are the tradeoff between accessibility (distance to CBD) and quantity of land, especially as a function of household income, and the effect on these of transportation costs. Transportation as a variable in influencing these location relationships is treated more fully in a number of transportation-oriented studies, e.g. by Kain.[6] This set of issues is formally embedded in metropolitan-wide location models, as in the influential Herbert–Stevens Penn–Dixie Model.[7]

Muth summarizes and expands this kind of emphasis in his important work, *Cities and Housing*.[8] He combines extensive econometric work on the spatial characteristics of housing markets—location patterns, density patterns, and especially rent gradients—with an analytic treatment of long-term competitive equilibrium for a homogeneous (except for location—CBD or multi-employment center accessibility) commodity with a single Cobb–Douglas production technology, and with long-run supply influence accorded only to new production. This competitive long-run equilibrium model is abstracted by Olsen,[9] and its implications for public policy are elaborated.

[2] Chicago: Univ. of Chicago Press, 1960.
[3] In Arnold Harberger (ed.), *The Demand for Durable Goods*, Chicago: Univ. of Chicago Press, 1960.
[4] W. Alonso, *Location of Land Use: Toward a General Theory of Land Rent*, Cambridge: Harvard Univ. Press, 1964.
[5] L. Wingo, *Transportation and Urban Land*, Washington: Resources for the Future, Inc., 1961.
[6] J. F. Kain, "The journey-to-work as a determinant of residential location", *Papers and Proceedings of the Regional Science Assn.*, p. 9. 1962.
[7] Herbert, J. P. and Stevens, B. H. "A model for the distribution of residential activity in urban areas", *J. Regional Science* 2, pp. 21–36 (Fall 1960).
[8] Chicago: Univ. of Chicago, Press, 1969.
[9] E. O. Olsen, "A competitive theory of the housing market", *American Economic Review*, 59 (Sept. 1969).

A number of studies have broadened the scope of what are essentially land use models by including variables other than single-dimensional accessibility. These models are attempts to explain rentals or market values of residential units. They include neighborhood variables (percent non-whites, median census tract household income, median education level, percent of units over 20 years of age, percent of units dilapidated, etc.), environmental variables (various pollution indices) as well as accessibility and housing unit characteristics (housing size, condition).[10]

The work of Kain and Quigley represents a full recognition of the multi-dimensionality of housing. They engage in a large empirical study with St. Louis data to examine the scope of multi-dimensionality and to organize multiple measurements into a representative set of influential factors through factor analysis.[11] This is important because of the complementary as well as substitutive relationships among housing components.

A different emphasis has been set by descriptive studies of particular sectors of the housing market, emphasizing attitudes, choices, physical conditions, demographic characteristics of occupants, successions of moves by a sample of occupants, etc. An influential work of this sort is by Sternlieb.[12] These studies, especially numerous ones focused on race in housing, have both presented facts about actual housing conditions and housing occupancy, and provided materials for understanding the segmentation (to some extent impermeable) of the housing market complex.

A highly influential early theoretical treatment of housing markets as segmented by quality level is Grigsby's *Housing Markets and Public Policy*.[13] This not only emphasizes heterogeneity, but ties it to a hierarchic linkage of quality submarkets, and indicates the nature of inter-submarket relations through an informative treatment of filtering. A considerable literature has developed the filtering concept further, but there has been some confusion as a result of multiple uses of the term. An article by Lowry attempts to clarify the situation.[14]

In a series of theoretical papers James Sweeney has formalized this concept of the commodity hierarchy and developed various market properties of such hierarchies.[14a]

The present author's comparative static model presented in the next section concentrates on durability, heterogeneity and convertibility, i.e. the importance of the pre-existing stock, its malleability to respond to changing market forces, and the quality-level segmentation of the market. It is an offshoot of a much more complex dynamic model

[10] Ridker, R. G. and Henning, J. A., "The determinants of residential property values with special reference to air pollution", *Rev. Econ. Statist.* **49**, pp. 246–57 (May 1967). Seyfried, W. R., "Location and the centrality of urban land values", *Land Economics*, **46**, pp. 329–33 (Aug. 1970). Nourse, H. O., "The effect of air pollution on housing values", *Land Economics* (May 1967). Straszhelm, M. R., "The demand for residential housing services", Harvard Institute of Economic Research, Discussion Paper No. 192, Sept. 1970, and *An Econometric Analysis of the Urban Housing Market*, New York, N.Y.: National Bureau of Economic Research, 1975; Bradbury, K., Engle, R., Irvine, O. and Rothenberg, J., "Simultaneous Estimation of the Supply and Demand for Household Location in a Multi-Zoned Metropolitan Area," in G. K. Ingram (ed.), *Residential Locations and Urban Housing Markets*, NBER Studies in Income and Wealth 43, 1977.
[11] Kain, J. F. and Quigley, J. M., "Measuring the value of housing quality", *J. Amer. Statist. Assoc.*, **65**, pp. 532–48 (June 1970).
[12] Sternlieb, G., *The Tenement Landlord*, New Brunswick, N.J.: Urban Studies Center, Rutgers, The State University, 1966.
[13] Philadelphia: The Univ. of Pennsylvania Press, 1963.
[14] "Filtering and housing standards: a conceptual analysis", *Land Economics*, **36**, No. 4 (Nov. 1960).
[14a] J. L. Sweeney, "A Commodity Hierarchy Model of The Rental Housing Market," *J. of Urban Economics*, **1**, pp. 288–323 (1974); —, "Quality, Commodity Hierarchies and Housing Markets," *Econometrica*, 1974.

currently being developed which pays attention to most of the characteristics discussed in Section II.[15]

Besides the theoretical-econometric approach of the present author,[16] the quality segmentation of the market complex, with attention to the importance of the existing housing stock and its conversion as supply forces, has been emphasized in the recent work at the Urban Institute headed by De Leeuw.[17] Another important emphasis of the present author's work, the heterogeneity of the housing package from the point of view of user tastes, has been the cornerstone of the very large empirical simulation model of intra-metropolitan location and housing by the National Bureau of Economic Research.[18] Unlike the present author's ongoing work, De Leeuw's study does not explicitly lay the foundation for quality segmentation in the patterns of demand and supply substitutability stemming from multi-dimensionality of the housing package, or attend to the problems involved in mapping the explicit relationship. On the other hand, the National Bureau's work does not attempt to map heterogeneity into a substitutability relationship that organizes both demand and supply responses along a single dimension (for example, to rationalize conversion of existing units).

This section, despite a brevity and selectivity which barely scratches the surface, makes clear that research efforts have proceeded in a variety of ways to increase understanding of urban housing phenomena. Different perspectives, different research techniques, different applications, prevent a real definition or location of the frontier, or even of the salient directions of advance. But while much is yet to be learned—a little of this will be discussed in Section V—much has already been learned.

B. A COMPARATIVE STATIC MODEL OF URBAN HOUSING

1. *Heterogeneity, substitutability and quality-level submarkets*

The point of departure of the present model is that the heterogeneity of housing segments the market into different submarkets. The different types of housing are in reality different, but related, commodities, linked together by different degrees of substitutability. We regard housing substitutability as generally a transitive ordering relation, i.e. housing units can be arranged linearly in terms of decreasing degree of substitutability. Although casual

[15] J. Rothenberg, "A dynamic model of urban housing markets", unpublished, June 1974.

[16] An example of econometric application of this approach is A. Butler, J. Pitkin and J. Rothenberg, "An econometric simulation model of metropolitan housing markets", paper presented at American Real Estate and Urban Economics Association Conference, Dec. 1972; same authors and George Galster, "A second generation microeconomic model of metropolitan housing markets", paper presented at Western Economics Association Conference, Las Vegas, June 1974; G. Galster and J. Rothenberg, "Notes on the specification of an aggregative model of metropolitan housing markets", Working Paper No. 129, Dept. of Economics, MIT, May 1974; J. Rothenberg, "An Approach to the Modelling of Urban Housing Markets, Part 1: Housing Demand," Working Paper No. 149, Dept. of Economics, MIT, Feb. 1975.

[17] F. De Leeuw and N. F. Elkanem, "The supply of rental housing", *American Economic Review*, **61** (Dec. 1971); F. De Leeuw, "The demand for housing: a review of cross-section evidence", *Rev. Econ. Statistics*, **53** (Feb. 1971); F. De Leeuw, "The distribution of housing services: a mathematical model", Working Paper 208-I, Washington, The Urban Institute, 1971; F. De Leeuw and R. J. Struyk, *The Web of Urban Housing*, Washington, D.C. : The Urban Institute, 1975; L. Ozanne and R. J. Struyk, *Housing from the Existing Stock: Comparative, Economic Analyses of Owner-Occupants and Landlords*, Washington D.C.: The Urban Institute, 1976.

[18] G. F. Ingram, J. F. Kain and J. R. Ginn, with contribution by H. J. Brown and S. P. Dresch, *The Detroit Prototype of the N.B.E.R. Urban Simulation Model*, New York, 1972; G. K. Ingram and Y. Oron, "The Production of Housing Services from Existing Dwelling Units," in G. K. Ingram (ed.), *Residential Locations and Urban Housing Markets*, NBER Studies in Income and Wealth, **43**, 1977.

examination suggests the existence of aberrations, such violation is not unique with housing: other multi-dimensional commodities show instances of intransitive preferences even by individuals, let alone group aggregates. As with most of these, one has little ground to expect widespread and serious exceptions to transitivity of substitutability as a market tendency.

The basic approach of this model argues that this linear structure of substitutability can be effectively represented by mapping the multi-dimensionality of housing package into a summary evaluational dimension called "the quality of housing". "Quality" approximates the overall attractiveness of housing packages from the point of view of average market transactions, considering size as well as the other structural and non-structural components of the package. Operationally, the mapping can be accomplished through abstracting consensual marginal tradeoffs by demanders *and* suppliers in the market at equilibrium positions. There are important practical problems associated with making actual measurements, but these are beyond the scope of the present chapter.

Quality level derivation sets a consensual tradeoff gradient for different units and thereby permits arraying these units in terms of differing degrees of substitutability. If B is of higher quality than A, and C of higher quality than B, then B is a closer substitute for A than is C. Units at the same quality level are very close substitutes in the market. These substitutability relations hold for supply as well as demand, because the market consensus we draw upon to generate the quality index refers to equal marginal tradeoffs among housing components by sellers as well as buyers. The assumption is that both buyers and sellers are willing and able to tradeoff along each dimension for others, buyers by choice of composition among different packages, sellers by production decisions in either new construction or conversion. The former tradeoffs are directed by relative preferences, the latter by relative costs. Utility and profit maximization goals, and high competition in the market, lead to an equilibrium in which the marginal tradeoffs of all participants are brought into equality with relative prices and thus with one another. This establishes similar gradients of substitutability for users and suppliers, thereby providing a means of weighting components of the housing package to define an index of quality which can be expected to hold approximately for situations which resemble the original compositional equilibrium (although not necessarily the other aspects of the original equilibrium).

This divides the market into submarkets separated by quality differences. Degree of substitutability, defined as quality difference, is thus established as a single dimensional linkage which organizes the whole market complex with respect to relative strengths of inter-submarket repercussions.

2. *Individual market equilibrium*

Despite characteristics of the housing market which suggest the importance and distinctiveness of dynamic adjustment problems, the present model is one of comparative statics. The author has developed a rather complex dynamic model, and some of its features will be sketched in the last section, which deals with appropriate directions for future research. But it is more cumbersome than is needed for the type of policy issues we have chosen to illustrate here; the static model is more succinct and does illuminate the salient relationships necessary to throw these policy issues into relief.

We shall point out adjustment sequences from time to time, but this is only meant for narrative suggestiveness, not as a substantive contribution. While a fully dynamic model is required for the most profound illumination of urban housing markets, a comparative static approach can capture important distinctive features and be expressible in considerably simpler, more analytically tractable terms.

The population of housing units is composed of "existing" units, produced before the present equilibrium period—E—and "new" units, built in the current period—B.

We distinguish a continuum of different quality-level submarkets, $Q_1, Q_2, \ldots$, as operationally defined above. These are average market substitution—"market hedonic"—levels, not simply different price levels, being identified in terms of the structure and non-structure components of the housing package we discussed earlier. Because of the imperfect substitutability between one level and all others each level has a price associated with it, and market changes may lead to changes in the relative prices between that level and the others. These levels define a form of market consensus, but are not equivalent to household utility levels, since they are predicated on linear substitution rates rather than allowing for the changing marginal tradeoffs presumed to be characteristic of household utility functions.

We assume each household has a utility function of the form:

$$U^j = U^j[\{Q, (R)\}, Z] \tag{1}$$

where Q and (R) together designate a housing unit of given quality level, Q, and relative composition of components of the housing package, the given vector of component ratios (R). Z is the composite commodity of all other goods (relative prices and therefore relative consumption of its constituents assumed constant over variations in housing–non-housing allocations).

We treat Z as the numeraire commodity, i.e. the price of Z is unity,

$$P_z = 1.$$

The budget constraint of the household is:

$$Y^j = P_i Q_i + P_z Z = P_i Q_i + Z \qquad i = 1, 2, \ldots \tag{2}$$

where P_i is the price of a housing unit at quality level i and Q_i is the set of all housing units m for which

$$\sum_{k=1}^{M} \hat{p}_k H_{km} = \hat{W}_i$$

where $\hat{W}_i$ is a theoretical expenditure level i, H_{km} is the quantity of housing component k in unit m, for each of the M components, and $\hat{p}_k$ is the imputed equilibrium price of component k, which serves as a weight in the quality level index $\hat{W}$.

The household is assumed to choose housing and Z to maximize U^j subject to its budget constraint. Its choice is not the conventional one of an optimal quantity of each commodity, where different quantities of a commodity can be obtained at a constant market price per unit of quantity. Since housing at different quality levels are multidimensionally different, they are different commodities, and they have different prices on the market. The household makes a threefold choice: (1) a particular allocation between housing and non-housing, (2) a particular quality of housing, (3) a particular internal composition of the housing package.

Each $\{Q, (R)\}$ is a separate commodity, and the household makes a set of simple yes–no choices among the set permitted by the budget. Given the set of imputed component prices and particular quality-level prices, one particular combination in this set will generally give the highest utility and will be chosen (in case of ties, a random process will select among them).

This choice of an optimal $\{Q, (R)\}$ can be represented by a household demand function. It is derived analytically by solving the first order conditions for utility maximization. Since we assume $(\hat{p}_1, \hat{p}_2, \ldots, \hat{p}_M)$ constant, $(\hat{R})$ is also constant for each household. So our demand function refers to optimal quality level:

$$^DQ^j = D^j[Y^j, (\hat{p}), (P)] \tag{3}$$

where $^DQ^j$ is that Q which maximizes U^j under these constraints, $(\hat{p})$ is the vector of equilibrium implicit component prices, (P) is the vector of given quality-level prices.

This demand can be aggregated for the total given population. Given the population's income distribution (Y^j), its utility functions (U^j) (all j), the vector of housing prices (P_H), each household will choose a unit at one particular quality level. This determines a total demand vector for the different quality levels:

$$D = \{D_1, D_2, \ldots\} \text{ where } D_i = \sum_{\text{all}_j} {}^DQ_i^j.$$

A number of units demanded at each quality level and the various internal compositions demanded are simultaneously determined.

3. *Individual builder and converter supply*

The model treats two types of supply responses. First is the actions of owners of existing units in offering their units at unchanged or changed quality levels. Second is the actions of builders in offering newly built units. It is a central tenet of the model that both types are influenced by the cost and revenue factors set by conditions in the different quality submarkets. To these we now turn.

(a) *Cost functions.* The annual costs of a unit newly built at quality level i by the nth builder is:

$$^n_BC(Q_i) = C^n_K(Q_i) + C^n_R(Q_i) \tag{4}$$

where $^n_BC(Q_i)$ are the total costs (annual flow) for a new unit at level i; $C^n_K(Q_i)$ the capital costs in annual flow terms (mortgage amortization of construction costs, interest-carrying costs, equity capital cost) for a unit at level i; $C^n_R(Q_i)$ are the recurrent annual costs (property tax, maintenance, repair, and operations for a unit at level i).

Omitting capital appreciations and depreciations (as falling outside the scope of comparative statics), the annual cost which the rth owner of an existing owner would incur by converting it from current level k to level i is:

$$^r_EC_k(Q_i) = C^r_K(Q_{0k}) + C^r_{K*}(Q_i : Q_k) + C^r_R(Q_i) \tag{5}$$

where $C^r_K(Q_{0k})$ is the annualized flow of aggregate sunk capital costs for r of the unit originally constructed at level 0 and converted to level k (if k was the original level it is simply the capital costs of level k), $C^r_{K*}(Q_i : Q_k)$ is annual value of the cost to r of converting a unit from level k to i, $C^r_R(Q_i)$ is the annual recurrent cost of maintenance and operation of a unit *at* level i. Thus, recurrent costs for the two types of units are assumed to be the same, insofar as they offer services at the same quality level: recurrent cost refers only to present, converted levels; but for converted units the original capital costs continue

76   *Jerome Rothenberg*

beyond conversion.[19] The two costs differ in their capital costs, where conversion units have a past sunk component and a current discretionary component (the cost of making the conversion from k to i); new units have only a single discretionary component, the full original capital cost of this unit. The variable cost of a new unit to offer services at i equals the total cost of the unit; for an existing unit to be converted to, and offer services at, i the variable cost is only the two discretionary components, the conversion cost and the recurrent cost.

The cost of conversion depends on whether a unit is converted to a higher, or to a lower, level. Upward conversion is treated straight-forwardly like investment in new construction. Downward conversion occurs both as an explicit investment of resources to refashion a unit, and as a deferral of part or all of maintenance expenditures so as to "run down" the quality of the unit to the desired quality level after a sufficient time. The first kind generally involves splitting one unit to obtain two or more units, each of lower quality. To avoid the notational and accounting complexities which this introduces we shall deal only with the second type (although *behaviorally* the phenomenon fits well in the model).

Downward conversion lowers the capital value of the unit. It does this by *saving* on maintenance; so conversion cost here is negative. Equations (6a) shows upward conversion, (6b) downward conversion and the notation differentiating them:

$$C_{K*}^r(Q_j : Q_i, Q_j > Q_i) = C_{K*}^r(Q_j : Q_i) > 0; \tag{6a}$$

$C_{K*}^r(Q_j : Q_i)$ is a direct investment of resources for converting from Q_i to Q_j.

$$C_{K*}^r(Q_j : Q_i, Q_j < Q_i) \equiv C_{K**}^r(Q_j : Q_i) = M^r(Q_j, Q_i) < 0 \tag{6b}$$

where $M^r(Q_j, Q_i)$ is the annual flow of the capitalized aggregate saving on deferred maintenance in achieving a decline in quality from Q_i to Q_j. Effectively, the real cost here is the opportunity cost of forsaking a higher for a lower market value for the property.

We now relate the size of $C_K(Q_j)$ to $C_{K*}^i(Q_j)$ and $C_{K*}^{i*}(Q_j)$ ... new construction to upward and downward conversion costs. If a builder wishes to build a new unit at Q_j he can select the most efficient way to do it. This way is more efficient than either building a unit at lower level Q_i and then converting it upward to Q_j or building a unit at higher level Q_i' and then depreciating it down to Q_j. Thus,

$$C_K(Q_{0i}) + C_{K*}(Q_j : Q_i) \geq C_K(Q_j) \leq C_K(Q_{0k}) + C_{K**}(Q_j : Q_k) \quad Q_i < Q_j < Q_k \tag{7}$$

Also:

$$C_{K*}(Q_j : Q_j) = 0 \quad \text{all } j. \tag{8}$$

These relations are seen in Fig. 1.

(b) *Revenue functions*

Each Q_i has a price, P_i, attached to it. This is the price for use of one housing unit at quality level i. (It can be interpreted either as the price charged by a building contractor to the investor–developer who hired him or the price charged by the latter to household users of the unit. We assume that the two prices are closely linked together.) We convert this price to an actual—where applicable—or imputed annual rental, with the lifetime of the unit as payout period and equal to that for the annual cost flows. Call this R_i.

Then $R_i - C_i$ is the total profit per year at Q_i; and $(R_i/C_i) - 1$ gives the annual rate of

[19] This is, of course, violated after housing units are sold for capital gains or losses. As noted above, we are neglecting such changes because of the comparative static nature of the model. Instead, *tátonnement* is assumed.

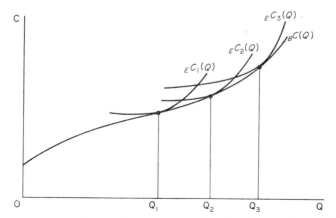

FIG. 1. The new unit cost function, $_BC(Q)$, is an envelope function of conversion cost functions. At Q_2, $_BC(Q_2) = {_E}C_2(Q_2) < {_E}C_1(Q_2)$ and $_BC_3(Q_2)$. Often also it will be the case that cost is less at some Q_J for conversions which begin closer to Q_J than for conversions which begin farther from Q_J, but this actually depends upon more specific features of the cost functions.

return at Q_i. This is a somewhat special sense, since the base includes maintenance expenditures; but these latter can be considered part of annual investment costs, since they represent an investment to maintain the value of the capital. True operating costs are assumed to be subtracted from gross rentals to give R_i as net rentals. We assume—in this comparative static context—that R_i and C_i are expected to be unchanged over the lifetime of the unit, for each Q_i, so long as it remains at that Q_i. Then max $(R_i/C_i) - 1$ is independent of the rate of interest used as a discount factor.

$$\left[i : \frac{R_i}{C_i} \geq \frac{R_j}{C_j}, \text{ all } j \neq i \right] = \left[i : \int_0^\infty \frac{R_{it}}{C_{it}} e^{-rt}\, dt \geq \int_0^\infty \frac{R_{jt}}{C_{jt}} e^{-rt}\, dt, \ldots \text{all } j \neq i, \text{ all } r \right]. \quad (9)$$

The function $R(Q)$ is a monotonic increasing function of Q, and it is independent of how a unit arrives at Q—whether through new construction or conversion. It must be noted again that $R(Q)$ is *not* a measure of Q, e.g. via

$$\frac{R(Q_i)}{R(Q_j)} = a \frac{Q_i}{Q_j} \text{ or } (R(Q_i) - R(Q_j)) = a(Q_i - Q_j).$$

R and Q are capable of independent changes. This is the important message of the imperfect substitutability of units across different quality levels. Events localized in one Q_i will have reverberations in other Q_j levels, but not perfectly equivalent ones: on balance, events having their initial impact at one level will tend to change the relations between that level and the others.

(c) *Individual and group supplier equilibrium*

In discussing demand we made no mention of the length of time necessary to bring about consumer equilibrium. In effect, we treated a consumer adjustment period as one long enough for all consumers to reach equilibrium. In doing so we abstracted from what we earlier deemed characteristic of the housing sector: namely, the costs of changing residence and the consequent long periods of tolerated disequilibrium positions. Somewhat the same is true for supply. True to the comparative static context, we treat the supply adjustment period as that which is necessary for builders to have "fully" responded to any new market situation by starting and completing whatever new structures they decide to build, and owners of existing units to have decided upon and completed whatever conversions of their units they desire. "Full" response by both types of entrepreneurs is a complex notion here, because the gestation period of both types of "production" is long, downward conversion through depreciation especially so, and prices have a chance to vary significantly during the period of adjustment—thereby providing a variety of signals to both users and suppliers of housing along the way. Unlike most markets with very small gestation periods, where "current" market prices give continuingly good signals about what supply response is "in the works", there is here a considerable problem for a supplier to find out how much new supply will be forthcoming in any part of the market, i.e. by how much, and in what directions, will a current set of prices change by the time his new or converted units reach the market.

As a comparative statics model, these essentially dynamic considerations are not supposed to matter. They do matter; in that mistakes can happen along an adjustment path. If these mistakes are difficult to undo, the final outcome will reflect them. New houses built, or existing units converted, in the wrong parts of the market, or in the wrong numbers, or households making wrong—if infrequent—moves cannot easily be corrected. Their "correction" in effect means that the adjustment process is not completed in the present period, or that the period itself is not completed: further changes in occupancies or in the flow of supply outcomes must take place. In either interpretation the very concept of an equilibrium is weakened. My own belief is that the equilibrium concept *is* much less informative than usual in such a long-drawn-out, continuing adjustment process where prices vary throughout. Accordingly, full analytic treatment of the issue comes in a dynamic model, not a comparative static one. But to repeat, the present version is intended only as a simplified view of some of the major emphases of the approach in general. As such, it does throw light on some policy issues, and its greater simplicity is therefore convenient. But it does not pretend to be a fully articulated treatment of many of the difficult problems that must be faced. Some of these are explicitly grappled with in the considerably more complex dynamic model which will be mentioned in the last section.

We may suppose that the following adjustment process underlies the period-by-period supply equilibrium. At the start of period t_0 there exists a given stock of housing units, distributed over the various quality levels,

$$S_0 = \{S_{10}, S_{20}, \ldots\}.$$

Associated with each quality level there is a price per unit,

$$P_0 = \{P_{10}, P_{20}, \ldots\}.$$

Assuming that suppliers expect these prices to continue (to avoid deeper dynamic issues about the formation and change of expectations), these define an $R(Q)_0$ function.[20] There exists also a set of opportunities defined by current production and conversion technologies, as well as a set of prices of construction inputs and relevant cost of capital for the industry. Together, these define the cost function for new construction at each of the quality levels, $_BC(Q)_0$, and the set of conversion cost functions specifying conversion costs to all other quality levels from each given starting level,

$$\{_EC_1(Q)_0, \, _EC_2(Q)_0, \, \ldots, \, _EC_n(Q)_0\},$$

to which $_BC(Q)_0$ is an envelope function.

---

[20] As is proper for a comparative static model, this assumes full price adjustment, i.e. that vacancy rate is not a market adjustment variable.

Suppliers of new units (and potential converters of existing units as well) are assumed to be price takers. They have two supply decisions to make: how many new units should they build, and at what quality level(s). (This "choice" among quality levels does not preclude actual specialization to particular levels by given builders, since we are speaking about supplier firms in general. A selection of Q_i means that Q_i-specialized firms will do the actual building, a selection of Q_j, that Q_j-specialized firms will do the building. Of course, for explicit treatment of such specialization we would have to drop the assumption that all firms face the same $C(Q)$ and $R(Q)$ functions and substitute a set of restricted $C(Q)$ assignments.) The decision about quantity of units depends on the interrelated questions of the rate of return in housing relative to returns elsewhere and the availability of financing. Since our central focus here is the quality-level distribution, we simplify the issue by shifting the decision from the individual to the aggregate level. Each firm is assumed to produce only one unit; its sole decision is at which quality level to build. (Consistency with the aforementioned specialization of firms is maintained in that differential profitability for different quality levels enables firms specialized to the higher profit levels to outbid others for scarce financing.) The total number of firms that find it profitable to engage in building—and therefore the total new units built—is determined by the following:

$$\Delta_B S = B(\bar{\rho}_H, \rho_H), \tag{10}$$

where $\Delta_B S$ is the total number of new units supplied, ρ_H is the marginal rate of return in housing as a function of the number of new units built, $\bar{\rho}_H$ is the cost of capital to the housing industry. This simply expresses the profitability of all housing investments for which the rate of return exceeds the opportunity cost of the financial capital used to make the investment. This can be modified slightly to permit the appearance of an absolute credit rationing to the industry.

The question of at which quality level to build is determined by each firm as the level that maximizes profits. Profit maximization in the present situation is subject to a form of budget constraint. Housing developers typically obtain most of their financing from specialized financial institutions. They compete for these funds against one another and against non-housing sectors. Because of institutional characteristics of the capital markets it is generally believed that there are effective ceilings for funds to the housing industry. Under such an overall constraint the internal competition for funds within the housing sector generates an implicit price higher than the cost of capital to the sector as a whole. Allocation within the sector rests on rate of return competition. So each firm's appropriate criterion for competitive success in obtaining funds is in terms of a rate of return on investment: each attempts to maximize its profit rate. Thus, suppose all firms could choose between an opportunity to invest \$30,000 at 20 percent return or 60,000 at 15 percent return. The total of annual profits of the second exceeds that of the first. But two developers choosing the first could outbid one developer choosing the second in seeking funding for the same total investment out of scarce overall funding resources.[21]

---

[21] A further elaboration of this is useful for examining some types of public policy. The funding ceiling can be stipulated as different for different parts of the housing sector. An obvious axis of differentiation is geographic. Another—as suggested by Robert Solow—is quality level of housing. Thus, capital market differences with respect to either will tend to generate different consequences for public policies that deal uniformly with credit. This raises the potential attractiveness of discriminatory credit policies, and provides an analytic instrument for evaluating their results. This elaboration can be accomplished by specifying a set of explicit funding ceilings or different implicit required rates of return in the different housing subsectors. Individual firms would still act to maximize rate of return, but the cutoff on successful bids, and therefore the number of successful projects, would differ in the respective subsectors.

80   *Jerome Rothenberg*

Thus, for each firm optimal quality is that for which the rate of return is highest:

$$\hat{Q} = \left\{ Q_i : \frac{R(Q_i)}{C(Q_i)} \geq \frac{R(Q_j)}{C(Q_j)}, \text{ all } j \neq i \right\} \tag{11}$$

(omitting subscript B for costs).

Let us assume that $R(Q)$ and $C(Q)$ are continuous functions, both monotonic increasing in Q. Then conditions for maximum positive rate of return which justifies new construction[22] are:

$$\frac{d \log R(\hat{Q})}{dQ} = \frac{d \log C(\hat{Q})}{dQ}, \tag{12a}$$

$$\frac{d^2 \log R(\hat{Q})}{dQ^2} < \frac{d^2 \log C(\hat{Q})}{dQ^2}, \tag{12b}$$

$$\int_0^{\hat{Q}} (\log R - \log C) dQ > 0. \tag{12c}$$

This can be seen in Fig. 2. Subscript 0 refers to time period t_0.

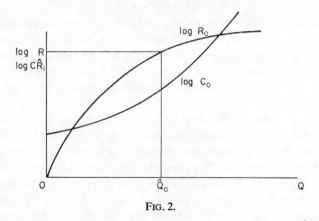

FIG. 2.

Assume that these conditions are fulfilled in the period we are examining for some $\hat{Q}$. This means that we have started at some previous equilibrium and disturbed the market so that either the $R(Q)$ or $C(Q)$ functions have changed to warrant new construction. Of course, new construction can be warranted as part of an equilibrium too if endogenous retirements of units from the housing stock form part of the equilibrium behavior of conversion suppliers.

If conditions (12) are fulfilled, the firm selects $\hat{Q}_0$ as the quality level at which to build (the slope of $R(Q)_0$ and $C(Q)_0$ are equal there). Since by our assumption all firms face the same $R(Q)$ and $C(Q)$ functions, *all* select the same Q_0 at which to build. This is based on the particular set of relative prices which determines the particular $R(Q)_0$.

Assume that there is a distribution of lags with which different firms respond to any change in market situation. (This assumption is necessary here to avoid the profound

---

[22] We implicitly assume only endogenous retirements from the stock of housing. Whether new construction exceeds retirements, i.e. whether new construction represents net increases in housing, depends on the conversion supply response.

problems of adjustment process which limit the usefulness of a static model in this area.) Then in the first subperiod some proportion l_1 of firms begin to build a unit at level $\hat{Q}_0$. When these units are completed they add to the stock available at $\hat{Q}_0$, so price in $\hat{Q}_0$ falls. This price decline decreases the corresponding portion of the $R(Q)$ function. The remaining $1 - l_1$ suppliers change their choice of most profitable level at which to produce—say it is $\hat{Q}_1$. Then l_2 of the remaining suppliers build at this level in subperiod 2. The increasing supplies here decrease $\hat{P}_1$ in the same way and a third best level is now chosen and acted on by l_3 of the remaining firms. The process continues in this fashion. So long as $l_1, l_2, l_3, \ldots$ are all very small percentages of the total of entrepreneurial adjustment, adequate flexibility will exist for the process to converge to a long-run equilibrium—no large irreversible errors will be created to generate continued oscillations. In this equilibrium the resulting $P_1, P_2, \ldots, P_n$ gives an $R(Q)$ function such that no producer either wants to build any additional units or could improve his profit situation by having built differently during the adjustment or by actually converting the unit he did build to a different level.

If this seems a bit cumbersome there is another interpretation of the equilibrating process that will serve. This alternative by-passes an actual intermediate sequence of adjustments. It assumes that max R/C determines not an actual building action but only a probability of such an action. For this interpretation the whole array of rates of return, R_1/C_1, $R_2/C_2, \ldots$, is important. The relative magnitudes determine the relative sizes of the probabilities of building:

$$\frac{\text{pr}_i}{\text{pr}_j} = \frac{\rho_i}{\rho_j} \tag{13}$$

where ρ_i is the rate of return at Q_i, pr_i is the probability of building a new unit at Q_i.

$$\int_0^N \text{pr}_i \, dQ_i = 1 \tag{14}$$

where 0 and N are the lower and upper boundaries of quality level.

From (10) we have the total number of new units being built, so the actual number at any Q_i is:

$$\Delta_B S_i = \text{pr}_i \, \Delta_B S. \tag{15}$$

The resulting supply response under this interpretation will change relative prices to the same degree as in the preceding interpretation. The supply–price configurations resulting should be the same in both versions.

In sum, we have argued that the supply of new units is determined by the following expression:

$$_B S(Q_i) = S(\bar{\rho}_H, \rho_1, \rho_2, \ldots, \rho_n) \text{ all } i. \tag{16}$$

The situation is quite different for existing housing units. Owners of these also seek to maximize their rate of return. At the time they came into existence they presumably represented the most profitable opportunities available. Once they are in existence the owner no longer faces the $C(Q)$ function with respect to the opportunities to convert each unit to various other quality levels. For a unit at each Q_i the cost constraints are reflected instead in the corresponding $_E C_i(Q)$ function, which generally lies everywhere above the

$_BC(Q)$ function except at Q_i, at which level the two functions are tangent,[23] and which therefore necessarily has a different slope. Thus, while owners of existing units all face the same $R(Q)$ function defining the revenue opportunities for converting each unit to the other quality levels, only owners of units at the same quality level face the same cost constraints. At each set of housing prices all producers of new units select the same target quality level as most profitable.[24] Here, on the other hand, only owners of units at the same quality level generally choose the same best destination. (More than one group might accidentally do so, however, given the specifics of revenue and cost opportunities.)

Conditions for rate of return maximization here differ slightly from those for new construction:

$$\frac{d \log R(\hat{Q})}{dQ} = \frac{d \log {}_EC_i(\hat{Q})}{dQ}, \tag{17a}$$

$$\frac{d^2 \log R(\hat{Q})}{dQ^2} \quad \frac{d^2 \log {}_EC_i(\hat{Q})}{dQ^2}, \tag{17b}$$

$$\int_{Qi}^{\hat{Q}} (\log R - \log {}_EC_i) \, dQ > 0. \tag{17c}$$

The only difference is in (17c), where the improvement in rate of return is not from the profit situation of no unit but of the starting situation, Q_i. This is because only *marginal* cost, not total cost, affects the conversion calculation: the original capital cost at Q_i is sunk and thus irrelevant to decisions about a conversion. While existing units are not necessarily cheaper than new units in terms of calculations about one quality level vs. another, they *are* cheaper *vis-à-vis* many target quality levels *vis-à-vis* overall use of resources: it will sometimes pay for an extra converted unit to offer services at some level k but not for some new unit to be produced at that level, despite a higher marginal cost for the former than the latter in terms of small quality-level differences—because only the sum of those marginal costs from initial i to k have to be spent as opposed to the full cost of building at k from scratch. Of course, the worthwhileness of conversion has to take into account the revenue situation as well. Uncommitted resources have an opportunity cost equal to the cost of capital $\bar{\rho}_H$; resources embodied in an existing unit have an opportunity cost equal to $R(Q_i)$. It is the joint consideration of the costs of *not* moving as well as moving that determines action.

The owner of a particular existing unit will choose to maintain his unit at the *same* level if there has been no change in revenue or cost factors from what it was when originally built, since then the equal slope necessary condition for maximization would still be fulfilled at the existing quality level (see Fig. 3).

Here, both the original $C(Q)_0$ and currently relevant $_EC_0(Q)_0$ functions have the same slope as $R(Q)_0$ at Q_0. So Q_0 remains the optimal level for all units at Q_0. Another level becomes more desirable only if conditions change $R(Q)$ and/or $_EC_0(Q)$. Thus, in figure 3, $\hat{Q}_0$ is the original optimum (equilibrium) R_0 and C_0, but with the shift of R to R_1, the new optimum level becomes $\hat{Q}_1$, supported by R_1 and $_EC_0(Q_0)$.

[23] We have, it will be remembered, assumed away capital gains and losses transactions by which a present owner of a unit may have annual capital cost obligations very different from that of the original owner when it was guilt.

[24] Or have the same quality level as maximally probable for new construction.

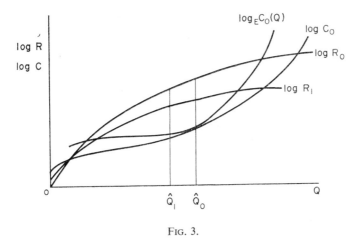

FIG. 3.

A shift in the $R(Q)$ or $_EC_1(Q)$ functions need not warrant a conversion, even if at the original equilibrium level $\hat{Q}_0$ the new functions are no longer parallel. This is because while conditions (17a) and (17b) may be satisfied at some new $\hat{Q}_1$, condition (17c) may not. $\hat{Q}_1$ is "locally" better than $\hat{Q}_0$ but not globally so: the rate of return is actually smaller at $\hat{Q}_1$ than at $\hat{Q}_0$. This is likely only rarely to occur, so we shall speak in what follows as if a shift in $R(Q)$ or $C(Q)$ which disrupts a previous parallel will generally warrant a conversion.

Thus, units at every other quality level Q_i will find shifting worthwhile only with a change in R and/or $_EC_i$. But since the conversion cost function differs for each quality level, converters at each level will wish to convert generally to a different destination level. So even in the first round supply adjustment activity, more than one level will tend to be affected. The anomalous dynamics of one-sided adjustment, as seen in new construction, is absent. Therefore, price changes during the adjustment process will reflect the variety of conversion supply actions in the works. Thus, we may use the initial round of conversions as a good approximation to the completely adjusted conversion supply situation.

The more difficult issue for this kind of supply response is: what percentage of the units at each quality level will choose to convert if conversion prospects look good with respect to any level other than where the unit now is? The answer is not to be discovered in the model. It is an empirical question. We may simply assume the existence of specific mobility frictions or lagged response factors specific to different types of property owner (e.g. owner-occupier vs. commercial owners), so that it takes some particular threshold profit differential before each type of owner is willing to shift his unit. (These thresholds may reflect differential access to financing, or credit rationing, as suggested above, as well as difference between consumer and producer orientation.) If these thresholds differ for different owners to convert their units from a variety of initial levels to a variety of destination levels, then we can formulate the percentage of owners who will convert as an endogenous variable dependent on the size of profitability differentials.

A further complication arises because owners of existing units are responding to the same market signals that new builders are, and shifting their units to a new destination is as much a bringing of new units to that level to compete with newly built units as any other newly built units aimed at that quality level. The treatment here is that price at each quality level responds equally to the appearance at that level of additional units via new construction *or* conversion. So the effects on price of either flow must be adjusted to by the other. More generally, entrepreneurs of both types must adjust to price adjustments that symmetrically reflect the total of all additional units appearing at any quality level, from whatever source.

To summarize, a change in either the revenue or cost side of the market opportunities will lead to a supply adjustment that has two forms, new construction and conversion. New construction adjustment reflect basically uniform constraints and opportunities,[25] conversion adjustments reflect the non-uniform constraints resulting from the systematic differentials of conversion cost to any level from a variety of different levels. Both adjustments are motivated by a search for maximum rate of return. The net gain of units at any quality level is the algebraic sum of new units and net conversion to the level from all other levels:

$$\Delta S_i = \Delta_B S_i + \sum_{j=1}^{M} \Delta_E S_{ji},\tag{18}$$

where $\Delta_B S_i$ is the number of new units constructed at Q_i, $\Delta_E S_{ji}$ is the net number of units converted from Q_j to Q_i.

4. *Price adjustment processes*

Suppose we begin with a general equilibrium throughout the housing market complex. This will be supported (characterized) by a vector of housing component and quality level prices—$\{(p), (P)\}$. Now let some exogenous change impinge on the market. Because of the somewhat shorter adjustment period usually attributed to users, we suppose this change originates on the demand side (but the same principles operate for supply-originated changes). Then, with the equilibrium at time t_0 we have a set of housing units distributed among the various quality levels, the equilibrium price and a new vector of housing demands: $(S_0, D_0, \hat{P}_0, \hat{p}_0)$. Since D_0 represents a change from the equilibrium, market-clearing D_{-1} demand vector, it will generate a non-zero vector of excess demands among the quality levels:

$$X_0 = D_0 - S_0 = \{D_{10} - S_{10}, D_{20} S_{20}, \ldots\} \neq 0 \tag{19}$$

We assume prices adjust on the basis of excess demand to clear the submarket complex:

$$\Delta P = f(D-S) \quad f' > 0. \tag{20}$$

These price changes will induce changes in both the amounts demanded and supplied, as indicated in the demand and supply relations developed above (for supply it is the shape of the $R(Q)$ function that is affected). Full equilibrium occurs when the induced changes lead to a situation where all quality submarkets clear, so that $X = 0$ and $\Delta P = 0$.

This general equilibrium has a number of dimensions. Assume that it calls for an unchanging number of units at each quality level. On the demand side the relative prices of different levels must equal a common marginal rate of substitution among users (preference tradeoffs). On the supply side these prices must make it unprofitable for either type of supply to change either the relative or absolute sizes of the stocks at different quality levels.

---

[25] Unless financing constraints differ systematically.

Thus, the prices for any pair of levels must: (1) in absolute size be related to costs of new construction so that expected rate of return from new construction equals the cost of capital to the industry; in relative size (2) be equal to the marginal conversion cost between the two levels and (3) the relative new construction cost between the two levels. These pairwise relations, moreover, must be consistent with the whole system of linkages among the various submarkets. Overall consistency must occur in the face of differences on the taste side and differences in technology on the supply side—new construction, upward conversion, downward conversion. It is achievable generally through variations in relative flows to and from different levels by both demanders and suppliers of different types.

IV. Application of the Model to Rent Control

The purpose of the present chapter is primarily to illuminate what are believed to be salient features of the housing complex which must be attended to in evaluating the consequences of different types of public policy. We do not pretend, or intend, to offer an exhaustive examination of housing policies or even an elaborate evaluation of any one policy. Rather, we shall simply indicate in schematic form how the analytic model presented above could be applied in systematic fashion to the evaluation of a public program. We have chosen rent control as our example partly *because*, relative to other types of policy, it is *not* usually thought of in connection with the critical market segmentation which we have emphasized above. To demonstrate that even such an apparently even-handed type of policy cannot avoid distinctive consequences due to market segmentation ought to be suggestive.

A. IMPOSITION OF RENT CONTROL

The main circumstance under which rent control seems to be resorted to is where there is a considerable excess demand for housing, especially rental housing, due to heavy immigration and/or sharp constraints on new building (as, for example, during wartime when building materials and/or labor are in very short supply).

Another conceivable circumstance is during a period of rapidly increasing cost of housing as a result of inflation of input prices (either for building or maintaining housing units). This seems a distinctly unreasonable ground for rent control, since: (1) the public understands the validity of the need for property owners to pass on genuine rising input costs; (2) such input cost rises are likely to affect many other types of production in the community as well: their control only in housing would be rank discrimination.

We therefore assume that it *is* heavy excess demand for housing (some or all kinds) that forms the rationale for imposition of rent control. We shall assume for simplicity that the excess demand applies uniformly across quality levels. We shall first examine the effect of rent control applied to all quality levels, then where controls are pin-pointed to only some quality levels but no others.

Case I. *All quality levels controlled*

A housing equilibrium is disturbed by rising across-the-board demand, and important constraints on new construction promises a long period of inadequate supply catch-up.

Starting with a population of rental housing units at different quality levels and their corresponding prices (rentals), $\{\hat{S}_1, \hat{S}_2, \ldots; \hat{P}_1, \hat{P}_2, \ldots\}$, we have at each level i, $\Delta D_i > 0$ and $\Delta S_i > 0$, but small. The result is a rise of prices at each level: $\Delta P_i > 0$. As a result, the $R(Q)$ function rises throughout its length.

Figures 4a and b show the several dimensions of the uncontrolled rental market's adjustment to this situation. In Fig. 4b (where D and S curves represent *mutatis mutandis* situations of all housing prices moving together) demand has risen from D_1 to D_2, amount supplied increasing only along an inelastic supply function S_1. So P_i rises from $\hat{P}_1$ to $\hat{P}_2$,

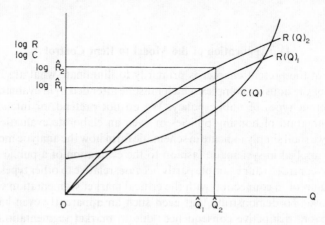

Fig. 4a.

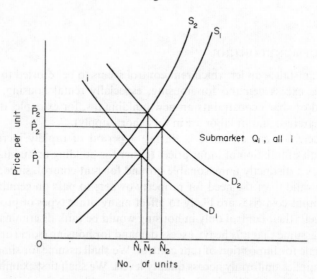

Fig. 4b.

and number of units supplied from $\hat{N}_1$ to $\hat{N}_2$. P_i increases at every Q_i, but by differing amounts depending on the elasticities of demand and supply. This rise in all housing prices pushes the $R(Q)$ upward (Fig. 4a) throughout its length, but not necessarily parallel to the old. The result is generally a shift in the relative profitability of new construction at the different quality levels. In terms of most profitable level, this shifts in Fig. 4a from $\hat{Q}_1$ to $\hat{Q}_2$—an increase in level here, but not necessarily so. So the pattern of new construction by quality level is affected also. Finally, the shift in $R(Q)$ changes relative profitability for different conversions by existing units (not shown). This leads to a new pattern of net conversion supply.

Let us suppose that as a result of the substantial price rises that would occur in such a situation rent control is imposed when the excess demand has become evident but before prices rise as part of the adjustment. Rent control can take many forms. For illustrative purposes we assume a form that approximates that of New York City. In this form: (1) all existing rental units are covered; (2) all newly constructed rental units are exempted; (3) increases in cost, whether from making capital improvements or carrying out higher levels of maintenance (but assuming away rising input costs), are allowed to be proportionately covered by higher rentals, but no higher.

1. *Impact on new rental units*

Despite not being covered by rent control, the construction of new rental units is affected indirectly in two ways. For the first, while the new unit is uncontrolled when it first comes into the market, the existence of rent control as a policy raises the possibility that controls may be extended to it at some later part of its life. Such subsequent extensions of control have been experienced in the real world, so it is not an idle surmise. If that occurs, the unit would from then on be constrained in its ability to take advantage of new market opportunities. Thus, in its overall lifetime it would represent a less valuable asset than without this possibility. Anticipation of such a decline in lifetime value makes it less valuable to its builder because it will be less valuable to its next owner (in anticipation of being less valuable to its next owner, etc.). So its expected rate of return to the builder is less for every current set of prices at which comparable units sell (or rent), and therefore the number that will be built decreases. This is true at every prospective quality level. In effect, we have a virtual shift in the *mutatis mutandis* supply function shown in Fig. 4b—decreased new construction at every price leads overall supply to fall from S_1 to S_2. The result is an equilibrium shown by $\bar{N}_2$, $\hat{P}_2$—less new construction and a higher price in the uncontrolled part of the market because of rent control.

The second effect concerns the competition of new rental units and existing rental units within each quality submarket. The direct effects of rent control on controlled units changes the pattern of conversions among the different quality levels. As a result, relative prices are different than they would have been, and so elicited new construction will be different as well.

2. *Impact on existing rental units*

The increased demand at every quality level raises price at all quality levels for uncontrolled rental units—as in Fig. 4a. We show this now for an existing—and thus controlled—rental unit beginning the period at level $\hat{Q}_1$ in Fig. 5.

In the initial situation, given $R(Q)_1$ and $_EC_1(Q)$ representing the relevant opportunities and constraints open to this unit, $\hat{Q}_1$ was the optimal level. The reference unit therefore starts here. In the new situation, if it were not subject to rent control it would be faced with

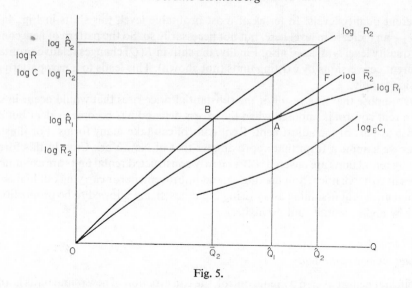

Fig. 5.

the opportunities of $R(Q)_2$, and would choose to be at $\hat{Q}_2$, which maximizes rate of return. (If prices rose proportionally at all quality levels, returns would still be maximized at $\hat{Q}_1$, since $R(Q)_2$ would be parallel to $R(Q)_1$, but at the price $\hat{R}_2$ higher than $\hat{R}_1$ as before.) But it cannot raise price above $\hat{R}_1$. So it is not in fact faced with the opportunities of $R(Q)_2$. What are its opportunities?

The new opportunities are defined by the details of the rent-control regulations. We assume that rent control permits covered units to be converted upward or downward in quality, and the new rental not to exceed the old plus the proportional amount of any increment incurred in connection with conversion. No requirements are made to decrease rentals in line with downward conversions. (This asymmetry is similar to price-control regulations where upward prices are limited to quality rises but downward prices are not required for quality declines. The regulations require real rate of return constancy in the upward direction but only nominal price constancy in the downward direction.)

Given these regulations the relevant revenue opportunities facing the unit are shown in Fig. 5 as OBAF (log $\bar{R}_2$). The frontier has three segments:

$$\bar{R}(Q)_2 \equiv \begin{cases} (1) \ R(Q)_2 \ (Q: 0 \le R(Q) \le \hat{R}_1), \\ R_1 \ (Q: R(Q)_2 = \hat{R}_1) \le Q \le \hat{Q}_1, \\ (3) \ \log \hat{R}_1 + \log {}_EC_1(Q: Q > \hat{Q}_1) \end{cases} \qquad (21)$$

The first segment is that part of the new uncontrolled function for rentals $R(\hat{Q})_2$ up to log $\hat{R}_1$—since none of these requires raising rents above $\hat{R}_1$. The second is simply the ability to keep charging $\hat{R}_1$, even though quality of the unit is anywhere between $\bar{Q}_2$ and $\hat{Q}_1$ (the real price-nominal price asymmetry mentioned above). The third is the ability to raise rents proportionally equal to higher costs when raising quality (so log $R(Q)_2$ is parallel to log ${}_EC_1(Q)$ to the right of Q_1).

At what level will the rate of return be greatest? First we examine this for each section of log $\bar{R}(Q)_2$. (1) In Section 3, log $\bar{R}(Q)_2 - \log {}_EC_1(Q) = \max[\log R(Q)_1 - \log {}_EC_1(Q)]$:

everywhere in this section the rate of return is the same as at $\hat{Q}_1$. (2) In Section 2, rates of return rise with *falling* Q, since $\log \bar{R}$ is constant while $\log {}_EC_1(Q)$ falls: the max here is at point B: $[Q : \log \bar{R}(Q)_2 = \log \hat{R}_1]$. (3) In Section 1, since both $\log \bar{R}_2$ and $\log {}_EC_1$ fall, the optimum can occur anywhere, depending on the relative shapes of $\bar{R}(Q)_2$ and ${}_EC_1(Q)$.

What has been established is that the rate of return at point B dominates that of all higher quality levels. How does it compare with the highest return in Section 1? In the not unreasonable case of an approximation to proportional price rises at all quality levels, $\log R(Q)_2$ is nearly parallel to $\log R(Q)_1$. Then the fact that $\hat{Q}_1$ was the chosen quality level at the outset means that it had a higher rate of return than any other. Express this in terms of $\hat{\rho}_1 \geq \rho_i$. The parallel upward shift of $R(Q)$ adds a constant premium return: $\rho_i + \delta$. Then B dominating A means that $\delta > \hat{\rho}_1 - \bar{\rho}_2$. The rate of return for any level in Section 1 is $\rho_i + \delta$. In order that $\hat{\rho}_i + \delta$ exceed $\bar{\rho}_2 + \delta$, it must be that $\rho_i > \bar{\rho}_2$. If $\log R(Q)$ and $\log {}_EC_1(Q)$ are second-degree curves this cannot happen: the farther a level is from $\hat{Q}_1$ the lower will be ρ_i, and all levels less than $\bar{Q}_2$ are farther than $\bar{Q}_2$ from $\hat{Q}_1$. Thus, B will dominate any alternative in Section 1 unless $R(Q)$ or $C(Q)$ have special shape, or prices rise proportionally more in Section 1 than in Section 2.

Whichever situation prevails, however, the owner of the housing unit will see advantage in decreasing its quality level at least to $\bar{Q}_2$ and possibly beyond. Thus, rent control gives each owner of an existing unit at any quality level inducement to convert the unit downward in quality while retaining its old nominal price—thereby raising real prices throughout. Each quality level will experience a loss of units through the downward conversion of some as a result of this systematic inducement; but it will experience as well a gain of units insofar as units from higher levels are converted down to it for the same reason.

What net pattern of conversions can be predicted? The net change of units through conversion for any quality level depends on the number of units originally located at relevantly higher levels relative to the number at this level, and the differences in threshold immobilities which influence the percentage of units that will actually convert in response to the profit differentials available. The only systematic hint to net changes here is that higher-income levels will tend to have fewer units at levels relevantly higher. Lower levels will tend to have many more units at relevantly higher levels, probably disproportionately so to the larger number of units at each of those low levels itself. While real predictions depend on actual data about the quality distribution of dwelling units, some presumption exists on the basis of the general character of that distribution that very high-quality levels will experience net conversion declines while moderately and quite low-quality levels will experience net conversion increases. Nothing *a priori* can be guessed about the large middle range.

In sum, at this first impact stage, rent control will include general disinvestment in rental housing capital by systematic downward conversions throughout the quality spectrum while holding nominal prices constant. This will raise real prices on rental units which have been converted. What secondary repercussions follow depend on the pattern of net conversions and new construction to the different quality levels. The size of the net conversion additions to any Q_i depends on:

(a) the number of units at relevantly higher levels than Q_i;
(b) the number of units at Q_i;
(c) the average threshold immobilities at these different levels;

(d) the relative rise of prices at the different quality levels both above and below Q_i. Large rises at lower levels increases the incentive to convert downward and increases the size of the desirable conversion.

The size of the additions to Q_i from new construction depends on:

(a) the absolute size of price rise at Q_i;
(b) the size of price rises at all other Q levels.

What is important here is the absolute size of the returns relative to the cost of capital, and the relative attraction of Q_i in comparison with the other quality levels.

3. *Other repercussions*

(a) The aforementioned pattern of new construction and conversion supply responses leads to the following situation. At each quality level we may distinguish three types of rental housing units: existing units which did not convert either to or from this level; units that were converted to this level from some level above; units that were newly constructed at this quality level. There will be two different prices. Both new units and converted units will have the higher uncontrolled price reflected in $R(Q)_2$; unconverted existing units will have the lower controlled price reflected in $R(Q)_1$. This shows that the downward conversion of existing units effectively decontrols those units. The dual-price situation persists because of the constraints imposed by rent control.

Since all three types of unit have the same quality, the existence of two prices leads consumers to have significant preferences among them. The controlled, lower-priced units are highly preferred. They come to have extremely low vacancy rates, large waiting lists and low turnover. Present tenants cannot expect to obtain so good a bargain in the uncontrolled portion of the market, and so may remain in these units even long after their desired *type* of housing has changed markedly. The match of tenant's characteristic and housing characteristics can come to decline appreciably as household characteristics change over time while households feel frozen to controlled units. Turnover, vacancy rates for uncontrolled—legally or effectively—units are considerably higher.

(b) Conversion and new construction are substitute sources of supply. If net conversions are generally negative for high-quality levels and positive at low and moderate levels (or whatever net pattern actually emerges), this tends to raise uncontrolled prices in the former and lower them in the latter quality ranges. Incentives for the distribution of new construction are influenced accordingly—increasing in the former and decreasing in the latter. Insofar as the surmised pattern of net conversions is correct, the impact on new construction further skews an already highly skewed supply mix between new construction and conversion: less new construction and more conversion (filtering) for lower levels, more new construction and less conversion for high levels.

(c) Up to now we have been speaking only about rental units. But just as new construction and conversion are substitute forms of supply, so too rental and ownership units are substitutes as well. The events in the rental part of the market will have an effect on the ownership part of the market. But more important, it is the existence of the ownership market as a reasonably close substitute use of resources that will significantly affect the events in the rental market.

The effect of new rental construction is probably more marked. We have noted that the expected lifetime rate of return on new rental units is likely to decline as a result of the onset of rent control, and that this would decrease the number of such new units built. The original tradeoff noted in this decline was between housing and non-housing uses of funds. In fact, the much closer tradeoff is between rental and ownership housing. The rate of return on new ownership units is not impaired by price control. So funds that would have gone in the rental direction shift to the ownership direction. The closeness of substitutability between the two sectors suggests a larger decline in rental construction, other things being equal, than in the housing–non-housing shift. On the other hand, the net decline of new rental construction is *less* than this initial impact. The substantial disinvestment of housing capital embodied in existing units will surely lead to a greater demand for housing qualities that can only be satisfied from the uncontrolled part of the market—new construction. With prices rising higher in these segments of the market than in the absence of rent control, more new construction will be encouraged here than upon the first impact of the program.

There is a similar net effect on existing units. In addition to the different rental quality-level options open to any existing rental unit there is for some a very real option to be converted to the ownership part of the market. This is the case especially for single-family houses. The lesser lifetime rate of return expected from a rent-controlled existence in the rental market can be by-passed by selling the property for ownership, since the forces leading to excess demand in the former probably operate in the latter as well, but without the profit-dampening operation of rent control. So shifts of units into the ownership market are likely to occur at all quality levels, but especially at middle and higher, since this is where household wealth situations make ownership feasible. For single-family houses the shift is easy. But it is not impossible for multiple-family houses as well. In these, newer forms of ownership, like condominium or cooperative arrangements, make the shift quite possible.

The net effect of these shifts is to decrease new rental construction at all quality levels somewhat more than indicated earlier; and to accentuate the loss of capital to the rental market. But this overall effect avoids some of the loss of capital to housing as a whole by substituting away from the incentive to convert downward in quality.

4. *Summary*

Nominal rent control of all quality levels has the following effects:

(a) Higher real prices at all quality levels than before the increase in demand for housing; but its weighted average somewhat lower after that by the rent control–modified supply responses, and the more so the greater the percentage of controlled units which failed to convert or move to the ownership sector.

(b) A much more rapid depreciation of the existing rental housing stock through widespread downward conversion of quality (a one-shot shift for each new change in demand).

(c) A two-price system: unconverted controlled units with rentals and quality frozen; converted controlled units and new units with real rentals risen above a no-rent control-free market level, the more so the larger the shift of new construction out of rental into ownership units.

(d) An effective extent of controls considerably smaller than the legal intent, either through conversions of existing units downward in quality or through their shifts out of rentals into the ownership market.

(e) A changed mix of new construction and net conversion additions at different quality levels.

Case II. *Controls at selected quality levels only*

Suppose the chief purpose of rent control is to protect the poor in a period of housing price squeeze rather than to control the whole rental housing market. Toward this end it is believed that only housing units inhabited by the poor should be subject to control. So the regulation imposes controls only on the lowest—say one-third—housing units. The same regulations concerning these controlled units apply as before. In addition, an originally controlled unit cannot climb out of controlled status by upgrading beyond the control boundary level.

1. Impact on new rental units

At the first stage there is basic similarity here as with the all-level controls. There is a significant difference, however. At the uncontrolled levels there is less fear by builders that new units may be some day subject to controls. So the uncertainty about this afflicts only units to be built at controlled quality levels. This means that the expected lifetime rates of return on new units in controlled levels falls not only relative to ownership units and non-housing investments but also relative to a closer substitute: new rental construction at the higher uncontrolled levels. The result could be a substantial shift of construction away from the controlled levels to the uncontrolled levels, as well as some to the two other alternative types. New construction in housing overall, or even to rental housing, need not be much affected, but only its distribution among quality levels.

The second stage results here, as in Case I, from the changes in relative stocks at the different quality levels stemming from control-induced conversions of existing units.

2. Impact on existing rental units

There is an important difference here from the all-level control system. This is shown in Fig. 6.

Q_u represents the upper boundary of quality level subject to rent controls; all levels above Q_u are uncontrolled. The appropriate $R(Q)$ function under these regulations is OBAFGJ (beyond Q_u unit owners face the free market $R(Q)_2$).

Owners of units above Q_u can respond to the free market $R(Q)_2$. So, for example, the unit beginning at $\hat{Q}'_1$ converts *upward* to $\hat{Q}'_2$ ($\max[\log R(Q)_2 - \log {}_E C_1(Q)']$). The upward shift is not intrinsic to the adjustment here: it depends on the particular shapes of $\log R(Q)_1$, $\log R(Q)_2$ and $\log {}_E C_1(Q)'$. It could just as well have declined. Units starting at other levels above Q_u are similarly affected, converting upward or downward or not at all, depending on the same factors, but always in response to the new $R(Q)_2 \div {}_E C_i(Q)$ relationship. What is important to notice is that there is no systematic incentive toward downward conversion. Moreover, the discontinuous decline of $R(Q)$ at Q_u (from G to F) will tend significantly to dry up normal downward filtering of units across the Q_u boundary.

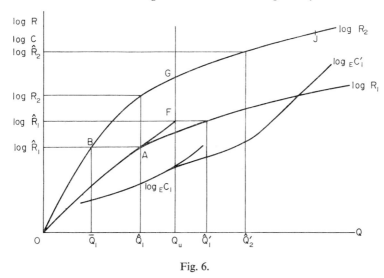

Fig. 6.

Owners of units at or below Q_u, on the other hand, have the familiar control-induced incentive to convert downward (from $\hat{Q}_1$ to $\bar{Q}_1$ in Fig. 5). So real prices rise to equal that of newly constructed units at these levels. The weighted real price rise here is, however, less than above Q_u insofar as some units below Q_u remain unconverted. When consideration is taken of the substantially greater new construction above Q_u than below it, this judgment may be reversed unless the percentage of units below Q_u which remain unconverted is quite sizable. Since this percentage depends on the size of the conversion attraction relative to threshold immobilities, it depends on the size of the excess demand acting upon the system (since that determines the rise of $R(Q)$, and the size of this rise directly affects the size of the differential gains from conversion).

3. *Summary*

(a) New construction supply is encouraged above Q_u beyond what is induced by the demand increase, since there is a shift out of the controlled levels into the uncontrolled levels. There is less substitution of new units for lost net conversions, and downward conversions out of the uncontrolled levels into the controlled are likely to be considerably decreased. It is discouraged in the controlled levels more than under the all-level control system because of the increased relative attractiveness of the uncontrolled levels.

(b) The downward filtering of units from levels above Q_u to levels below Q_u is likely to be quite substantially decreased relative to the all-levels control system. This will tend to raise real prices more than otherwise and somewhat offset the net discouragement here to new construction.

(c) In the controlled levels will occur the usual control-induced disinvestment of housing capital through systematic downward conversion. This, in conjunction with the big decrease in filtering from the uncontrolled levels, implies a decline—possibly large—in the average quality of units for the poor—and at higher real rental levels. Only the bulk of the unconverted units will serve the poor at unchanged real costs.

(d) Net effects. In comparison with the all-level rent-control program the control of low-quality housing alone clearly damages the poor. It results in a lower supply of units to them from both new construction *and* net conversion, and worsens the quality distribution of those units that do remain.

V. Agenda for Future Research

At the end of Section IIIA we concluded that much had been learned about urban housing. To reverse the earlier statement, nonetheless, much has yet to be learned. To the author's knowledge, no substantial research effort has succeeded in formulating an analytic framework and securing empirical estimates of a model which incorporates all or even most of the characteristics described in Section II. The author's own theoretical formulation of a dynamic model is one of the most ambitious in this respect, but has a long way to go to be suitable for either efficient manipulation or operationalizing toward econometric estimation. Most of the major work in the field proceeds on drastic simplifications for both purposes. Desire for analytic tractability has often taken the form of characterizing housing as analogously as possible to the representative conventional industry, since the properties of such an industry—positive and normative—are well understood. The constraints entailed in the effort toward empirical estimation are especially disabling since the data requirements for even modestly complex models are well beyond what is available. The result is typically very marked compromises in the richness of the model.

1. *Formulation of a dynamic model*

Selection of elements to be included in a dynamic model is important because the complexity of such a model rapidly gets out of hand, and some types of issues can be more happily embedded in an analytic instrument than others. The author's model emphasizes a number of key facets. In addition to the three mainstays of the comparative statics model presented here—durability and convertibility of pre-existing stock, heterogeneity, quality-level segmentation of market—special attention is given to the frictional costs for consumers to change housing, the informational needs and substantial but different gestation lags in different forms of supply response, the non-structure—especially neighborhood—components of the housing package, the flexibility and reversibility of demand and supply actions, the linkage of supply and demand where a participant must both buy and sell in order to fulfill his participation, the constraints due to various forms of non-market intervention, the adaptational function of vacancy changes relative to price changes in the market.

Frictional costs for demanders and large variable lags for suppliers have the effect of making active participation in the market by users sporadic and supply adjustments at any time incomplete. Thus, both the units actually available for trade and the match of these units with users are highly random. Moreover, forced mismatches at any time are unlikely to be quickly corrected because of the same barriers against continuous active participation on the user side and lagged responses on the supplier side. The past throws its shadows ahead. Disequilibrium situations are likely to be created and perpetrated, giving way to new forms of disequilibrium. Market adjustment processes are to be seen as tendencies toward equilibrium, not equilibrium actualizations.

The non-structure aspects of the housing package emphasize the variety and extent of externalities that may impinge on housing users and suppliers alike. Important kinds of resource immobilities and inadvertent rapid changes may be accounted for by these—as, for example, the difficulties of unslumming neighborhoods via rehabilitation or spot renewal, or the vicious circle of neighborhood decline and owner abandonment of structurally sound buildings.

Governmental interventions affect permissible technologies for construction of housing at different quality levels; presumed maintenance standards; zoning restrictions for exclusions and inclusions, with resulting deeper segmentation among the submarkets; and inadvertent private land use changes resulting from direct government actions within the land market—as, for example, dislocations from highway construction.

The importance of vacancy rate changes instead of prices as the market's first line of adjustment to market changes affects the signals transmitted to active and potential market participants as to what adjustments are called for; and it affects the welfare impacts of market changes on these participants.

All of these elements, as well as more conventional ones like mortgage market imperfections have a salience that should be captured within the analytic schema, but in a way that does not shut down the possibility of reasonable prediction. This is a difficult order. The author's ongoing efforts will certainly not foreclose the field to other kinds of attempts. It constitutes an item of real priority for future research.

2. *Empirical estimation*

This is perhaps an even more difficult task than the aforementioned. First and foremost, the data necessary for giving empirical content to even relatively simple models are either not available or are undependable. Many items are not collected, or are collected only sporadically, or on incomparable or incomplete bases. The greatest lack is probably for time series. Many bodies of data come into being as part of special studies, and these are a one-time operation, so the data exist as islands in time, totally surrounded by an absence of further collection. Our continued emphasis on the importance of dynamic phenomena points up the seriousness of this deficiency.

Considerable effort by researchers will have to go into demonstrating the need for particular additional bodies of data—so as to influence public agencies to extend their statistical activities—and in many cases to developing the data themselves. In this they should act as much as possible as agents for the long-run needs of the research community as a whole, not simply to meet their own special research needs of the moment. To facilitate this, suppliers of research funds must understand that the present serious data deficiencies in the field require heavy investment activity on a high priority basis if there is to be significant improvement. Yet not a great deal may result from direct data-dredging operations. Much of it will have to come as by-products of more theoretically oriented research. To link these efficaciously to the long-run development of widely available empirical information is a worthy agenda item.

3. *Public policy*

We have said little directly about public policy in this section. Yet the thrust of the entire chapter is that good public policy analysis requires an understanding of the system on which it is intended to impinge. The substance of our discussion of an agenda for further research is that the models through which the effects of alternative public policies must be screened need considerable improvement if their use is not to mislead public authorities more than they enlighten them. While a great deal of direct research attention must go to the clarification of different types of policies themselves and to often profound questions of administration, such questions have been outside the more general scope of the present chapter. Our message, then, is the need to bring more of what seems distinctive of the urban housing complex into the direct fine light of analysis and measurement.

4. *Policy and Policy Models in Transportation*

EDMUND J. CANTILLI

Transportation as an element of urban policy analysis, urban analytical method, urban design, or urban planning resolves itself into two major areas of formal study, one of which appears to be a subset of the other. The two areas are *traffic*, concerned basically with surface *vehicular* traffic (private autos, taxis, buses, trucks), and *transportation*, concerned generally with all forms of urban transport, passenger and goods (cargo), private, commercial, and public.

Reasons for the dichotomy are, among others:

the greater visibility of surface traffic,
the greater direct impact of surface traffic,
the greater extent of a technology for surface traffic.

Component Modes

Urban transportation can be defined in terms of its component modes:

motor vehicle,
rail rapid transit,
air,
waterborne.

Beginning with the last listed, waterborne transportation in the urban context is minimal and experimental. Cities located on rivers perennially consider new systems of rapid commuting based on new developments in marine propulsion: water-jet engines, hydrofoils, air-cushion, etc. But the difficulties of regular, scheduled, consistent waterborne transportation in the urban context (except for Venice, Italy) seem enormous. Problems of weather, visibility, water surface conditions, flotsam dangers, pollution, and docking and terminal facilities, have proven too great to overcome, except in the few cases of urban ferry systems, which have usually survived because of a difficulty in replacement by bridge or tunnel. Those which exist, however, present terminal facilities which are an element of the urban pattern.

Air transport is little more integrated into the urban pattern. Generally it is located on the outskirts of town (or at least where the outskirts were at the time of first establishment of the airport), and, generally, air transport is not a part of the *fabric* of urban transportation: it serves intercity, interstate, or international traffic demands. There is an element of commuting in that there are some few executives who leave for another city on Monday to return on Friday (New York–Washington; New York–Boston). It is not then the *air traffic* which is an element of the urban pattern, but the terminal facilities (airports), and the means used getting to them. With air travel, then, the urban element may be the city streets or expressways used to transport passengers to airports, or the rapid transit systems with links which serve the same purpose. There are additional links, air links using helicopters, and their locations, generally in downtown areas, can be of some significance in urban policy analysis. But their impacts are necessarily minor.

Rapid transit is of greater impact on the urban fabric, and in recent years it has become a major element of urban policy. In the last generation most urban rapid transit systems, whether rail or bus, have come under the control of public operating bodies. The economics of operation (and maintenance, and replacement, and capital funding) have developed in such a manner as to make it unattractive for private enterprise to build, develop, or operate subways or even, more recently, bus lines. The rising gap between the cost of operation of an urban transportation system and the income from fares charged to patrons using the system, has forced governments, local, state, and even federal, to take a greater and greater hand in local urban systems. This development, of the ever greater use of subsidy funds, tax funds, for the mass transportation systems of urban centers across the country, has engendered a debate on the basic purpose, merits, and need for urban mass transportation. Figure 1 shows the increased gap as it developed from about 1962. Patronage has been decreasing at a rapid rate since World War II (see Fig. 2). This is one major reason for the transit problem.

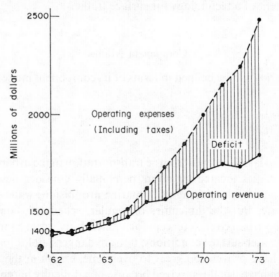

FIG. 1. Results of transit operations, 1962–73. 1973–1974 *Transit Fact Book*, American Transit Association, Washington, D.C., 1974, Fig. 1.

The *motor vehicle* has, more than any other transportation mode, changed the appearance, livability, purpose, and safety of the urban scene. While rapid transit, railroad, and interurban trolley lines can be said to have affected the development of cities in the latter nineteenth to early twentieth centuries, encouraging the beginnings of towns along rail lines and at stopping places, no transportation phenomenon freed the individual in such a manner as to permit development in any *location*; permitting the "spread city", the "slurbs" of post-World War II; allowing the overrun of prime agricultural lands within sight of major cities (Nassau County–New York; San Fernando Valley–Los Angeles) to be

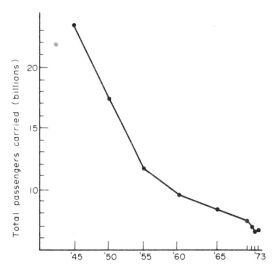

Fig. 2. Patronage trends, 1945–73. 1973–1974 *Transit Fact Book*, American Transit Association, Washington, D.C., 1974, Fig. 2.

swallowed up and paved over. The motor vehicle, more than any other form of transportation, has forced major rethinkings of urban policy in the short space of 40 years. Unlike other urban transport modes, the motor vehicle embraces elements of *personal* transportation (the private automobile), *commercial* transport (the taxicab and the truck), and *public* transport (the bus).

Planning "Balanced" Transportation

The ideal of "balanced" transportation has received lip service of late. There exists no method for planning balanced transportation, a phrase which suggests a nice balance among the elements of transportation modal possibilities, in a city, in a metropolitan area, in a region, a state, or a nation. The "balance" suggested is one between private vehicles and public mass transportation, implying that such a balance exists and can be found. But the balance in New York City must be greatly different from that in Los Angeles; in New York, while fewer than one-third of the commuters use private cars, monstrous traffic jams occur; in Los Angeles, bus lines cannot long endure. This brings us to the basis of all transport: land use.

Urban planners can debate a kind of chicken-or-egg precedence: does transport, or a movement system, determine the shape and character of specific land uses, and thereby determine the shape and character of a city? Or does the logical juxtaposition of specific land uses, scientifically located and designed, decide the quality, character, and conception of the transport system which serves them? In the context of this debate, a "balance" in transport in the urban context can be seen as the proper weighting of transportation mode, capacity, speed, character, appearance in relation to its service of land use: highly concentrated areas (commercial, industrial) can be served by highly concentrated transport modes; dispersed or low-density land uses are best served by individual personal vehicles or vehicles which serve small groups (buses).

In this context, where do other modes fit in? It can be seen that water-based transportation, except for remaining ferries (and, again, Venice), cannot contribute greatly to the urban "balanced" network without extensive development and improvement in this mode's technical and marketing capabilities. Conceivably, water "buses" along a river could replace land buses running on the Interstate highway which parallels the river, or the (reactivated) railroad line which runs in the river valley. But to equal or beat the time either of the above two examples take in their regular shuttle runs would require a fleet of expensive hydro-foil boats, new terminal (docking) facilities, and the assurance of surface transport connections at the terminal. This is almost as far beyond reasonable expectation as the installation of a monorail system in midtown Manhattan, ignoring the existing subways and surface bus lines.

Air transport again is not part of an urban transport pattern. The major airports are peripheral *clients* of an urban system, and STOL and VTOL ports, wherever they may be located in downtown areas, serve the major airports. The *needs* of airports *became* a part of the urban transport pattern, but provide little to the daily ebb and flow of passenger or freight movement which binds the various parts of an urban center together.

The balance, then, is between motor vehicle and rail, and, analyzing the situation a little deeper, the balance is found among *elements* of motor vehicles and rail modes. The elements in question are:

> private auto,
> taxicab,
> truck,
> bus,
> rail rapid transit,
> commuter rail.

Each of these sub-elements can be further refined:

Private auto

Auto use for recreation only
In this case there may not be conflict with peak-hour traffic (beach- or visit- or shopping-directed); or there may be conflict (race track or theater traffic).

Auto use for commuting to work only
This is the major consideration in the urban context, since it demands the greatest capacity, and has the greatest economic and environmental effects.

Auto use in business
This segment will add to peak-hour traffic, then be in evidence on city streets throughout most of the day.

"Official" auto use
Official city cars can add appreciable numbers to peak-hour problems, usually for no good reason.

Rental cars for any of the above purposes
Rented vehicles may swell the ranks of the above categories, or they may be replacements for any one of them, on a temporary basis.

Combinations of the foregoing
The same auto in the same day may be used for combinations of the above purposes.

Taxicab

"Cruising" taxicab
The cab which cruises the city streets seeking a client adds apparently useless vehicle-miles to the city streets, using energy aimlessly, and producing prodigious amounts of environmental damage.

"Car service" (*responds to phone call only*)
A somewhat more reasonable approach to use of city streets, energy, and pure air, but generally only one passenger is carried at a time.

"Limousine" service (for special events)
Similar to the "car service", except that larger vehicles are used, and larger groups are carried (weddings, funerals). The nature of much of limousine use, however, is to degrade the quality of general traffic, due to the vehicle's size and usually lower-than-average speed.

Truck

Private "pickup" trucks
Such vehicles are generally not found in the mainstream of peak-hour traffic, but are related to specific activities throughout the day and throughout the city.

Panel (delivery) trucks
Again, these vehicles rarely conflict with mainstream traffic except where they service urban commercial areas already overloaded with parked vehicles.

Mail trucks
Mail vehicles, of all sizes, can be considered a special group since they are so numerous, are "above the law" in many respects, and are ubiquitous.

Emergency vehicles
The special conditions under which these vehicles are required and permitted to operate make them a major component of the overall transportation makeup of a city.

Construction, maintenance, special-purpose vehicles
These may seriously affect overall flow depending upon where and under what circumstances they are used.

Large-load, single-chassis vehicles
Large, single-unit trucks in the urban texture present a major problem in that they may be underloaded, they take up inordinate street space whether parked or moving, and maneuvering can be time-consuming and therefore expensive.

Tractor-trailers
These are special-purpose vehicles, built for large-capacity, long-range carrying ability, and even more out of place in interior portions of cities than other large trucks.

Bus

City bus

These vehicles are generally specific to a "run" or an area, with designated stops and, usually, schedules.

Charter (special-group) bus

Charter vehicles will usually have a single (or few) origin and destination, and a designated high-type route, removing them from major effects on street traffic.

Commuter bus

The bus entering the center city from suburbs or beyond will have few stops within the city, generally at an off-street terminal.

Rail Rapid Transit

Subway

The subway is removed from the surface, and its only disadvantages are inflexibility to changing conditions, age, maintenance, noise, and crowding.

Elevated

Elevated systems are passé but they remain, with some of the same advantages and disadvantages of subway systems, but saddled with the additional drawback of the ability to blight the area they pass over.

Surface train; trolley

Some surface rail systems remain (especially in foreign countries), and the recent "energy crisis" made them a subject of nostalgic reconsideration.

Commuter rail

Suburb–center city

The railroad commuter is generally in a higher economic class, and the railroad enters the city (it may be elevated, surface, or subway, or all three) and stops at a central terminal.

Within city limits

The areas through which the railroad passes have usually fallen into economic depression, and the railroad serves a foreign group (racially, economically). Often, too, there is no basis for a "reverse-commute" of inner-city residents to the suburbs.

Inter-city

Inter-city commutation is still rare and, utilizing the same trackage (usually) as suburban commuter movement, adds little to the urban problem.

Transportation Planning Models

Trip generation is the first area of transport planning in which some capability for forecasting movements is necessary. The simplest approach to modeling is based on the assumption that travel is orderly, that the amount of travel produced or generated by each zone is related to some measure of land-use activity in the zone. In an early application of this principle, trip production rates were defined for each major land-use category. This simple approach was replaced by multiple linear regression analysis, with a predictive equation of the general form

$$Y = a + b_1 X_1 + b_2 X_2 + \ldots b_n X_n$$

where Y is the dependent variable and equals the number of trips attracted to, or originating from, the zone. This can be stratified into home-based and non-home-based trips.

$X_1, X_2, \ldots, X_n$ are the independent variables and are variables such as population, car ownership, household income, number of persons employed, etc.

Trip distribution is the second area of transport planning in which forecasting requirements have resulted in modeling techniques. The trips produced by each origin zone (i) are distributed among all destination zones (j). The earliest forms of this model were growth-factor models: the forecasted numbers of trips between a pair of zones (T_{ij}) was based on a measured number of trips (t_{ij}) and modified by a factor (A) representing the change expected in future trip making:

$$T_{ij} = t_{ij}(A).$$

Variants of this method have been developed, but none of them can handle major changes in land use. For this purpose the "synthetic" or "analogous" distribution models were developed. The *gravity model* is one of these.

The gravity model is based on Newton's laws, and was first used for retail location as "Reilley's law of retail gravitation".[1] The general equation is:

$$T_{ij} = a_i b_j g_i A_j f(D_{ij})$$

where T_{ij} is the number of trips from zone i to zone j,

$\quad D_{ij}$ is the distance (or travel time) from zone i to zone j,

$\quad g_i$ is the number of trips *generated* in zone i,

$\quad A_j$ is the number of trips *attracted* to zone j,

and $\quad a_i$ and b_j are values formed by successive iterations.

This model has to be calibrated to find a value for the term $f(D_{ij})$, which describes the *observed* travel pattern. Early values were simple inverse exponential functions of the distance from zone i to zone j, but later ones are travel-time factors derived empirically for each trip purpose and for each trip origin.

The *entropy*[2] model is a recent improvement of the gravity model, of the form:

$$T_{ij}^{mp} = a_i^p b_j g_i^p A_j e^{-\beta_p c_{ij}^m}$$

where m is the mode of travel,

$\quad p$ is the type of person (car-owner or non-car-owner),

$\quad c_{ij}^m$ is the cost of travel between zones by mode.

Another form of "synthetic" model is the *intervening opportunity* model. It is based on the relative locations of destination zones, and provides the probability of a driver finding an "acceptable" destination in a given zone as a function of all possible destinations in all other zones nearer to i than j:

$$T_{ij} = p_i[e^{-LT} - e^{-L(T+T_j)}]$$

[1] W. J. Reilley, *The Law of Retail Gravitation*, New York, 1931.

[2] A. G. Wilson, A. F. Hawkins, G. J. Hill, and D. J. Wagon, "Calibration and testing of the SELNEC transport model". *Regional Studies*, Vol. 3 (1969).

where T_{ij} is the number of trips from zone i to zone j,

   p_i is the number of trip origins in zone i,

   T is the total number of destinations closer to i than j,

   T_j is the total number of trip destinations in zone j,

   L is the probability that some other destination will satisfy the needs of a given driver (empirically derived).

Modal split and *trip assignment* are two more recent areas in which work has been continuing in model-building. "Modal split" refers to the division between transportation "modes" or types, i.e. private auto, bus, rapid transit, etc. "Trip assignment" refers to the selection of the actual *route* expected to be taken by specific groups of travellers. Diversion curves and graph theory have been used in this attempt.

The uses of models have developed from the need to predict the usage of major motor-vehicle routes, generally rural or inter-city, during the period 1950–70. Applications of such models within urban areas are more recent, and less accurate due to the nature of the models and the diffusion processes within cities.

Sectors of Responsibility

Responsibility for the effectiveness of urban transportation, its efficiency, safety, and environmental acceptability, can be apportioned among three groups: the political (governments at all levels); the private (business groups); the individual.

The *individual* has little direct responsibility, except from a regulatory standpoint (adherence to laws, ordinances, regulations) and a moral standpoint (modal choices based on environmental impact, energy requirements, etc.). On the one hand (regulation), individuals can reasonably be expected to adhere to regulatory requirements, except as such requirements overbalance the economics of an individual's livelihood: taxes and tolls can reach levels of individual, i.e., public, resistance.

Private organizations have a greater area of effectiveness in control over events, and thereby a greater measure of responsibility. Large organizations may operate bus lines, fleets of trucks, fleets of passenger cars. The efficiency with which such fleets are operated, the avoidance of duplication and congested periods and facilities, will directly impinge upon the overall efficiency of an urban transportation "system". Private buses may compete for city street space with city buses; trucks may disrupt peak-hour commuting periods; and autos can add to already overloaded facilities at inappropriate times. Individual operators of trucks and buses can be more difficult to meld into the network of transport; individuals may be more likely to carry less-than-capacity loads, to operate at the worst hours of the traffic day, or to operate inefficient, unsafe vehicles which derogate the environment inordinately. Private organizations also have moral responsibilities in modal choice, which, however, devolve to economic choices even more rapidly than do individual choices.

Political, or public, agencies have, if not the greatest responsibility in the sphere of urban transportation policy, then the greatest capability for implementation of universal policy. Only governmental agencies, through the use of political, regulatory, and fiscal control, can work directly toward the ideal or transportation "balance" discussed earlier. But laxity in enactment and enforcement of urban planning and transportation policies which aid balance, and the tendency (stronger in the U.S. than elsewhere) to leave much decision making in the private sector, lead to and perpetuate problems of congestion and environmental degradation.

Elements of Policy Analysis

There are four major areas providing the indicators needed to analyze, evaluate, and measure the effects of policy in the urban transportation field. They are:

economics (fiscal),
efficiency (satisfaction of purpose),
comfort and convenience (community values),
environmental effects (social and ecological).

ECONOMICS

With the decline in passenger volume and the increase in deficit operation, cost is not as useful a tool in measuring the effectiveness of urban mass transportation as it once was. The ultimate measure of private enterprise, the profit, is long gone. In its place, cost-benefit ratios must include "utility" measures to counterbalance the excessive weight of cost versus benefit. Fiscal considerations are still valid in measuring *aspects* of a facility operation, however, and *cost* is still the ultimate measure against which to rate *performance*, which, however, must be measured in terms beyond pure dollars. Except for those few major transit operations still in private hands, fiscal balance is no longer the overall measure of policy success it was once. It is now an element in a quadripartite approach to measurement.

EFFICIENCY

This aspect implies the comparison of planned utility or effect with actual utility or effect. Efficiency measurement requires a listing of facility purpose and an analysis of how close actual purpose approaches planned or theoretical purpose. Some of the more obvious, basic purposes of urban transportation systems are in terms of:

volumes—of vehicles, of passengers, of trains; to be compared to designed and intended *capacities*;
speeds—for comparison with design speeds;
densities—of vehicles, of pedestrians;
accessibility—to vehicles, to stations, to stops, to ultimate destinations;
origin-and-destination—served by the facility, by population age and economic groups.

COMFORT AND CONVENIENCE

Items of this aspect include:
scheduling—relationships of schedules to desires and needs of patrons;
information—availability, comprehensibility of signs, maps, schedules;

physical constraint—heights of steps, slope of stairs, push force of doors, acceleration, deceleration, handholds, visibility, seat size and shape;

internal environment—temperature, noise, dust, odor, safety, security, lighting.

ENVIRONMENTAL EFFECTS

The latest element of policy analysis in urban transportation involves the effects of facilities on the external environment. The "environment" consists of everything, animate or inanimate, in the universe. It is more than "air pollution" or "water pollution", although it can be said that the impacts of the "emissions" or emanations or other factors from the presence of a transportation facility *act through* air, water, soil, and man-made environments. Impacting factors resulting from the introduction of transportation facilities can be listed as:

    gases,
    liquids,
    particulates,
    other by-products (rubber particles, etc.),
    de-icing salts,
    noise,
    physical presence.

The factors can impact three primary elements of the environment:

    air (including meteorological phenomena),
    water (and soil),
    man-made environment.

By vitiating, disturbing, or destroying any of the primary elements, the following secondary elements are affected:

    plants,
    animals,
    man.

Man can be included with *animals* from a purely physical standpoint; air pollution causes emphysema, etc., but man is a separate element in that his *social* structure and psychological behavior are also affected.

In the purely *ecological* sphere, elements to be considered include size and value of natural systems (ecosystems); numbers and species of wildlife affected; plant communities affected, etc. In the urban context, it is *parks* and *lawns* and *street trees* which are primarily to be considered.

In the *social* sphere, there exist purely socio-economic elements, such as:

    families relocated,
    housing affected,
    business/industries affected,
    effects on employment/goods movement accessibility,
        effects on tax abuse base, property values and the purely socio-psychological:
        community cohesion,
        community/individual attitude,
        residential mobility,

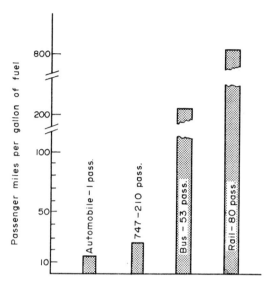

FIG. 3. Energy efficiency. 1973–1974 *Transit Fact Book*, American Transit Association, Washington, D.C., 1973, Fig. 7.

annoyance/irritation,
access to community facilities,
pedestrianism.

Safety is a major element in the environmental impact area as concerns transportation in the urban context. Safety is a major problem with surface traffic, because of the inherent pedestrian–vehicle conflict. Safety is therefore a prime indicator in the urban transportation policy analysis scheme: numbers and rates of fatal, injury, and property-damage accidents, for all modes.

An even more recently developed means of evaluating transport policy decisions is that of energy consumption. Figure 3 rates basic transport modes by "energy efficiency". They could as well be rated by accident rates or emissions or capacity, but in terms of energy consumption, there is no doubt of the superiority of rail mass transportation.

Analysis of the effectiveness of urban transportation policy decisions covers a broad spectrum of considerations, ranging from planning decisions to operating and maintenance decisions. That transportation is a major element of the urban policy field is without question, since every aspect of urban life is affected or colored by some means of transportation, from walking to a corner store to the noise of an airplane overhead interfering with a telephone conversation. Transport involves every area of modern urban living: work, shopping, recreation, medical/dental, entertainment, and purely purposeless travel. That a major interest in this sphere must be taken by policy-makers must also be without serious question.

Suggested Readings

Cantilli, E. J. *Programming Environmental Improvements in Public Transportation*, D. C. Heath & Co. (Lexington Books), Lexington, Massachusetts, 1974.

Cantilli, E. J. and Falcocchio, J. C. *Transportation and the Disadvantaged*, D. C. Heath & Co. (Lexington Books), Lexington, Mass., 1974.
Cantilli, E. J. and Shmelzer, J. L. *Transportation and Aging*, U.S. Department of Health, Education and Welfare, Washington, D.C., 1970.
Eldredge (ed.) *Taming Megalopolis*, Doubleday-Anchor, 1967,
Farris, and McElhiney, *Modern Transportation, Selected Readings*, Houghton Mifflin, 1973.
Klein, G. E. *et al. Methods of Evaluation of the Effects of Transportation Systems on Community Values*, Stanford Research Institute, 1971.
Meyer, J. R., Kain, J. F., and Wohl, M. *The Urban Transportation Problem*, Harvard University Press, Cambridge, Mass., 1965.
Miller, *Urban Transportation Policy, New Perspectives*, D. C. Heath & Co. (Lexington Books), 1972.
Munby, *Transport—Selected Readings*, Penguin Books.
Murin, W. J. *Mass Transit Policy Planning*, D. C. Heath & Co. (Lexington Books), Lexington, Mass., 1971.
Owen, W. *The Accessible City*, Brookings Institution, Washington, D.C., 1972.
Smerk, *Urban Transportation: The Federal Role*, Indiana University, 1966.

PART III

Essential Urban Services

5. *Strategies for Applying Formal Planning Tools to Program Decisions in Public Education*

JAMES McPARTLAND

There may be more at stake in financial and human terms for decisions about educational programs than about any other public functions or services. Yet, in principal, the planning and decision-making problems in public education are no different from those in other areas: to specify the likely benefits of a wide range of program alternatives and to choose the best one within the limitations of available resources. While general mathematical models and procedures have been developed by systems analysts to deal with problems of this general type, the ease of application of these formal approaches will differ with the realities of the particular situation. In education, the problems of direct application have often appeared insurmountable.

While the cost-benefits perspective has influenced the existing informal educational planning process and the terminology of the systems analyst is used by educational decision-makers,[1] the technical problems of applying formal quantitative tools for program decisions have resisted any working solutions until very recently.[2] These problems have been mainly that the mathematical formulations require more specific data and knowledge than could reasonably be supplied or estimated.

This chapter will describe three major information requirements of most formal approaches to planning which have posed technical roadblocks to applications in educational program decisions, and present some working solutions that have been recently proposed or attempted in each case. In describing these practical compromises, a general iterative strategy for educational planning will be developed, whereby weaker planning tools are used at first to direct attention to sources of improved information. These data can then be collected and fed into the following round of planning to permit the use of somewhat stronger tools.

A Politically Recognized Need

The decisions made regularly at all levels of government regarding public education affect large numbers of people and involve huge sums of money. In this country, the annual expenditure on public elementary and secondary education exceeds 50 billion dollars.[3] Over 40 percent of the annual expenditures of state and local governments goes for public education, which is more than three times the average outlay for other functions in their budget.[4] Moreover, the vitality and growth of an entire city or region may depend on the success of program decisions in education, because the willingness of a work force to enter or remain in an area is strongly influenced by the kinds of schools they believe to be available for their children.

111

With so much at stake, state legislatures and educational agencies have recently called for better information to justify the current expenditures and to guide policy decisions concerning the schools. State legislatures have been enacting "educational accountability" laws that require regular reports on the functioning of public education.[5] State departments of education and some local school districts have been developing new testing programs, new analysis tools, and reporting procedures to aid decision-making procedures concerning school programs. A 1973 survey discovered thirty states actually operating assessment programs to gather and report measures of educational outcomes, and all the remaining states planning to develop and institute some type of assessment and accountability programs in the future.[6] Sixteen of the thirty states with functioning programs are required by law to operate their assessment programs, and in the others the idea originated in the state educational agency. Thus, the need for better information and precision in educational planning has been clearly recognized. The pressures of state and local accountability laws and assessment reports are major reasons to expect serious advances in educational planning methods.

A General Planning Model and its Data Requirements

Educational program planning is defined in this chapter as the process of identifying the school practices which best accomplish the desired educational outcomes, given the available resources that can be used in school programs.[7] This definition simply expresses the system analyst's criteria of cost-benefits in the educational context, and there are several general mathematical models that formalize the problem and techniques for arriving at solutions. But any of these formal models require some way of dealing with the following questions:

1. What are the desired *educational outcomes*, the priorities among them, and how are they to be measured accurately?
2. What is the *educational process* through which the available alternative school practices and policies are related to the development of the desired outcomes for particular kinds of students?
3. What is the *relative cost* of establishing specific kinds of the alternative school practices and policies?

In the terminology of the systems analyst, the three questions involve specifying the "objective function" and the "production function" in education, together with any constraints that the real world places on the values that the variables in these functions may assume.[8] The objective function specifies the priorities among the desired outcomes of education, including all aspects of student learning and development as well as the outcomes of remaining within the budget. Thus, questions 1 and 3 above involve specifying the objective function. In the formal planning models, the objective function is the thing to be "optimized" by choosing among alternative education programs. The production function expresses the way changes in school variables (such as aspects of facilities, curriculum, staff, and social environment) and student input variables (such as family background and earlier learning) are related to increases in each educational outcome. Thus, question 2 above is concerned with specifying the production function. As one analyst has expressed it: "The idea behind an objective function is to assign a numerical value (utility) to every (relevant) state of the world; the decision problem is to maximize that function subject to budget and operational [production function] constraints."[9]

In its most simplified expression the "objective function" is represented as:

$$b_1 y_1 + b_2 y_2 + \ldots + b_c y_c + \ldots + b_n y_n = Y \tag{1}$$

where b_i is the priority attached to increasing each outcome y_i. One of these outcomes, y_c, is the level of cost, so that the associated b_c would ordinarily be a negative number to indicate that increased cost is negatively valued.[10] The decision sought is one which maximizes Y, given the operational and resource constraints of the system.

The production function is represented as:

$$a_{11} x_1 + a_{12} x_2 + \ldots + a_{1m} x_m = y_1,$$

$$a_{21} x_1 + a_{22} x_2 + \ldots + a_{2m} x_m = y_2,$$

$$\vdots \tag{2}$$

$$a_{c1} x_1 + a_{c2} x_2 + \ldots + a_{cm} x_m = y_c,$$

$$a_{n1} x_1 + a_{n2} x_2 + \ldots + a_{nm} x_m = y_n$$

where x_i are certain characteristics of school and non-school factors and a_{ij} are the coefficients expressing the relationship between x_i and y_j.

There will be certain constraints set on the values of x_i and y_i, of the form

$$x_i \geq 0 \qquad i = 1, 2, \ldots, m,$$

$$y_j \geq 0 \qquad j = 1, 2, \ldots, n,$$

$$0 \leq y_c \leq C \quad \text{where } C \text{ is the total budget limit.}$$

However, such a simplified expression of the objective and production functions would need to be modified to reflect such probable realities as (a) unit increases of most outcomes will not be equally valued along the entire scale (non-linear terms are needed in (1)) and (b) production functions would be different for certain schools and communities (some interaction terms are needed in both sets of equations).

To completely specify the values of these functions in education is a task involving overwhelming obstacles. Thus, some middle ground must be sought between rejecting formal planning methods altogether in favor of subjective impressions, or accepting the formal planning methods only after all of the equations and data can be completely specified or approximated. Because the realities of existing knowledge are different for each of the three questions listed above, different working solutions and strategies are emerging in each case.

Strategies for Specifying and Measuring Outcomes

The first step in any educational planning and evaluation system is to clarify the outcomes that are desired from the schools. Then, to be useful in formal planning activities, accurate methods of measuring the outcomes should be determined, and there should be some agreement on the relative priorities of the outcomes.

The actual state of affairs concerning educational outcomes far from satisfies this ideal. There are a large number of outcomes that schools are expected to promote in students. Besides imparting the basic skills in standard subjects, schools are expected to influence students' personal-social development and attitudes. However, there is no agreement about which outcomes must be included as school objectives for *all* students, which outcomes are worthwhile but of secondary importance, and what priorities exist among various levels of achievement on each of the several objectives.[11] Moreover, only a small number of the outcomes that have been suggested can presently be measured. Cognitive achievement can be tested in many subject-matter areas, but instruments to accurately gauge most non-cognitive outcomes either do not exist at all or are in very early stages of development. Thus, serious difficulties exist in both specifying and measuring educational outcomes.

Examples of the complexity of actually specifying objectives can be drawn from some state and local efforts to more precisely list and define the principal goals of their public schools. These exercises demonstrate the multiplicity and breadth of educational outcomes which are widely desired. In Maryland, a "needs assessment" study was conducted to survey members of different citizen groups and estimate the relative importance they attach to various goals for the public schools.[12] A sample of 11,000 Maryland citizens participated and judged ten general student outcomes and thirty-seven specific student outcomes to be important. These outcomes range from development of skills in traditional subject areas (e.g. "knowledge of mathematical concepts", "mastering of reading skills") to attitudes and personality attributes (e.g. "respect for self and the rights of others", "capability of self-development and self-direction") and positive reactions to school life ("has had opportunities to explore and participate in activities for personal enjoyment and development"). Other examples of educational objectives have been expressed both in terms of minimum levels to be accomplished by all students completing a course of study in the public schools, and with regard to the desired distribution of a range of outcomes or opportunities in the student population.[13]

Although many objectives have been named, the only generally accepted and reliable measures that are widely used in the schools at this time are the standardized achievement tests of cognitive learning.[14] These tests include the commercially developed batteries used in most districts (of which the Iowa Tests of Basic Skills, the Stanford Achievement Tests, and the Metropolitan Achievement Tests are the most popular), and recently developed test exercises developed especially for certain states and localities. Although these tests are used only in assessing the restricted goals of cognitive learning, their use in educational planning and assessment systems has not been without controversy about their completeness and technical problems of their comparability.[15]

There are certainly dangers in using available tests because they are convenient but measure only a limited number of desired outcomes. This use creates incentives in the schools to overemphasize the outcomes which are being measured at the expense of outcomes which are not being measured. But some accurate knowledge seems better than none, so most state assessment programs have been following the strategy of using achievement tests alone, but acknowledging their shortcomings and warning against over-reactions. The implicit reasoning is that the outcomes measured by the available tests are generally agreed to be of high priority as school objectives. The question then becomes how to use the available test scores to learn most about alternative educational programs and policies.

There are two major procedures to correctly use test score results for program planning so as to provide the most information possible: (1) adjust test scores for student inputs, and (2) develop statistics to reflect program impact on the distribution of outcomes and on particular kinds of students, as well as on the average students.

THE USE OF ADJUSTED TEST SCORES

Unless some specific adjustments are made to student achievement test scores, these results cannot be used to gain knowledge about the effectiveness of school programs. The inference may not be valid that the schools or districts with the highest test averages have the best instructional program. This is so because students from different kinds of families or with different academic starting points are *not* randomly distributed across the schools, but family background and initial performance factors are strongly related to students' present performance on achievement tests. For example, students from economically disadvantaged families are not equally likely to be found in each school, and such students will score lower on tests on the average because of their family disadvantages even though they may receive exactly the same educational program as more advantaged students.

Thus, showing that a school has low unadjusted test scores probably tells more about the kinds of students who attend the school than about the quality of the instructional program. Before any statement from test score results can be made about the relative success of alternative school programs, adjustments must be made to standardize for the background and starting points of the students served by the different schools. The "value added" by schools over and above what students enter school with needs to be identified.[16]

It is noteworthy that most of the recent state educational assessment reports present test score data in the form of *unadjusted* averages for the separate schools and school districts in the state. While such reports describe the level of learning in the state on the subjects covered by the tests, and locate where the students with the most need attend school, the unadjusted averages do not say anything about whether the test results are caused by the school programs or by non-school factors.[17] The recent research on achievement tests has indicated that much more of the variation in student test scores is accounted for by non-school factors than by a difference in school programs,[18] so that these reports probably *only* describe where the students from disadvantaged families attend school without indicating anything about which schools may have the best program.

Several approaches to adjusting test scores for student inputs will be discussed in later sections of the chapter.

USE OF STATISTICS IN ADDITION TO THE MEAN

Given that an instrument exists to measure a desired student outcome and that this measure can be standardized for student inputs, which statistics should be used to provide indications of the effectiveness of a school's program? In other words, how should the individual student scores on an adjusted measure be combined into a meaningful statistic indicating school effectiveness?

The usual statistic selected is the arithmetic mean (or average) of the student scores in the school. In fact, the mean is often the only summary statistic used. A recent RAND study suggests several other statistics besides the mean to gauge a school's program.[19] This study argues that there are some important school program objectives that can best be examined by statistics of intraschool *distributions* of scores. Some of these statistics indicate the effect of schools on equalizing performance and increasing mobility, others deal with school effectiveness with the most disadvantaged and most advantaged students, and others are concerned with assuring achievement of certain minimums by all. Examples of these statistics include measures of spread (such as the standard deviation or interquartile range), indicators of distortions in the distribution (such as skewness), and proportions of students below a specific achievement score.

Although most of the suggested statistics that consider the distribution of scores have not yet been applied to educational assessment data, there are some early indications that such measures are not as much affected by non-school factors as are the mean or medium. Because of the unresolved problems of statistically adjusting for student inputs, this property of low correlation with student input factors is of great usefulness in clearly assessing the impact of school programs.[20] The next section addresses problems of separating school and non-school influences, and the estimation of educational production functions.

Strategies for Specifying the Educational Process

Even if the problems of identifying and measuring the desired educational outcomes in order of priority were completely solved, planners still could not make decisions about school programs without detailed knowledge of the educational process. Educational program decisions involve choices for all operational and managerial aspects of the instructional program. This includes curriculum, facilities, materials, staffing patterns, student assignment policies, and the organization of authority, rewards, and tasks to be used in schools. To make these choices requires knowledge of how specific changes in each aspect of the instructional program will affect the desired outcomes.

This knowledge does not exist now, and it is doubtful that educational research will soon provide detailed knowledge of how a large number of school factors are related to student outcomes. The problem is not that past research has been poorly executed or that the technical tools to conduct such inquiries are not available. In reality, the way types of schools and students are distributed does not provide the kinds of scientific comparisons that are needed to improve our knowledge of the educational process without random experiments with school children. Because variation across schools in most aspects of the instructional program is restricted and because students from various backgrounds are not randomly distributed across the school differences which do exist, recent research has been hampered. When most schools are alike and when more disadvantaged students attend the same schools, it is not possible to find large independent school effects on learning. Moreover, when small differences in one aspect of the instructional program are in fact correlated with the existing differences in other aspects—when the schools with the best teachers also tend to have the best materials and curriculum, for example—then research is further stymied. Such correlations, when sufficiently high, prevent leaning about the *separate* importance of specific components of the educational program. In short, we do not understand the details of how specific aspects of schools are related to student learning. Researchers need to find or create comparison cases that offer the possibilities of increasing this knowledge.

Because knowledge of the educational process is required in order to apply formal planning tools, what does this mean for educational planning? Again, some middle ground strategy is needed rather than either altogether rejecting formal quantification in the planning process or waiting until research provides better estimates of all the separate parameters of the educational process. Such a strategy is emerging from both researchers and state educational assessment groups, from such centers of recent activity as Educational Testing Service, RAND, and the state assessment programs in California and New York.[21]

The broad strategy is to divide the problem into two stages. First, *identify exemplary schools* by controlling for student input factors to schools and noticing schools that consistently achieve more than expected given their student inputs. At this stage no attempt is made to measure the specific program attributes that are most important to success, only to locate the most successful schools. Second, *study these exemplary schools* to learn what particular aspects of their instructional programs are different from other schools. The program aspects that are most distinctive in the exemplary schools then becomes candidates for more rigorous research evaluation, and for dissemination to other schools. After careful evaluation, when a few particular program aspects are definitively identified as true parameters of the educational process, these variables can be added to the student inputs in the following planning year as controls when identifying further exemplary schools. With both student inputs and verified program aspects controlled, a continued study of exemplary schools should add further program aspects to our knowledge of the educational process. By this reasoning, with each successive cycle of planning, we will be bootstrapping our way to more precise knowledge of the educational process, while at any given year achieving some guidance for further research and for policy experiments based on the best available knowledge.[22]

In other words, the strategy is to separate the two technical problems of (1) adjusting school outcome measures for the differences in student inputs and (2) estimating the program characteristics that are related to school effectiveness after student inputs are taken into account. The remainder of this section will describe the recent work on how to approach each of these problems, and list the advantages and disadvantages of this general strategy.

METHODS FOR IDENTIFYING EXEMPLARY SCHOOLS

Recent efforts to identify exemplary schools or districts have been attempting to solve the same general problem with the same general approach. The efforts vary only in the details of the general approach. The general problem is that there are a group of schools or a group of school districts for which the same measures of educational outcomes have been collected from all the students involved. (At present, the available measures have been standardized achievement scores.) The task is to isolate the school effects on these outcomes from non-school influences, and identify the schools or districts that consistently show a substantially larger (or a substantially smaller) effect than the others in the group.

The general approach is in three steps. First, an equation is estimated that expresses the relationship between non-school factors and each of the educational outcome measures. This equation is obtained through least-squares multiple regression analysis, where the outcome measure is regressed on the non-school factors to obtain an expression of the form:

$$y = a + b_1 x_1 + b_2 x_2 + \ldots + b_r x_r \tag{3}$$

where y is the outcome measure, x_i are the non-school input measures, and b_i are the associated regression coefficients giving the average amount of change in y for a unit increase in x_i. In other words, estimated values of a (the general intercept) and the b_i are obtained through multiple regression analysis to represent the average relationship between non-school input factors and a selected educational outcome.

Second, predicted (or "expected") mean achievement scores are obtained for each school or district by substituting the values of x_i of the particular school or district into this regressions equation. The difference between this predicted mean score and the actual mean score obtained by the school or district is an estimate of the degree to which a school is an over- or under-achiever relative to its student inputs. This difference (or residual) value has been called the "student development index" or "performance index" or "performance indicator" by researchers who have used this approach.

Third, in order to take into account the random errors of estimation that are always involved in both the predicted and actual components of the difference score, criteria are established for identifying the exemplary schools on the basis of the size and consistency of the difference scores. In other words, the probabilities of random error in the difference score estimates are acknowledged, and the only schools or districts to be identified as exemplary are those whose estimated difference scores are large and consistent enough to have only a small chance of being produced solely by the random errors of measurement.

This general approach to arrive at predicted or expected outcomes and residual scores is a familiar general application of multiple regression analysis that has been used frequently in other areas. Thus, the unanswered questions and differences of opinion are not about the general multiple regression approach, but about the application to educational processes; what variables to use as input measures, and whether the correlations in education create biases toward certain schools.

There are many areas of disagreement about how to apply the general approach. For example, the ETS researchers believe that the prediction equation should be based on individual student data while others have performed the multiple regression analysis on the data of school or district averages.[23] There are serious disagreements over the non-school input factors which should ideally be used in defining the prediction equation and obtaining predicted and residual scores. The input variables which have been suggested or used include: (a) the same or different outcome measures from previous years, (b) measures of student family socio-economic status (such as parents' education, occupation, income, family size, and race), and (c) some concurrent student measures on a so-called "ability" test. Some have argued that *only* previous year's test scores should be used as inputs (which is the same as using an average achievement growth score to measure school effectiveness). Others have argued that both previous test results and family socio-economic status are appropriate, but concurrent "ability" tests should never be used as input variables.[24] Finally, there are differences of opinion on the importance of requiring consistency of several estimates as well as size before identifying a school as exemplary. Some research at RAND, by developing methods of examining consistency and demonstrating its usefulness, has been very important in this regard.[25]

At the present time these many questions are being answered by a practical rather than technical approach: the variables, level of analysis, and the kind of consistency checks being used are the ones which are readily available. Further work is needed to evaluate the consequences of using approximate techniques and measures, and to provide practical methods for checking the advisability of certain short-cuts in particular applications.

There are other general limitations about this application of multiple regression to education which will be discussed at the end of this section.

METHODS FOR STUDYING PROGRAMS IN EXEMPLARY SCHOOLS

The reason for identifying exemplary schools is to gain knowledge of the elements of school programs that are most important for promoting desired student outcomes. Although there are no existing examples that show how to most profitably follow-up the identification of exemplary schools with studies of their programs, several possibilities are evident.

As a beginning, the over-achieving schools can be compared to the average school or to the under-achieving schools on the basis of readily available numerical data about school programs. Such data may be public information, such as school size and per-pupil expenditure, or it may be information collected through follow-up surveys of the particular schools, such as teacher experience and use of individualized instruction in reading. One advantage of comparing only over- and under-achieving schools is that new data on program characteristics would only be collected from a fraction of the schools in the system or state. However, there are real disadvantages of depending on survey data alone for the follow-up studies of exemplary schools.

We do not have sufficient knowledge at present to anticipate the kinds of program variables that make or cause an unusually effective school. The search at this time should be very open-ended, and a survey approach alone is not well suited for this goal. Survey instruments usually require preconceptions about what variables are to be studied rather than an open-minded search. While surveys can certainly provide some valuable data with which to investigate the exemplary schools, most survey instruments offer only crude measurements of the least subtle aspects of a situation. To the extent that program aspects causing the exemplary schools cannot be anticipated beforehand, or to the extent that they involve detailed aspects of the life of the school, survey data will probably miss the necessary information.

Not only would many potentially important variables be ignored in a formal survey, but there is the danger that a variable measured in a survey may incorrectly be seen as important when it is merely correlated with an unmeasured program element that is actually producing the unusual effects. Such mistakes are always possible when certain aspects of educational programs happen to be found together in existing schools even though there is no causal relationship between them. Surveys that consider only a small number of variables are especially vulnerable. Less-restricted investigations that permit access to a wide range of program information will allow researchers to be alert to these errors and to consider rival hypotheses about causes of unusually effective schools.

For these reasons, it is wise to rely on more open-ended studies of exemplary schools than survey data alone could provide. In addition to formal data from surveys, exploratory case study methods should also be used to study unusually effective schools.[26]

After exemplary schools have been identified, experienced teams of observers and researchers should spend time in these schools in an effort to understand the life of these schools and what is truly different about the operation of their programs. The goal should be to discover those program elements that appear to differentiate the over-achieving schools that could be adopted in other school locations to derive the same benefits. Several expert observers should make separate judgments in each case to guarantee the reliability of the observer reports.

From the formal analyses of available data or new survey data on program differences and the case study reports, some program elements should be identifiable as *candidates* for increased investment and dissemination to other schools and systems. The final step is to put these candidates to the test by conducting careful studies of their effects in other schools. If the candidate program elements are truly part of the educational process, then other schools who use these elements should improve in the desired outcomes. This prediction should be tested by careful evaluation studies of the use of the program elements in other schools. Although the recent history of evaluation research in education has not been one of careful scientific methodology, it is vital that candidate program aspects of exemplary schools be studied with serious attention to scientific requirements.[27] The knowledge suggested by identifying exemplary schools and exploratory analyses of the programs in such schools can be secured only through such studies.

ADVANTAGES AND LIMITATIONS OF THE TWO-STAGE APPROACH

While there are some major advantages of this strategy for gaining knowledge about the educational process, there are also some limitations to be acknowledged.

The major advantages of the approach are (a) it separates school program factors from student inputs, (b) it is practical, (c) it does not make assumptions about the educational process beforehand that go beyond our present knowledge, and (d) it offers a technically suitable strategy for gaining positive knowledge.

As was pointed out earlier, it is necessary to adjust for student inputs—such as socio-economic status and initial level of achievement—in order to learn which aspects of the *school* program are most important for educational outcomes. This basic requirement is fulfilled by this approach since the first stage is designed to make the necessary adjustments for student inputs. It is practical because the data requirements to apply the approach are limited and feasible. The approach can be initiated with any set of schools that uses the same achievement test, a condition that presently exists within most single school systems and which can ordinarily be accomplished in a short time across most states. The only data required in addition to student test scores in order to identify exemplary schools are measures of student inputs such as previous year's test results and/or estimates of socio-economic status and racial composition. These data are often available in school system files or can be reliably estimated without enormous difficulties. The information on school programs needed in the second stage of the approach need only be obtained on a subset of the schools—those which have been identified as over-achievers and a sample of schools for comparison. Thus, the data requirements are feasible in most systems and states to apply the two-stage approach: it takes advantage of data already being collected and focuses the needs for most of the additional required information on a small fraction of the schools.

The approach also acknowledges that little is known about which aspects of school programs are most important for educational outcomes, and avoids premature assumptions about this question. After unusually effective schools have been identified in the first stage of the approach, the investigation of the program aspects which may explain the effectiveness is to be open-ended and broad-reaching.

Perhaps most important of all, this approach of comparing programs from a selected set of schools may succeed in providing positive knowledge where previous research has failed. Previous research investigating test score outcomes, such as the Coleman study, have concluded that on the average school program differences do not explain very much. This conclusion may be correct, yet does not negate our proposed strategy. The existence of some truly exceptional schools and some important program elements is not inconsistent with the recent research results. The research only implies that exemplary schools for test-score outcomes are at best limited in number, although some may exist. Thus, by getting away from dealing with the average difference between schools, this strategy of concentrating on unusually effective schools holds promise for producing positive contributions to knowledge where other more general research strategies might not.[28] When other outcome measures which may be less responsive to non-school influences become available the strategy becomes especially promising.

The limitations of knowledge gained by studying existing schools in this way derive from certain realities of school differences rather than from technical defects in the techniques being proposed. As long as one is working with existing school programs, there are no alternative techniques without these limitations.

Obviously, before evidence can be obtained that an experimental program is producing real improvements in desired outcomes, such a program must appear in the schools under study. By their nature most experimental programs are conducted on a small scale in a single school in a single subject and classroom, rather than in an entire grade or in many schools. As such, their effectiveness may be overlooked when the search is only at the school level or when only one school has the program. The implication is that experimental programs with rigorous evaluations may be a *separate* source of important knowledge about the educational process, and need to be examined in the educational planning process apart from any other information that is collected.

Somewhat less obvious is that if some truly important aspect of the instructional process exists in *all* schools, it will not be uncovered by this search strategy. The only way to learn that some program element is effective is to be able to compare cases with and without the element. Thus, if all schools had equally excellent reading textbooks, this factor would not appear important for producing good reading-test scores. If this example were true, it clearly would be a tragic mistake to substitute the investment in reading textbooks for some other school element on the basis of the finding that textbooks did not distinguish an overachieving school from an underachieving one. Yet the danger of such misinterpretations exist under this approach, which is a search for relationships which will be absent when there is simply no variation in variables as well as when there is no true causal connection. Thus, it is more convincing to reject an element of school program as unimportant on the basis of both of two kinds of comparisons: the finding of no difference in the program element between schools with unequal outcomes and the finding of a significant difference in the program element between schools with similar outcomes.

A third limitation was mentioned earlier as a reason to not rely on surveys without case studies to uncover the most important program aspects: the fact that one aspect may appear important when it merely happens to be found together with other program aspects which do have important effects. There is no way to rigorously test which particular program aspect in a cluster of several is truly important and which is a coincidental companion of the important ones, without establishing or finding comparison cases with different combinations of the aspects in the cluster. Because these experiments are likely to be impractical, it is helpful to consider the detailed process through which each aspect might affect the desired outcomes. This consideration may allow a judgment about the most likely candidates to be the causal elements.

Finally, the possible correlations between student input variables and school program variables may introduce significant bias into the identification of exemplary schools in the first place. Under the proposed multiple-regression technique, the student input factors that are used to standardize schools will also standardize schools on the basis of the program aspects which are highly correlated with student inputs. This would mean that over- and underachieving schools would be identified after both student inputs and certain program aspects were taken into account, and it would be impossible to learn about the potential importance of those program aspects. For example, suppose a relatively small school size was important for student learning, but that the smallest schools had the highest proportion of economically disadvantaged students. In this example, when the analyst controls for student socio-economic status to identify unusually effective schools, he is also controlling for school size (because the variables are correlated in reality). The exemplary schools identified are those that are unusually productive after both inputs and school size are controlled, although the analyst might believe it is only inputs that are standardized.[29] The danger of overlooking school size as an important program aspect in this hypothetical example is obvious. To guard against this bias, it is necessary to become aware of the school aspects which are highly correlated with inputs; also, it may often be helpful to identify exemplary schools along the entire range of the student input measures, even though the size and consistency criteria for such identification may need to be somewhat different for the high and low socio-economic student bodies. In this way, the chances of controlling on a school aspect because it is correlated with student inputs is somewhat reduced.

In summary, the two-stage approach of first identifying unusually effective schools and then studying the selected schools in a resourceful and open manner is a practical method of dealing with the current level of ignorance about the educational process. But because the approach depends upon the natural variations and relationships which exist in schools, it has the limitations that any technique will have using these data. These limitations can cause the inclusion of unimportant program elements as well as the overlooking of important ones, so the analyst must be sophisticated in his approach. In addition, it is important to have a continuing program of experiments to study initial judgments and to examine experimental variations which are not widespread in the schools.

Strategies for Estimating Costs

There are few examples of formal planning tools being used to choose among program alternatives in order to actually minimize costs. Levin, in his cost-effectiveness analysis of teacher selection, provides an example that shows the relative difficulties in estimating costs for educational planning.

In his analysis, Levin used simplified specifications of educational outcomes and the educational process.[30] Using results obtained earlier from the Equality of Educational Opportunity survey, he chose one achievement test as the educational outcome, and he considered only those aspects of the educational process represented by the relationship between average student-achievement test scores and two teacher variables—teacher verbal score and teacher experience. The estimated relationship specified that for each additional point of teacher verbal score, student achievement increased by .179 points for white students and .175 for blacks, while the comparable achievement increment for each additional year of teacher experience was .060 and .108 for whites and blacks, respectively.

Using data for teachers from the same survey, Levin estimated "earnings functions" for teachers which showed that about $24 of annual salary was associated with each additional point of verbal score and about $79 with each additional year of experience. Putting these earnings functions together with the production function estimates allowed Levin to show the relative costs of improving student achievement under alternative hiring and promotion policies. A strategy of obtaining teachers with high verbal scores, compared to obtaining more experienced teachers, was estimated to be five times less expensive for a given test score increment of white students and ten times less expensive for black students.

The Levin example illustrates that specifying costs of alternatives for program planning is a complex process involving the estimation of explicit relationships between costs and unit changes in specific program aspects. To do this for even a few program variables will require extensive data on real variations in the variables and their accompanying costs. However, data with sufficient variations may only be available if information from a number of years or from a number of districts is brought together.

As was true for the problems of specifying the educational process, some practical short-cuts and approximations can often be made in estimating costs of alternatives. These suggestions, which are detailed elsewhere,[31] appear to follow a few general rules. First, clearly identify the program alternatives that are most likely to be considered, so that only a few variables within a limited range that are associated with these alternatives need to be costed out. For example, previous analyses of the educational process may have suggested four major alternatives being considered for new programs in a district: (1) smaller class sizes, (2) diversified staffing with aides and master teachers, (3) transportation of students to achieve greater socio-economic mix in student bodies, and (4) the construction of open-space areas for learning centers with accompanying individualized materials and staff in-service training. Cost estimates would be needed only for these four changes in the particular planning cycle. Second, establish the comparability of total costs of complete alternative programs, and estimate the "incremental costs" of each alternative from a "base case" of the current program. Then a total cost can be established for each alternative by combining the incremental and base costs. Third, rough estimates will often suffice for certain program alternatives, depending on the particular circumstances and budget categories.[32] Finally, planning decisions often do not require knowledge of the optimum combination of program elements, but only indications of the rank orderings of cost-benefit of a few total program packages.

Application of Planning Tools in Special Cases

There have been some special cases of educational planning where formal tools have been applied successfully or, at least, generated interesting conclusions. These are special cases because they do not focus on student learning or instructional programs, which are the usual major planning concerns. These cases are important because they are real attempts to use formal tools in actual situations in the educational setting, and demonstrate well many of the problems and prospects of the systems approach in education.

Probably the most successful special cases have been what McNamara has called "demographic applications".[33] These include problems of: bus routing and assignment of students, given the present location of schools and student populations;[34] the location and size of future schools, given current and projected centers of school-aged population;[35] the repair and replacement of school equipment, given the recent history of equipment purchases;[36] cafeteria menu planning, given nutritional objectives;[37] and master schedules of classes and students, given course requirements, class-size restrictions and the number of staff and students.[38] Perhaps the most interesting applications of this general type have involved the assignment of pupils to schools to achieve desegregation in racial and ethnic distributions, given predetermined constraints on the maximum travel time for any given student, where the added goal was to minimize the daily total transportation time.[39]

Another important special case involved an application of planning tools to state educational finance programs to determine an optimal state-aid plan, given particular objectives of equalization of expenditures and utilization of state and local resources.[40]

These special cases demonstrate that formal tools can be of considerable aid to educational planning, when the necessary data is obtained to adequately specify the outcomes, processes, and costs involved. On the other hand, some special case applications of cost simulation methods in higher education have caused some to argue that the use of formal mathematical models may be less accurate, less direct, and more expensive than the traditional planning approach of relying on judgments of experienced educators.[41] With regard to the major decisions in education, experience with formal planning tools is only beginning to accumulate. The next few years should tell whether the major planning tasks for state and local educational programs can be significantly improved with formal tools and efficient data estimation strategies.

Notes

1. The use of PPBS (Program Planning and Budgeting System) and MBO (Management by Objectives) are examples of how the perspective of the systems analysts have influenced informal educational planning. If these perspectives are followed, planners strive to be much clearer in verbally defining objectives, and listing alternative programs with their estimated costs. Even though these activities do not reach the level of formalization of mathematical approaches to be discussed in this chapter, they hold a potential for improved planning. See, for example, Cook (1966), Drew (1967), Glennan (1969), Haggart (1972), Hartley (1968), and Lane and Kyle (1968).
2. Of course, there are many political and social forces which may account for the persistence of limited, informal, or subjective planning practices in public education. These include the narrow restrictions on program alternatives created by accrediting agencies and post-secondary entrance requirements, the actions of powerful professional interest groups who might stand to lose from more exacting evaluation procedures, the traditional bureaucratic separation of responsibilities along subject-matter specialities, and the strict tradition of local district and school autonomy for program evaluation and decisions. For discussions of other social and political conditions affecting educational planning and decision making, see Sisson (1969), Benson (1967), and McNamara (1970, p. 435).
3. U.S. Office of Education, *1972 Digest of Educational Statistics*, p. 22, table 22.
4. U.S. Office of Education, *1972 Digest of Educational Statistics*, p. 26, fig. 5.
5. See the publications of the Cooperative Accountability Project (1973a, b) and of the Education Commission of the States (1973) for a description of accountability legislation in the states. See also, Lessinger and Tyler (1971).
6. Educational Testing Service, 1973.
7. There is an important distinction between planning for educational program decisions and human resource planning. The latter attempts to clarify relationships of the total educational system in a nation to economic and social development, by projecting the manpower needs of desired future economic and social conditions so that the requisite size and outputs of the nation's schools and colleges

can be determined. Such human resource planning has been conducted in other nations with planned economies (McNamara, 1971, pp. 427–9; Bereday and Laufwerys, 1967; Parnes, 1962; UNESCO, 1964). In this chapter we are not concerned with this approach, but deal with decisions concerning the type of program to be conducted in the public schools.

8. See Klitgaard (1973), Bowles (1970), Levin (1970), and McNamara (1970) for a discussion of the problem in these terms.
9. Klitgaard (1973, p. 11).
10. More precisely, there would be several cost factors in the equations, ones for each of the separate aspects the school program being purchased.
11. See Klitgaard (1973, pp. 15–18) for a discussion of how it is unlikely that agreement on these priorities will be achieved in education.
12. Title III of the 1965 Elementary and Secondary Education Act, which supports programs in state education agencies, requires that participating state agencies conduct a needs assessment. See Maryland State Department of Education (1972) as one example.
13. See Coleman (1968) for a discussion of the objective of "equality of educational opportunity". See Klitgaard (1973), pp. 12–13) for a discussion of possible distributions of achievement which may be valued.
14. This may be changing, however, as noted in the ETS 1973 survey of state assessment programs, where at least twelve examples of measures of non-cognitive outcomes were found in use. The four which were most prevalent were: attitudes toward school, self-concept, citizenship, and career orientation. See also Tyler (1973).
15. Subject-matter specialists have found the existing commercial tests to measure only some of the outcome objectives in their field, when a list of subject-matter objectives is examined such as the ones produced by National Assessment of Educational Progress (Finley *et al.*; and Womer, no dates). A different problem arises, frequently for program comparisons within a state, on the basis of commercially produced achievement tests, since several different and non-comparable test series may have been chosen for use by the separate districts of the state. This difficulty has prompted the recent development of an "anchor test" and translation scores between the most common commercial tests in certain grades (Jaeger, 1973).
16. See Dyer (1972) for development of the "value added" concept in education.
17. The test results alone do make clear where the poor students happen to attend school (though not anything about which schools have the best programs) and some eight states have used this data to allocate funds to districts. But such decisions are based on where the *need* is greatest, not on where the educational *program* is working. It is possible under this policy that the most totally ineffective school programs receive the most money to continue to make the same mistakes. For further discussion see Barro (1970).
18. See, for example, Jencks *et al.* (1972) and Coleman *et al.* (1966).
19. Klitgaard (1973).
20. For the same reasons of importance, there is hope that some of the exercises being developed by National Assessment of Educational Progress will be more related to school programs and less to family-background factors than existing test-scale scores. This hope is held because the exercises are *more specific* to school instruction than the summary scores of many standardized test batteries, reflecting present knowledge which is more likely to be learned in school than elsewhere. For example, studies have shown variations in math scores to be more related to school than family compared to reading scores, presumably because many aspects of maths are specific skills not taught or practiced very much outside of school.
21. See Dyer (1970), Klitgaard and Hall (1973), California State Department of Education (1972), and University of the State of New York (1972).
22. *Ibid.*
23. Compare Dyer (1970) and Dyer *et al.* (1969) to California State Department of Education (1972) and Hilton and Patrick (1970).
24. Dyer (1970).
25. Klitgaard and Hall (1973).
26. See Forehand *et al.* (1973, pp. 23–6).
27. See McDill *et al.* (1972) for a discussion of evaluation research in public education.
28. Klitgaard and Hall (1973, pp. 1–2).
29. See Forsyth (1973) and O'Connor (1972) for discussion of similar points. There is a separate source of possible bias when previous years' test scores are used as input variables when identifying exemplary schools. This is the result of the well-known statistical phenomenon of "regression to the mean".
30. Levin (1970).
31. Haggart (1972), especially chapter 3, 5, and 8. See also the discussion of the strategy of defining "equal-cost alternatives".

32. There are methods for analyzing when to be most concerned about precision; see Haggart (1972).
33. McNamara (1971).
34. Shapley *et al.* (1966), Newton and Thomas (1969).
35. O'Brien (1969), Ploughman (1968).
36. Ploughman (1968).
37. Lutz (1968).
38. Oakford *et al.* (1967).
39. Clarke and Surkes (1968); Lefkowitz and D'Epsopo (1967), Heckman and Taylor (1969).
40. Bruno (1969).
41. This conclusion was drawn by Hopkins (1971) with regard to departmental planning in universities, although this author found merit in mathematical planning models for other university decisions. For other examples of the use of formal planning tools in higher education see Fox (1972), Fox and Sengupta (1968), and Koenig and Keeney (1969).

References

Barro Stephen M. (1970) "An approach to developing accountability measures for the public schools." *Phi Delta Kappan*, **52**, 196–205.

Benson, C. S. (1967) "Economics and education." *Review of Educational Research*, **37**, 96–102.

Bereday, G. F. and Laufwerys, J. A. (Eds.) (1967) *The World Yearbook of Education 1967: Educational Planning*. London: Evans Brothers Ltd.

Bowles, S. S. (1970). "Towards an educational production function." In W. L. Hansen (Ed.) *Education, Income and Human Capital*. New York: Columbia University Press.

Bruno, J. E. (1969) "An alternative to the use of simplistic formulas for determining state resources allocation in school finance program." *American Educational Research Journal*, **6**, 479–514.

California State Department of Education (1972) *California State Testing Program 1970–1: Profiles of School District Performance*. Sacramento: Office of Program Evaluation and Research.

Chirikos, T. N. and Wheeler, A. C. (1968) "Concepts and techniques of educational planning." *Review of Educational Research*, **38**, 264–76.

Clarke, S. and Surkis, J. (1968) "An operations research approach to racial desegregation of school systems." *Socio-Economic Planning Sciences*, **1**, 259–72.

Coleman, James S. (1968) "The concept of equality of educational opportunity." *Harvard Educational Review*, **38**, 7–22.

Coleman, James S., Campbell, Ernest Q., Hobson, Carol, McPartland, James, Mood, Alexander M., Weinfeld, Frederick D., and York, Robert L. (1966) *Equality of Educational Opportunity*. Washington: Government Printing Office.

Coleman, James S. and Karweit, Nancy L. (1972) *Information Systems and Performance Measures in Schools*. Englewood Cliffs, New Jersey: Educational Technology Publications.

Cook, Desmond L. (1966) *Program Evaluation and Review Technique. Applications in Education*. Office of Education Cooperative Research Monograph No. 17, Washington, Government Printing Office.

Cooperative Accountability Project (1973a) *Legislation by the States: Accountability and Assessment in Education*. Denver.

Cooperative Accountability Project (1973b) *Characteristics of and Proposed Models for State Accountability Legislation*. Denver.

Crandell, R. H. (1969) "A constrained choice model for student housing." *Management Science*, **16**, 112–20.

Cronbach, Lee J. and Furly, Lita (1970) "How we should measure 'Change'—or should we?" *Psychological Bulletin*, **74**, 68–90.

Drew, Elizabeth B. (1968) "HEW grapples with PPBS." *The Public Interest*, **8**, 9–24.

Dyer, Henry S. (1970) "Toward objective criteria of professional accountability in the schools of New York City." *Phi Delta Kappan*, **52**, 206–11.

Dyer, Henry S. (1972) "The measurement of educational opportunity." In Frederick Mosteller and Daniel P. Moynihan (eds.) *On Equality of Educational Opportunity*. New York: Random House (Vintage Books).

Dyer, Henry S., Linn, Robert L., and Patton, Michael J. (1969) "A comparison of four methods of obtaining discrepancy measures based on observed and predicted school system means on achievement tests." *American Education Research Journal*, **6**, 591–605.

Education Commission of the States (1973) *1972, Legislation and Achievements: Accountability Assessment and Testing*. Denver: Department of Research and Information Services, Education Commission of the States.

Educational Testing Service (1973) *State Educational Assessment Programs, 1973 Revision*. Princeton.

ERIC Clearinghouse on Educational Administration (1970) *Models for Planning: Analysis of Literature and Selected Bibliography*. Eugene, Oregon: University of Oregon.

Fennessey, James (1973) "Using achievement growth to analyze educational programs." Report No. 151, Center for Social Organization of Schools, Johns Hopkins University.

Fennessey, James (1974) "Understanding 'fan spread' in achievement measures." Report No. 168, Center for Social Organization of Schools, Johns Hopkins University.

Finley, Carmen J. and Berdie, Frances (1976) *The National Assessment Approach to Exercise Development*. Denver: National Assessment of Educational Progress.

Forehand, Galie A., Marco, Gary L., McDonald, Frederick, J. Murphy, Richard T., and Quirk, Thomas J. (1973) *An Accountability Design for School Systems*. Princeton: Educational Testing Service Research Bulletin, June.

Forsyth, Robert A. (1973) "Some empirical results related to the stability of performance indicators in Dyer's student change model of an educational system." *Journal of Educational Measurement*, 10, 7–12.

Fox, K. A. (ed.) (1972) *Economic Analysis for Educational Planning: Resource Allocation in Nonmarket Systems*. Baltimore: Johns Hopkins University Press.

Fox, K. A. and Sengupta, J. K. (1968) "The specification of econometric models for planning educational systems: an appraisal of alternative approaches." *Kyklos*, 21, 665–94.

Glennan, Thomas K., Jr. (1969) "Systems analysis of education." In *Proceedings of 1969 Invitational Conference on Testing Problems*. Princeton: Educational Testing Service.

Haggart, Sue A. (ed.) (1972) *Program Budgeting for School District Planning*. Englewood Cliffs, New Jersey: Educational Technology Publications.

Hartley, Harry J. (1968) *Educational Planning—Programming—Budgeting. A Systems Approach*. Englewood Cliffs, New Jersey: Prentice-Hall.

Heckman, L. B. and Taylor, H. M. (1969) "School rezoning to achieve racial balance: a linear programming approach." *Socio-Economic Planning Sciences*, 3, 127–33.

Hilton, Thomas L. and Patrick, Cathleen (1970) "Cross-sectional versus longitudinal data: an empirical comparison of mean differences in academic growth." *Journal of Educational Measurement*, 7, 15–24.

Hopkins, David S. P. (1971) "On the use of large-scale simulation models for university planning." *Review of Educational Research*, 41, 467–78.

Jaeger, Richard M. (1973) "The national test-equating study in reading (The Anchor Test Study)." *NCME Measurement in Education*, 4.

Jencks, Christopher, Smith, Marshall, Acland, Henry, Bane, Mary Jo, Cohen, David, Gintis, Herbert, Heyns, Barbara, and Michelson, Stephan (1972) *Inequality: A Reassessment of the Effect of Family and Schooling in America*. New York: Basic Books.

Klitgaard, Robert E. (1973) *Achievement Scores and Educational Objectives*. Santa Monica, California: RAND.

Klitgaard, Robert E. and Hall, George R. (1973) *A Statistical Search for Unusually Effective Schools*. Santa Monica, California: RAND.

Koenig, H. E. and Keeney, M. G. (1967) "A prototype planning and resource allocation program for higher education." *Socio-Economic Planning Sciences*, 2, 201–15.

Lane, R. E. and Kyle, D. W. (1968) "The application of systems analysis to educational planning." *Comparative Education Review*, 1, 39–56.

Lefkowitz, B. and D'Espopo, D. A. (1967) "Analysis of alternative methods for improving racial balance in a school district." A paper presented at the 31st meeting of the Operations Research Society of America.

Lessinger, Leon M. and Tyler, Ralph W. (1971) *Accountability in Education*, Worthington, Ohio: Charles A. Jones Publishing Co.

Levin, Henry M. (1970) "A cost-effectiveness analysis of teacher selection." *Journal of Human Resources*, 5, 24–33.

Lutz, R. P. *et al.* (1968) "Taking the heat off the school lunchroom." A paper presented at the Annual Conference of the American Institute of Industrial Engineers.

Maryland State Department of Education (1972) *Goals and Needs of Maryland Public Education*, Baltimore: Maryland State Department of Education.

McDill, Edward L., McDill, Mary S., and Sphere, J. Timothy (1972) "Evaluation in practice: compensatory education." In Rossi, Peter (Ed.) *Evaluating Social Programs*, New York: Seminar Press.

McNamara, James F. (1971) "Mathematical programming models in educational planning." *Review of Educational Research*, 41, 419–46.

Merwin, Jack D. and Womer, Frank B. (1969) "Evaluation in assessing the progress of education to provide bases of public understanding and public policy." In *NSSE Yearbook. Educational Evaluation: New Roles, New Means*, Chicago: University of Chicago Press.

Newton, R. M. and Thomas, W. H. (1969) "Design of bus routes by computer." *Socio-Economic Planning Sciences*, **3**, 75–85.

Oakford, R. V., Allen, D. W., and Chatterton, L. A. (1967) "School scheduling practice and theory." *Journal of Educational Data Processing*, **1**, 16–50.

O'Brien, R. J. (1969) "Models for planning the location and size of urban schools." *Socio-Economic Planning Sciences*, **2**, 141–53.

O'Connor, E. F., Jr. (1972) "Extending classical test theory to the measurement of change." *Review of Educational Research*, **42**, 73–97.

Parnes, H. S. (1962) *Forecasting Educational Needs for Economic Cooperation and Development*. Paris: Organization for Economic Cooperation and Development.

Ploughman, T. (1968) "An assignment program to establish school attendance boundaries and forecast construction needs." *Socio-Economic Planning Sciences*, **1**, 243–58.

Shapley, L., Fulkerson, D., Horelick, A., and Weiler, D. (1966) *A Transportation Program for Filling Idle Classrooms in Los Angeles*, Santa Monica, California: RAND.

Sisson, R. (1969) "Can we model the educational process?" *Socio-Economic Planning Sciences*, **2**, 109–19.

Tyler, Ralph W. (1973) "Assessing educational achievement in the affective domain." *NCME Measurement in Education*, **4**.

Unesco (1964) *Economic and Social Aspects of Educational Planning*, Paris: United Nations Educational, Scientific and Cultural Organization.

U.S. Office of Education (1973) *Digest of Educational Statistics, 1972 Edition*, Washington: Government Printing Office.

Werts, C. E. and Linn, R. L. (1970) "A general linear model of studying growth." *Psychological Bulletin*, **73**, 17–22.

Womer, Frank (no date) *What is National Assessment?*, Denver: National Assessment of Educational Progress.

University of the State of New York, State Educational Department, Bureau of School Programs Evaluation (1972) *New York State Performance Indicators in Education, 1972, Report*, Albany, New York, Sept.

6. *A Dynamic Model for Policy Studies in Community Health Service Systems**

JULIUS SURKIS

Introduction

Advances in the field of medicine have enabled the treatment and cure of many previously fatal diseases. The general availability of adequate health care for the average person has not kept pace with these major advances despite the continued rise of expenditures for health and medical care. In fiscal 1965 the expenditure for these services totaled $38.4 billion or 5.9 percent of the Gross National Product. Since 1955 the annual expenditure has increased by 112 percent. It is estimated that by 1975 health services will account for 7.0 percent of the Gross National Product.[1]

The size and growth of these expenditures are sufficient reasons to devote greater effort to examine the decision-making processes within the various health-care systems. E. G. Mesthene, head of the Program on Science and Technology at Harvard, traces our failure to cope with health care, as well as other major urban problem areas, to the institutional inadequacy of traditional approaches.[2] Therefore, it is not sufficient to study only the existing health-care systems but one must try to define and evaluate innovative approaches as well.

In reviewing the application of operations research and allied techniques in the area of health care system modeling one encounters two basic approaches:

(a) *Analytical models.* We find a concentration of papers that use the "birth and death process" which treats the changes in the state of a system over time. Typical of this approach are papers that deal with hospital and doctors' office appointment systems;[3, 4] relating admission rates and length of stay in a hospital to the bed census.[5, 6] Other statistical techniques have also been widely used. An example of this class of application relates patient descriptors to demand for hospital services using multiple regression and factor analysis.[7]

(b) *Simulation models.* In this area we note operational models of maternity wards, outpatient clinics and operation room scheduling.[8–10]

These efforts only try to cope with a small fragment or subsystem of existing health-care systems. Recently there have been some proposals to simulate comprehensive health-care systems, but these are still in a definition stage.[11, 12] Even these comprehensive models have neglected the interactive information feedback nature of health-care systems. As Flagle points out: "a complete and viable health care system should make use of cybernetic or information feedback models; these models may contain links and elements that are

---

* Taken from the dissertation submitted to the Faculty of The Polytechnic Institute of Brooklyn in partial fulfillment of the requirements for the degree of Doctor of Philosophy (Operations Research), 1972.

not formally present in real world systems."[13] In the health-care area we have not found any studies that pursue this approach. However, cybernetic or feedback systems have been used to describe the behavior of the firm by Cyert and March,[14] Bonini,[15] and Forrester.[16]

This highly complex social problem of health care is beset by continually rising expenditures which have not produced a significant improvement in the quality of medical care for the average person. There has been a limited attempt to study the problems of health care using statistical and operations research techniques. The restricted scope of these applications is apparent in the aforementioned references. Therefore, there is a need to develop models which encompass the essential elements that make up a health-care system and evaluate new institutional alternatives.

It is the purpose of this study to develop a macro-model of a community health-service system which can be utilized to simulate various organizational structures and policies. The aim of the model will be to test an innovative approach for the delivery of health care to communities. The health-care system will be viewed as a feedback or "closed" system. In such a system, the focus is on interactions within the system where outputs influence inputs, and past actions have a bearing and exert control over future actions. The interacting components of the health-care system will be the community, the health center, and the user sector generated from the community.

The structure and adaptive behavior of the system over a period of time will be studied using the methodology developed by Forrester called *Industrial Dynamics*.[16–18]

We have chosen to explore the delivery of health-care services to communities because health-care services, however financed and planned, are ultimately implemented at the community level and thereby serve a particular community. Group practice or group health plans have been available for some time. Recently, there has been a national emphasis on a particular array of formula-grant, project-grant programs to states, localities, and private sector institutions stressing a community-directed effort. Among these, the Neighborhood Health Center programs sponsored by the Office of Economic Opportunity hold promise for bringing innovations to the evolution of community-oriented health-care services.

The Neighborhood Health Centers are aimed at ghetto areas to provide comprehensive family health care with facilities and resources up to the hospital level. Like group health plans, this approach is intended to provide continuing care to the community; and by affiliations with hospitals, coordinate aspects of services not available at the health center. The stress is on ambulatory preventive care. The team approach is used to deliver health care.

The Neighborhood Health Centers, at various phases of implementation in the Metropolitan New York area, were used as the basis for the development of the model. However, the actual model of the study represents an idealization of these centers and can be viewed as representing a generalized community health service system.

The model developed in this study will try to evaluate the impact on the system of changes in the community, changes in family registration policies, resource allocation decisions, budgetary decisions as well as the effect of organizational problems such as personnel training and hiring. This impact will be measured in terms of such variables as: number of persons receiving care, cost of a visit, segment of the community using the health center, etc.

The emphasis in the modeling has been to reflect the interrelated changes over a period of time that occur in the community, at the health center, and among the user groups. We have not attempted a specific definition of quality of care or a health index. Some of the system output variables can be utilized to construct and evaluate these.

It is hoped that viewing the health-care system at the community level and stressing the feedback mechanisms that exist between components will contribute to a better understanding of such systems and provide a realistic planning tool in their design.

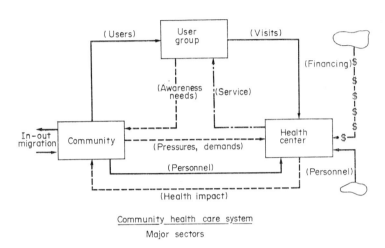

Community health care system

Major sectors

FIG. 1.

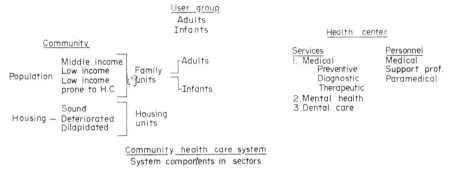

Community health care system
System components in sectors

FIG. 2.

System Definition

In trying to study the behavior of the community health service system, it is essential to establish a suitable framework. The central processes involved in studying the dynamic behavior of this system should reflect the interrelated changes that occur in the community, at the health center and among the user groups that are generated (Fig 1).

The community defined in terms of demographic, physical and social aspects relevant to a health orientation generates the major demand variable, the user flow, in response to the health services. The health center defined in terms of its resources, its budgeting, planning and operational aspects will generate services that are the perceived needs of the community. The user group depending on the type of community that generates it, and the kind of services that are offered, will react and interact with these system components. In addition to these physical flows of users, services, and funds which are easily recognizable in the actual real-life system, there are a set of information flows that play a major role in the behavior and dynamics of the system. The actual needs of the community, the perception of these needs by the health center, the motivation of the users which depend on information related both to the community and the health center operations are some of the information flows that are considered in the structure of the system.

1. COMMUNITY SECTOR

The community is defined in terms of its demographic, physical, and social aspects that are relevant to a health orientation (Fig. 2).

The population attributes such as ethnic distribution and the distribution of age groups are factors that have a bearing on the health needs of the community. Within the model, we have considered three groups (middle income, low income, low income prone to health care) and basically two age groups (adults, infants). The educational and economic state of the community has been tied into these six groups of population. This is a simplifying assumption and may have to be treated in greater detail in future models. The population attributes may be altered by the in and out migration from the community. The implications of such a flux on the health state of the community and its influence on the utilization of health services are obvious. If there is excessive movement in the community, there will be no permanence in the relation established between the community and the health center. This would also affect community organizations adversely. The population movement is related to the physical aspects of the community. As housing deteriorates, the more affluent segment of the community tends to leave the community and lower-income level segments move in. This tends to generate overcrowding in housing units which creates further physical decay, which may result in further dislocations in population. The model focuses on this interrelationship since it is assumed that this aspect is vital for the health service system that is being studied. We are aware that this may be an oversimplification and additional cause and effect relationships may be incorporated.

In the model, the population of the community is viewed as experiencing internal and external changes. Internal changes will be reflected by births and deaths while external changes will be related to migration into and out of the community. Since different segments of the model require varying degrees of detail on population, the model will track both individual and family units within the three population groups. Migration will be measured in terms of family units. As indicated in the beginning of this section, the main influence in the community flux will be housing conditions. This might set into motion influx accelerating factors which would depend on the growth of certain population segments. However, this might be counteracted by a housing-congestion factor. The individual population figures will consider birth and death rates as well as infant mortality rates. Influx rates which were in terms of family units will be converted to individuals. Eventually, the health services would have a bearing on these population parameters. In the model we consider two age groups: infants up to the age of 3 and adults. This again is a simplification, but is considered sufficient to focus on specific aspects of infant mortality and infant care, which are quite distinct from the treatment of adults. It can be argued that the population should be broken down in terms of dysfunction groups related to health with a more extensive age breakdown. The level of such detail is questionable in a model such as the one being studied since our basic interest is to gain some insight into the dynamic behavior of a community health-service system at a strategic level.

The physical aspects of the community are described by three categories of housing: sound, deteriorated, and dilapidated. We consider normal aging of housing which may be accelerated due to congestion brought about by overcrowding and influx of low-income groups.

The social aspects of the community will be identified in the organizations that exist within the community. These organizations can play a vital role in influencing the health aspects of the community. The state of these organizations is influenced by the stability of the community which in turn depends on movement in and out of the community.

2. HEALTH CENTER SECTOR

The range of services at the health center will be considered in two major categories: medical and specialty services. Each one of these major categories will be broken down into significant segments that are necessary to provide sufficient detail to highlight the dynamic interactions that exist in the overall health-services system. It is assumed that the major goal of a health center is to provide basic ambulatory care with emphasis on preventive medicine and therapy. It is also assumed that the health center is affiliated to some degree with a major hospital center to which the complex and rare cases are referred.

The delivery of medical and specialty services at the health center will be carried out by means of health teams.

In considering the modeling of the health center, it was assumed that the financing of the center would be provided by an outside agency and would be a fixed amount for each budgeting period with fractional increases. It is further assumed that the health center cannot influence the amount budgeted. However, depending on the type of center, it may have varying degrees of independence in the allocation of the budget to various services within the center.

In modeling the health center, the area of medical services was subdivided into preventive care, diagnostic care, and therapeutic care segments. It was assumed that these areas would be serviced by medical teams. Each team would service all three areas based on certain decision rules.

In the model, the composition of a medical health team would include full-time or part-time internists, pediatricians, obstetricians, gynecologists—who are grouped as professional support personnel—as well as clinical aides, home health aides, receptionists, appointment clerks, and interviewers—who are classified as paramedical personnel.

Each class of personnel will have a single salary level. To keep the scope of the model within bounds, the user categories were divided into adult and infant segments. These two groups would seek to utilize center services based on need that is a function of the community and the quality of services at the health centers. These considerations are discussed in the user sector. The model assumes that preventive care entails preliminary examinations directed to detecting cancer, diabetes, tuberculosis, and venereal disease. Preventive care also is assumed to include well-baby clinics and immunization. The resources needed to supplement these services will include laboratories and X-ray facilities. The area of diagnostic care will entail in-depth examinations and complete diagnostic X-ray units with complete laboratory units as well as consultations within the center, and specialty consultations with affiliated hospitals. It can be seen that the resources for these services will have to be more complete and comprehensive than the preventive care area. In the model we are assuming that the quality of these services will depend on the level of affiliation with outside hospitals. Therapeutic services will require the same resources as preventive and diagnostic services and will provide routine treatment at the center as well as giving examinations and re-evaluations for previous treatments and diagnostic examinations.

The pharmacy of the health center will also be considered to be within the category of therapeutic services.

Special services at the health center will be viewed in two major segments: mental health, including preventive and rehabilitation of narcotic and alcoholic addiction, and dental-care services. Each of these specialty service areas will again operate through the vehicle of the team concept. The mental-health teams will include a full- or part-time psychiatrist, psychiatric social workers, and family aides. The dental-care team will be composed of a dentist, a dental hygienist, operating assistants, and auxiliary assistants.

In addition to these operating teams the model considers administrative, line supervision personnel as well as laboratory and X-ray resources and research and information services at various levels depending on the funding.

The health center sector of the model reviews the gross personnel requirements of the center at every budget period. The requirements are matched against available funds. Adjustments based upon decision rules which differ with center types are made, and allocations for each additional team type are determined. This initiates the recruitment cycle for the different categories of personnel. Before becoming fully productive, personnel go through training and adjustment periods at the center. The processing rates for each service area at the center are influenced by the productivity of the teams, demand for services, and the quality of auxiliary services.

The modeling of the health center will now be described in more detail.

The desired resource level for center services is based upon the utilization of each service area. The additional team requirements for each service is then determined by taking into account the previous requests that are in process, being recruited, and actually at the center. The model also assumes that the net additional requests are accumulated until they amount to a fraction of a team and are forwarded for budget considerations. Then periodically the budget allocation takes place. Trial expenditures are calculated on accumulated team needs for each service area. These are matched against funds that will be available from the coming budget. If the funds are sufficient, the accumulated team requests are authorized. Otherwise, the requests would have to be readjusted and scaled down to the funds that are available. The available funds are scaled down in proportion to the needs for each service type modified by factors that might put a special emphasis on certain services. These factors might be related to center orientation or community pressures. Then once the budget allocations are authorized the appropriated personnel recruiting gets under way. The recruiting for the medical, mental health, and dental-care teams each proceed with three different categories: medical personnel including M.D.s, psychiatrist, dentists; support professionals including social workers, nurses, and paramedical personnel including aides and secretaries. The model is so designed as to provide different recruitment delays, related to type of team, category of personnel, and the number that is being recruited. In the personnel area, the model also accounts for personnel leaving the center. There is a normal departure rate of personnel which is augmented by stress factors due to overwork or center conditions.

In arriving at the processing rates for the various types of services at the center, the model considers the productivity of the teams. In determining this parameter, the number of various groups of personnel that are actually at the center and their level of competence is considered. This actual adjusted figure and the number of personnel that have been approved and funded are used to form a ratio which indicates the discrepancy in each personnel group. Empirical relationships are postulated that indicate the effect of the discrepancies on team productivity. Then the team productivity is determined by using these contributing productivities. Using these productivity figures, the ideal processing rate and number of teams that have been funded, the processing rate for medical, mental-health, and dental-care teams are calculated. These are monthly processing rates. The processing rate of medical teams is then broken down into preventive, diagnostic, and therapeutic care sectors. This is based on center policies and an adjustable fraction of processing that can be shifted to either sector based on congestion that might arise due to demand.

3. USER SECTOR

This component of the system is generated through the interaction of the community and the health services. Once established, it will have a bearing on the community and the health services.

Two classes of user groups are defined in the system: adults and infants. A more detailed description of multiple classes in different states of dysfunction with various transition probabilities could have been adopted, but this would only tend to add to a great deal of detail without contributing to the overall objectives of the model. So instead, we chose to reflect the "need" that the adult- and infant-user classes would have for various types of services. This need would be a function of the community.

The users originate the community. Through initial registration drives, user families will have contact with the services offered by the health center. At this stage, the system tracks the users in family units in order to adjust the user pools properly for population changes that occur in the community: new births in the user population that would join the infant-user pool, infants that join the adult-user population and the effect of migration out of the community that would have to be reflected as losses from the user pools. In the experimental centers that are in operation, it was noted that not all families and individuals registered actually utilize the center facilities. Therefore, the model recognized various factors that have a bearing on registered families that actually become users. User motivation considers the quality of housing in the community and the stability of the population. As the quality of housing deteriorates, it will have an adverse effect on motivating people to use health services.

The stability of the population will have a bearing because excessive in and out movement from the community will affect user motivation adversely. The model recognizes that an interrelationship exists between housing and population stability. This is taken into account when the flux index for the community is calculated.

The way in which the community views the health center has a bearing on user motivation as well. The model considers the effect of backlogs at various services and the attractiveness of physical facilities.

The system keeps track of user families, but since it is the individuals who utilize the center facilities, the adult- and infant-user pools are defined in terms of individuals.

It is assumed that individuals initially go through a preventive examination then join their respective user pools. In converting user families to individuals, the income groups and their respective family sizes are considered. The arrival of infants into the infant-user pool from the user families is assumed to be in proportion to families with infants in the community. The departure of adults and infants from the user pools due to emigration will reflect the movement occurring in the community.

In addition to inflow and outflow from the user pools, there is going to be an interchange between the pools since infants grow up to join the adult pool and the user families have infants that join the infant-user pool. The magnitude of these flow rates are determined by a parameter that considers the state of the community and its mix as far as birth rates and transition from infants to adults are concerned.

There are internal flows from the user pools to the various types of services offered at the health center and flows from these services back to the user pools.

For each type of service, we will consider a normal visit frequency by the user. This will be a time-dependent relationship which will be a function of how long the health center has been in operation. This relationship implies a learning-curve effect. Thus, if only this factor were to be considered, the visit frequencies would tend to increase as time went on. However, usually there are some countervailing effects that play a role such as the user view of backlog at the specific services. Delays and rescheduling of appointments will have an adverse effect on the frequency of visits. The model considers another factor which tries to account for the actual need of the community for the particular kind of service. For instance, as a community deteriorates physically and economically, people will become less concerned with routine check-ups and medical care in general, but may have the need for services to treat addiction and similar problems. So even if the center has been in existence for some length of time, and even if the center is operationally adequate, demand for preventive care may be depressed due to the state of the community. The model also considers the effects of related services. For instance, in the case of diagnostic-care users, a percentage of those that have gone through preventive care will utilize diagnostic care after a suitable lag period. Similarly, for therapeutic care the users will be augmented by the effect of users that have gone through diagnostic-care treatments. Users that have come to a particular service area at the center are not returned to the user pool immediately. They are detained in an intransit status to avoid double counting and also to take into account delays that may result from congestion. In the model we have a flow that goes from the user pools to each of the appropriate service areas at the health center and we have flows that come from the intransit state from each service area back to the user pools.

4. FEEDBACK LOOPS IN THE SYSTEM (Fig. 3)

LOOP 1: Decay in housing will decrease community attractiveness which will tend to lose higher-income population segments causing congestion in housing and further decay in the housing situation. (+)

LOOP 2: As housing congestion increases, it will act as a deterrent for further influx into the community thus decreasing the population flux. (−)

LOOP 3: As the population turnover of the community decreases, the community organizations will tend to flourish and expand. (+)

LOOP 4A: As the turnover of the population decreases, and the health center starts making inroads into the community and the community organizations are strengthened, user motivation will be improved which will bring more new users to the health-center facilities. (+)

LOOP 4B: The increase of users will create congestion in services at the center. (−)

LOOP 5: Depending on health needs of the users (needs are assumed to be a function of the community) and the spectrum of services offered at the health center, the users will take advantage of services by return visits, thus increasing congestion. (+)

LOOP 6: As center congestion increases user discontent begins to mount which affects the continuity of services since users neglect visits which tends to reduce center congestion. (−)

LOOP 7: As user visits at the center increase, the stress upon the staff increases, which gives rise to staff discontent, which affects team productivity adversely, decreasing processing. (−)

LOOP 8: As the center utilization increases, the discrepancy between actual and desired team requirements puts pressure on funding authorities to increase the periodic funding to the center. The community organizations depending on their strength may amplify the pressure to increase the funding. (+)

LOOP 9: The allocation of funds to various center facilities is based on the center organization and the strength of the community in exerting its specific demands. The allocation gives rise to the recruiting of new personnel, which tends to decrease the discrepancy in personnel needs, improve team productivity, and increase processing. (+)

Model Definition

In this paper we will not attempt to present all the details of the model equations for the community, health center and user sectors. These can be found in ref. 19. Instead we will include system flows with all the relevant level, rate, and auxiliary equations symbolically identified (Figs. 4, 5, 6, 7).

Policy Studies Using the Model

Using the system definition and description developed in the previous sections, the model was coded in the DYNAMO language and subjected to considerable experimentation to explore various policy alternatives in community-service systems. We will present some of these results to indicate the kind of experiments that can be performed with a model such as the one developed in this study. The data used in the model such as budgets, type and number of personnel in each team were obtained from community health centers in the Metropolitan New York area. As indicated in the introductory section of the study, these centers contain fragments of the total system as idealized in our model. Therefore, in examining the dynamics of such a system one cannot validate it with actual experimental data since most of the real systems are in their infancy of development and extensive data bases are non-existent.

The emphasis in our experimentation with the model was focused on the sensitivity of the idealized model to changes in parameter values and decision policies. In performing this

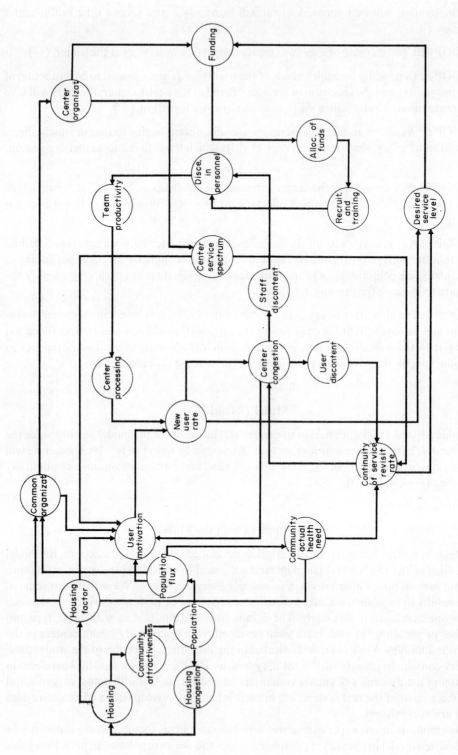

FIG. 3. System feedback loops.

sensitivity analysis, one can attempt verification on the basis of "relationships and inter-actions that are believed to be there in the real system but have evaded quantitative meas-ure" as Forrester suggests.[16]

The results discussed in this section assume a stable middle-income community in which we have explored the sensitivity of many controllable parameters and policies. This ex-ploration had to be selective since an exhaustive experiment would have involved around 300 separate runs requiring approximately 50 hours of IBM 360/50 computer time. All the model simulations were run for a period of 30 years, and the increment of time used was 1 month.

We will discuss, in detail, the impact of a system parameter and a decision policy. In the conclusion we will refer to other results obtained by the model experimentation.

1. SENSITIVE PARAMETER

Estimating demand for services

In the model we employed a parameter, DRF (Desired Resource Factor). Depending on its value, this parameter could overstate or understate the magnitude of the desired team requirements for planning purposes. (Assigning a value greater than 1 to DRF would tend to overstate requirements and assigning a value less than 1 would understate the desired team requirements. Setting the value of DRF equal to 1 would reflect desired requirements without distortion.)

We will comment on some of the results for DRF at these levels: .7, 1.0, 1.5. The model simulation was performed for an initial annual budget, BBU = $700,000. Observing the statistics for total number of visits, we note that when the team requirements are under-stated the total number of visits is lower than the other cases (Table 1).

This is to be expected since we would have fewer teams funded. The interesting phen-omenon appears when we observe the cost per visit figures (Table 2).

It appears that starting with the 15th year (180 months) of the simulation and continuing thereafter the cost per visit is higher when we "underplan". When the desired team require-ments are overstated, the cost per visit is higher during the start-up period but becomes significantly lower after the first 5 years. After 15 years of operation the difference between DRF = 1.0 and DRF = 1.5 (normal and overstated) is not very significant.

Observing the backlog ratios (Figs. 8, 9, 10) for various services during the first 5 years we note that they exhibit a similar pattern for all three cases of DRF. After this initial

TABLE 1. CUMULATIVE VISITS (THOUSANDS)

| Time, | DRF | | |
months	.7	1.0	1.5
60	47.8	51.3	58.6
120	138.6	165.3	206.2
180	273.7	356.0	386.4
240	449.8	603,0	603.3
300	661.6	869.1	863.7
360	912.0	1169.6	1165.4

TABLE 2. COST PER VISIT (DOLLARS)

Time, months	DRF		
	.7	1.0	1.5
60	13.01	14.21	15.95
120	6.53	6.72	5.68
180	3.88	3.77	3.14
240	2.70	2.47	2.40
300	2.15	1.87	1.90
360	1.74	1.56	1.58

stage, for DRF = .7, there is a periodic peaking effect following the addition of the teams of the center.

Backlog ratios decline when more teams are added. Another contributing factor to the periodic decline of backlog ratios is a decline in incoming patient loads due to dissatisfaction and congestion. For the cases where DRF = 1.0 and DRF = 1.5, there appears a

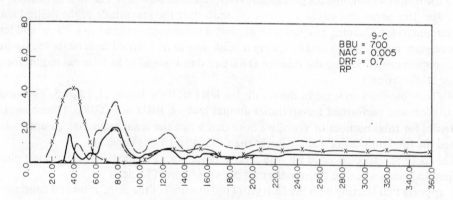

FIG. 8. Backlog ratios—Case 9.
— —Backlog ratio for preventive care; ——— backlog ratio for diagnostic care; – – – backlog ratio for therapeutic care; —×—backlog ratio for special service 2.

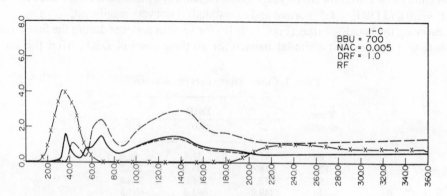

FIG. 9. Backlog ratios—Case 1.
— — Backlog ratio for preventive care; ——— backlog ratio for diagnostic care; – – – backlog ratio for therapeutic care; —×— backlog ratio for special service 2.

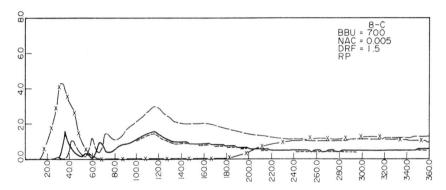

FIG. 10. Backlog ratios—Case 8.
— — Backlog ratio for preventive care; ——— backlog ratio for diagnostic care; – – – backlog ratio for therapeutic care; — ×— backlog ratio for special service 2.

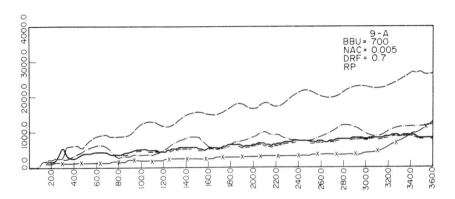

FIG. 11. Incoming adult user rates—Case 9.
— — Adult user rate to preventive care; ——— Adult user rate to diagnostic care; – – – adult user rate to therapeutic care; — ×— adult user rate to special service 1; —.— adult user rate to special service 2.

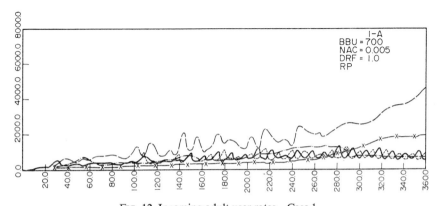

FIG. 12. Incoming adult user rates—Case 1.
— — Adult user rate to preventive care; ——— adult user rate to diagnostic care; – – – adult user rate to therapeutic care; — ×— adult user rate to special service 1, —.— adult user rate to special service 2.

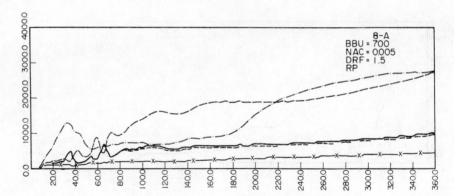

FIG. 13. Incoming adult user rates—Case 8.
— — Adult user rate to preventive care; ——— adult user rate to diagnostic care; – – – adult user rate to therapeutic care; — × — adult user rate to special service 1; —.— adult user rate to special service 2.

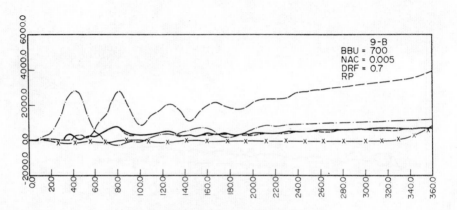

FIG. 14. Adult user intransit levels—Case 9.
— — Adults intransit from preventive care; ——— adults intransit from diagnostic care; – – – adults intransit from therapeutic care; — × — adults intransit from special service 1; —.— adults intransit from special service 2.

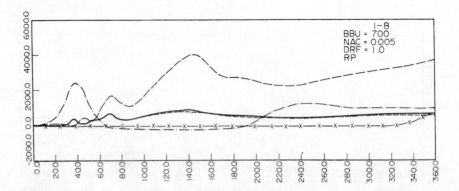

FIG. 15. Adult user intransit levels—Case 1.
— — Adults intransit from preventive care; ——— adults intransit from diagnostic care; – – – adults intransit from therapeutic care; — × — adults intransit from special service 1; —.— adults intransit from special service 2.

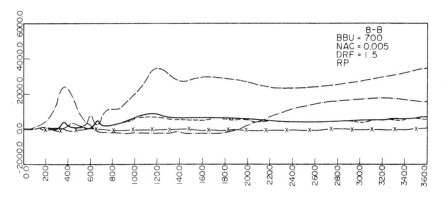

FIG. 16. Adult user intransit levels—Case 8.
— — Adults intransit from preventive care; ——— adults intransit from diagnostic care; – – – adults intransit from therapeutic care; — × — adults intransit from special service 1; —.— adults intransit from special service 2.

major peak for services around the twelfth and tenth years respectively. By the fifteenth year of operation we note an equilibrium condition as far as the backlog ratios are concerned. However, the various services do not exhibit respectively congruent backlog ratio levels with variations in DRF.

The incoming user rates (Figs. 11, 12, 13) exhibit interesting aspects which are not reflected in the backlog ratio figures. Whereas in the backlog ratio figures the normal and the overstated cases had similar characteristics, we note that the incoming users that generate this behavior are quite different. It can be seen that the incoming users that generate this behavior are quite different in each of the three cases.

The intransit user level (Figs. 14, 15, 16) reflect a pattern similar to the backlog ratios since backlog ratios play a major part in determining intransit user levels.

2. SENSITIVE DECISION POLICY

Variation in operational policies

The allocation of processing capacities to services that utilize the same resources exhibits the sensitivity of the model to operational policies that change the decision by which allocations are accomplished. In the area of medical services we have preventive care, diagnostic care, and therapeutic care which utilize the efforts of the medical teams. The decision rule by which the processing capacity for each of these services is determined influences the behavior of the model.

We experimented with two policies: (a) regulate the allocation of the medical team processing capacity to preventive, diagnostic, and therapeutic care services on the basis of backlog ratios. The allocation will be reviewed periodically (every 6 months). The service that has had the higher backlog ratio would get a higher proportion of the processing capacity. Let us call this the "regulated" policy since the backlog ratios will be regulating the allocation of the processing capacity. (b) utilize a fixed proportion of processing capacity for each medical service. The proportion could be chosen to be an approximation of potential use of each service. Let us call this the "fixed" policy.

Experimental runs were made at various budget levels and "desired resource factor" levels. In this section we will focus on the case where we have an initial budget of $700,000 and a DRF = 1. We will examine the impact of the "regulated" and "fixed policies". The intransit levels (Figs. 17 and 18) show the implication of these policies. For the regulated policy preventive-care intransit levels rise to 4000 and then decline and after that have a rising tendency again. The diagnostic and therapeutic-care intransit levels remain around 1000. For the "fixed" policy diagnostic and therapeutic-care intransit levels go up to 5000 and 1000, respectively, while for preventive care the intransit level remains zero.

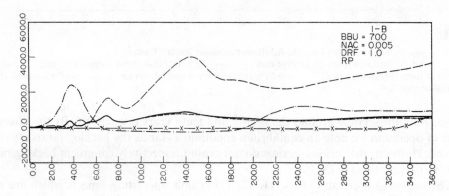

FIG. 17. Adult user intransit levels—Case 1.
— — Adults intransit from preventive care; ——— adults intransit from diagnostic care; – – – adults intransit from therapeutic care; —×— adults intransit from special service 1; —.— adults intransit from special service 2.

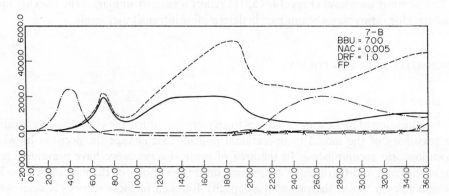

FIG. 18. Adult user intransit levels—Case 7.
— — Adults intransit from preventive care; ——— adults intransit from diagnostic care; – – – adults intransit from therapeutic care; —×— adults intransit from special service 1; —.— adults intransit from special service 2.

We note that the backlog ratios reflect similar differences in behavior (Figs. 19, 20). In looking at the aggregated incoming adult users (Figs. 21, 22), we note higher figures for the "regulated" policy indicating that this policy attracts more users. Comparing the cost per visit figures we note that the "regulated" policy is slightly more economical (Table 3).

TABLE 3. COST PER VISIT (DOLLARS)

Time months	Regulated	Fixed
60	14.21	15.82
120	6.72	6.49
180	3.77	3.84
240	2.47	2.67
300	1.87	1.89
360	1.56	1.56

We have tried to point out the sensitivity of the system to various scheduling policies rather than advocate the superiority of either one of the policies discussed.

Obviously, there are trade-offs with either policy or any other policy that can be suggested. It is interesting to note that this operational policy has received a great deal of attention in the literature concerning simulation studies related to health-care systems.

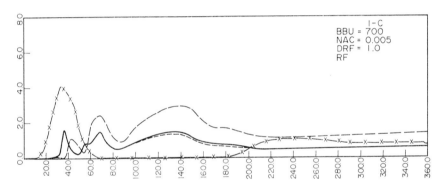

FIG. 19. Backlog ratios—Case 1.
— — Backlog ratio for preventive care; ——— backlog ratio for diagnostic care; – – – backlog ratio for therapeutic care; —×— backlog ratio for special service 2.

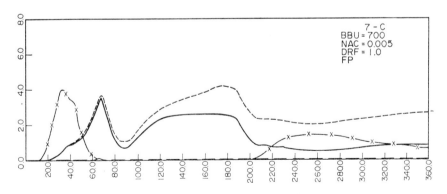

FIG. 20. Backlog ratios—Case 7.
— — Backlog ratio for preventive care; ——— backlog ratio for diagnostic care; – – – backlog ratio for therapeutic care; —×— backlog ratio for special service 2.

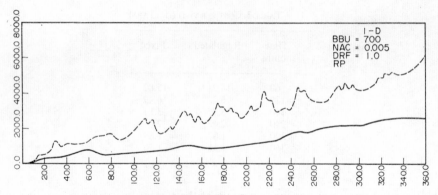

FIG. 21. Aggregated incoming adult users—Case 1.
— — Medical services; ———— special services.

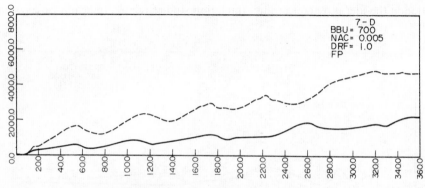

FIG. 22. Aggregated incoming adult users—Case 7.
— — Medical services; ———— special services.

Conclusion

The model developed in this study has tried to define the basic structure of a health-care system by emphasizing the interacting components such as the health center, the community, and the user groups. The model was coded in the DYNAMO language and subjected to considerable experimentation. The details of some of these experiments and the results were presented in the previous section.

The results are significant in that they provide multi-faceted answers to difficult questions that health planners face. For example, increasing the annual budget of the health center by as much as 40 per cent does not produce uniformly better results. As one would expect these additional funds help, but for services that are in demand, the center still experiences periodic congestion. By observing the model output variables such as various backlog ratios, incoming user rates, and other outputs over a period of years the health planner can get a better understanding of the impact of budgets on the overall health system.

The experimental results reveal another interesting aspect concerning the estimates for resources required at the health center. For example, in planning, managerial decision may effect the entire operational system by overstating or understating their personnel resource requirements. Experiments with the model provide us with the relative impact of such magnification or reduction on many aspects of the system. We find that understating the desired resources is more expensive in the long run: the cost per visit is higher for the understated case as compared to the normal; the normal and overstated resources are quite similar. However, the incoming user pattern that generates this behavior in backlog ratios is very different in each case.

The analytical and simulation research efforts briefly reviewed in the Introduction showed a heavy emphasis on operational policies that deal with scheduling of resources. In our experimentation, we used a "regulated" and a "fixed" resource allocation policy. Results show that the behavior of the model is very sensitive to different scheduling policies. This confirms the importance of this operational aspect in the design of a health-care system. Once again, the model can compare the relative merits of many such alternative policies and enable the planner to evaluate cost-benefits and trade-offs.

Some short-term decisions such as the duration and intensity of initial registration drives can have a long-term impact on the behavior of the health-care system. The impact of these different registration drives results in significantly different incoming user rates, and backlog ratios.

After establishing some of the sensitive parameters and policies in a typical community health-care system, we performed some experiments where some of these sensitive system elements were varied simultaneously. For example, a gradually higher user registration rate with a normal resource-requirement policy. The model output indicated that under the higher registration rate, 92 percent of the families were registered. This could be deduced intuitively. However, we also found that under the normal registration policy with the magnified resource requirements policy we had more visits per person at only a slightly higher cost. This is an unexpected result.

Other experiments with the model revealed some results that are pertinent to the model structure. A great deal of effort was spent to model the recruitment and training aspects of various personnel categories. Varying parameters relevant to this segment of the model showed no effect on the system behavior. Results like these indicate where the model can be further aggregated to reduce the computational burden without any loss to the relevance of the model.

As far as the validity of the present model is concerned, we would like to discuss briefly the justification for its basic components, its behavior characteristics which can be related to real systems, and lastly, the causes and symptoms exhibited by the model which can be seen in "real world" health systems. We are taking this approach because the explicit verification of the simulation experiments cannot be undertaken since in reality there is no facsimile of our model.

The structure of the system, consisting of the community, user sector, and the health center, was arrived at by a very careful consideration of the nature of interrelationships existing in a community health-service system. In the literature, one finds models that consider the operation aspects of a health center with a user stream. This is not a sufficient representation since the user stream and its demands change with time. Part of this change may take place in the community which generates the user stream. Changes may also occur within the user stream because of the impact of the health services.

Our model considers all the operational aspects of a health center: budgets, personnel, specialization of services, productivity of teams, and decision rules for operation. The range of the budgets, the type and number of professional and paramedical personnel in each specialization unit are all based on actual data and team descriptions obtained from two of the health centers in the New York Metropolitan Area. The community component of our model was based on the Red Hook Community in Brooklyn, NY. The housing data on number and condition of units, population, and ethnic breakdown, together with various birth and mortality rates, were abstracted from census data (tracts 85, 57, 59, 55 and NYC Department of Health statistical sources (health area 41). The community model was tested independently of the other components to simulate a period of 30 years (1940–70). The model experiments described in this study used the state of the community as it existed in 1940. The third component of the system, the user sector, is influenced by the community and the health center and, in turn, influences the other two components. Its members are part of the community and yet evolve into an entity influenced by the health center. The evolution and impact of the user sector became apparent to us by the examination of patient visits, and patient return visit statistics obtained from the Neighborhood Medical Care Demonstration Project of Montefiore Hospital in the Bronx, NY. These statistics were studied in conjunction with the type and experience level of medical teams handling these visits at the health center. These helped conceptualize the interactions between the users and the health center. By attending the community health advisory group meetings over a period of 2 years we were able to witness the growth of user needs into user demands while the health centers were developing. The "community actual need index" and "user motivation" relationships in the model were an attempt to quantify the interaction between the community, user sector, and health center. The impact of congestion and waiting were approximated from patient and user interviews conducted at the Child and Youth Care Project at Roosevelt Hospital.

In the previous paragraph, we have attempted to trace the development and justification of each major system component independent of the total system behavior. We further feel that the limited experiments with the model exhibit certain stability characteristics, growth tendencies, and time-phased relationships that bear a close resemblance to actual systems. For example, with a normal budget structure and a reasonable user registration rate, the model does exhibit a stable behavior after about 10–12 years of operation. Despite some severe restrictions imposed on the system in terms of funds or resource allocations, the user group exhibits growth tendencies in the model (incoming user rates and user family figures in the previous section). This phenomenon is easily verifiable in real world health systems. The same type of stable growth tendencies can be observed in the personnel levels of the health center facilities. This expansion and growth in personnel levels is analogous to actual health-care organizations. In the model we also note some time-phased relationships such as a surge in service backlogs resulting in expansion of facilities which, in turn, operate at lower load capacities. Users take advantage of the more comfortable and attentive service facilities. This results in a build-up of incoming users and backlogs which generate another cycle of growth at the center. This type of "action–reaction" phase can be observed in some existing health clinics.

In the experiments summarized at the beginning of this section and some of which were described in detail in the previous section, we feel that the model was able to show some of the troubles and difficulties that actual health-care systems exhibit. We studied various initial registration policies with the model. The strain on facilities of intense initial registration was witnessed at an actual health center when it was tried for a limited time period. The model experiments verify this aspect. However, we have no actual data to verify the long-term effects exhibited by the model. The model also shows, quite dramatically, the impact of scheduling policies at the center. The micro models that appear in the literature confirm the critical nature of facility scheduling in health-care systems. This was also found to be the case by the author in his attempts at developing responsive, regulated operational rules at the Child and Youth Care Project at Roosevelt Hospital.

It should also be indicated that many of the relationships such as team productivity as a function of various personnel categories, community actual need index with its various influence factors, and the influence of backlogs on user delays were arrived at after lengthy discussions with health center directors, sociologists, and community groups.

We have only explored the health center component of the model in great detail. To obtain a complete understanding of the system behavior, experimentation is warranted with the community component as well. The experiments that were run used a stable middle-income community. We feel that the model may reveal interesting behavior patterns for different community types. This is left for future research.

In designing health-care system models at the regional or national level, the model developed in this effort could be used as a subsystem. The model may also serve as a guide to pinpoint critical data to be collected to evaluate health-care systems. Some examples of such data are community reaction factors to health care, operational data regarding backlogs and intransit user estimates.

In conclusion, we have attempted to model a complex social system using a novel approach. Experiments with the model indicate that interesting and useful insights can be gained concerning the behavior of a comprehensive health-care system.

References

1. Merriam, Ida C. "Social welfare expenditures 1964–1965." *Social Security Bulletin*, Oct. 1965.
2. *Annual Report of Science and Technology Program—Harvard University*, Harvard University Press, 1970.
3. Welch, J. D. "Appointment systems in hospital outpatient departments." *Operations Research Quarterly*, **15** (Sept. 1964).
4. Fry, John. "Appointments in general practice." *Operations Research Quarterly*, **15** (Sept. 1965).
5. Balintfy, Joseph L. "A stochastic model for the analysis and prediction of admissions and discharges in hospitals." *Management Sciences, Models and Techniques*, Vol. 2, edited by Churchman and Verhulst, New York, Pergamon Press, 1960.
6. Bithell, J. F. "A class of discrete time models for the study of hospital admissions systems." *Operations Research*, **17** (Jan.–Feb. 1969).
7. Das, Rhea S. "Service gate information and prediction of demand for hospital services." *Opsearch* (India), **1** (July 1974).
8. Kennedy, F. D. and Woodside, M. B. *The Maternal and Infant Care Simulation Model*, Vol. III, Public Health Service Contract No. 108–26–269, Mar. 1968.
9. Fetter, R. B. and Thompson, J. D. "The simulation of hospital systems." *Operations Research*, **13** (Sept.–Oct. 1965).
10. Davis, Gordon J. "A model for improvement of operating room utilization", Master's Thesis, University of Florida, 1961.
11. Milly, G. H. and Pocinki, L. S. "A computer simulation model for evaluation of the health care delivery system." National Center for Health Services Research and Development Report HSRD-70, June 1970.
12. Kennedy, F. D. "The development of a simulation model of a community health service system." Public Health Service System Contract No. 108–26–269, Mar. 1968.
13. Flagle, C. D. "Integrating models of health care systems (Abstract). *Operations Research Bulletin*, **18** (Fall 1970).
14. Cyert, R. M. and March, J. G. *A Behavioral Theory of the Firm*, New Jersey, Prentice-Hall, 1963.

15. Bonini, Charles P. *Simulation of Information and Decision Systems in the Firm*, Chicago, Markham Publishing Co., 1967.
16. Forrester, J. W. *Industrial Dynamics*. Massachusetts, The MIT Press, 1961.
17. Forrester, J. W. *Principals of Systems*, Massachusetts, Wright-Allen Press, 1969.
18. Forrester, J. W. *Urban Dynamics*, Massachusetts, The MIT Press, 1969.
19. Surkis, Julius, Ph.D. Thesis, Department of Operations Research and Systems Analysis, Polytechnic Institute of Brooklyn, 1972.

7. Quantitative Studies in the Provision of Three Essential City Services—Fire Protection, Sanitation, and Emergency Medical Services

SAMUEL J. BERNSTEIN AND ISRAEL PRESSMAN

Introduction

The more than 20,000 local governmental units in the United States spend about 100 billion dollars annually on the delivery of municipal services. The present chapter attempts to review the development and utilization of formal approaches in three major municipal service delivery areas: fire protection, sanitation, and emergency medical services. These are chosen to complete a profile of representative models which have been developed for improved service performance. In each, the various dimensions of the service delivery areas will be indicated. Representative quantitative approaches will be defined, potential solutions will be shown and weaknesses in design and information will be detailed where appropriate. Resulting is a state-of-the-art review closely following the precedent-setting work of the National Science Foundation in the Research for Applied National Needs Division Program on Policy Related Research. We are grateful to both the RANN staff and respective professional evaluators for assisting us in formulating this composite review. Professors Plass and Marks and Ms. Dolyns were of particular importance in making this chapter a reality. Their contributions constitute the basic input material.

I. Fire Protection: Resource Allocation in Fire Supervision

A twofold objective may be defined for fire protection whether it be urban or rural: fire prevention and fire suppression. In the first case the objective is to prevent fires from occurring and in the second to effectively respond to fires by extinguishing them. Although of equal importance from a public policy perspective, greater efforts to date have been expended in the development of quantitative approaches for improving fire-suppression capacities. This development stems from conditions more or less peculiar to the urban environment: the dramatic increase in the number of reported fires in urban centers and the urban public's perception of needed increases in fire-suppression capacity for local-neighborhood fire companies. In addition, the methodological problems related to formalizing an approach to fire prevention are indeed difficult. Consequently, under the fire suppression objective, five major subject areas were identified and at least sixty-five major quantitative studies were reported in the last decade by the Fire Protection Evaluation Report of the National Service Foundation. In contrast, only two studies to date were reported in the area of fire prevention. The five dimensions of study included: Resource Allocation in Fire Suppression, Effectiveness Criteria for Allocation, Fire Information and Command and Control Systems, Administration of Fire Protection Service, and

151

Management Issues in Urban Fire Protection. The present review will focus on the resource-allocation aspects of fire suppression because it directly involves issues and concerns relevant to the actual service delivery. Moreover, the studies reported in this area are demonstrative of the utilization of quantitative techniques. It should be noted, however, that the scope of our review is limited by length considerations.

1. POSITIONING PROBLEMS IN FIRE SUPPRESSION

Quantitative approaches in resource allocation focus on positioning, repositioning, and dispatching of men and equipment to fire alarms. By far, the largest part of the collective effort has been concerned with positioning "home-base" location for fire-fighting companies. Model building in this area may be said to begin with the pioneering work of Valinsky in the early 1950s.[1] Utilizing an historical approach, Valinsky postulated that the positioning of "home-base" fire companies in New York City could be determined in four sequential general steps according to the following guidelines: A set of positions may be developed which satisfied minimum response distance acceptable by the National Board of Fire Underwriters. Burnable material in each part of the city may be determined in order to increase protection for areas with higher risk of fire. (This may result in shifting some of the initial positioning.) The last two steps involve further refinement of positioning on the basis of ability to respond to short-term emergencies and the performance of a proposed positioning plan in major emergencies when multiple fire units are occupied.

Following the historical/inductive approach of Valinsky are the mathematical positioning approaches which may be catalogued in terms of the homogeneity or heterogeneity of regions. Homogeneous regions are those where demand for fire service occurs uniformly in all parts of the region and all alarms may be considered analytically, at least, of equal importance. Heterogeneous regions are those where there is substantial variation in the fire rate and/or the importance of the alarms.

Location of facilities in homogeneous regions has generated a considerable body of systematic research, of which fire protection may be considered one dimension. Primary amongst the studies in fire protection is the work of the Rand Institute of New York City.

At the outset, the Institute staff focused on response time as the crucial determinant of effective and efficient fire protection. This is a reasonable approach given the already established network of fixed home-bases for fire companies in the city. Kolesar and Blum (1973)[2] generalized the concept that average or expected response could be expressed by a version of the basic formula: expected distance $= 2/3\sqrt{(A/n)}$ where A is the region area under consideration and n is the number of suppression units assigned to the region. When the number of suppression units is replaced by the average or expected number of units available when an alarm is sounded, the expected number of units available in turn can be calculated as the total number, n, minus the average number busy on calls. If

$\mu =$ the average time (in hours) required by a company to service an alarm and return to its usual position,

$\lambda =$ the average number of alarms per hour,

the average number of units available can then be calculated by the mathematical expression:

$$(n - \lambda\mu).$$

Kolesar and Blum thus argue that an approximate formula for the expected response distance associated with assigning n units to a region of area A can be given by:

$$\binom{\text{expected}}{\text{distance}} = (\text{constant})\sqrt{\left(\frac{A}{n - \lambda\mu}\right)}.$$

In a computer simulation, the attempt was made to validate the formula under more realistic circumstances characteristic of New York City's South Bronx neighborhoods. The results conformed fairly well to the predictions obtained from the model as shown in Fig. 1.

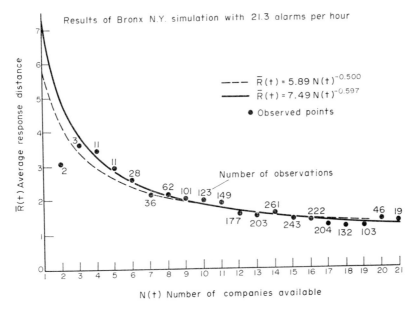

FIG. 1. Comparison of estimated and simulation response distances by number of available companies. (Source: Kolesar and Blum[2].)

Kolesar and Walker (1973)[3] expanded the research on response time by relating it with response distance. The resultant inequality formula emerges:

$$\binom{\text{response}}{\text{time}} = \begin{cases} (\text{constant}_1)\sqrt{\left[\binom{\text{response}}{\text{distance}}\right]}; \text{ if distance} \leq 2 \text{ miles,} \\ \\ (\text{constant}_2) + (\text{constant}_3)\binom{\text{response}}{\text{distance}}; \text{ otherwise} \end{cases}$$

By combining this approach with the earlier "square-root" formula for expected response distance, Blum derived an approximate formula for expected response time. The computer simulations attempting to validate the approach show the following: one, even where demand is not homogeneous, the results of the homogeneous model provide a good estimation; two, further quantitative research must be taken to set the base for deciding optimal location of facilities on the basis of minimum response time.

Rider (1974)[4] formulated the following approach to the optimal location question (see Table 1).

TABLE 1. RIDER'S MODEL FOR DIVIDING COMPANIES AMONG SUBREGIONS

Formulation

$$\text{Minimize} \quad \sum_i \lambda_i \left[h_i c_1 \left(\frac{A_i}{n_i - \mu_i \lambda_i} \right) \frac{c_2}{2} \right]^\beta,$$

s.t. $\sum_i n_i = N,$

where
λ_i = alarm rate in area i,

h_i = hazard factor in area i,

A_i = land area of area i,

n_i = the number of units to be assigned to area i,

c_1, c_2 = constants associated with the response time estimating formula,

β = the tradeoff parameter for controlling effects of extremes in performance in some areas.

Optimal solution

$$n_i = \lambda_i \mu_i + \lambda_i^2 h_i^{\nu\beta} A_i^{(1-\nu)} \left[\sum_i \lambda_i^2 h_i^{\nu\beta} A_i^{(1-\nu)} \right] [N - \sum_i b_i],$$

where $\quad \upsilon = \dfrac{2}{c_1 \beta + 2}.$

Source: Rider[4].

Optimal locations dictated by this approach can be loosely summarized as: "allocate to each region a number of units equal to the sum of the average number busy ($\lambda_i \mu$) and a portion of the remaining forces which increases with alarm rate, hazard and area of the region." Guild and Rolling (1972)[5] pursued this line of work of a square-root relationship between response distance and average area assigned to n fire companies. They also included economic considerations involving the overall cost to society of a fire-suspension allocation program. In general, their estimate of cost per fire to society when units are assigned to fire suppression in an area is:

$$
\begin{pmatrix} \text{expected} \\ \text{cost/fire} \\ \text{of maintaining} \\ \text{companies} \end{pmatrix} + \begin{pmatrix} \text{cost/hour} \\ \text{of} \\ \text{burning} \end{pmatrix} \left[\begin{pmatrix} \text{expected waiting} \\ \text{time due to} \\ \text{waiting for the} \\ \text{primary unit} \end{pmatrix} + \begin{pmatrix} \text{expected travel} \\ \text{time to and} \\ \text{from the fire} \\ \text{scene} \end{pmatrix} + \begin{pmatrix} \text{expected} \\ \text{service} \\ \text{time at the} \\ \text{fire scene} \end{pmatrix} \right]
$$

Although various constraining conditions limit the applicability of this approach, the basic problem stems from the lack of validation.

Returning to the question of optimality of location, Larson and Stevenson (1972)[6] demonstrated that the exact positioning of fire units does not greatly (15–20 percent) affect the resulting response time and that approximation formulas of the square-root genre described above provide satisfactory results if the objective is "essentially optimal" positions.

When the region to be protected has a heterogeneous demand (variation in the rate and importance of alarms in different parts of the region), the positioning problem becomes more difficult because of the additional variables to consider and their unknown nature. Raouf's study (1972)[7] of Windsor, Canada, for example, presented an approach for this case. Using historical information about the rate and seriousness of fire alarms in the district, Raouf calculated the value of a location as the weighted sum of the rectilinear distances from the location to the points where fires occur. Weights are provided by the number of man-hours spent fighting the fire. This solution is a practical one, being that the computations are fairly simple. Also, it permits periodic checking of fixed locations of suppression forces as well as the development of new positioning for new districts. Building on this approach, Santone and Berlin (1970)[8] calculated responses for the City of East Lansing by determining the shortest time-path to different geographic fire points through a computer representation of the city's street network. Similarly, Hogg (1968)[9] minimized overall average response distance for a rebuilt Glasgow in the 1980s given a particular number of companies to be positioned.

The Metropolitan Dade County Florida Fire Department study[10] describes an extension of Santone and Berlin's approach to locate fire stations in the Miami area. This procedure begins with: (1) an indication of which current stations cannot be moved, (2) a number of new stations to be located and a set of initial positions for these stations, (3) the frequency of alarms in each subregion of the county, (4) a table of the lengths of the shortest travel-time paths between all major intersections in the county through a computerized representation of the actual street pattern, and (5) a list of the "desired travel times" calculated for each subregion on the basis of the size and land use in the subregion. The procedure then attempts to improve on the initial set of locations for the "movable" stations. Improvements are measured in terms of reducing the overall "exposure" of the region, i.e. the sum of the products of the frequency of alarms in each subregion and the percentage by which the actual travel time from the subregion to the nearest station fails to meet the desired travel time criterion. Station locations are then restricted to the intersections in the traffic network representation. Mathematically this objective function is given by

$$\min_{A_k} \sum_j p(j)[\min_{i \in A_k} d(i,j) + q(j)\min_{i' \in A_k, \ i' \neq i} d(i',j)$$

where A_k = any set of R possible positions,

$\quad p(j)$ = the probability of a given alarm coming from demand point j,

$\quad q(j)$ = the probability of an alarm at demand point j will require multiple companies,

$\quad d(i,j)$ = the estimated representations from position i to demand zone j.

Another study which used the concept of covering fixed locations is the work of Mitchell (1971)[11] in Fullerton, California. Like most of the services studies, Mitchell divided the region into a set of demand districts or nodes, selected a number of units to be positioned, and then designed districts which minimized overall average response time to the pattern of alarms which had been experienced in the region. A number of other limitations, such as a maximum possible expenditure for suppression services, were discussed, but none were actually employed in the districting procedure.

The important characteristic of Mitchell's work which distinguishes it, however, is the attempt to include the response of more than one company in the overall average being minimized. At each demand point, he calculated the response performance of a given plan as the response time from the closest position in the plan plus the response time of the second closest, weighted by the chances that a second unit would be needed in alarms at that demand point. The chances of a second unit being needed was estimated from the history of alarms at that location. As can be seen, the mathematics for this approach is indeed complicated.

A final formulation of the fixed location type is the one applied by Stacey (1973)[12] in Dayton, Ohio. Like the authors above, Stacey modeled the positioning problem as one of allocating a given number of companies over possible locations in a way which would maximize the service to a set of demand points. The positioning plans were constrained to provide given levels of "protection" to each point, and to accommodate limitations on available company bays at the locations where units could be positioned. A set of dimensionless measures of the seriousness of risk, each weighted by the reciprocal of response distance, provided the indices of "protection" used in these constraints, and the procedure sought to maximize total protection.

TABLE 2. STACEY'S FORMULATION OF THE POSITIONING PROBLEM

Maximize:
$$\sum_i \sum_j p_{ij} x_j,$$

s.t.
$$\sum_j x_j \leq d,$$

$$\sum_j p_{ij} x_j \geq C_i \quad \text{for all } i,$$

$$b_j^1 \leq x_j \leq b_j^2 \quad \text{for all } j$$

where
- x_j = the number of units assigned to station j,
- b_j^1 = the minimum number of units which can be assigned to station j,
- b_j^2 = the maximum number of units which can be assigned to station j,
- d = the total number of companies available,
- P_{ij} = a dimensionless measure of the protection afforded demand point i by a company at station j (inversely proportional to the travel distance from i to j),
- C_i = the minimum level of protection acceptable at demand point i.

Source: Stacey[12].

Stacey's formulation embodies many of the constraints incorporated in earlier approaches discussed above. Like Hogg's work, the formulation accounts for combining companies into station locations with limited numbers of bays. As in the Dade County approach, consideration is given to a desired level of protection for each demand point; and like Mitchell's formulation, some weight is given to the protection offered by units other than the closest to each demand point.

The principle difficulty with Stacey's formulation is the complication that optimal solutions may very well require fractional numbers of companies at some locations and the complexity of implementing the "protection" constraint concept. Unless some suitable interpretation of say 2.6 companies at location *i* can be made, the fractional solutions which may be produced by Stacey's approach would have to be rounded to yield a meaningful positioning plan. Rounding may destroy the cardinal optimality of the positioning plan. More importantly, the dimensionless nature of Stacey's protection measures makes it very difficult to specify the requirements C_i. The C_i do not correspond directly to any measurable quantities in the fire environment. Moreover, when these numbers of candidate positions and the number of demand points increase beyond 50, the exact procedures become impractical. On balance, Hogg's suggestion that, "heuristic procedure would have produced almost as good results as those of the exact scheme and would have required far less computation time" must be taken as a serious exhortation to Stacey as well as to this type of large-scale policy analysis generally.

2. REPOSITIONING POLICIES

In turning to the other dimension of resource allocation, we approach a most complicated aspect of decision making in fire suppression, that of dealing with an emergency situation. When a substantial number of fire-suppression companies in an area are unavailable because they are involved already with serious fires, it may be necessary to reposition or "move-up" some available units to avoid leaving an area entirely unprotected. Although "moving-up" is a common practice, the NSF Fire Study indicates that only the Rand Institute systematically dealt with this problem. The collective effort of the Institute revolves about the work of Swersey, Kolesar, Walker and Shinner and Chaiken.

The first attempt to formalize the repositioning problem is attributed to Swersey (1969)[13] who utilized a "warehouse location" approach borrowed from the field of operations research. His formulation selected the repositioning scheme which minimizes a combination of city-wide response time after the repositioning and the cost of company movements. This formulation is shown in Table 3. Some alternative schemes for solving the problem were considered by Walker and Shinner (1969).[14] Included in these were schemes for obtaining approximate, heuristic solutions. Results indicate that the heuristic approach provides solutions which are nearly as good as the exact technique. This holds, especially when the time required for an exact repositioning design is too long for consideration. Chaiken (1970)[15] further penetrated the reality of repositioning and argued that the attempt to solve the problem on the basis of minimization of city-wide average response time was inadequate because fire marshalls reposition on the basis of "some minimum coverage to neighborhoods". To correct for this, he proposed a four-step optimization procedure which included local constraints that any repositioning had to satisfy while a city-wide minimal level of coverage is obtained. The four steps are sequential and may be summarized as follows:

Step 1. Define the need for relocation . . . when none of the three closest companies to some neighborhood is free to respond to new alarms.

Step 2. Select the empty company locations which must be covered by a repositioning . . . mathematical formulation to assure that each neighborhood has one of its closest three company locations covered.

TABLE 3. SWERSEY'S FORMULATION OF THE REPOSITIONING PROBLEM

Minimize:

$$\sum_j \sum_i \alpha_{ij} x_{ij} + \sum_j Cyj(1 - 0j).$$

Subject to:

$$\sum_j x_{ij} = b \qquad \text{for each } i,$$

$$\sum_i x_{ij} \leq kyj \qquad \text{for each } j,$$

$$\sum_j yj = m,$$

$$yj = on1 \qquad \text{for all } j,$$

$$0 \leq x_{ij} \leq 1 \quad \text{for all } i \text{ and } j,$$

where $yj = \begin{cases} 1 & \text{if company location } j \text{ is to be occupied} \\ 0 & \text{otherwise,} \end{cases}$

$x_{ij} = \begin{cases} 1 & \text{demand region } i \text{ is covered by a unit at company location } j \\ 0 & \text{otherwise,} \end{cases}$

b = the number of surrounding companies which provide some measure of protection to any demand region,

k = the number of demand regions,

C = the fixed cost of any company movement,

α_{ij} = a response time "cost" of having a unit a location j cover demand region i,

$O_j = \begin{cases} 1 & \text{if company location } j \text{ is presently occupied} \\ 0 & \text{otherwise} \end{cases}$

Source: Swersey[13].

Step 3. Determine companies which should be moved from their home base to empty positions being covered ... mathematical formulation to reposition unoccupied companies within the constraints of maintaining minimum neighborhood coverage and minimize city-wide average response time after repositioning. The basis for this approach is in the "square-root" formulation discussed in home-base locations of the previous sections.

Step 4. Consider the cost in terms of distance required to relocate ... mathematical formulation.

Although Kolesar and Walker (1972)[16] indicate satisfactory results from the application of this model to a "very busy night of July 4, 1969 in New York City", various analytical and administrative conditions complicate implementation. Analytically, the four-step sequential procedure compounds the error potential and consequently steps 2 and 3 might be combined. Such a combination, however, would increase the computational difficulties and would delay the necessary solution of the repositioning problem beyond usefulness. Administratively, the Rand procedure may be suited only for large jurisdictions, for only they can afford the necessary computer hardware. In smaller and less dense jurisdictions it is simpler to gain expanded coverage by relocating companies in accordance with the heuristic principle of repositioning the smallest companies first in cases of emergency.

3. DISPATCH POLICY

Complementing the positioning and repositioning dimensions of fire suppression is the assignment of available companies to incoming alarms—dispatching. Two subquestions have received attention here: how many companies should be dispatched to an initial alarm and which units should be sent?

At present, the administrative response of fire jurisdictions to the question of how many to send is generally fixed for various alarm types. If one of the senior officers of the responding company determines that the fire-fighting force is inadequate, a second and higher-order alarm is called in for additional units. This process is then repeated as necessary.

Again, the work of Swersey (1972)[17] and the Rand Corporation may be said to provide the dimensions of a "flexible response" approach to dispatching policies in regard to how many pieces of equipment to send. In such an approach the number of units to be dispatched to an alarm depends on a number which changes as units become busy. Specifically, the Rand work has considered the following elements:

1. The probability that an alarm is serious, i.e. the likelihood that the alarm will require more than a minimal, one-company response.
2. The number of units available in the surrounding area at the time the alarm is received.
3. The relative weight or value attached to the response time of the first-arriving versus the second-arriving unit.
4. The rate of alarms in the area surrounding the location of the alarm.

In Swersey's study, the essential problem is described as one of deciding between rapid response of the closest unit and rapid response of the second-arriving unit. Larger numbers of units also are discussed, but the issues seem the same as for the one versus two decision. In the case of two units, if only one unit is dispatched to a fire, the arrival time of the second (when it is needed) is delayed by the time for the first unit to reach the fire scene and request help. Thus, first response is relatively rapid, but second response is delayed. On the other hand, if two units are dispatched initially, the response time of the second unit is reduced, but a price is paid in the first response. The second unit which is not needed at the fire scene is out of service for the time required to reach and return from the fire scene. Thus, fewer units in the area are available for new alarms, and the average response time for first responding units will be correspondingly higher.

After investigation of a number of possibilities, Swersey concludes that the most convenient dispatch rule is the one given in Table 4. Simply stated, the decision on whether to send one or two units should be based on whether the probability, s, that a given alarm is serious is greater than or equal to a calculated threshold, or criterion value. If s is larger than the calculated value, two units should be sent. Otherwise, one unit should be sent.

The criterion value, in turn, depends on the factors (1) through (4) discussed above. As the number of units busy in a region increases, or the alarm rate (i.e. chances of more alarms in the immediate future) becomes larger, the rule tends to dispatch fewer companies. As the anticipated seriousness of the alarm or the weight placed on the arrival of the second unit increases relative to the response of the first unit, the rule tends to dispatch more companies immediately.

Carter and Swersey (1973)[18] investigated a slightly modified version of this decision rule by simulating different dispatch policies for the South Bronx, which experiences a relatively high alarm rate.

These simulation experiments generally supported the value of considering the availability of response units in a flexible dispatch rule instead of being restricted to a fixed dispatch policy. The greatest gain appears to have been derived from explicit investigation

TABLE 4. SWERSEY'S RULE FOR HOW MANY TO DISPATCH

Criterion:

$$s^* = \tfrac{1}{2}(\min\{1,s_u\} + \min\{1,s_l\}) + w,$$

where

w = a workload factor $(0 \leq w \leq 1)$,

$$s_u = \lambda\left(\frac{\alpha}{1-\alpha}\,\Delta T_{1/2} + \Delta T_{2/2} + \Delta T_{\min/2}\right)\bar{s},$$

$$s_l = \lambda\left(\frac{\alpha}{1-\alpha}\,\Delta T_{1/1} + \Delta T_{2/1}\right)\bar{s},$$

λ = alarm rate in the region around the present alarm site,

α = the weight attached to the response of the first unit as compared to the second,

s = the expected probability of a serious alarm in the region around the present alarm site,

$\Delta T_{i/k}$ = the estimated increase in the response time of ith units caused by dispatching a second unit to the present alarm when the number busy is assumed equal to the expected number when k units are always dispatched,

$\Delta T_{\min/k}$ = the estimated increase in the response time of the closest unit caused by dispatching a second unit to the present alarm when the number busy is assumed equal to the expected number when k units are always dispatched.

Policy:

Send 2 when $s \geq s^*$

Send 1 otherwise

where s = the probability the present alarm signals a serious fire.

Source: Swersey.[17]

---

of the probability that an alarm signals a serious fire. By ruling out multiple response to alarms that are almost certainly not serious, the dispatch rule measurably increases the availability of fire companies.

Since the probability that an alarm is serious forms such an important part of their proposed dispatch rules, the Rand researchers also performed considerable research on the prediction of this probability. In Carter and Rolph (1973)[19] an extensive statistical analysis compared formulas for forecasting the probability that an alarm is serious.

Four different types of statistical approaches were considered. They included combinations of:

1. Direct estimation from the historical pattern at a particular alarm box, as opposed to partial attention to the historical pattern of boxes in the immediate area.
2. Estimation of the probability that an alarm is serious directly, as opposed to first estimating the probability an alarm implies a fire in an occupied structure and multiplying this probability by the chances that an alarm in an occupied structure is serious.

An historical approach results which considers the following factors as determinative of an alarm's seriousness:

The history of alarms involving fires in occupied buildings at the particular alarm box.

The history of alarms involving fires in occupied buildings at surrounding boxes.

The historical chances that a fire in an occupied building is a serious fire.

The season of the year when the alarm is received.

The time of day when the alarm is received.

On balance, the part of the Rand work which would appear to have wider application is the explicit consideration in dispatch decision rules of the probability that an alarm is serious. Even if the immediate availability of surrounding units and related criteria can be ignored in the dispatch decision, it may be desirable to have predetermined first responses for particular neighborhoods—one for alarms likely to be minor and a second for alarms likely to be more serious. Such a dispatch policy would employ the forecasting aspects of the Rand work, but not the decision rules. In jurisdictions where such a scheme might be appropriate, an additional problem arises. That is the willingness of fire-protection officials to dispatch a potentially inadequate first response to a call from an alarm box with a history of false or inconsequential alarms. While such policies are informally followed by some fire departments in their "problem neighborhoods", it would appear that formalization of such a dispatch plan could create many political and organizational conflicts.

The other dimension of the dispatching question involves the question of which units to send. To a large extent the response is determined by fire jurisdictions on the basis of the "closest available units". For small jurisdictions where fire companies are generally available the rule seems satisfactory. Research, therefore, is concentrated on large and busy urban type fire-protection jurisdictions. The work of Carter, Chaiken and Ignall (1972)[20] at Rand is demonstrative. Although their studies are primarily involved with the drawing of optimal boundaries the findings may be applied in the analysis of dispatching policies involving two cooperating companies. The rationale for this is that questions of optional boundaries and optional dispatch policies are almost identical in the case of two cooperating fire companies.

Results in a general sense indicate that the best dispatch policy depends on the work load of two or more units such that when units are not busy the policy is always to send the closer company. As one of the companies becomes busier than the other, it may be desirable occasionally to dispatch the less busy unit even if it is not nearer to the alarm. The policy is optimal because it leaves the remaining busier unit available to respond to an additional alarm.

Ignall (1974)[21] extended this research and formulated a complete rule for which units to dispatch. In particular, he considers the question, "Which N of the $2N$ units in a given region should be dispatched to an alarm?" Like the earlier work, Ignall makes the assumptions that the number of alarms arise according to the Poisson probability distribution, with different alarm rates for different points in the region. More significantly, he continues to assume that the time a given company is in service on a particular alarm is independent of the locations of both the alarm and the fire house where the company is stationed. This assumption has the effect of ignoring the tendency of the response time being part of in-service time to be longer when more distant units are dispatched.

Within these assumptions, Ignall investigates rules for the best units to dispatch under criteria varying from a simple average of response times of all responding companies, to averages weighted more heavily on the response of the first units, and then to averages including weighting for the balance of workload between companies. A statement of the problem of finding the units to dispatch under any of these weighted objective functions is shown to be a very large linear program (see Table 5).

Various problems, however, complicate the application of Ignall's large-scale linear program: (1) the calculations necessary for solution are too time consuming for response to individual alarms; (2) the data scheme requires a management information system

Samuel J. Bernstein and Israel Pressman

TABLE 5.

Criterion for company j on an alarm of type k at point x:

$$t_j^* = t_j(x) + \theta_j \{1 + (r - 1)\}P_k$$

where $t_j(x)$ = the time for unit j to respond to point x,

r = the ratio of the value of response time at serious fires to response time at other fires,

P_k = the probability an alarm of type k is serious,

θ_j = a balancing factor increasing with the workload of company j.

Policy:

If n units are required, send the units j with the n smallest t_j^*.

Source: Ignall.[21]

which is not in existence even in most larger fire jurisdictions; (3) the limited testing showed improvements in workload balance between companies without significantly increasing average response time, however, the implications are limited only to very large and very busy fire districts.

4. SUMMARY

Where suppression companies should be positioned, what companies should be dispatched and how companies should be repositioned during fire emergencies are the basic service delivery questions in the area of fire suppression activities with which we started out. A sample of major efforts have been reviewed in this regard closely following the National Service Foundation Report of Policy Related Research in Fire Protection. An overview reveals the following picture.

By far, the largest part of the research has been concerned with positioning "home base" locations for suppression companies. This research has produced:

A relatively well-validated set of simple mathematical formulas for rough or preliminary positioning, which are derived from the homogeneous demand case where the alarm rate is assumed constant over the entire region being studied, but can be more widely applied.

A collection of more detailed and complex formulations which position companies at sets of fixed positions.

A limited number of probabilistic results which have implications for the performance of positioning plans in environments where the nearest company to an alarm is not always available.

Taken together, these results appear to largely exhaust the possible approaches to the positioning problem, but much more experience with the techniques is required to more thoroughly identify their strengths and weaknesses. It would be particularly useful to have further evidence on the degree to which the quality of the resulting positioning plan is improved when the simple formulas available from the homogeneous case are replaced by the more complex covering, or fixed location schemes.

A considerable amount of research also has been performed (largely by the New York

City Rand Institute) on rules for assigning companies to alarms. This research has demonstrated the value of considering the probability that a given alarm signals a serious fire. A set of optimal (under appropriate assumptions) decision rules has resulted for both questions: "How many of each type of company to dispatch?" and, "Which particular units should be assigned to form the desired number of dispatched units?" These decision rules do not always assign the closest available units.

Pending more widespread implementation, it appears that this research on dispatch provides fairly satisfactory answers to the above questions. However, it is not clear whether rules other than the commonly used "assign a predetermined number of the nearest units" rule are necessary except in very large cities. When company workloads are low, the more complex decision rules collapse into this simple widely used policy.

The New York City Rand Institute also has performed much of the basic research on the repositioning problem, i.e. temporarily moving free companies into areas left unprotected when a large number of companies are occupied at serious fires. This research has produced a simple and intuitive scheme for computerized repositioning which appears to meet the needs of New York City. Some modification of the approach probably would be required to fit the environment in other small jurisdictions. Moreover, the repositioning problem is probably only complex enough to require more than dispatcher's judgement in large fire jurisdictions.

Finally, a number of computer simulation routines have been developed which permit more "realistic" testing of complete suppression allocation policy alternatives. Where these routines have been employed, they appear to have yielded worthwhile insight. However, many of the details of the simulations have not been thoroughly validated, and it is not clear that a relatively complex and expensive effort to develop a simulation can be justified in other than the very largest fire jurisdictions. For the future, validation is the prescription of quantitative research activities.

II. Emergency Medical Services: Ambulance Transportation

Emergency medical care is concerned with urgent unscheduled medical events which may threaten a patient's life and/or result in extended disability. Formal quantitative approaches for planning, measuring performance and emergency medical transportation have been developed. Our emphasis in this review is on the latter because it involves actual service delivery issues and because effective and efficient transportation is an essential link in saving a person's life in an emergency.

In analyzing issues in emergency medical transportation from the quantitative perspective, the contributions may be catalogued sequentially as: (1) the demand for the service; (2) location of facilities; (3) dispatching; and (4) the number of ambulances needed. Our review follows this order.

1. THE DEMAND FOR SERVICE

Hisserich (1969) shows that per capita demand for public ambulance service is a linear function of socio-economic characteristics of the census tract.[22] Using least-square regression techniques he found that in general, census tracts with low-income, nonwhite families, high unemployment rates and elderly people or children tend to generate many more calls for ambulance service. Within this framework, several submodels, using similar techniques, were developed to predict different types of ambulance service calls; for automobile accidents, other accidents, dry runs, cardiac, and poison cases. Although the methodology was validated in Los Angeles, and would seem transferrable to other municipalities, evidence for applications elsewhere is lacking.

Based on Hisserich's efforts, Deems (1973)[23] proceeded to comprehensively analyze the efficacy of socio-economic data for predicting ambulance demand. Two separate approaches were used: a first-order linear regression and a second-order non-interacting regression. In both cases, different emergency ambulance service calls could be predicted as well as overall demand.

Prediction was considered for total calls, drug intoxication, obstetrics/gynecology, auto trauma, other trauma, cardiovascular, other medical, and dry runs. Using a first-order model with thirty-four variables the lowest coefficient of determination was .74 for obstetrics/gynecology and the highest was .95 for drug intoxication. A second-order, non-interacting model using a reduced number of variables (6 to 15) was investigated. The lowest and highest coefficients of multiple determination were .76 for obstetrics/gynecology and .92 for drug intoxication. Total calls had a coefficient of determination of .93 in the linear model and 190 in the second-order model. Significant variables in the linear model were total tract average, tract averages per population, percentage of unemployed males, median family income, number of housing units, housing units per population, and number of workers who either drive or ride to work as a passenger in an auto. The most significant variables in the second-order regression equations were percentage of tract in commercial use, unemployed males, median family income, percentage of age groups 3 to 34 who are enrolled in school, total housing per population, total acreage per population.

Of the socio-economic approaches to predict ambulance demand, the Deems methodology is most comprehensive; however, the findings are less than universal. They correlate only in part with those of Hisserich in Los Angeles and seem to contradict those of Gibson's Chicago study (1973).[24] The regressions, however, show that socio-economic factors may be identified and demand predicted. At some future point in time, pursuant to a series of such validated studies, an effective demand for service list may be constructed with far-ranging applicability to regions showing similar characteristics.

2. LOCATION OF FACILITIES

The ambulance location problem involves positioning base facilities so that the average response time for a total ambulance transportation system is at a minimum even when demand peaks.[25, 26] Response time is further constrained to prevent degradation of service to any of the various subareas within a region. In this sense, the location problem is similar to that of fire suppression. However, little effort is reported on emergency repositioning so important in fire suppression.

Volz's (1970[27] and 1971[28]) work in Washtenaw County, Michigan, analyzes the problem of deployment in a semi-urban setting. In this study, the county was divided into a grid of 1-mile squares. All calls within a square were assumed to originate at a single point within the square and an ambulance was always assumed to be available. Using data on the spatial distribution of calls without regard to time, ambulance velocity, type of road, and the probability distribution of the number of available ambulances, the author considered solutions with and without a constraint on maximum response time. Optimal locations of base facilities were obtained as a function of the number of ambulances available with and without response time constraints.

Fitzsimmons (1973)[29] addresses the ambulance location question from the perspective of minimizing the mean response time for the total system. Following the example of other service studies utilizing the Poisson distributions, the Fitzsimmons model assumes a Poisson distribution of service time. The input data for the model consists of: (1) the distribution on number of busy ambulances, $P(i)$; (2) the probability of "j" particular ambulances being busy, $P(j)$; (3) the mean response time given "i" busy ambulances as a function of i, $R(i)$; (4) the mean response time if an ambulance is dispatched from the hospital, RH; (5) the probability of patient being taken to hospital "k" (as a function of k), $G(k)$; (6) mean arrival rate, a; (7) mean service rate, s; (8) mean ambulance speed as a function of distance travelled, v; and (9) the number of ambulances, N.

Shown below is the formulation of the model:

Mean response time for system (RBAR)

$$= \sum_{i=0}^{N-1} P(i)R(i) + \left(1 - \sum_{i=0}^{N-1} P(i)\right)RH,$$

where $P(i) = e^{-a/s}(a/s)^i/i!$,

$\quad R(i) = \sum_{j \in Bi} - p(j)\gamma(j)$,

$\quad RH = \sum_{k=1}^{k} G(k) \sum_{m=1}^{M} f(m)|h(k) - x(m)|/v$,

where B_i = number of combinations of N ambulances taken i at a time,

$\quad \gamma(j)$ = mean response time given "j" particular busy ambulances $j \varepsilon B$,

$\quad f(m)$ = probability of an incident in the district,

$\quad h(k)$ = location of the "k" hospital, $k = 1 \ldots K$,

$\quad x(m)$ = location of the centroid of the M elements in the emergency ambulance service area.

Among Fitzsimmon's findings are the following:

1. Dispersed ambulance deployment is superior to single central station deployment, a finding previously reported by Savas in New York City in 1970.
2. Optimal deployment can significantly improve response time by at least 12 percent of a uniform deployment.
3. Optimal deployment is a function of incident rate.
4. Consideration must be given to secondary deployment, or redeployment.
5. One central dispatch command is more desirable than many independent dispatching commands.
6. Use of a selective retrieval policy of transporting special cases to more distant, better equipped hospitals yields only a 1 percent increase in mean response time.
7. An adaptive deployment policy (redeploying based on system state) can improve system response time.
8. The probability of an empty system decreases with large systems.

9. When uncertainty exists about the distribution of incident locations, ambulances should be deployed uniformly throughout the region.

10. With a single ambulance, optimal location is at the median for each variable.

Some of the assumptions in the Fitzsimmons' model appear to be more restrictive than in others. For example, other models use a response time which is dependent upon ambulance location and/or incident location. In Fitzsimmons, response time is a function of whether the ambulance is at its base or hospital when dispatched and the number of other busy ambulances. Moreover, hospital transfer delay and mean ambulance speed are considered constant and the probability that all ambulances are busy must be small.

The Fitzsimmons' approach, despite its limitations, has been validated through a related simulation in Los Angeles, and the model also has been incorporated into a computerized algorithm for ambulance location CALL, Computerized Ambulance Location Logic, and effectively applied in the design of an ambulance system for Melbourne, Australia.

In a series of similar studies of ambulance service in New York City, Savas (1969),[30] Gordon and Zelin (1970)[31] focused on improvements in service which could be achieved by dispersing the city's ambulance fleet. Using simulation techniques, the effect of a single ambulance satellite station was found to result in improved system response time but only marginal improvements in round-trip time. A dispersed ambulance system with and without satellite was then analyzed and found superior to the existing deployment. Savas thus concludes in favor of a completely dispersed ambulance system with exact locations being determined periodically by analyzing the distribution of demand. This flexible dispersion policy is then shown to hold for both cost and cost-effectiveness criteria.

Swoveland (1973)[32] developed an ambulance location technique by dividing a region into zones which are approximated by single central points. The procedure locates one ambulance at a node so as to minimize the average response time for the ambulance system in that region. Assuming that the closest ambulance to an incident is busy, a "branch and bound" technique called probabilistic enumeration is then used to obtain an optimal solution. The analytics of this approach is shown below:

Let N = a finite set of nodes;

     $R_k \subset N$ = a collection of K non-empty regions $k = 1 \ldots K$;

     ρ = an assignment, i.e. a mapping from $\{1 \ldots K\}$ to N such that $\rho(k) \in R_k$.

           Thus, ambulance k is located at node $\rho(\mathrm{k}) \in R_k$;

     Γ = collection of all assignments;

and for each assignment $\rho \in \Gamma$,

           $v(\rho)$ = the expected response time under assignment ρ.

The problem is then stated as $\min_\rho \varepsilon_\Gamma v(\rho)$.

If the closest ambulance is always available the problem becomes the "K-median" problem, i.e.

$$v(\rho) = \sum_{i \varepsilon N} P_i[\min_k d(\rho(k), i)],$$

where P_i = prob. of a call from node i and

$d(j, i)$ = travel-time from node j to node i.

A more realistic result is based on the "Stability Hypothesis", i.e. values of $W_\rho(i, q)$ are independent of ρ, where $W_\rho(i, q)$ = the fraction of total calls per day arising at node i and serviced by the q closest ambulance.

The result is approximately

$$v(\rho) = \sum_{i \varepsilon N} \sum_{q=1}^{k} w(i, q) d(l_\rho(i, q), i)$$

where for assignment ρ, $l_\rho(i, q)$ is the node $\rho(k)$ and where k is the qth closest ambulance to node i.

By using branch and bound techniques the problem reduces to calculation of the mean $\bar{v}$ over a subset Γ_1 corresponding to subregions S_k, $k = 1, \ldots, k$. Thus,

$$\bar{v} = \frac{1}{m} \sum_{\rho \varepsilon \Gamma_1} \sum_{i \varepsilon N} \sum_{q=1}^{k} w(i, q) d(l_\rho(i, q), i),$$

where m = no. of assignments in the subcollection.

A simulation was conducted to validate the model.

A major methodological benefit emerging here is that there was no need to assume the availability of the ambulance. Other simplifying assumptions, however, are made; for example, priority of assignment is not considered, dispatch of ambulance on route to home base is not considered, and provisions for cancellations are not accounted for.

Toregas and ReVelle (1971)[33] and 1972)[34] in their location model modified minimum response time by incorporating a maximum-delay constraint. By aiming to minimize the number of facilities, and solving through integer programming, the base locations are provided as a by-product.

Let S = minimum response time,

N_i = set of nodes within S of i that can provide acceptable emergency services to i,

d_{ji} = distance j to i.

Thus, $N_i = \{j | d_{ji} \leq S\}$.

The problem is to minimize the total number of facilities used (z) or min $z = \sum_{j=1}^{n} x_j$, s.t. $\sum_{j \varepsilon N1} x_j \geq 1$

where $X_j = \begin{cases} 0 & \text{if no facility is established at point } j, \\ 1 & \text{if a facility is established at point } j. \end{cases}$

Because the model assumes response capacity for each facility at all times and does not permit interaction among ambulances, its utility for generalization is limited in terms of real work consideration.

A unique approach to location problems has been taken by Schneider (1971)[32] who uses a man/computer interactive system. The system is called ADLOC (Ambulance Dispatch Center Locator). A cathode-ray tube displays a network of the city streets and displays the number of incidents for each intersection. The user inputs a location scheme through a keyboard terminal and light pen. The computer evaluates the user's selection by computing total travel time and longest trip. Two computer algorithms—heuristic in nature—then can be called by the users to improve these two measures. The author's hypothesis is that this man–computer interactive scheme can produce near optimal solutions, which rival those technically derived. Their experimental procedure neither confirms nor denies this hypothesis.

Two interesting features emerge from Schneider's approach. One, that there is potential in developing a generalized computer package, which may be modified for different localities. Two, structured heuristic findings may be of equal value to complicated analytical approaches requiring large amounts of data generally unavailable to administrations as was shown in the case of fire suppression. Limiting the utilization of this approach, however, are simplifying assumptions such as availability of nearest ambulance, lack of consideration of spatial and temporal variations, use of a hypothetical demand, provision of little information as to the nature of the algorithms determining optionality.

Larson and Stevenson (1971)[36] questioning the previous approaches to facilities location, based on response time developed a simple model based on mean travel time to analyze the effects of different facility locations and district boundaries for service delivery. They found that when demand was spatially homogeneous, the mean travel time resulting from a random distribution of facilities was only 25 percent over the mean travel time for optimally distributed facilities. Addressing the question of determining boundaries or "districts" for two facilities, they found that the location of the non-fixed facilities and district boundaries, whether units were independent or cooperative, had little effect on the mean travel time of the ambulance system. The authors conclude that mean response time thus may be an insensitive factor for gauging facilities locations.

Larson and Stevenson further showed that minimal mean intradistrict travel distance $E(D)$ may be obtained by designing the district as a square rotated at 45° with the facility's position at the center of the rotated square.

The mean travel is $2/3\sqrt{(A/2)}$ where A = total district area. If there are N square districts and A is the area of district i and $A = 1$ then

$$\text{mean travel distance} = E(D) = \sum_{i=1}^{N} 2Ai/3A\sqrt{(Ai/2)}$$

with min $E(D)$ occurring when $A_i = 1/N$.
Thus,

$$E^*(D) = 2/3\,(2N)^{-1/2} \approx .471/\sqrt{N},$$

and the mean travel distance from a service request to the nearest facility is

$$E^*(D) = 1/4\sqrt{(2\pi/N)} \approx .627/\sqrt{N}.$$

Following Larson's lead, Hoey,[37] Blum,[38] and Coyle[39] did not consider response time in determining ambulance locations for the cities of Boston, New York, and Atlanta respectively. Hoey divided the day into five segments and determined the number of ambulances needed for each segment. Final allocations for each segment of the day were made by analyzing the average percentage of time secondary ambulances were used during peak-hour secondary ambulance usage and utilization.

Blum and Coyle, using census tract data, target response times, and mean ambulance velocity, estimated, by a series of complicated calculations, optimal locations. In each of these three cases, the conclusions are still tentative in light of the previous studies showing significant improvements in facilities' locations stemming from response-time-based models.

3. DISPATCHING POLICIES

Keeney (1972)[40] addressed ambulance dispatching as typical of the larger set of dispatching problems characteristic of public services delivery, for ambulance facilities, the model may be described as follows: Service regions are subdivided into districts where each is assigned the service of one ambulance. All locations in a district are closer in terms of time or distance to the ambulance assigned than to any other ambulance in any other district. Assuming that all ambulances are available, an intuitive procedure is presented for districting a region which permits determining second, third, and fourth closest ambulance facilities.

Let F_i = facility $i(1 \ldots n)$ which are optimally distributed. If F_{n+1} is added, then the only changes in the assignment, associating locations with facilities are those whose locations were formerly in the district of F_i and are now in F_{n+1}.

Rules are presented for redistricting with both internal and external boundaries and for districting a region with n facilities. In addition, a method for identifying the second or third nearest facility is outlined.

The procedure presented by Keeny is mathematically descriptive rather than analytic and seems to work. Limitations include: lack of validation and failure to account for frequency of calls. Such a failure can result in a degradation of overall systems response time as shown in fire-suppression dispatching. The method, moreover, does not address the problems of ambulance coverage deriving from location.

Jarvis (1973)[41] developed a model for developing optimal dispatching policies for up to twelve units by partitioning a service region into areas called atoms. Calls originate from any atom and arrive according to the Poisson distribution. The number of calls from disjointed atoms are considered independent random variables. Within the region there are a fixed number of companies to provide emergency service. The service time for any unit in any atom follows the exponential distribution. Minimizing mean response distance for each combination of busy and free units in the region by atoms is the objective.

Jarvis reports that although workload is not considered explicitly by the model, workload imbalances derived from always dispatching the closest unit, may be improved using solutions obtained from the model. The weaknesses in the model stem first from the assumption that service time follows an exponential distribution and, second, that validation studies are not shown.

Carter, Chaiken and Ignall (1972)[42] made a classic contribution to understanding of dispatching problems in fire suppression as shown in the previous section. A fruitful avenue of research might involve the extension of their work to ambulance service.

4. THE NUMBER OF AMBULANCES NEEDED

The problem of determining the number of ambulances needed, in a particular community, independent of the location problem, was modeled by Bell and Allen (1969).[43] Their approach was based on a queuing concept that the calling population vies for a service provided by a limited number of ambulances. If a call for service encounters all ambulances, it must wait in a queue. Elements of the queue are served on a first-come first-serve basis as ambulances become free. Assuming the requests for service can be modeled by the Poisson distribution and the mean for this distribution identified, a formula which approximates waiting time distribution is derived:

Let λ = arrival per hour,

$1/\mu$ = mean service time.

Let the service time distribution be of general form such that the probability that service takes no longer than t hours is

$$\int_0^t f(y)\, dy.$$

For a Poisson arrival process, general service distribution, a first-come first-served basis and a single server (ambulance) the probability (steady state) that there are n customers in service is

$$\rho^n \exp(-\rho)/n!$$

where $\rho = \lambda/\mu$.

If there are n ambulances in the system, then we get immediate service if there are $(n-1)$ or less customers in the system. This is estimated by

$$\text{Prob. of } (n-1) \text{ or less} = \sum_{j=0}^{N-1} \rho^j \exp(-\rho)/\rho!$$

The probability that an arriving customer must wait more than X hours is approximated by

$$\left[\int_x^\infty (t-x)t^{-1}f(t)\, dt\right]\rho \exp(-\rho) + \{1 - (1+\rho)\exp(-\rho)\}$$

where it is assumed that only two ambulances are in the fleet and the service time is $t \geq x$.

The authors determine the minimum number of ambulances required to provide immediate service for 95 percent and 99 percent of the calling population. The authors validate their model when service time is exponential. But the test does not validate the model for the more general case of service time. Further analysis with simulation might answer their question.

Stevenson (1968)[44] developed two models for determining the number of ambulances required to serve a region. In the "primary model", ambulance service is provided by a single source. In the secondary model, ambulance service is provided from a primary source as long as primary ambulances are available. When all primary ambulances are busy, ambulance service is provided by a secondary source. Service time in the primary model is assumed to be exponentially distributed (which has not been found to be a valid assumption).

In both models, calls for service arrive according to the Poisson distribution. Stevenson uses the secondary model to determine the optimal mix of primary ambulances to minimize the total expected cost. The cost model assumes that secondary ambulances are called upon at a fixed cost per call. This secondary model is one of the few models encountered which explicitly accounts for cost of system operation.

Stevenson's and Bell's models suffer from three limitations. First, provision is not made for temporal variation in demand. Failure to account for this results in the potential for ambulance service falling below an acceptable level: particularly where there are significant temporal variations in demand for service, as shown in urban areas. Second, calls for service are assumed to be uniformly distributed throughout the service region. This has been shown to be an invalid assumption by several investigators. Third, these models do not account for the effects of system performance on ambulance locations.

In conclusion, the work of Siler (1972)[45] is cited as an example of a general-purpose simulation of emergency medical transportation system which has been validated with actual emergency medical data. The simulation is designed to be used by individuals with limited programming experience. To start the simulation, the user models his environment by using the data by type of emergency, time of occurrence, location, time of reporting, informant, mode of notification, number of injured, as well as the types of injuries and their severity. Given this information, a set of dispatching policies may be selected in order to determine which emergency medical facility to use, the modes of transit available and the most efficient route. This simulation appears to be an excellent beginning for general-purpose simulation in emergency medical services.

5. SUMMARY

As compared with the results of research in fire suppression, emergency medical transportation findings are seemingly less conclusive. The bulk of accomplishment comes primarily in two areas: facilities location or ambulance bases, and demand for service. To a lesser degree dispatching and fleet size studies have resulted in new tools for improved administration. Several promising methods have been cited to solve the ambulance location problem. Although each purports to solve the problem, implementation is problematic because validation studies are weak or non-existent. Nevertheless, some of the primary spillovers of location studies have enabled dispatch policies which minimize mean response time while constraining for maximum delay. In regard to demand for service, the work of Hisserich and Deems demonstrates how key demographic factors can be used to predict demand for ambulance service. Yet a consistent set of forecasting indicators has not been shown which could be applied across the board. In dispatching, models were shown to enable balancing work loads and showing where imbalanced work loads would be more beneficial. Lastly, in questions of fleet sizes, queuing models were shown to be effective.

Further research may be said to demand attention for integrating findings in order to generalize approaches that have greater than case-study implications. Also required is a greater emphasis on cost analysis.

To effectively utilize the already available models on location and dispatching as well as to optimize future utilization, it is important to study the organizational context in which the models are expected to work. In this regard, Professor Hyrum Plass has suggested the consideration of central authorities which have control over all aspects of the ambulance service. Without the existence of such an authority, he argues, none of the "optimal policies" generated by models could be implemented in either larger or smaller cities.

In most of the efforts reviewed, it became clear that the quantitative approach proceeded by attempting to solve a specific local problem in emergency medical service transportation.

In many cases, improved performance resulted. However, there is a dearth of findings which indicates that optimal policies from one area can be successfully transferred to another area. To be able to generalize findings and thereby to evolve proven "software packages" is an essential area of further research.

Last in emergency ambulance service, a major problem is the ability to distinguish the gravity of calls for service. In fire suppression, a similar situation exists and attempts have been made to evaluate seriousness of fire calls in different regions and to assign the appropriate fire-fighting response. There is a similar research need in emergency medical service to screen calls which do not need the service, reduce the "prank" calls, queue non-emergency/non-urgent calls and provide preliminary treatment advice during response delay.

III. Sanitation: Solid Waste Management

INTRODUCTION

Six major areas dimension the field of solid-waste management:

1. Level of service to users of sanitation systems.
2. Productivity and work procedures for collection.
3. Collection technology.
4. Transport, scale, and systems design.
5. Processing technology.
6. Disposal technology.

Formal approaches for improved service delivery revolve primarily about two of these dimensions: Service level problems and Productivity problems. As compared to fire suppression and emergency medical transportation, the problems of solid waste are less complicated for three reasons. First, response time is not a relevant measure for effective performance. Second, optimization is only by region and subregional concerns are not relevant. Third, hardware improvements contribute to a large measure to improve sanitation service; for example, the larger, quieter compactor truck. Cognizant of these differences we begin this review with the problems of determining adequate service levels.

1. LEVEL OF SERVICE FOR USERS OF SANITATION SYSTEMS

A. *Collection frequency*

Collection frequency and cost are probably the most important variables in citizen perceptions of effective level of sanitation servicing. Hirsch[46] (1965), in a seminal study, estimated waste collection cost using frequency and other collection characteristics as determining variables. His method, later emulated by many researchers[47, 48] involved defining an "idealized average cost function" for refuse collection service as follows:

$$AC = f(A; Q_1, Q_2, Q_3, Q_4, Q_5; D, U, H, B, Y, K, F; L, T)$$

where AC = average annual residential refuse collection cost per ton,

A = annual amount of residential refuse collected,

Q_1 = weekly collection frequency,

Q_2 = pickup location,

Q_3 = nature of pickup,

Q_4 = disposal method,

Q_5 = type of hauling equipment,

D = pickup density,

U = residential–non-residential land use mix,

H = hauling distance,

B = number of people per pickup unit,

Y = per capita income,

K = nature of contractual arrangement,

F = type of financing,

L = factor price level, and

T = state of technology and productivity.

Since reliable data was not readily available to measure A, a proxy variable, N, the number of residential pickups, was used in the model from which the average annual residential refuse collection cost per pickup, is derived.

Hirsch's conclusions show that an increase in frequency of collection from weekly to twice weekly leads to a cost change in the order of 70 percent. Marks and Liebman (1970)[49] in related work consider the effect of increased waste collection as a variable impacting on cost and frequency. Their basic analytics are reported below.

Let K = number of sources of waste,

S = amount of waste at the kth source,

J = number of disposal points,

D_j = maximum capacity of jth disposal point,

I = set of intermediate facility points,

F_i = fixed charge at facility i,

V_i = variable charge at facility i,

Q_i = capacity of facility i.

Given these conditions the problem is to find the minimum total cost of facilities and trans-shipment. Mathematically, this may be accomplished in the following program format:

$$\text{Min} \quad \sum_{i=1}^{m} F_i y_i + \sum_{i=1}^{m} \sum_{j=1}^{n} C_{ij}^* X_{ij}^* + \sum_{i=1}^{m} \sum_{k=1}^{p} C_{ki}^{**} X_{ki}^{**},$$

S.t.

$$\sum_{i=1}^{m} X_{ki}^{**} = S_k \qquad k = 1 \ldots p,$$

$$\sum_{j=1}^{n} X_{ij}^{*} = \sum_{k=1}^{p} X_{ki}^{**} \qquad i = 1 \ldots m,$$

$$\sum_{j=1}^{p} X_{ki}^{**} \le Q_i Y_i \qquad i = 1 \ldots m,$$

$$\sum_{i=1}^{m} X_{ij}^{*} \le D_j \qquad j = 1 \ldots n,$$

$X_{ij}^{*}, X_{ki}^{**} =$ non-negative integers,

$y_i = (0, 1).$

where $\quad y_i = \begin{cases} 1 & \text{if the } i\text{th facility is built} \\ 0 & \text{otherwise,} \end{cases}$

$x_{ij}^{*} =$ flow from i to j,

$x_{ki}^{**} =$ flow from k to i,

$c_{ij}^{*} = c_{ij} + r_j =$ unit cost of transfers from i to j,

$c_{ij} =$ unit shipping cost from i to j,

$r_j =$ unit variable cost for using disposal j,

$c_{ki}^{**} = c_{ki} + t_k + v_i,$

$c_{ki}^{'} =$ unit shipping cost from k to i,

$t_k =$ unit variable cost for using source k.

The effect of frequency on waste generation was studied by Quon *et al.* in Chicago (1966).[50] This team looked at two wards of the City where portions of the wards had their frequency of collection varied from once to twice weekly. Data was then gathered on the weights of refuse collected in the various sections of the wards and three calculations were performed to determine solid-waste generation. In the first calculation collection frequency was constant and at known collection intervals. The refuse production, $P(t)$, was found from the equation

$$P(t) = \frac{\bar{X}_t}{t}$$

where $t =$ period in days and

$$\bar{X}_t = \text{mean of } X_t \text{ with}$$

$$X_t = \frac{w}{\sum_{j=1}^{m} U[BL(j)]} \qquad j = 1, \ldots, m,$$

where X_t = refuse quantity in pounds per living unit per period,

w = refuse weight of one truckload,

$U(BL)$ = no. of living units in the block BL,

$BL(j)$ = name of block collected by the truck, and

m = total no. blocks collected by the truck.

The second calculation was performed using an average collection interval $\bar{t}$ with

$$\bar{t} = \frac{\sum_{j=1}^{m} t_j}{m},$$

$$X = w/\sum_{j=1}^{m} \{U[BL(j)]t_j\},$$

and

$$X = \begin{cases} X_1 & \text{if } \bar{t} \geq 5 \\ X_2 & \text{if } \bar{t} < 5. \end{cases}$$

The first category received once-a-week service.

The second category received twice-a-week service.

The third calculation was performed considering areas with different frequencies of service and the sum total of all refuse collected from each area was determined.

Results of Quon seem to conform with the general expectation that daily solid-waste generation decreases with increased time between collections. Increased collection frequency, from once to twice weekly, however, results in a 35 to 40 percent increase in solid-waste generation. Given the inability to define the dispositional characteristics of persons to waste disposal it is impossible, as Professor Marks says, to explain and/or to give accurate estimates of the increase to be expected from an increase in collection frequency. Service pricing is discussed next as a determinant person's solid waste disposal dispositions.

B. *Service pricing*

How different pricing schemes influence the behavior of users of solid-waste services is a major substudy area of MacFarland (1972) who found that the quantity of solid waste collected depended on the price of the service with variation greater for commercial collection than for household collection. For example, an increased user fee of 10 percent correlated with a 5 percent drop in quantity of waste generation by household. Unanswered in MacFarland's study is the question of where does the waste go. Little more is known at present than the intuitive response of more litter. Both Clark (1971)[51] and MacFarland (1972)[52] showed cost increases in the order of 30 percent resulting from backyard rather than curbside collections.

Place of pickup was shown by Stone (1969)[53] to be related also to crew size. His findings reveal, as might be expected, that one-man crews are incompatible with backyard collections. Greco (1974),[54] being spurred by the recent fuel crisis, then related fuel consumption to place of pickup along with collection frequency. Results obtained from his statistical approach for a sample of 10,000 homes serviced, are shown in Table 6. Clearly, the preferred alternatives include curbside pickups and once per week collections for a 6-day week.

TABLE 6. TRADE-OFF CONSIDERATIONS FOR COLLECTION SERVICE LEVELS

	10,000 homes serviced							
	Once per week				Twice per week			
	5-day week		6-day week		5-day week		6-day week	
Number of trucks required	8	5	7	4	12	7	10	6
Gallons of gasoline consumed per day if all trucks are gas	320	200	280	160	480	280	400	240
Gallons of diesel consumed per day if all trucks are diesel	192	120	168	96	288	168	240	144

(1) 260 stops per truck per day assumed for one/week, rear-door service.
(2) 350 stops per truck per day assumed for twice/week, rear-door service.
(3) 450 stops per truck per day assumed for once/week, curb side service.
(4) 600 stops per truck per day assumed for twice/week, curbside service.
(5) Fuel consumption of 24 gallons per truck per day assumed for diesel-powered equipment.
(6) Fuel consumption of 40 gallons per truck per day assumed for gasoline-powered equipment.

Source: Greco.[54]

C. *Storage methods*

Turning to the last determinant of service level we find that Stone's work (1969)[55] is the watershed. Involved in this study are statistical comparisons evaluating bags, standard containers, home and industrial compactors and garbage incinerators. It may be concluded from a methodological perspective at least that few new techniques or new procedures have been developed here.

By way of summary it may be said that the determinants of solid-waste sanitation service level most amenable to quantitative and formal approaches or simulations are collection frequency, pricing and cost, and place of pickup. Other dimensions such as solid-waste collection and storage methods do not show any significant utilization of these techniques. The least understood dimension in this regard is the behavioral and attitudinal disposition of the service user.

2. PRODUCTIVITY

Productivity which is the second major area of quantitative analysis in solid-waste management involves the relationship of amount of work achieved to effort. Three focal points have guided the research endeavors here: measurement, crew size, and crew scheduling and routing. Routing encompasses the larger amount of research appearing in a series of problems ranging from what is a fair day's work, division of the community into tasks, to the actual design of routing.

A. *Measurement*

Sanitation crew productivity can be effectively achieved by improved measurement of daily time and weight data, if routes are well defined. For example, the National Commission on Productivity suggests five basic measures for gauging improved effectiveness of collection systems which are based on time and weight data. These are:

1. Total tons collected/crew collection hour.
2. Households served/crew collection hour.
3. Cost/ton collected.
4. Cost/household served.
5. People served/truck week.

Clark and Grillean (1974)[56] demonstrates the types of productivity gains which may be achieved by improved data collection and management-control techniques. These include reductions in budget on the order of 50 percent, reduction in crew size and a decrease in service level without a garbage pile-up. Although causation of the benefits are not shown, it appears that both improved management control through better routing and more effective use of productivity measures on truck weight and the like were crucial contributors to improved performance.

Absenteeism as an element in productivity was studied behaviorally by Shell and Shupe (1974) in Covington, Kentucky.[57] By statistically analyzing the personal histories of refuse-collection workers the authors showed the following results: older employees did not have the expected decreased absenteeism; more dependents led to more days away from work; absenteeism was positively related to the number of jobs held previously. Although the results of this effort are limited by the fact that the data base was from one smaller city, they are incisive and provide a base for indicating the value of further analysis of absenteeism, particularly as it relates to different work rules.

Partridge and Harrington (1974)[58] through statistical techniques related collection time per stop to the types of containers being collected. They found that collection was faster on the first trip of the day than on succeeding trips, probably because of fatigue. Like absenteeism, the effect of fatigue on productivity remains a fertile research area.

Through the use of ergonomics—i.e. how the body uses energy and what is a person's capacity for work—the beginnings of research findings are emerging in this regard. For example, Alpern,[59] using these techniques, concludes that proper pacing might increase productivity by 10 percent and that reducing energy per stop tends to raise productivity. Although this effort may be considered primitive it clearly shows the potential for developing models which related easily measured actual body conditions with work productivity in refuse collection.

The effect of different work rules, i.e. total hours and incentives, on productivity was simulated by Wersan (1971) for Winnetka, Illinois (incentive), and Chicago (total hours).[60] The models simulate individual trucks in the collection process, and calculate various efficiency measures for work accomplished. One important result is the suggestion that the variability of waste generation may have a major effect on incentive systems. A simple example of this would be a community with very large seasonal variations in waste generation which tried to use the same task assignments (or districts) all year; the crews would be very underutilized in the months with less generation. Similar problems in task assignments can be expected if the waste on the routes varies greatly from week to week or between routes; use of a total hours system or some higher level incentive system such as weekly route or reservoir routing would be desirable. These tend to equalize the fluctuations so that the crews would not work 10 hours on one day, and $4\frac{1}{2}$ the next. The sort of thing that could happen in a highly variable system.

In the Chicago model relay policies of crews loading multiple vehicles were simulated, and it was found to cost slightly more than the traditional system. But, the policy led to a major decrease in missed collections because on-route productive time was higher.

In a related effort, Tanaka statistically investigated the costs of various payment incentive systems, to improve productivity. Highest efficiency in solid work collection was found to be a total hours system with overtime allowed in some cases for a fixed pickup rate. Remaining unanswered in Tanaka's analysis is the basic tradeoff question of the balance between overtime and incentive time in choosing a fair day's work. It may be concluded that productivity measurements are in the early stages of formulation. Much remains to be accomplished in order to formulate a consistent set of standards for work productivity in solid-waste management.

B. *Crew size and crew schedule*

The key representative study of crew size is by Stone (1969),[61] whose salient aspect is a detailed survey of six garbage-collection systems (four public and two private). A composite or summary result of this work is shown in Fig. 2 which relates collection time to number of cans at each pickup stop for each of the six collection systems. From this figure it may be implied that collection time appears to increase linearly with the number of cans picked up, in all systems with each additional can adding about 0.2 minute for the one-man crews and 0.1 minute for the three-men crew system. The result is that a one-man

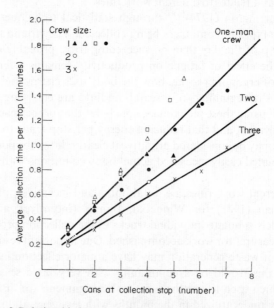

FIG. 2. Relationship between collection time and crew size*. (Source: Stone.[61])

crew system appears to be more efficient, in terms of man-hours per ton collected, than a larger crew of two or three. Two one-man crews, the studies thus indicate, could collect more tons per day than one two-men crew in the communities under study. In all of this, Stone found that the travel time remains constant at about 20 percent of work time.

In another aspect of the study, Stone used time and motion analysis to attempt a model of the collection process, in order to develop standards for the different types of collection. His results here seem to be in agreement with the field survey; however, they are still fairly tentative and relate primarily to more sparsely populated suburban areas. In higher-density areas these results might not be representative.

In the related issue of crew scheduling or the assignment of men to jobs, Shebanek (1974)[62] utilized a questionnaire to determine which crew members liked to work together. These men were grouped together in work teams, and increased productivity was reported for Covington, Kentucky, however, results were not validated elsewhere.

A more formal approach was utilized by Altman and Beltrami (1971)[63] to assign crews for houshold refuse collection in New York City. Their multiple objectives were to design schedules which would effectively meet the demand, cut down on missed collections, lower cost, and also lead to better working conditions by increasing the number of long weekends (at least two days off sequentially, preferably three) and minimizing within the strict union rules on total shifts and hours that a single crew could work per week. Analytically, the approach was in the following programming format:

Let n_i = number of crews assigned to refuse collection for ith shift and jth day

p_{ij} = tons collected/crew for ith shift and jth day.

Then the amount actually collected on day j is q_j

$$q_j = \sum_{i=1}^{2} p_{ij} n_{ij}$$

and the amount of missed collection on the jth day is

$$m_j = \max(f_j + m_{j-1} - q, 0)$$

where f_j = refuse available at curbside of the jth day.
The problem is then

$$\min f(\bar{n}) = 1/2 \sum_{j=1}^{7} mj^2 + \delta C(\bar{n}),$$

$$\text{s.t.} \quad n_{2j}(n_{ij} - M) = 0,$$

$$r_j = N - \sum_i n_{ij}$$

$$5N \le \sum \sum n_{ij} \le 6N$$

$$0 \le n_{ij} \le M$$

$$\sum_{i=1}^{2} n_{ij} \le N$$

where $\bar{n}$ = a vector with 14 components, the n_{ij}'s,

M = max. no. of trucks available on any shift,

r_j = no. of crews on recreation on the jth day,

$C(\bar{n})$ = weekly cost in dollars,

δ = measures relative significance of dollar cost vs. social cost,

N = maximum no. of personnel to be assigned.

Ignall, Kolesar, and Walker (1972)[64] further expanded the linear program model for sanitation crew assignment within similar constraints to the above in the following form:

Let M = number of trucks available,

N = total number of crews assigned to the district,

f_j = amount of refuse, placed on the street just prior to the first shift in day j, $j = 1, 2, \ldots, 7$,

m_j = amount of uncollected refuse at the end of day j,

m_{ij} = number of crews assigned to shift i in day j (our choice), $i = 0, 1, 2$ (0 is non-collection work on day shift, 1 is day shift collection, 2 is night shift collection),

P_{ij} = productivity of one crew on shift i, day j (measured in amount of refuse collection per shift),

c_{ij} = payroll cost of a crew on shift i, day j,

r_j^* = minimum number or crews who will be given day j off, then

Problem I.

minimize

$$\sum_{i=1}^{2} \sum_{j=1}^{7} c_{ij} n_{ij} + w \sum_{j=1}^{7} m_j$$

s.t.

$$n_{ij} \geq 0 \qquad i = 0, 1, 2; j = 1 \ldots 7$$

$$m_j \geq 0 \qquad j = 1 \ldots 7$$

uncollected refuse:

$$m_j \geq m_{j-1} + f_j - \sum_{i=1}^{2} n_{ij} p_{ij} \qquad j = 1 \ldots 7$$

days off:

$$\sum_{i=1}^{2} n_{ij} \leq N - r_j^* \qquad j = 1 \ldots 7$$

truck availability:

$$n_{ij} \leq m \qquad n_{2j} \leq m \qquad j = 1 \ldots 7$$

use of all available crews:

$$\sum_{i=1}^{2} \sum_{j=1}^{7} n_{ij} \geq 5N$$

If we define N_{kij} as the amount of garbage generated on day k that is picked up by crew ij, then by $N_{ij} = \sum_k N_{kij}/P_{ij}$ we get:

Problem II:

minimize
$$\sum_{k=1}^{7} \sum_{j=1}^{7} \sum_{i=1}^{2} N_{kij} t_{kij} + \sum_{j=1}^{7} n_{0j} c_{0j}$$

s.t. $n_{0j} \geq 0 \qquad j = 1 \dots 7$

$N_{kij} \geq 0 \qquad$ for all l, j, k

$$\sum_{j=1}^{7} \sum_{i=1}^{2} N_{kij} = f_k \qquad k = 1 \dots 7$$

$$\sum_{k=1}^{7} (N_{kij}/p_{ij} + N_{k2j}/p_{2j}) + n_{0j} \leq N - r_j^* \qquad j = 1 \dots 7$$

$$\sum_{k=1}^{7} N_{kij}/p_{ij} \leq M \qquad i = 1, 2$$

$$\sum_{j=1}^{7} \sum_{i=1}^{2} \sum_{k=1}^{7} N_{kij}/p_{ij} + \sum_{j=1}^{7} n_{0j} \geq 5N$$

The major problem with both the Beltrami and Ingall studies is the lack of real testing and validation which could result in implementation.

Lofy (1971),[65] applying less formal techniques to the crew assignment problem, showed results which might be implemented more easily. In Table 7, Lofy's results are shown. The main suggestion emerging is to the intentional scheduling of unbalanced work loads such that high productivity crews are assigned to dense areas. This results in a most efficient collection of solid-waste material.

TABLE 7. CREW ASSIGNMENT AND PRODUCTIVITY

		Density of collection route		
		'Dense' (tons/day)	'Average' (tons/day)	'Sparse' (tons/day)
Crew productivity	"high"	14.4	12	9.6
	"medium"	12	10	8.0
	"low"	9.6	8.0	6.4

Route assignment 1: "high" 'sparse' and "low" 'dense' = 9.6 + 9.6 = 19.2 tons.
Route assignment 2: "high" 'dense' and "low" 'sparse' = 14.4 + 6.4 = 20.8 tons.

THEREFORE:
It is better to assign a high productivity crew to a dense area, where collection is easier.

C. Routing

Of the various dimensions of productivity analysis in solid-waste management, the most developed is that of routing. Major efforts have been expended over a long period of time in the following subareas: choice of a fair day's work, route balancing, and minimizing mileage. An entire chapter could be devoted to detailing these efforts alone. However, space consideration permits a mere overview of the state-of-the-art.

The decision as to what makes a reasonable route entails determining equal amounts of work where possible and the method for choosing a fair assignment. Hudson (1973) describes the use of census data, which is readily available for estimating waste generation and collection time.[66] This work parallels the prediction of ambulance demands discerned by Deems (1969) in the study of emergency medical transportation. Betz and Stearns (1966)[67] looked at the choice of the number of services in a day's work and related it to the trade-off between incentive time and overtime. These authors assumed incorrectly, however, that productivity would remain constant, which is not valid.

Route-balancing procedures involve converting work required in any specific area into routes. The basic goal is to define a set of areas which will require equal amounts of work and will also be easy to collect and supervise. Contiguous and compact districts aid in achieving ease of collection and supervision. The many methods developed for this task fall within two classes: those analytically soluble and those soluble by computer. Structurally, at least, route balancing is accomplished analytically using graphs: put the time or quantity requirements per block face on a map and draw boundaries which indicate routes. The computer districting approach does exactly the same thing but requires more preparation of data, and the creation of districts more rapidly. However, many times it is limited by common sense. On balance, Marks reports that computerized methods have not the superiority of graphs for route balancing.

Related to balancing is the question of minimizing mileage, left-hand turns, and going the correct way in a one-way street and safety. Shuster and Shur (1974)[68] developed a method for reducing the number of left-hand turns in a route by making clockwise (right-hand) loops wherever possible. This is shown in Fig. 3.

Stricker and Marks (1971) developed a sequential approach involving districting first and routing second.[69] The basic output is the choice of which streets should be travelled twice and which only once to minimize travel. Liebman followed a slightly different

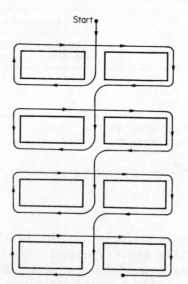

Fig. 3. Routing pattern showing clockwise loops for one-side collection. (Source: Shuster and Shur.[68])

sequential approach.[70] Mileage is first minimized for the whole collection area. Cycles— or groups of blocks—are then derived, each with a required amount of work. Using various criteria such as which streets to travel twice, minimum left-hand turns, etc., mileage can be kept to a minimum. The comparative advantages of the latter approach is in cases of large numbers of blocks per route, otherwise the districting approach might be used first. The problems with both models are: the lack of a solid technical formulation and the lack of any validation.

The last aspect of the routing involves the determination of waste or refuse pickups from fixed points while travelling the least. In the literature this problem is known as node-routing. Marks concludes that the work to date in this aspect of solid waste collection reduces itself to an application of Clarke-Wright's (1964) algorithm. Analytically, the structure of the algorithm is shown below.[71]

Given:

$$X_i \quad = \text{trucks } i = 1 \ldots n,$$

$$C_i \quad = \text{capacity } i = 1 \ldots n,$$

$$Q_j \quad = \text{loads to be determined } j = 1 \ldots m,$$

$$P_j \quad = \text{destination points } j = 1 \ldots m,$$

$$P_0 \quad = \text{depot or origin,}$$

$$d_{y,2} \quad = \text{distance between points } y \text{ and } z.$$

The object is to minimize the total distance covered by the trucks satisfying the capacity and load restrictions. The C_i are ordered such that $C_{i-1} < C_i$ and it is assumed that $C_i \ll \sum_{j=1}^{m} q_j$. The solution technique is based on the Danzig and Ramser method (1959) and is solved by an iterative procedure.

Beltrami and Bodin (1974) extended the basic algorithm to provide greater flexibility in pickups by including containers with different frequencies of location and inserting institutions like schools and restaurants on residential routes.[71] The strength of this approach is that modification, after initial studies are made, is fairly easy. The weakness is in the fact that if starting and ending points of the route are widely separated the model does not work well. By implication, then, it may be said that in denser urbanized areas the model is effective. Clark and Goddard (1973) in a simulation study of Cleveland showed in this regard that costs of hauling refuse increases with declining density.

Summary

Collection, frequency, user costs, and place of pickup were shown to be the basic determining characteristics of service levels on solid-waste collection systems. How these interrelate resulting in improved performance or productivity was shown next. Measurement for productivity involved data items like load weights, collection times, pickup locations, vehicle mileage. Their improved utilization by management would lead to gains in the following dimensions of systems performance: facilities utilization, crew size, crew scheduling, costs of operation, place of pickup, and quality of service. Further evidence marshalled, suggests that higher productivity can be achieved with crews under the incentive system, but that careful management is necessary to give an acceptable quality of service. With a total hours system, higher quality service may be easier to achieve, but the cost also might be higher. Incentive systems may also reduce absenteeism. One basic problem in incentive systems, however, is the balancing of workloads on the different routes. Ergonomics, the study of how energy is used in the body, may give some insight into the size of a reasonable day's work, and routing procedures may aid in generating areas with equal workloads.

Techniques for routing are available which can lead to collection areas with equal workloads and greatly reduce vehicle mileage, without requiring a computer (although they generally were developed for computer implementation). These methods are easy to apply and flexible, and should probably be used if major rerouting is planned. However, to insure efficiency of service delivery, the findings of Greco on work balancing must not be ignored.

For curbside pickup in all but the most congested areas, crew size of two has been shown to be probably sufficient. For backyard pickup, three-man crews have been shown to be desirable. In areas where high densities of waste are found, larger crews may be desirable, although containerization may be an alternative. In terms of crew scheduling, computerized approaches have not been shown to be more effective than structured heuristic and analytical approaches.

The need for future research, ignoring the equipment and technological issues, involves improved evaluation approaches and strategies for implementation.

In the former category, systematic analysis and better evaluation of present operation is involved. A major obstacle to date in this endeavor has been the lack of information which may be easily quantifiable—not an uncommon problem. Management information systems appropriately designed will enable more fruitful research in productivity studies, alternative forms of organizational structure, impact studies of service changes involving frequency, pricing, etc., as well as different site locations.

In the latter category new methods are required for developing: prediction of quantity and composition multi-objective decision procedures for systems design, implementation strategies, new technologies and MIS waste reduction and recovery.

IV. Conclusions

Quantitative policy analysis of essential urban services may be said to have taken great strides toward maturity in the last 15 years. This has resulted in major inroads being cut in two substantive dimensions of urban public administration: public management systems and actual services delivery. Methodologically, these have come about through the increased use of system approaches blending many tools and techniques from various disciplines like economics, operations research, public administration.

The present review of quantitative approaches has focused on a sample set of service delivery problems: specifically, the allocation of men and fire-fighting equipment in fire suppression, transportation in emergency medical services, and solid-waste management. In each case, an attempt was made to provide an in-depth trend analysis revealing how quantitative studies developed to their present state. In addition, attempts were made to report potential benefits to the respective service administrators. A review was thus provided showing in substantial detail a description and explanation of various models forming an integrated picture of the state-of-the-art.

At this point it is imperative to integrate the findings in terms of a composite set of organizational implications for guiding administrators as well as future researchers and students. By generalizing we are sacrificing the essential detail; however, it is felt that a general overview is worth this tradeoff at the conclusion.

First and possibly foremost is the need to develop implementation strategies. At present, public administrators do not see "systems" type studies as part of management. As a result consultants promulgate models and formulate solutions to service delivery problems. The consultants leave and projects dissipate. The net effect is to leave the agency or department no better off than when it started. Without major efforts on organizational implementation problems, little benefit may be expected to accrue in terms of improved performance. As a starting point, improved communication between systems analyst and administrator ought to be a focal point of attention.

Improved information maintenance and retrieval may be considered a correlated requisite if quantitative analysis is to make major contributions to improved urban administration. Two thrusts are conceived in this regard. First, all large-scale model endeavors in service delivery require large-scale data bases that are easily updated. To a large extent these are lacking in most municipalities and/or service delivery jurisdictions. Second, the type of data required for modeling endeavors are not of the same form which administrators consider essential. In the different service areas research needs to be undertaken to define modified information and record-keeping formats to benefit both systems analysts and administrators.

Organization design in service delivery is of major significance. At present in almost all service delivery jurisdiction, an organizational paradox exists. The service is delivered by a multitude of small and semi-independent units on the one hand and a central authority controls on the other. Such patterns of relationships tend to complicate accountability and inhibit the development and utilization of new approaches to problem solving. In order to optimize the limited resources available to municipalities new organizational modes must be studied. Some beginnings have been made in this regard with the various charter revision studies across the nation.

In conclusion, research is necessary to identify the organizational conditions under which systems analysis and operations research tools can be best utilized in the design of management systems and the allocation of men and facilities. Particular emphasis here should be on including administrators in the formulation as well as the implementation strategies for quantitative analysis and the development of common terminologies easily understandable by both technicians and users.

Validation of models and validation criteria for effective performance are most probably the weakest links in model utilization by administrators. This arises because administrators doubt a model's utility. The eventual purpose of validation would be the development of reliable or "proven" software packaging adaptable to a variety of administrative and jurisdictional settings. As a by-product, the resistance to the use of models by administrators would be lessened.

In sum, not enough research attention has been paid to the linkages between mathematically derived optimal solutions and the practical solutions to problems which must be made to work in an organizational setting. This concluding comment has aimed to indicate some of the more salient features involved in suturing the presently broken linkages in order that greater utilization of quantitative approaches may obtain and, thereby, improved service delivery.

References

1. Valinsky, D. "A determination of the optimum location of fire-fighting units in New York City." *Operation Research*, **3**, 494–512 (Nov. 1955).
2. Kolesar, P. and Blum, E. H. "Square root law for response distances." *Management Science*, **19**, 1368–78 (Aug. 1973).
3. Kolesar, P. and Walker, W. E. "Measuring the response characteristics of New York City's fire companies." Draft Report no. R-144 9-NYC, NYC Board Institute, Dec. 1973.
4. Rider, K. L. "A parametric model for the allocation of fire companies: formulation, solution and interpretation." Report no. WN-8551-HUD/NYC, NYC Rand Institute, Mar. 1974.
5. Guild, R. D. and Rollin, J. E. "A fire station placement model." *Fire Technology*, **8**, 1, 33–44 (Feb. 1972).
6. Larson, R. C. and Stevenson, K. A. "On insensitivities in urban redistricting and facility location." *Operations Research*, **20**, no. 3, 595–612 (May–June 1972).
7. Raouf, A. "An evaluation of the placement of fire stations in a city: a case study." Paper presented at the 41st National Meeting, Operations Research Society of America, Apr. 1972.
8. Santone, L. C. and Berlin, G. N. "Location of fire stations." *Systems Analysis for Social Problems*, edited by Blumstein, A., Kamrass, M. and Weiss, A. B., Washington Operations Research Council, 1970.
9. Hogg, J. M. "Planning for fire stations in Glasgow in 1980." Report no. 1/68, U.K. Home Office Scientific Advisory Branch, Oct. 1968.
10. "Station Location Model." Unpublished report of the Metropolitan Dade County (Florida) Fire Department.
11. Mitchell, P. S. "Efficient allocation of fire department resources, Part I." *Fire Technology*, **7**, no. 3, 237–42 (Aug. 1971).
12. Stacey, G. S. "The allocation of resources in municipal fire protection." Unpublished dissertation, Ohio State University, 1973.
13. Swersey, A. J. "A mathematical formulation of the fire engine relocation problem." Report no. D-18682-NYC, NYC Rand Institute, June 1969.
14. Walker, W. E. and Shinnar, S. "Approaches to the solution of the fire engine relocation problem." Report no. D-19519-NYC, NYC Rand Institute, Nov. 1969.
15. Chaiken, J. M. "Suggested algorithm for computerized relocation of fire companies." Report nos. D-19619, D-18682, D-19619, NYC Rand Institute, Mar. 1970.
16. Kolesar, P. and Walker, W. E. "An algorithm for the dynamic relocation of fire companies." Report no. R-1023-NYC, NYC Rand Institute, Sept. 1972.
17. Swersey, A. J. "Models for reducing fire engine response times." Unpublished dissertation. School of Engineering and Applied Science, Columbia University, 1972.
18. Carter, G. M. and Swersey, A. J. "Simulation tests of fire department initial dispatch strategies." Report no. WN-8335-NYC, NYC Rand Institute, Aug. 1973.
19. Carter, G. M. and Rolph, J. "New York City fire alarm prediction models I: Bos reported serious fires." Report no. R-1214-NYC, NYC Rand Institute, May 1973.
20. Carter, G. M., Chaiken, J. M., and Ignall, E. "Response areas for two emergency units." *Operations Research*, **20**, no. 3, 571–94 (May 1972).
21. Ignall, E. "Response areas for fire-fighting units application." Draft working paper, NYC Rand Institute, Mar. 1974.
22. Hisserich, John C., Lave, Lester, and Aldrich, Carole. *An Analysis of the Demand for Emergency Ambulance Service in an Urban Area*, EMS Working Paper no. 2, UCLA, Emergency Medical Systems Project, 1969, 27 pp.
23. Deems, John M. *Prediction of Calls for Emergency Ambulance Service*, Thesis, Atlanta: Georgia Institute of Technology, Aug. 1973, 91 pp.
24. Gibson, Geoffrey, "Evaluative criteria for emergency ambulance systems." *Social Science and Medical Journal*, **7**, 425–54 (1973).
25. Fitzsimmons, James Albert. *Emergency Medical Systems: A Simulation Study and Computerized Method for Deployment of Ambulances*, Dissertation, UCLA, School of Business Administration, 1970, 207 pp.
26. Hoey, Jan Morris. *Planning for an Effective Hospital Administered Emergency Ambulance Service in the City of Boston*, Document No. RR-01-73, Cambridge: Massachusetts Institute of Technology, Operations Research Center, Sept. 1973, 151 pp.
27. Volz, Richard A. *Optimum Ambulance Location in Washtenaw County, Michigan*, Ann Arbor: University of Michigan, Highway Safety Research Institute, 1970, 20 pp.
28. Volz, Richard A. "Optimum ambulance location in semi-rural area." *Transportation Science*, **5** (2), 193–203 (May 1971).

29. Fitzsimmons, James A. "A methodology for emergency ambulance deployment." *Management Science* **19**, 627–36 (Feb. 1973).
30. Savas, E. S. "Simulation and cost-effectiveness analysis of New York's emergency ambulance service." *Management Science*, **15** (12), 608–27 (Aug. 1969).
31. Gordon, Geoffrey and Zelir, Kenneth. "A simulation study of emergency ambulance service in New York City." *Transaction of the New York Academy of Sciences*, **32**(4), 414–27, Series II (Apr. 1970).
32. Swoveland, C., Oyeno, D., Vertinsky, I., and Vickson, R. "Ambulance location: A probabilistic enumeration approach." *Management Science*, **20** (4), 686–98 (Dec.), Part II, 1973.
33. Toregas, Constantine, Swain, Ralph, Revelle, Charles, and Bergman, Lawrence. "The location of emergency service facilities." *Operations Research*, **19**(6), 1363–73 (Oct. 1971).
34. Toregas, Constantine and Revelle, Charles, "Optimal location under time or distance constraints." *Papers of the Regional Science Association*, **28**, 133–43 (1972).
35. Schneider, Jerry B. and Symons, John G. *Locating Ambulance Dispatch Centers in an Urban Region: A Man–Computer Interactive Problem Solving Approach*.
36. Larson, Richard C. and Stevenson, Keith A. *On Insentivities in Urban Redistricting and Facility Location*, Final Report, New York City Rand Institute, 1971, 24 pp.
37. Hoey, *op. cit.*
38. Blum, Mark S., Leonard, Michael S., Pittman, Julian V., and Whelan, David C. *Ambulance Placement Strategies for Emergency Medical Systems*, Atlanta: Georgia Institute of Technology, Health Systems Research Center, (Jan. 1974), 133 pp.
39. Coyle, John W., Blum, Marks S., and Reinbolt, Orien L. *An Improved Emergency Medical System for Metropolitan Atlanta*, 2 vols., Atlanta: Georgia Institute of Technology, Health Systems Research Center, 1973, 566 pp.
40. Keeney, Ralph L. "A method for districting among facilities." *Operations Research*, **20**(3), 613–18 (May–June 1972).
41. Jarvis, James Patrick, *Optimal Dispatch Policies for Urban Sewer Systems*, Document no. TR-02-73, Cambridge: Massachusetts Institute of Technology, Operations Research Center, 1973, 133 pp.
42. Carter, M., Chaiken, Jan, and Ignall, Edward. "Response areas for two emergency units." *Operations Research*, **20**, 571–94 (May–June 1972).
43. Bell, Colin E. and Allen, David, "Optimal planning of an emergency ambulance service." *Socio-Economic Planning Sciences*, **3**, 95–101 (1969).
44. Stevenson, Keith A. *Emergency Ambulance Services in U.S. Cities, An Overview*, Document no. TR-40, Cambridge: Massachusetts Institute of Technology, Operations Research Center (Aug. 1968), 37 pp.
45. Siler, Kenneth F. "A PL/1 model of an emergency medical system." AIS Working Paper no. 73-8, UCLA, Accounting and Informations Research Program, 1972, 19 pp.
46. Hirsch, W. Z. "Cost function of an urban government service: refuse collection." *The Review of Economics and Statistics*, **47**, 87–92 (1965).
47. Marks, David H. *Evaluation of Policy-Related Research in the Field of Municipal Solid Waste Management*, Massachusetts Institute of Technology (Sept. 1974), 364 pp.
48. Environmental Protection Agency, Office of Solid Waste Management Programs. *Decision-Makers Guide in Solid Waste Management*, Cincinnati: USEPA, 1974 (SW-127).
49. Marks, D. H. and Liebman, J. C. *Mathematical Analysis of Solid Waste Collection*, Public Health Service Publication No. 2104, Washington: U.S. Government Printing Office, 1970.
50. Quon, J. E., Tanaka, M., and Charnes, A. "Refuse quantities and frequency of service." *J. San. Eng. Div., Proc. ASCE*, **94**(SA2), 403–20 (Apr. 1968).
51. Clark, R. M., Grupehhoff, B. C., Garland, G. A., and Klee, A. J. "Cost of residential solid waste collection." *J. San. Eng. Div., Proc. ASCE* **97**(SAS), 563–8 (Oct. 1971).
52. McFarland, J. M., Glassey, C. R., McGauhey, P. H., Brink, D. C., Klein, S. A., and Colveke, D. G. *Comprehensive Studies of Solid Waste Management Final Report*, Report 72-3, Sanitary Engineering Research Laboratory, College of Engineering and School of Public Health, University of California, Berkeley, 1972.
53. Stone (Ralph) and Company, Inc. *A Study of Solid Waste Collection Systems Comparing One-Man with Multi-Man Crews*, Public Health Service Publication no. 1892, Washington: U.S. Government Printing Office, 1969.
54. Greco, J. R. "Comparative evaluation of fuel requirements for residential collection service levels." *NSWMA Technical Bulletin*, **5**(1), 1–4 (Jan. 1974).
55. (Ralph) Stone and Company, Inc., *op. cit.*
56. Clark, R. M. and Gillean, J. L. "Systems analysis and solid waste planning." *J. Env. Eng. Div., Proc. ASCE*, **100**(EE1), 7–24 (Feb. 1974).
57. Shell, R. L. and Shupe, D. S. *Personel History and Absenteeism for Solid Waste Collection/Disposal Workers*, Preliminary Report, EPA Grant R801617, May 1974.

58. Partridge, L. J., Jr., and Harrington, J. J. "Multivariate study of refuse collection efficiency." *Journal of Environmental Engineering Division, Proc. ASCE*, **100**(EE4), 963–78 (Aug. 1974).
59. Alpern, R. "Ergonomics and refuse collection." Los Angeles: Bureau of Sanitation (unpublished).
60. Wersan, S., Quon, J. E., and Charnes, A. *Mathematical Modeling and Computer Simulation for Designing Municipal Refuse Collection and Haul Services*, Cincinnati: USEPA, 1971 (S.W. 6r.g., PB-208 154).
61. (Ralph) Stone and Company, Inc., *op. cit.*
62. Shebanek, R. B., Shell, R. L., and Shupe, D. S. "Increase productivity through crew assignment," presented at the American Institute of Industrial Engineers, Inc., 25th Annual Conference and Convention, New Orleans, May 22–4, 1974.
63. Altman, S., Beltrami, E., Rappaport, S., and Schoepfle, G. K. "Nonlinear programming model of crew assignments for household refuse collection." *IEEE Transactions on System Man and Cybernetics*, SMC-1(3), pp. 289–91 (July 1971).
64. Ignall, E., Kolesar, P., and Walker, W. "Linear programming models for crew assignments for refuse collection." *IEEE Transactions on Systems Man and Cybernetics*, SCM2(5), pp. 664–6 (Nov. 1972).
65. Lofy, R. O., "Techniques for the optimal routing and scheduling of solid waste collection vehicles." Unpublished Ph.D. Thesis, University of Wisconsin, 1971 (UN 71-25485).
66. Hudson, J. F., Grossman, P. S., and Marks, D. H. *Analysis Models for Solid Waste Collection*, Research Reports, Research Report R73-47 Department of Civil Engineering, MIT, Cambridge, MA: 1973.
67. Betz, J. M. and Stearns, R. P. "Discussion of simulation and analyses of a refuse collection system by J. T. Quon, A. Charnes, and S. J. Wersan." *J. San Eng. Div. Proc. ASCE*, **92**(SA3), 17–26 (June 1966).
68. Shuster, K. A. and Shur, D. A. *Heuristic Routing for Solid Waste Collection Vehicles*, Cincinnati, United States Environmental Protection Agency, 1974.
69. Stricker, R. and Marks, Ditt. "Routing for public service vehicles." *Journal of Urban Planning and Development Division, Proc. ASCE*, **97**, 165–78 (Dec. 1971).
70. Liebman, J. C. and Male, J. W. *Optimal Routing of Solid Waste Collection Vehicles*, Department of Civil Engineering, University of Illinois, Champaign–Urbana, 1973.
71. Clarke, G. and Wright, J. W. "Schedule of vehicles from a central depot to a number of delivery points." *Operations Research*, **12**, no. 4, 568–81 (July–Aug. 1964).

8. *Police Service and the Criminal Justice System*

JOHN H. HERDER*

Background

Police service in this country developed long before much attention was given to systems. Yet those early departments tended to follow similar paths of development. The evolution of the Department of Police Service in New Haven, Connecticut, is a typical example. Police service started as the night watch during colonial times. Although the night watch varied in its effectiveness over the years, it did serve to deal with the frequent collisions between students in the local college and youths in the town. The night watch also was kept busy settling the disputes that arose whenever a fire broke out in the town. The various fire companies often spent more energy fighting for the right to put out the fire than fighting the fire itself.

Sometime before 1860 the growing city experimented with a day policeman for a short interval, but the innovation proved to be unpopular. By the time the Civil War started, however, the need for a permanent police organization was clear. The presence of large bodies of soldiers with nothing much to do and plenty of money to spend stimulated the rapid development of "rest and rehabilitation" resorts. Violations of law and order became a common occurrence. Bounty jumpers and the bustle of the wartime street scenes aroused the citizens to support the introduction of a police department. New Haven had outgrown the night watch. The innocence of the small Puritan colony was lost for ever.

In 1861 the state legislature passed an act authorizing the city to organize a police department. The initial activity of the new department was patrol. As the city grew, precinct stations were established one by one until there were six altogether. But as the motor car replaced foot patrol and radio replaced the signal light and call box, the precincts closed one by one. Today they are considered to be obsolete.

Surprisingly, shortly after the department was organized in 1861, a number of uniformed officers were ordered into plainclothes and assigned to detective duty. Released from patrol duty, these men were able to devote more time to the investigation of major crimes in the city. It was not until 35 years later, however, that the detective division with three permanent men was officially established.

Inevitably, traffic became a police responsibility. Horse-drawn vehicles set their own pace and generally found their own way. The police department simply handled the licensing tasks. There were 875 public (horse-drawn) vehicles licensed by the department in 1893. Only 25 years later there were 700 automobiles registered in New Haven. In that same year seven pedestrians were killed by automobiles. Handling traffic had become part of police service. In 1924 a traffic commission was established.

* Dr. Herder is head of Herder Associates, a civil systems management consulting firm, Hamden, Connecticut. A former college president and Bell System executive, Dr. Herder has worked extensively with local police departments on organization and operations problems. Dean Goodman, a graduate student at Yale University, assisted in the preparation of this material.

Youth problems have always been a part of police service. The chief of police, writing the year the department was organized, said, "I regret being compelled to notice a constant increase in juvenile offenders in the city, as most of the arrests for theft have been boys under the age of 18 years, and some of them under the tender age of 10 years." Eighty-five years later a youth division was created.

These are some of the landmark events that characterize the evolution of one urban police department. The department started from small beginnings and only gradually and reluctantly acquired those complex structural features and systems characteristics which are so evident today.

Enormous Complex

Police service is recognized today as part of a system called the criminal justice system. To understand the part police service plays in that system, it is advantageous to consider first more general systems in which police and the criminal justice system may be embedded.[1] Policing is a service function.

Many efforts have been made to define and describe the objectives of police service. Most of them, however, are not output oriented, and consequently are difficult to apply to an analysis of the structure of the criminal justice system. For example, the International City Managers Association lists five police objectives[2]:

1. Prevention of criminality.
2. Suppression of crime.
3. Apprehension of offenders.
4. Recovery of property.
5. Regulation of non-criminal conduct.

Another somewhat longer list also illustrates the traditional kinds of objectives statements[3]:

1. Prevention of crime.
2. Investigation of crimes.
3. Apprehension of violators.
4. Presentation of criminals for adjudication.
5. Services to the public.
6. Enforcement of non-criminal ordinances.
7. Regulation of activity within the public way.

A more definitive list, which is output oriented, was prepared by Szanton[4]:

1. Control and reduction of crime.
2. Movement and control of traffic.
3. Maintenance of public order.
4. Provision of public service.

These functions comprise police service in the typical American city. They are part of the service functions performed in the broader urban system. Looking at the urban system as an information system, Charnes *et al.* identifies four main function systems: service, private, public, and management. Beginning with the external environment, the information reaches the system primarily through the urban managers, voluntary organizations, and the media. From these points the information flows reach each of the functions and influence and interact with the elements of service functions, including police.

Charnes defines the four functions in this way:

1. Service function systems—information systems involved in the provision of governmental managed services, such as police and judicial, fire protection, health care, education, transportation, etc.
2. Management function systems—information systems involved in the administration of the urban area, both operational management and strategic management.
3. Private functions systems—information, systems that are privately owned and privately managed, including radio, television, newspapers, telephones, private health systems, etc.
4. Public functions systems—information systems that are non-private and non-public such as religious groups, social clubs, environmental groups, and many others.

As the authors acknowledge, this classification scheme is arbitrary and simplistic. The sharp lines shown in Fig. 1 and implied by the labels create compartments that do not actually exist. One information system blends into others. Moreover, this total design is an area in which there is surprising little formal knowledge. Analytical efforts have focused on isolated systems, as this chapter will amply demonstrate. Largely ignored, for example, are the roles of voluntary organizations, such as auxiliary police and fire, and perhaps even more significantly, private systems, such as private guard services and private investigative services.

The report of the President's Commission on Law Enforcement and Administration of Justice declares that, "The criminal justice system is an enormous complex of operations". One of the models of the criminal justice system[2] prepared for the Commission shows a simplified yet comprehensive view of the movement of cases through the criminal justice system. There are four institutions through which the cases pass: police, prosecution, courts, and corrections.

The process begins with crime. Obviously, there are undetected crimes and unreported crimes. They fall outside this system. Only those crimes observed by the police and those reported to the police that they choose to act upon provide the initial input. The police undertake an investigation, either by the patrolman or plainclothesman, which in some cases leads to an arrest and booking. At this point, the prosecution process begins with the initial appearance and preliminary hearing and the charge.

The process divides into four major pathways: felonies, misdemeanors, petty offences, and juvenile offenses. The juvenile process represents a separate process in which the police have substantial leeway to handle, more so than the adult processes. Police often hold informal hearings and dismiss or adjust many juvenile cases without further processing.

In the cases of felonies and misdemeanors the charge is filed by the prosecutor on the basis of information submitted to him by the police or by citizens. The information step is an alternative to grand jury indictment. Some states have no grand jury system; other states seldom use the grand jury. The information step is often used in felonies, and is almost always used in misdemeanors. The indictment leads to arraignment, trial, and sentencing.

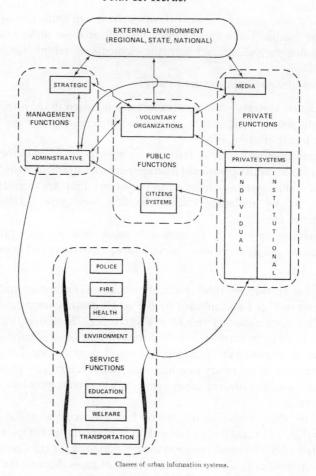

Classes of urban information systems.

FIG. 1. Classes of urban information systems.

At this point the corrections process begins. Corrections involves both imprisonment and probation. And often, in the case of felonies and juvenile offenses, parole is used. Finally most cases finally move out of the system.

Actually, cases are disposed of at various points in the system. The differing weights of line indicate the relative volume of cases disposed of along the way, but this is only suggestive since no nationwide data to support these weights exists. Some cases are simply not solved or the individual is not arrested. In some cases, the arrested person is released without prosecution or the charges are dropped or dismissed. A grand jury may refuse to indict. Of course, once tried the accused may be acquitted.

This system was not designed or built in one piece at one time. As time has passed, layer upon layer of institutions and procedures have accumulated. Parts of the system, such as the magistrates' court, trial by jury, and bail, are part of a long cultural heritage. Other parts—juvenile courts, probation and parole, even the professional policeman himself— are relatively new. As a whole the system represents an adaptation of the English common law to the American political system.

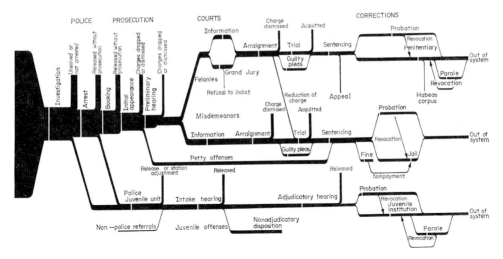

FIG. 2. A general view of The Criminal Justice System.

Since the landmark study by the President's Commission on Law Enforcement and Administration of Justice, numerous attempts have been made to define and describe the system more accurately. It quickly became evident as the thinking developed and models were proposed that the "enormous complex" was not a single "criminal justice system" but a number of systems and an even greater number of interrelationships. The purpose of this chapter is to describe the police service system, illustrate a number of the subsystems that have been developed since the commission study and, finally, identify the important elements of the system that have yet to be incorporated in the analyses.

Police Patrol

Patrol is the core activity of police service. The patrol force is primarily responsible for the prevention of crime and the protection of life and property. The effectiveness of patrol service depends in large measure on the extent to which patrol activities are successful in removing or at least reducing opportunities to commit crime. A police department tries to deploy its patrol manpower in such a way as to create the impression of omnipresence. When criminal incidents occur despite preventive patrol efforts, then the patrol conducts an investigation of the incident, hopefully to identify and arrest the perpetrator.

Beyond the control of crime itself, patrol forces control the flow of traffic, enforce traffic laws, and investigate accidents. Because of the volume and character of traffic work, a separate organization within the police department usually is created to handle this work. Patrol also provides citizen services such as first aid, emergency escort, settling domestic disputes, quieting noisy parties and handling lost and found property.

Police patrol activities include ten general tasks:

1. Patrolling—usually in radio patrol cars and sometimes on foot, the patrolman moves about his assigned sector seeking to reduce the opportunity for potential offenders to violate the law successfully. Deterrence through ever-present police patrol and the

prospect of speedy police action once a report is received are important to crime control and a sense of community security.

2. Observing—the patrolman tries to know the habits of people living in his sector and to be familiar with the streets, yards, alleys in each neighborhood. He seeks to discover open doors and windows, unsafe conditions, questionable characters, and traffic violators.

3. Supervising public gatherings—the patrolman frequently is assigned to attend or be near public meetings or events. He also supervises spontaneous gatherings at a fire or an accident or other incident to maintain order and, if necessary, prevent violence.

4. Providing field services—a citizen may personally contact an officer on patrol and request help. The patrolman regularly inspects business establishments (the "door check") and homes on his beat that are temporarily left vacant. He may give directions or offer assistance. He often renders first aid.

5. Answering complaints—most requests for police services come from citizens who telephone police headquarters. The patrolman is dispatched to every conceivable type of emergency. Since the police department functions 24 hours a day, 7 days a week. it is often the only governmental agency the citizen can turn to for help when he needs it.

6. Investigating—in large police departments the tasks of police investigation are usually divided between patrol and detectives. The patrolman performs only the preliminary investigation and the detailed follow-up is performed by the detective.

7. Collecting and preserving evidence—the patrolman is responsible for preserving as nearly as possible in the condition he finds it evidence at a crime scene. Careful identification and preservation of physical evidence is an essential part of successful prosecution of offenders.

8. Arresting offenders—most of the arrests a patrolman makes are at or near the scene of a crime. He may on occasion also make an arrest by warrant.

9. Preparing reports—a vital product of the work of a patrolman is the incident report or accident report that he prepares. A substantial amount of a policeman's time is spent writing reports of his activity.

10. Presenting court testimony—the patrolman is often a witness in criminal cases. He not only testifies about the evidence of the case, he also must be prepared to answer cross-examination. The efforts of a police officer in enforcing the law are ultimately fulfilled by the successful prosecution of a case in court.

Because of its crucial role in law enforcement and in public attitudes about police service, the patrol function has been the subject of study and analysis for many years. One of the earliest proponents of measuring police performance in some systematic fashion was O. W. Wilson. He advocated using a set of hazard formulas—situations that might potentially require police service—to determine the allocation of police manpower. In order to assign his patrol force in response to a frequency distribution of incidents, or hazards, requiring police attention, Wilson notes that the police administrator must rely on accurate information, i.e. the total flow of data to the police chief that will enable him to plan effectively.[6] The need for management information has led to the development of rather technical police information and statistics systems in many departments.

The allocation of a police patrol force is essentially a problem involving the optimal utilization of a scarce resource and in this sense can be viewed as a strict administrative policy decision made by the police chief in response to his overall objectives. Larson[7] examines in some detail the structure and performance of a hypothetical police response system. In situations involving calls for service the optimal police response is the one that minimizes delay time between the request for and the arrival of police service. To accomplish this Larson suggests that the administrator implement various operational policies to (1) reduce the average travel time; (2) limit dispatcher error probability; (3) minimize the necessity of complaint queueing; (4) cut down on non-essential paperwork. He goes on to explain that the administrative decisions involved in pursuing these objectives are largely based on some measure of cost-benefit analysis.

Average travel time can be reduced in several ways. Many of the alternatives are, however, costly. Frequently, it is not feasible, due to budgetary constraints, to simply increase the number of available patrol units. A more realistic approach is one that considers the utilization of patrol units on hand in a more advantageous manner. Larson, considering this problem in a model he refers to as a "patrol allocation algorithm", examines travel time models that are within the control of the police administrator. The administrator can control the shape of the sectors which must be patrolled. Assuming that the positions of the patrol unit and the incident are independent and uniformly distributed and that travel distance is right-angle, indicating an urban street grid, it is mathematically demonstrated that for comparable sectors, elliptical formats have the lowest mean travel time. Next in order are diamond-shaped sectors and finally rectangular forms.[8] This is not by any means a compelling argument for adopting a patrol plan using only elliptical sectors. Irregular shapes imposed upon an urban grid are likely to produce wasteful overlaps, and furthermore, these models consider a plan involving only intra-sector dispatching.

Larson considers models that would allow intersector dispatching. Such a format, however, challenges the traditional concept of sector/beat identity. The police administrator must assess the trade-off between potential reduced response time versus the loss of sector identity before making a policy decision in this area. Larson suggests, in his analysis, that intersector dispatching is preferable to sector identity. Certain traditional concepts of one man, one sector are, he notes, brought to question by results predicting large amounts of intersector dispatching, and the predicted amounts have been verified through experiment. Sector identity should perhaps be replaced by some sort of regional identity. Or, even more drastically, the very method of assigning units to rigid, non-overlapping areas should be discarded. Some type of overlapping sector plan would acknowledge that delivery of police service to an area is the responsibility of several units. It would provide a more continuous level of preventive patrol and could not significantly change anticipated travel time as long as some sort of compensatory repositioning, either uniform or fixed-point, is utilized.[9]

In terms of limiting dispatcher error probability, the probability of dispatching other than the closest car with present manual dispatching systems is a function of sector geometry, utilization factors, and the type of position estimation being used. Using an automatic car locator model, a reduction in travel time resulting from the near elimination of dispatcher error should average between 10 and 20 percent. The gain here is, however, difficult to quantify fully, and consequently, the cost justification for implementing an automated command and control system is one which the police administrator finds difficult to determine.

Another mathematical approach to the question of police resource allocation can be found in Shumate and Crowther.[10] They consider the problem of dispatcher delay queueing in terms of event probabilities, thereby providing the police administrator with useful clues about the likelihood of any outcome for a given demand situation. The model they use assumes strict intra-sector dispatching and relies upon past data from various departments to reach certain important value coefficients. They determined that the average time to service any call, i.e. perform a task, is 25 minutes, and the average rate at which events requiring police attention occur is .018 per minute.[11]

$$P(n/x) = \frac{e^{-x}x^n}{n!}$$ (the probability of some number of events—n—occurring where the average rate per unit time is known)

It can be shown that:

$$P(0/.45) = .638$$

$$P(1/.45) = .287$$

$$P(2/.45) = .064$$

$$P(3/.45) = .010$$

This model shows that the probability of the second event occurring while the first is still being serviced is .287. Another way of expressing this is to say that 28.7 percent of the events that occur will have to be delayed while the patrol unit finishes servicing the event it is already working on. If 800 events occur in any given time period, then 28.7 percent or 230 of them will experience a delay of $12\frac{1}{2}$ minutes in receiving service. The figure of $12\frac{1}{2}$ is reached by taking an average of the 25-minute time allocation allotted to each service call—a reasonable estimate since it is impossible to predict when in the 25-minute period the second event will occur. By similar calculations it can be shown that the probability of two events occurring in the 25-minute period during which a call for service is being answered is .064. The response to 6.5 percent of all calls will be delayed by $37\frac{1}{2}$ minutes ($12\frac{1}{2}$ plus an additional 25 minutes to service the first call waiting in queue).[12]

Once the probability of one or more additional events occurring before the first can be serviced has been calculated, a measure of the frequency and size of delays that will be encountered can be made.[13]. An even more precise method is suggested in which the model considers the fact that while tasks are waiting in queue the probability of additional events occurring increases. Table 1 is derived from calculating the probability of "n" events being in queue awaiting service when any event occurs. This calculation is done using a constant which expresses the ratio between the average interarrival gap and the average time required to service an event (25 minutes) (Table 1). By using a table of values for this constant, i.e. varying the interarrival gap times through policy formulations such as sector changes, patrol strength increases, etc., many useful questions can be answered regarding the likelihood of delays of varying magnitude occurring.[14]

Patrol effort is generally proportional to reported crime occurrence; but at the same time police administrators agree that the intercept probability for patrol is very small. Larson, in an optimal random patrol model, notes that the probability of a patrol car passing the scene of a crime of duration 3 minutes is less than 12 percent; detection, of course, is far less likely. The probability of intercepting a crime of duration 1 minute could not be expected to exceed 1 in 60. There are at least two important implications of this result. First, the task of detecting crimes in progress cannot be assigned solely to patrol. Second, the crime-deterrent aspect of patrol is brought into question.[15] Consequently, police must rely upon cooperative citizens, alarm devices, and other detectors to increase the detection/ apprehension probability associated with crime.

TABLE 1.

Number of events	Delay in minutes	Probability of exactly *n* events	Probability of *n* or less	Probability of *n* or more
0	0	0.5450	0.5450	1.000
1	12.5	0.3140	0.8590	0.4550
2	37.5	0.1041	0.9631	0.1410
3	62.5	0.0278	0.9909	0.0369
4	87.5	0.0069	0.9978	0.0091
5	112.5	0.0017	0.9995	0.0022
6	137.5	0.0004	0.9999	0.0005
7	162.5	0.0001	1.0000	0.0001
8	187.5	0.0000	1.0000	0.0000

In the tradition of O. W. Wilson, who was once Superintendent of the department, the Chicago, Illinois, Police Department has developed effective systems techniques for the allocation of resources.[16] An Operations Research Task Force was established in 1968. It consisted of four civilian analysts and seven police officers. The approach of the task force to the problem of resources allocation was[17]:

1. Understand Chicago as an environment in which law-enforcement activities take place.
2. Examine overall police resource allocation in the light of community criteria.
3. Analyze the functional aspects of law enforcement response to calls for police service and aggressive preventive patrol.

The major activities of police service are analyzed in three subsystems: response force, preventive force and the follow-up force.[18] The *response force* is the police subsystem which responds to calls for service (the "complaint call"). The probability that the response force will apprehend an offender is a function of the time elapsed between the time the crime is committed and detected, the department is called, the call processed by the dispatcher and the travel time of the assigned car. Evidence indicates that the apprehension probability is a decreasing function with respect to elapsed time.[19]

The preventive force is essentially the patrol function described above. That is, the preventive force tries to give the impression through policemen in uniform and driving marked cars of omnipresence. The preventive force does premise checking, inspecting parked cars for valuables, removing drunks from the street, etc.

The follow-up force seeks to apprehend criminals through the investigative process. It also handles the case following the booking of an offender.

Figure 3 illustrates the interactions of these three forces in police functions as they are conceptualized in the Chicago Police Department.

The outputs of the reactive force are arrest and service to the public. The probability of arrest is expressed as a function of elapsed time and the tactics used. The outputs of the preventive force are arrests and the impact on the decision to act. The probability of apprehension is a function of elapsed time, probability of detection and tactics used. The outputs of the preventive force are arrests and the impact on the decision to act. The probability of apprehension is a function of elapsed time, probability of detection and tactics used. The output of the follow-up force is arrest, the probability of which is

Development of Police Systems Inputs and Outputs

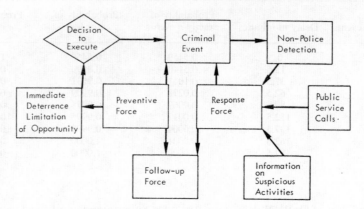

FIG. 3. Development of police systems inputs and outputs.

dependent on elapsed time and methods used. Finally, all of these functions are dependent on the type of crime.

With this frame of reference in mind, the task force sought how to best assign patrolmen to police districts "so as to cause the average crime rate in a city to be as small as possible". The mathematical model used for achieving this distribution is presented by Shoup and Dosser.[20]

The Shoup-Dosser model assumes the city to be divided into two sectors with corresponding average rates Z_1 and Z_2. The average crime rate is the number of crimes of a specific type committed over a set time interval, such as a police watch (an 8-hour shift). The effectiveness of a patrolman is different in each sector. This is accommodated by the constant numbers K_1 and K_2. If t policemen are assigned to sector one, they will have effectiveness tk_1. When t policemen are assigned to sector one, the average crime rate in that sector is Z_2/tk_1. Therefore, the total average rate for the two-sector city is

$$\frac{Z_1}{tk_1} + \frac{Z_2}{(T-t)k_2}. \tag{1}$$

To be applicable to a city like Chicago, the problem becomes determining the best distribution of T policemen in a large number of sectors. This is determined by means of a more general solution.

General Solution

Consider the following definitions:

n: number of police districts in the city,

i: the police district number $i = 1, \ldots, n$,

Z_1: average number of crimes (per unit time) in police district i ($i = 1, \ldots, n$),

k_i: an effectiveness constant for a patrolman in district i,

t_i: the number of patrolmen assigned to district i.

The object is to minimize the total average crime rate in the city with a fixed total police force of T. Therefore, we wish to minimize.

$$\sum_{i=1}^{n} \frac{Z_i}{t_i k_i} \tag{2}$$

subject to

$$\sum_{i=1}^{n} t_i = T. \tag{3}$$

Form

$$F = \sum_{i=1}^{n} \frac{Z_i}{t_i k_i} + \lambda \left(\sum_{i=1}^{n} t_i - T \right) \tag{4}$$

and obtain the set of $n + 1$ equations

$$\frac{\partial F}{\partial t_i} = -\frac{Z_i}{t_i^2 k_i} + \lambda = 0, \quad i = 1, \ldots, n. \tag{5a}$$

$$\sum_{i=1}^{n} t_i - T = 0. \tag{5b}$$

From (5a) it follows that,

$$t_i = \sqrt{\frac{Z_i}{\lambda k_i}} \quad i = 1, \ldots, n. \tag{6}$$

and

$$\sum_{i=1}^{n} t_i^2 = \sum_{i=1}^{n} \frac{Z_i}{\lambda k_i}. \tag{7}$$

Solving for λ in expression (7) gives,

$$\lambda = \frac{\displaystyle\sum_{i=1}^{n} \frac{Z_i}{k_i}}{\displaystyle\sum_{i=1}^{n} t_i^2}. \tag{8}$$

Now

$$\sum_{i=1}^{n} t_i^2 = T^2 - 2 \sum_{i<j} t_i t_j. \tag{9}$$

From (6)

$$t_i t_j = \frac{1}{\lambda} \sqrt{\left(\frac{Z_i Z_j}{k_i k_j} \right)}. \tag{10}$$

Substituting (10) into (9) and then substituting (9) into (8) gives

$$\lambda = \frac{\displaystyle\sum_{i=1}^{n} \frac{Z_i}{k_i}}{T^2 = \frac{2}{\lambda} \displaystyle\sum_{i<j} \sqrt{\left(\frac{Z_i Z_i}{k_i k_j} \right)}}. \tag{11}$$

Solving (11) for λ gives

$$\lambda = \frac{\sum_{i=1}^{n} \frac{Z_i}{k_i} + 2 \sum_{i<j} \sqrt{\left(\frac{Z_i Z_j}{k_i k_j}\right)}}{T^2}$$

$$= \frac{1}{T^2} \left(\sum_{i=1}^{n} \sqrt{\frac{Z_i}{k_i}} \right)^2. \tag{12}$$

Finally substituting λ from (12) into (6) gives the optimum distribution of the t_i over the n districts to minimize the average crime rate,

$$t_i = T \frac{\sqrt{\frac{Z_i}{k_i}}}{\left(\sum_{i=1}^{n} \sqrt{\frac{Z_i}{k_i}} \right)} \quad \text{for } i = 1, \dots, n. \tag{13}$$

Additional refinements are possible. Normalizing each district, adding the risk to the individual and introducing a weighted crime index can be made part of the analysis. The calls for service in a sector can be normalized per policeman by dividing the events by the size of the assigned force, C_1 and C_2. The risk to the individual can be taken into account by dividing the population in the sector, D_1 and D_2.

$$\frac{t_1}{t_2} = \sqrt{\left(\frac{Z_1 K_2 C_2 D_2}{C_1 D_1 K_1 Z_2} \right)}$$

or, to simplify notations,

Let

$$Z_1^* = \frac{Z_1}{C_1 D_1}$$

so that

$$\frac{t_1}{t_2} = \sqrt{\left(\frac{Z_1^* K_2}{K_1 Z_2^*} \right)}$$

The Z_1 reflect different types of crimes which may have differing levels of seriousness to the people in the community. If in Sector 1 there are A crimes of weight a, B of weight b, C of weight c, etc., then the weighted crime index for the district becomes

$$Z_{1w} = aA + bB + cC + \dots$$

and the optimal allocation becomes

$$\frac{t_1}{t_2} = \sqrt{\left(\frac{Z_{1w}^* K_2}{K_1 Z_{2w}^*} \right)}.$$

Figure 4 shows a schematic representation of the effect of using a 6708-man force in the Chicago Police Department under conditions of "equal efficiency" (described above) and "different efficiency" (the ratio of felony arrests to manpower).

Incidentally, this discussion of allocating police patrol resources is from the report of the Operations Research Task Force of the Chicago Police Department entitled *Allocations of Resources in the Chicago Police Department*.[21] The report represents an excellent case

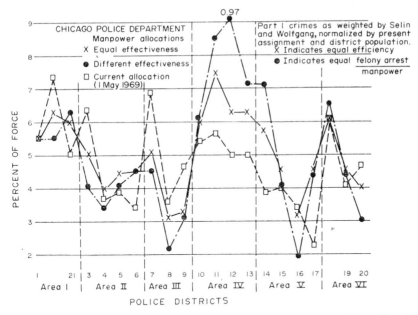

FIG. 4. Schematic model of Chicago patrol force allocation using "equal effectiveness" and "different effectiveness" conditions against Part I or "index crime". Allocations use weighted workloads but are not subjected to a mathematical optimization process. In the diagram crossed lines denote "equal effectiveness" assignments; circled lines denote "different effectiveness" resulting from the ratio of felony arrests/manpower. The Part I crimes are weighted according to Selin and Wolfgang and normalized by present assignment and district population. Current allocations, square-marked lines, are accurate for May of 1969.

study of a major police department. Covered are such topics as allocating patrol resources, the police response function, the preventive function, a demonstration experiment in resource allocation involving strategic patrol and PPBS as an allocation tool.

Police Information Systems

The flow of information is one of the important factors in shaping the police function. The police administrator is dependent upon the flow of data on which to base his decisions regarding future police directions. Two basic kinds of information are essential to his decision-making task:

Operational data—field data; measures of the effectiveness of regular operating procedures and of meeting demands imposed by unusual occurrences.

Management data—budgetary, fiscal, and manpower allocations; personnel staffing and organizational structuring; training needs; community attitudes and relations; criminal justice system integration and coordination.

The two organizational divisions in a police department that have the greatest responsibility for assembling, organizing, and evaluating information are the records and communications unit (in some departments these functions appear in separate units) and the planning unit. As a part of a larger administrative process, planning is designed to answer questions about efficiency, policy alternatives, and the effectiveness of new techniques. Planning is a bridge between the management of police services and police operations.

ALERT I operated by the Kansas City, Missouri, Police Department is an example of a records and communications system that provides essential operational and management data for police decision-making. ALERT I employs seven subsystems:

1. Court docket system—docket and officer notification.
2. Arrest system—statistics and histories.
3. Offense report system—name of victim and statistics and history of incident.
4. Criminal information system—warrants, wants, and warnings.
5. Traffic-ticket system.
6. Vehicular accident-report system.
7. Applicant system—licenses obtained through the police department.

Information is readily accessible to police personnel through the use of remote terminals. Like any records and communications system, ALERT I enables the department to execute several important functions: (1) general communications; (2) the processing and storage of information; (3) accessing of information for investigative functions; (4) dispatching of personnel in crime prevention work; (5) the development of a management information base for evaluation and planning. But in contrast to a manual system, ALERT I is able to reduce response time by eliminating manual intervention and limiting dependence on the dispatcher. By producing hard copy at the terminal, it eliminates the repetition of information requests. With respect to the patrol function, it reduces the administrative duties of the patrol officer by gathering information at the time of occurrence, and furthermore it enhances privacy and security by reducing voice communications.

One element in a fully computerized police data system that has been slow in developing is the vehicle locator. If patrol cars are to be dispatched efficiently and expeditiously, the dispatcher must know exactly where the cars are at all times. In the typical manual dispatch system this is not possible. The impressive locator boards displayed in front of the dispatcher can show by sectors whether a patrol car is available for assignment, on assignment, or not available for assignment. They cannot show the specific location of the patrol car. The only way a dispatcher knows where a car is located is to ask the operator. In a busy communication center this is time consuming and frustrating.

Several means of vehicle monitoring have been explored: triangulation, where a series of radio antennas help to locate the vehicle; the signpost method, which identifies a vehicle's location each time it drives by a signpost; and a digital input procedure, where the patrol officer is responsible for indicating his own location from time to time.

FLAIR (Fleet Location and Information Retrieval system) uses inertial guidance or dead reckoning to monitor car locations.[22] This is being developed for the Wichita, Kansas, Police Department. The design goal of the system is to provide accuracy to within plus or minus 50 feet for 95 percent of the time. Other design goals were to display locations of all vehicles in the fleet on a city-wide basis as well as on an incident-oriented basis, provide vehicle identification, and whether it is in or out of service. The system transmits the so-called "10 code" (officer in trouble or in an emergency situation) and indicates the exact location of this problem. Finally, the system displays either in real-time or at time-collapse speed the situations that occurred the day before.

The use of computer technology facilitates the adoption of a systems approach to the problem of traffic engineering, one of the more easily quantifiable functions sometimes assigned to the police. With two very clear goals in mind—ensuring maximum safety and promoting the facility of use—police and traffic engineers can deal with the traffic problem as an input–output relationship. By accumulating statistical data regarding accidents, violations, parking, and traffic flow, the trained analyst can offer specific recommendations for traffic planning. Accident occurrence can be plotted on a grid showing the precise location where existing traffic patterns and usages have caused unsafe conditions to develop. Specific recommendations for police-enforcement actions or traffic repatterning can be made. Similarly, suggestions for the placement of traffic-control devices—stop signs and lights, one-way streets, warnings, etc.—can be made on the basis of hard data. Of equal importance is the fact that certain outputs of this system serve as important court information inputs. The processing of traffic offenders can be expedited by the utilization of computerized data.[23]

Another vital aspect of police work that has recently come to be dealt with in a systems approach is manpower management.[24] The recruitment and selection of new police officers is significantly aided by the comprehensive processing of results collected from tests, character investigations, psychological examinations, and medical reports. Data can be gathered that will apprise the police administrator of special skills or significant deficiencies that any of the men in his command may possess. Having some indication of skills, aptitude, and motivational levels, enables the police administrator to make important decisions shaping the careers of the men he commands. Certain types of training—compensatory or otherwise—can be suggested. Assessments of promotional potential and leadership ability can be more accurately rendered. Information regarding a man's field performance can be assembled to give an indication of his ability to perform under stress conditions. Information useful in structuring a career development approach can facilitate the implementation of experimental techniques in police system organization. Related tasks can be consolidated into various functions-oriented command units. Greater specialization can be encouraged by creating different grades within the various ranks. Efforts can be made to develop a better working environment for the performance of police duties.

Another model for the use of specialized technology in police work is known as the COPPS (computer-oriented police planning system) management information technique[25] (Fig. 5). This model stresses an approach that enables the planner to monitor workload statistics compared with available police resources and then to arrive at estimates for meeting future police assignments and priorities.

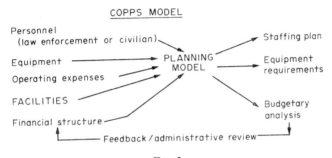

COPPS MODEL

Fig. 5.

The many-layered and partitioned criminal justice system often creates problems where the separate institutions interface. The problems often become acute with the passage of time, as institutions change and conditions in the environment change. An example of a systems study that attempted to overcome the problems at the institutional interface is the systems analysis of prisoner transportation in Connecticut.[26]

Transporting prisoners is a problem that has been shared by the police departments in the state of Connecticut for many years. The problem was particularly serious for the smaller departments that do not have overnight lock-up facilities. But all the departments shared in the responsibility for transporting their prisoners from the lock-ups to the courts and return.

The task of moving prisoners back and forth was costly in time and manpower for the local police departments. In smaller departments the loss of two or more officers for most of a day represented a serious drain on patrol and traffic manpower.

The study defined and examined in detail three existing "systems" of prisoner transportation: transporting prisoners to and from the Circuit Courts, performed by the local police, among others; transporting prisoners to and from the Superior Courts, performed by the sheriffs, among others; and transporting prisoners to and from the courts and state correctional institutions, performed by the Correction Department.

One of the central issues was the legal responsibility with respect to inmates while in courts, detentions, prisons, etc. It turned out that no single agency had overall responsibility for the transportation of prisoners within the state. The study reviewed the statutes and recommended the desired changes, based primarily on the results of the systems analysis.

In order to develop as realistic a model of prisoner movement as possible, data were collected from actual prisoner-movements statistics between correctional institutions, courts, and police departments. The data were tabulated on the IBM 1130 computer and flow models of prisoner movement were developed and tested on the CDC 6600 computer. In order to determine the best routing to move prisoners to area collection points, the problem was adapted to the solution of the "Transshipment Problem" as reported by Order.[27] This method of solution is an extension of the linear programming technique of solving transportation problems involving shipment of goods from origin points to destinations. The technique produced optimal routes for moving prisoners to collection points. Two separate networks were developed—the local network which collected prisoners from the police departments and dropped them off at local courts; and statewide network which moved prisoners from the correctional institutions to the local courts.

Courts and the Criminal Justice System

Much of the effort of the police is aimed at the successful prosecution and conviction of the criminal. In order to show the relationships between the police and the courts, several systems applications to the court functions are examined.

Every component of the criminal justice system depends upon access to information in the performance of its functions. Consequently, systems that can accomplish the vital functions of gathering, accessing, processing, and evaluating data are of great value. Computer technology is presently being used by the Office of the United States Attorney General to expedite prosecution. This system, known as PROMIS (Prosecutor's Management Information System), provides several important kinds of information: (1) defendant,

(2) crime data, (3) arrest data, (4) charge data, (5) court processing data. The availability of this information facilitates investigative work, aids in coordination with Federal level prosecution and also helps the Attorney General and his staff monitor the workload and performance of Federal prosecutors.[28] Through the use of simulation models, it is possible to make projections of the impact of administrative policy decisions on the performance of the prosecutor's office, i.e. the impact of increasing manpower resources at the prosecutor, investigator, clerk, etc., level.

Another systems-oriented approach to the administration of justice is COURTRAN, a model designed by the Federal Judicial Center. COURTRAN is a software computer system that provides information-support services for court management. It stores data pertaining to (1) criminal court operations; (2) civil court operation; (3) criminal court research; (4) civil court research. It tabulates various administrative costs incurred in the court on the basis of specific court function, e.g. cost of fixed overhead expense, salaries, cost per type of prosecution, cost of administrative delay, etc. In effect, COURTRAN is a high-level programming language designed to interpret and execute various statements made through court documents. Despite its seemingly great value as a tool for improved court management, it has been extremely limited in its implementation by the fact that technology has traditionally been forced to accommodate itself to the existing environment.

Much of the introduction of technological advances into criminal justice administration has been accomplished through the creation of information networks linking several related functions in the overall system. One such example is the Florida Crime Information Center (FCIC). The FCIC provides law-enforcement officials with two basic kinds of computerized data; on-line and off-line. The on-line information includes (1) wanted persons; (2) criminal histories; (3) vehicle information; (4) property information. The off-line information, which is accumulated and stored through a batch processing technique, includes (1) intelligence information; (2) uniform crime report information; (3) state investigative reports; (4) budgetary information and other administrative aids.

One of the most significant aspects of FCIC is that it is interfaced with other computerized state and national files, e.g. vehicle registrations, motor vehicle data, NCIC, and SEARCH, to create a rather broad information base for administrative tasks in criminal justice. This approach is a significant step toward the development of a total criminal justice system.

Toward a Total Criminal Justice System

There are two basic approaches that can be taken in formulating a model for a total criminal justice system. One views the criminal justice system as a simple production process—a linear accumulation of costs flowing from a single arrest (Fig. 6). This linear approach is essential to an economic analysis of crime.[29]

Another approach, referred to as the feedback model, measures the cost to the system per criminal career as a function of the probability of some given measure of success, e.g. recidivism rates, against certain variables (Fig. 7). This feedback model shows how the system performs in relations to the measure of recidivism. By utilizing a crime-switch matrix[30] (a tool for determining the likelihood that any arrestee will be rearrested for one of the seven FBI Index crimes), the recidivism probability can be determined and the subsequent cost of the system for any arrestee who is released at a given state in the criminal

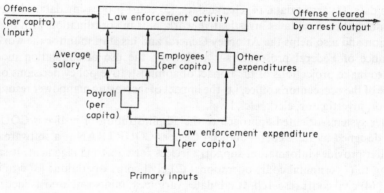

FIG. 6.

justice process is estimated. This model, of course, has several limitations. Future criminal behavior is assumed to be a function solely of age, previous offense, and disposition—a broad statement. Also, the delay between arrests is viewed as being exclusively a function of the disposition. While these assumptions are clearly too sweeping, the overall model seems to have some validity as a tool in the planning process provided that necessary inputs can be quantified in some fashion.[31]

A steady-state linear model can be used to compute costs and workloads at the various processing stages and to establish manpower requirements to meet these expected workloads. The workload can be defined as the annual demand for service at the various processing stages (courtroom hours, detective man-hours, etc.); the manpower requirements are derived from the workload by dividing the annual working time per man (or other resource); total operating costs are allocated to offenders by standard cost-accounting procedures.

The independent flow vector to the model, which must be specified as input, is the number of crimes reported to police during one year. The outputs are the computed flows, costs, and manpower requirements that would result if the system were in steady state. Each processing stage is characterized by vector cost rates (per unit flow) and branching probabilities (or ratios). The input flow at each processing stage is separated into the appropriate output flows by element-by-element vector multiplication of the input flow and the branching probability where

$F_{i,m}$ = number of offenders associated with crime-type i entering processing stage m during one year,

$F_{i,mn}$ = number of offenders associated with crime-type i following route n out of processing stage m, and

$P_{i,mn}$ = probability that an offender associated with crime-type i input at stage m will exit through route n ($\sum_n P_{i,mn} = 1$).

A look at the prosecution and courts submodel of the linear production system allows us to see a schematization of this process (Fig. 8). This submodel calls for four classes of branching probabilities which refer to:

1. Whether or not the defendant reaches the trial stage.
2. The type of trial (or whether dismissed at trial stage).

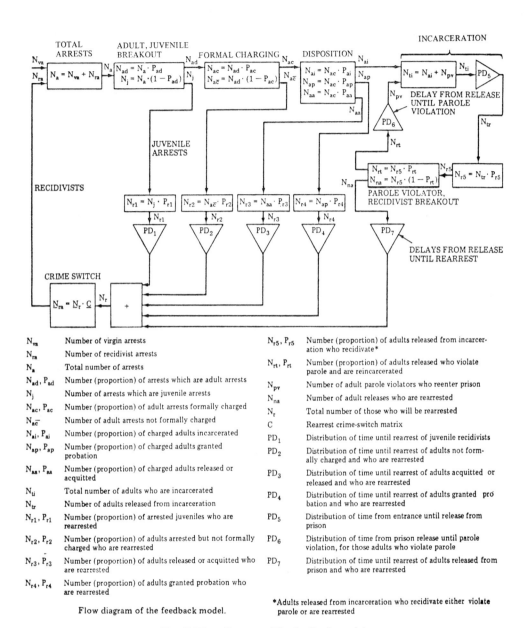

Flow diagram of the feedback model.

N_{va}	Number of virgin arrests
N_{ra}	Number of recidivist arrests
N_a	Total number of arrests
N_{ad}, P_{ad}	Number (proportion) of arrests which are adult arrests
N_j	Number of arrests which are juvenile arrests
N_{ac}, P_{ac}	Number (proportion) of adult arrests formally charged
$N_{a\bar{c}}$	Number of adult arrests not formally charged
N_{ai}, P_{ai}	Number (proportion) of charged adults incarcerated
N_{ap}, P_{ap}	Number (proportion) of charged adults granted probation
N_{aa}, P_{aa}	Number (proportion) of charged adults released or acquitted
N_{ti}	Total number of adults who are incarcerated
N_{tr}	Number of adults released from incarceration
N_{r1}, P_{r1}	Number (proportion) of arrested juveniles who are rearrested
N_{r2}, P_{r2}	Number (proportion) of adults arrested but not formally charged who are rearrested
N_{r3}, P_{r3}	Number (proportion) of adults released or acquitted who are rearrested
N_{r4}, P_{r4}	Number (proportion) of adults granted probation who are rearrested

N_{r5}, P_{r5}	Number (proportion) of adults released from incarceration who recidivate*
N_{rt}, P_{rt}	Number (proportion) of adults released who violate parole and are reincarcerated
N_{pv}	Number of adult parole violators who reenter prison
N_{na}	Number of adult releases who are rearrested
N_r	Total number of those who will be rearrested
C	Rearrest crime-switch matrix
PD_1	Distribution of time until rearrest of juvenile recidivists
PD_2	Distribution of time until rearrest of adults not formally charged and who are rearrested
PD_3	Distribution of time until rearrest of adults acquitted or released and who are rearrested
PD_4	Distribution of time until rearrest of adults granted probation and who are rearrested
PD_5	Distribution of time from entrance until release from prison
PD_6	Distribution of time from prison release until parole violation, for those adults who violate parole
PD_7	Distribution of time until rearrest of adults released from prison and who are rearrested

*Adults released from incarceration who recidivate either violate parole or are rearrested

FIG. 7. Flow diagram of the feedback model.

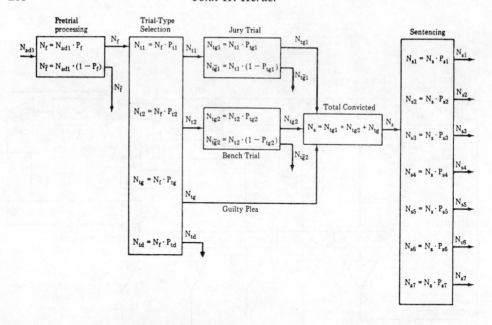

FIG. 8.[32]

N_{ad1}	The number of adult arrests who are formally charged by the magistrate.
(N_f, P_f)	The number of adults formally charged who receive a Superior Court felony disposition.
$(N_f, 1 - P_f)$	The number of adults formally charged who do not receive a Superior Court felony disposition.
(N_{t1}, P_{t1})	Number of defendants who reach trial stage and who receive *jury trials*.
(N_{t2}, P_{t2})	Number of defendants who reach trial stage and who receive *bench* or *transcript trials*.
(N_{tg}, P_{tg})	Number of defendants who reach trial stage and who plead guilty.
(N_{td}, P_{td})	Number of defendants who reach trial stage and who are dismissed or placed off calendar.

(N_{tg1}, P_{tg1})	Number of defendants who receive jury trials who are found guilty.
$(N_{tg1}, 1 - P_{tg1})$	Number of defendants who receive jury trials who are not found guilty.
(N_{tg2}, P_{tg2})	Number of defendants who receive bench or transcript trials who are found guilty.
$(N_{t^-2}, 1 - P_{tg2})$	Number of defendants who receive bench or transcript trials who are not found guilty.
N_S	The number of defendants who are sentenced.
(N_{Sj}, P_{Sj})	The number of sentenced defendants who receive sentence type j $(j = 1, 2, \ldots, 7)$.

3. The trial verdict.
4. The sentencing decision.

Having determined the flow through each processing stage, it is possible to determine the total costs simply as a product of the unit costs and flow rates. Costs can be separated into pretrial and trial costs; and, for each, court and prosecutor's costs.

The linear model, however, is not without its limitations. First of all, it assumes a steady-state system in which none of the variables are exogenous. Clearly, this is not the case in the real world. The environment in which such a system would operate is one that is marked by variable demand properties which would undoubtedly have some influence on the performance of the model. Just what the impact would be, however, is, at this time, still unclear.

What is particularly interesting about these two models is that they implicitly accept the importance of the integrative and coordinated aspects of criminal justice information. Once this approach has been accepted, it is possible to attack problems in criminal justice administration as shortcomings in a system whose function it is to supply decision-makers with vital management information.

Criminal justice operation must, in fact, utilize both linear and feedback approaches in formulating an optimal systems design for problem-solving. One such combined model, known as JUSSIM (Justice Simulation), recognizes that in order for the models to be useful in dealing with problems where the knowledge of cause and effect relationships is poor (as is certainly the case in the criminal justice system) a feedback apparatus must be established between the model and the decision-maker.[33]

JUSSIM is essentially an integrative computer program with specific applications in criminal justice planning. It assumes a steady-state linear model and provides feedback data at various stages in the overall process. Each processing stage has workload measures that are associated with manpower and other available resources. In order for the simulator to produce hard data relating output to unit input, the planner must determine what questions he wishes to explore, what assumptions he can justifiably make, what changes in the system he wishes to consider, and what output measures he wants to study.

A more detailed example of a justice simulation model can be seen in the Philadelphia/ Alaska Justice Improvement Simulation Model (Fig. 9). This model, known as PHILJIM, is a general computer model for the simulation of a total state and metropolitan criminal justice system—from police processing through court procedures with various release and detention options for defendants, to correctional dispositional and referral alternatives.[34] The principal benefits of this mode are that:

1. it permits a thorough understanding of present system operations by providing a "snapshot" of performance on a system-wide scale;
2. it facilitates comprehensive diagnoses of criminal justice system problems by utilizing simulation techniques;
3. as an operational model, it enables public officials to experiment with changes in criminal justice system procedures/allocations without actually making the changes.

Several large metropolitan areas currently have operational computerized data systems, some, in fact, functioning as system-wide information centers. One of the more sophisticated examples of such a system is the Kansas City model, the ALERT II format—an outgrowth of the previously described ALERT I police computer system. A schematic diagram of this system and a close-up of the municipal court information component depict just how comprehensive such a system can be. (Figs. 10, 11).[35]

By gathering, organizing, and evaluating data from such a system, it should be possible to estimate statistically the parameters of various outputs in a production function model. Indeed, the production function approach to law enforcement serves to emphasize a very important point. If offense rates are increasing, expenditures on law enforcement must be increased fast enough or else system effectiveness will fall.[36]

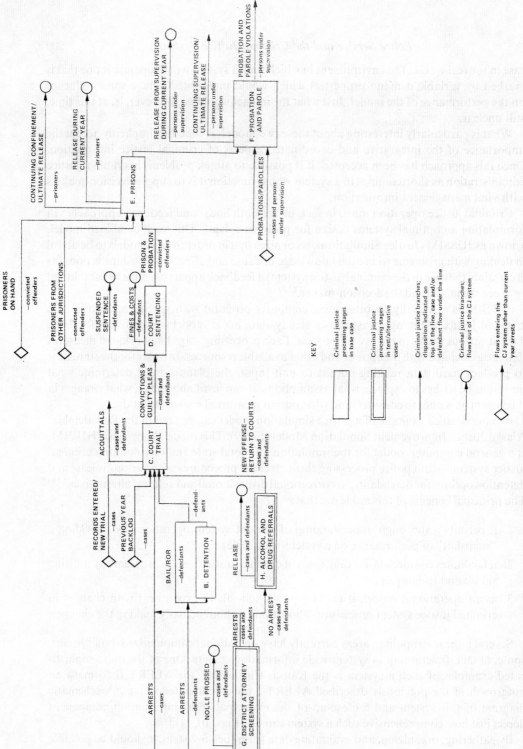

FIG. 9. Flow diagram of the Philadelphia/Alaska illustration of the Justice improvement simulation model.

KEY

☐ Criminal justice processing stages in base case

▭ Criminal justice processing stages in test/alternative cases

↑ Criminal justice branches; disposition indicated on top of the line, case and/or defendant flow under the line

◯ Criminal justice branches; flows out of the CJ system

◇ Flows entering the CJ system other than current year arrests

A. POLICE ARREST AND APPREHENSION

NO ARREST
—cases and defendants

POTENTIAL ARRESTS
—cases

G. DISTRICT ATTORNEY SCREENING

ARRESTS
—cases

ARRESTS
—cases and defendants

NOLLE PROSSED
—cases and defendants

NO ARREST
—cases and defendants

H. ALCOHOL AND DRUG REFERRALS
—cases and defendants

RELEASE
—cases and defendants

B. DETENTION
—defendants

BAIL/ROR
—defendants

RECORDS ENTERED/NEW TRIAL
—cases

PREVIOUS YEAR BACKLOG
—cases

ARRESTS
—cases

—defendants

C. COURT TRIAL
—cases and defendants

ACQUITTALS
—cases and defendants

NEW OFFENSE—RETURN TO COURTS
—cases and defendants

CONVICTIONS & GUILTY PLEAS
—cases and defendants

D. COURT SENTENCING
—defendants

SUSPENDED SENTENCE
—defendants

FINES & COSTS
—defendants

PRISON & PROBATION
—convicted offenders

PROBATIONS/PAROLEES
—cases and persons under supervision

E. PRISONS

PRISONERS ON HAND
—convicted offenders

PRISONERS FROM OTHER JURISDICTIONS
—convicted offenders

CONTINUING CONFINEMENT/ULTIMATE RELEASE
—prisoners

RELEASE DURING CURRENT YEAR
—prisoners

F. PROBATION AND PAROLE

RELEASE FROM SUPERVISION DURING CURRENT YEAR
—persons under supervision

CONTINUING SUPERVISION/ULTIMATE RELEASE
—persons under supervision

PROBATION AND PAROLE VIOLATIONS
—persons under supervision

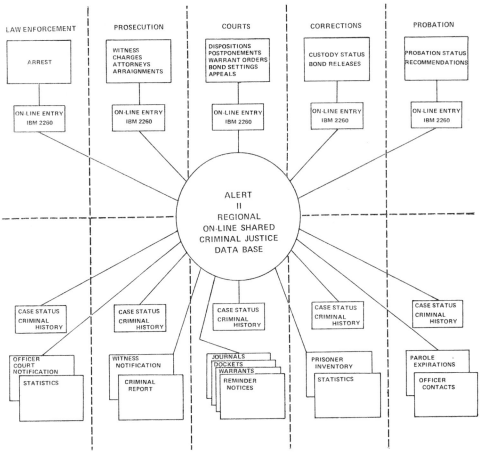

FIG. 10.

In Search of a Manageable System

While a good many problems can be solved by quantitative methods, it would be a mistake to assume that quantitative methods can be applied indiscriminately to police problems with the expectation that they will invariably produce improved decision-making. To so assume would be to confuse technique with the substantive process of administrative decision-making. After all, the goals and values which are at the heart of all police problems are human goals and values. In this realm, any method or technique must be regarded as a tool controlled by and subservient to those who use it.[37]

The question raised here by Shumate and Crowther is one that is particularly germane to any discussion of systems analysis in criminal justice. What, in fact, are the limitations of quantitative analysis in this setting? How does one cope with the problems of design and analysis when dealing with public systems? Without a doubt, measures of effectiveness for various public policy alternatives are hard to specify and perhaps even harder to evaluate. Constraints on available options are ambiguous. Furthermore, local measures of economy and administrative efficiency may be but a small part of an appropriate set of criteria.[38]

Even so, there is a place for a systems approach to criminal justice administration. Resource allocation, particularly in police work, is a problem that concerns factors such

John H. Herder

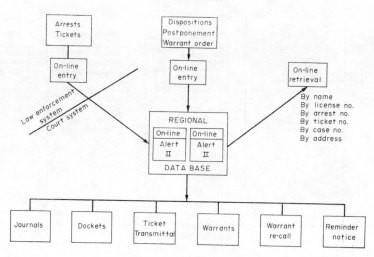

FIG. 11. Municipal court system.

as the amount of time necessary to perform a designated function and the optimal use of resources with designated function and the optimal use of resources with which to do it. It is important also for the administrator to be able to state his goals in operational terms. One aim of any administrative policy is to achieve a higher level of productivity. Since administrative decisions are going to be made anyway, it makes sense to provide the administrator with a systematic total flow of data so that he is able to make *informed* decisions based on some sort of predictive analysis regarding their impact.

The increased operations and management data that can be anticipated through the use of a systems approach to criminal justice functions will not necessarily uncover ways to reduce law enforcement costs. They may, in fact, show that additional expenditures should be made. Most important, however, they should, if properly utilized, lead the way to more effective utilization of existing resources and more advantageous ways of meeting future demands. The criminal justice system will always be limited by the fact that it is a component subordinate to the wishes of the larger political system, and as such stands to be perennially buffeted by the harsh reality of the fact that ". . . Policy makers at one level may simply not be providing sufficient resources to combat crime, while policy makers at another level may not be taking sufficient action to maintain economic opportunities for an important segment of the population."[39]

Human values must be kept in mind. There are technical problems as well. One limitation of the systems approach is the ease with which one accepts the scope of the system presented. Obviously, a system is an abstraction. Giving the particular system the benefit of the doubt that might arise because of the abstracting process, makes the reader too willing to accept the universe as defined by the system.

In recent years public police have received a great deal of attention and analysis. Yet this analysis has examined only half of the policing effort in this country. There are 800,000 public and private security personnel in the United States. Only half of this number are public police. Of the $8.7 billion dollars spent annually on the policing effort, expenditures on public police account for only half.

What is the other "half"? It certainly does not show up in the analyses and systems reviewed in this chapter. Private security forces are guards, investigators, patrolmen, guards who respond to burglar alarms, and many others who perform a variety of legitimate security functions. How are these roles to be considered in the total criminal justice system?

The private police industry is the subject of an extensive five-volume study prepared by Kakalik and Wildhorn[40] of the Rand Corporation. The Rand study attempts to categorize public and private security forces by the services they perform and the degree of police powers they possess.[41]

Obviously, the public police have full "peace-officer" status and are responsible for enforcing all state and local statutes in their jurisdictions, usually towns, cities, and counties. There are other law-enforcement personnel employed by local, state, and federal agencies—guards employed by a contract security agency who have limited or no police powers, to "special-purpose" police, such as transit police, housing authority police, even campus police at some state universities. Between these two extremes are police at airports, harbors, parks, sanitation departments, and state and suprastate agencies. These police usually have some law-enforcement powers.

Wholly within the private sector are contract forces providing security or in-house forces who work exclusively for the store, bank, or manufacturer who employs them. These forces provide guard service, roving patrol, armored-car escort, central station alarm, and many investigative services.

In some cases, these forces overlap. How, for example, is the public police officer to be considered in the systems analysis who moonlights and still retains his full police powers while working for the private contractor or utility?

If these were isolated cases, then the analysis could be permitted to ignore them. But they represent *half* of the police effort in the country. A number of questions are identified in the Rand study that have not been answered. In fact, serious answers have not even been attempted.

How should public and private security forces be coordinated?

How effective are private and special-purpose public security forces?

If most (in some studies, over 95 percent) of the alarms that reach the police are false, how can this waste of police manpower be reduced?

Are there effective alternatives to campus police?

Are there effective alternative approaches to reducing business burglaries, shoplifting, pilferage?

What are the reasons users of private security employ particular security measures?

What is the prevalence of problems (such as abuse of power) in public and private police organizations?

Until the Rand study, the private police effort in the country was largely overlooked. It needs now to be made a part of the analysis of the total criminal justice system.

Related to the problem of private security forces is another area of interest: the role of voluntary organizations in police service. Many smaller police departments have active auxiliary police organizations. These organizations are usually social in nature, but many members perform police services as part of the regular force on weekends and during special events. This extra manpower, usually serving without compensation, represents voluntary police, somewhat like voluntary firemen.

There are differences, however. While many fire departments, even in some cities, could not function without the volunteer fireman, the voluntary policeman is largely ignored. In fact, the opinion among "professional" police and their organizations is to eliminate auxiliary forces. Many criticisms are leveled at the auxiliary by the police themselves: they lack training; training of auxiliaries is costly; the auxiliary is tired after working all week for his regular employers; and similar complaints.

What is the role of citizen input in police service? One of the marked failures among police departments is the failure to build a sound community base of interest and support for police work. Many departments discover too late that citizens have no confidence in or respect for the department. The usual strategy employed to overcome this citizen hostility, especially in cities, is a "communications" program. An enhanced auxiliary organization could be another means to develop community support. Minority groups, students, women could all participate in providing police service by this means. By overlooking the citizen role in the delivery of police service, the systems analyst has reinforced the isolation of the police service from the citizenry.

This may turn out to be a minor issue in face of the potential threat to the entire system posed by the issues of class and race. Does the criminal justice system discriminate against poor people and blacks? How does this question get examined in a systems analysis? How can a system show, for example, that most of the men in correctional institutions are black? How can a system show that "crime" occurs mostly in poorer neighborhoods, among the poor (many of whom are also black)?

Even at the most elementary level striking differences in the way the system operates appear. If the drunk found on the sidewalk, for example, is poor, he will be locked up "to sober up". He may even receive a short sentence in jail for his own good. If the drunk found on the sidewalk is well dressed, most likely the policeman will take him home or to a doctor.

This trivial but frequent occurrence foreshadows a more dramatic example. A young black caught robbing a gas station of $75 or $100 may get 5, even 10, years imprisonment. A board chairman who pleads guilty to stock fraud that made him $10 million and cost investors $200 million receives a 1-year sentence and is paroled in 4 months. This sentence comes despite the prosecutor's plea for substantial punishment "to deter white-collar crimes". The judge found that the chairman's character (some would read "class") had redeeming features.

The police do not themselves get involved in so-called white-collar crimes often. Police spend most of their crime fighting effort with people from their own social-class level or lower. These are the so-called "Index crimes". Our society is substantially more relaxed about the crimes the wealthy commit than about the crimes the poor commit.

This contradiction becomes most understandable when both definitions of crime are kept in mind. The first definition is the obvious one: "an offense against public law which provides a penalty against the offender". There is a second definition which is probably more to the point: "an offense against the social order or a violation of the mores that is dealt with by community action. . . ." Until systems analysis penetrates the social nature of crime and the criminal justice system, it does not portray the system accurately. When administrative decisions are made on the basis of a biased system, the decisions will be less valid than if the data base were unbiased. The challenge facing the analyst and citizens generally is to perceive of the criminal justice system in terms that reinforce the democratic ideal.

Notes

1. Charnes, A., Kozmetsky, G., and Ruefli, T. "Information requirements for urban systems." *Management Science*, **19**, No. 4, Part 2, pp. P-7-20 (Dec. 1972).
2. *Municipal Police Administration*. Chicago: International City Managers Association, 1961.
3. Leahy, F. *Planning-Programming-Budgeting for Police Departments*. Hartford: Travelers Research Center, Inc., 1968.
4. Szanton, P. "Program budgeting for criminal justice systems." In *Task Force Report: Science and Technology*, p. 3. Washington: Government Printing Office, 1967.
5. *The Challenge of Crime in a Free Society*, pp. 8–9. Washington: Government Printing Office, 1967.
6. Wilson, O. W. and McLaren, R. C. *Police Administration*, pp. 365–7. New York: McGraw-Hill, 1972.
7. Larson, R. C. *Urban Police Patrol Analysis*, p. 131. Cambridge: The MIT Press, 1972.
8. *Ibid.*, pp. 125–6.
9. *Ibid.*, pp. 264–5.
10. Shumate, R. D. and Crowther, R. F. "Quantitative methods for optimizing the allocation of police resources." *Journal of Criminal Law, Criminology and Police Science*, **57**, No. 2, 197–206 (1966).
11. *Ibid.*, pp. 204–5.
12. *Ibid.*, pp. 204–5.
13. *Ibid.*, p. 205.
14. *Ibid.*, p. 205.
15. Larson, *op. cit.*, p. 147.
16. Bottoms, A. M., ed. *Allocations of Resources in the Chicago Police Departments*, Washington: Government Printing Office, 1972.
17. *Ibid.*, p. xiii.
18. *Ibid.*, pp. 7–10.
19. *Ibid.*, p. 22.
20. Shoup, C. S. "Standards for distributing a free governmental service: crime prevention." *Public Finance* **19**, No. 4 (1964).
21. Bottoms, *op. cit.*
22. "Vehicle locator draws on space techniques." *The Data Communications User*, p. 28 (July 1973).
23. Wilson, *op. cit.*, pp. 443–8.
24. Wilson, *op. cit.*, pp. 245ff.
25. Cooper, G. *Proceedings of the International Symposium on Criminal Justice Information and Statistical Systems*. Project Search, 1972.
26. Herder, J. H., Larson, A. E., and Kanaga III, L. W. *Prisoner Transportation in the State of Connecticut*. Hamden: Herder, 1973.
27. Order, A. "The transshipment problem." *Management Science*, **2**, No. 3, 276–85 (1956).
28. Cooper, *op. cit.*, p. 385.
29. Phillips, L. and Vatey, Jr., H. "An economic analysis of the deterrent effect of law enforcement on criminal activity." *Journal of Criminal Law, Criminology and Police Science*, **63**, No. 3, 334.
30. Blumenstein, —. and Larson, R. C. "Analysis of a total criminal justice system." In Drake, A., Kenney, R. L., and Morse, D. M., eds. *Analysis of Public Systems*, pp. 318–19. Cambridge: The MIT Press, 1972.
31. *Ibid.*, p. 321.
32. *Ibid.*, pp. 322–3.
33. Cooper, *op. cit.*, p. 467.
34. Cooper, *op. cit.*, p. 479.
35. Cooper, *op. cit.*, pp. 113–14.
36. Phillips and Vatey, *op. cit.*, p. 335.
37. Shumate and Crowther, *op. cit.*, p. 206.
38. Drake, Kenney, and Morse, *op. cit.*, pp. 77–8.
39. Phillips and Vatey, p. 342.
40. Kakalik, J. S. and Wildhorn, S. *Private Police in the United States: Findings and Recommendations*. Santa Monica: The Rand Corporation, 1971.
41. Kakalik and Wildhorn, *op. cit.*, pp. 2–4.

PART IV

The Amenities of Urban Life

9. *Quantitative Analyses of the Performing Arts*

THOMAS GALE MOORE

Quantitative analyses of the performing arts are surprisingly rare. Most articles and writings concerning the arts are either purely descriptive or simply bemoan the poor financial state of the arts. The level of analysis tends to be that found in popular journals. Such writings will report on foundation giving to the performing arts or the level of governmental subsidies. Econometrics or quantitative techniques have been used rarely.

There are several reasons why sophisticated techniques have been used so infrequently to analyze the performing arts. For one thing the arts in total generate an insignificant proportion of national income. Researchers have emphasized the problems of "more vital" industries that contribute more to income and employment.

Also the performing arts are not one industry but several with different problems and different institutional structures. The performing arts consist of such diverse activities as ballet, opera, the theater, chamber music, and symphonic music. This is such a diverse group that operates on such a small scale that the U.S. Census does not even publish data on the activities separately. Generally each performing arts activity consists of small groups of individuals, none of whom has the resources nor motivation to support research into its problems.

Most of the analysis on the performing arts has assumed that the problem was a need for more money and that the answer was government subsidies. More sophisticated approaches have pointed out that the performing arts are highly labor intensive. In a growing economy this results in costs going up more rapidly for the performing arts than for the economy generally. As wage rates rise in the economy, they force up wages in the performing arts. Productivity improvements tend to be rare in these areas and hence, costs match the rise in wage rates. A Vivaldi concerto takes as many musicians today as it did in the eighteenth century.

Actually there have been fantastic productivity improvements in exhibiting the performing arts to the general public. The development of motion pictures provided the public with the opportunity to see drama, comedy, and music at a fraction of the cost of a live performance. Television has reduced the cost even further. Recordings provide the public with the opportunity to listen to Bach or Beethoven played by the finest musicians at less than the cost of a seat for one performance at a local symphony. Thus the argument that there cannot be any significant productivity improvements in the performing arts is only valid for the *live* performing arts.

The live performing arts are in essence handicraft industries existing in a mechanized world. They are analogous to the hand-knitted sweater industry. As long as the industry is defined to be hand-knitted sweaters, productivity cannot be great and prices and costs must rise sharply with wage rates. But if the definition is the sweater industry then productivity can play a role and wage rates can rise without forcing prices up.

Thus the live performing arts are by definition the handicraft portion of the industry.

They are a luxury good. Inevitably prices and costs will rise with wage rates in these areas. As a consequence the problems of the performing arts—hereafter by the performing arts is meant the live performing arts—are seen as the inevitable result of a growing economy. Little can be done to hold down ticket prices without increasing support for the arts from either private philanthropy or government subsidy. The inevitable result is that most writing on the problems of the arts have concentrated on either private aid or public aid for the performing arts.

There are four studies of different aspects of the performing arts that have gone beyond the superficial analysis given above and which have also attempted to use somewhat more sophisticated techniques to analyze the issues. These studies, which will be reported on below, are: William J. Baumol and William G. Bowen, *Performing Arts: The Economic Dilemma*,[1] Thomas G. Moore, *The Economics of the American Theater*,[2] Casimir S. Skrzypczak, "Is there a Niche for a Major Symphony with its own Symphony Hall on Long Island?"[3]; Edward J. Steadman, "Advertising Media Selection via Linear Programming".[4]

BAUMOL & BOWEN

The purpose of the Baumol & Bowen study was to "explain the financial problems of the performing [arts] groups and to explore the implications of these problems for the future of the arts in the United States".[5] In the course of their study they gathered a great deal of data on audiences for the performing arts, on revenues, on costs, on deficits of various performing arts organizations, and on the sources of financial support for various groups. They found that the audience for all segments of the performing arts are composed of individuals considerably better educated, more wealthy, and more likely to be professionals than are individuals generally. While they collected data on income and on ticket prices, they did not attempt to estimate price or income elasticities of demand.

They found that over the long run costs, primarily performer salaries, moved up faster than did prices. Revenues, however, have tended to rise only with the price level. These two trends resulted in a growing earnings gap that had to be filled with private or public gifts and grants.

The reasons for the rapid escalation in costs have been set out above but why revenues tended to lag is not so obvious. In the post-war period, except for the Metropolitan Opera, ticket prices of performing arts organizations have gone up only with the cost of living [p. 270]. Baumol & Bowen gave several explanations for this phenomena; none of which is completely satisfactory. They mention that managers of performing arts organizations are reluctant to raise ticket prices because it conflicts with their sense of social responsibility. They wish to encourage the poor, students, and young people to attend. No doubt some managers felt this way but it certainly does not explain why profit-seeking managers of Broadway productions failed to raise prices. Baumol & Bowen also indicated that they believe that demand for the performing arts, notwithstanding the excellent substitutes, is

[1] New York: The Twentieth Century Fund, 1966.
[2] Durham, NC: Duke University Press, 1968.
[3] Chapter III, *Community Support of the Performing Arts—Selected Problems of Local and National Interest*, Ed. Allan Easton, Hofstra University Yearbook of Business, Series 7, Vol. 5, 1970, pp. 163–202.
[4] Chapter IV, *ibid.*, pp. 203–51.
[5] *Ibid.*, p. 4.

inelastic [p. 274]. Yet at the same time they argued that a major factor holding down prices was the fear by managers of performing arts organizations of buyer resistance to higher prices [p. 277]. In other words Baumol & Bowen concluded that while demand was price inelastic, managers did not believe it was.

This point is crucial to their thesis. Baumol & Bowen indicated a growing gap between income and costs and concluded that more government support would be necessary to fill this gap. Yet if demand is inelastic then the gap could be filled by higher ticket prices. Since the audience for performing arts are generally drawn from the most affluent sector of the economy, according to their statistics, there would seem to be little ethical objection to higher prices. Baumol & Bowen even compare the performing arts with institutions of higher education which have raised their fees considerably faster than prices generally in the post-war period. If such institutions can ethically do so then why not the performing arts.

Inelastic demand, however, may be insufficient to justify higher ticket prices for at least some of the performing arts. Demand for Broadway tickets, Moore found (see below), is inelastic, yet no single Broadway impressario can raise his scale much out of line with other shows for fear of losing much of his business. That is the demand for tickets for a single organization is likely to be considerably more elastic than the demand for performances generally. While this argument is undoubtedly valid for Broadway, it has less validity for most other areas of the performing arts, where often the local organization has a virtual monopoly on professional caliber live performances.

In any case, a serious gap in our knowledge about the state of the performing arts results from the lack of evidence on the elasticity of demand facing most organizations. Is the demand elastic or inelastic for the Cincinnati Symphony Orchestra, for example?

As was mentioned above, Baumol & Bowen found that the income gap has been growing. Since costs can be expected to rise faster than the general price level and assuming ticket prices do not go up any faster, the performing arts organizations they concluded will increasingly be squeezed. They reported on the amount of private giving to the performing arts and present some data on government support. They estimated the "gap" in the future and indicated the amount of private philanthropy that could be expected and concluded that there would still be a shortfall that only government support could fill.

Baumol & Bowen estimated earned income for the performing arts by fitting a trend line to past earnings of eleven major orchestras over some base period, and by assuming that this rate would continue for all forms of the performing arts. They projected a higher and lower figure depending on the base period chosen. To this they added an assumed increase in the number of performing arts organizations (three major orchestras, five metropolitan orchestras, two smaller opera companies, a doubling of regional repertory theaters, a 25 percent increase in dance activity) [p. 553]. They similarly estimated growth rates in expenditures based on historical trends for major symphonies. Growth rates for private contributions were also based on past trends in giving. Again a higher and lower estimate was projected by using different base periods. The net result was that the income gap in 1975 was estimated to be between 5.6 million and 26.3 million [p. 401].

Baumol & Bowen concluded that increased government support for the arts, especially from the Federal Government, is more likely to close this gap than is either increased private giving or higher ticket prices. Since their book was published the Federal Government through the National Endowment for the Arts has been contributing to performing arts organizations. In fiscal 1972, the Federal Government spent over $33 million on promotion of the arts—mainly in the form of grants—a sum considerably larger than the minimum gap projected by Baumol & Bowen for 1975.[6]

Baumol & Bowen claimed that the growing gap between earned income and costs over the last few decades has been met by increased private contributions. It is possible that growing private contributions will continue to meet the gap. However, there is another hypothesis that seems consistent with the data. That is that costs will rise to meet income from all sources. If, for example, another million dollars is raised for the Metropolitan Opera, the deficit will rise by a million dollars as more touring is undertaken, singers are hired for more money, ticket prices are not raised, more elaborate scenery is purchased, more adventurous and less appealing productions are mounted, etc. Under this hypothesis no practical amount of Federal aid will eliminate the economic crisis of the performing arts. More aid may mean higher incomes for performers, musicians, authors, and choreographers without much improvement in quality of performances. If the supply of the individuals with the requisite skills is inelastic as Moore (see below) argued then more government aid may have only a marginal impact on quality with the major result being larger incomes for those with the highest abilities.

More research therefore is needed to define the elasticity of supply of the performing arts. Moore has developed data on this for Broadway but there is no knowledge for other areas of the performing arts. It is possible that Federal subsidies have prevented a disastrous decline in the performing arts or have led to a tremendous increase in the number and quality of performances. It is also possible that it has simply led to higher costs most of which are the result of larger payments to those most in demand.

Certainly Baumol & Bowen were correct in concluding that the long-run outlook for the live performing arts is dim. With a growing economy, personal incomes will continue to rise and with them the income of performers, musicians, and the like. As these go up so must costs of the performing arts organizations. Just as rising standards of living are replacing handicraft goods everywhere, eliminating domestic servants, pricing haut cuisine restaurants out of the market, so in the future society must either devote an increasing proportion of national income to the live performing arts or see them shrink and become the province only of the rich.

In an appendix to their study, Baumol & Bowen presented the only econometric work in their book [pp. 479–81]. Here they attempted to estimate the degree of economies of scale for major symphony orchestras. They ran three sets of regressions to measure economies of scale. The first model consisted of the following equation:

$$E/C = a + bC$$

where E is total expenditure, C is number of concerts and a and b are constants. They found that for ten of the eleven orchestras, b turned out to be negative and that in nine cases it was significantly different from zero at the 95 percent level. From this they concluded that there were economies of scale. Unfortunately no such conclusion is warranted. If there were no economies of scale and expenditures were perfectly correlated with the number of concerts, b would be zero. But if the relationship between expenditures and number of concerts is not perfect, if there is any randomness in the relationship, b will be biased downward. The more randomness, the more bias. Hence it is possible, although not probable, that the observed negative relationship stemmed simply from some randomness between total expenditures and number of concerts.

[6] *Budget or the United States Government*, Fiscal Year 1974, Appendix, p. 916.

Baumol & Bowen reported on adding another term to the above relation to represent time. This they asserted caused an improvement in the behavior or the b coefficients. All eleven became negative and significantly different from zero at the 95 percent level. They reported that for eight of the orchestras the coefficient of time was positive, suggesting an upward drift in costs over time. Since their costs were deflated by the minimum-salary level, this implied an upward drift in costs in excess of that to be expected from the rise in wage rates. However, only six of the time coefficients were significantly different from zero at the 95 percent level.

The most interesting regression equation fitted was:

$$E/C = a + bC + vC^2.$$

This quadratic equation permitted the estimation of a U-shaped curve with a unique minimum efficient size. They found that the b was always negative and in eight cases the v was positive. In six of the cases both the b's and v's were significant at the 99 percent level. For five cases they gave the results (in one case there was some ambiguity in the data). The cost minimizing number of concerts ranged from 94 to 155 with the median being 109 and the mean being 120. *A priori* there would seem to be no reason why the minimum cost number of concerts should differ significantly from one major orchestra to another. It would have been interesting therefore if Baumol & Bowen had pooled their data and estimated an industry-wide cost-minimizing number of concerts.

Baumol & Bowen fitted the same general regression equation using expenditures on artistic personnel alone rather than total units costs. They reported a significant improvement in the results with an increase in the cost-minimizing number of concerts per season. They concluded that unit administrative costs begin to increase at a smaller number of concerts than for musician salaries.

Baumol & Bowen's study was a major contribution to the literature on the performing arts. It presented a great deal of data not available before. It thoughtfully analyzed most of the issues. Yet outside of running a few simple linear regressions, it utilized no econometric techniques or other mathematical techniques. It was not intended to be a major contribution to quantitative analysis. Baumol & Bowen were seeking to reach a wider audience than simply that of academic researchers. At the same time they found no need for sophisticated mathematical models or tools.

MOORE

Moore studied the legitimate theater exclusively. His study concentrated on the New York stage though he did look into both summer stock and repertory companies scattered around the country.

While he noted that the theater is plagued with rising costs due to its essential handicraft nature, there have been additional factors adversely affecting the theater. The theater has been subject to three shocks in this century that have decimated it. The first shock was the development of silent motion pictures and the automobile. Together these factors killed the small town professional theater. The public could get cheaper entertainment on the silent screen and they could more easily travel to bigger cities for better live performances. It should be noted that the substitution of motion pictures for the road shows of that period probably on net resulted in little loss of quality. Most road shows offered tripe that would never see a stage light today.

The second blow to the theater was the addition of sound to motion pictures in 1927. "The Jazz Singer" and the movies that followed devastated Broadway. From an average of about forty-seven shows playing in a typical week in February 1927, the number declined to about eighteen in February 1934 at the heart of the depression [p. 148].

The third and final blow was television. Actually television broadcasting had a much larger impact on motion pictures than on the remnant of theater that still existed. But the theater suffered also.

Television and motion pictures affected the theater in two ways. They diverted audiences from the more expensive handicraft portion of the entertainment business to the cheaper but more mechanized media of movies and then television. With the introduction of each substitute the theater has had to concentrate on providing higher-quality drama, comedy, and musicals than offered by the substitute mediums. To some degree, a similar process affected motion pictures with the introduction of television. Motion pictures ceased being a mass entertainment medium and moved towards becoming an art form with higher standards.

But the effect of motion pictures and television was not simply to divert audiences, they also diverted the skilled talent from the theater to their own medium. Since the theater to survive had to provide the highest quality and since the mass mediums could afford to pay for skilled directors, authors, actors, and actresses, their talents were actively bid for and their incomes rose substantially.

In fact Moore reported that from the 1920s to 1961, playwrights' earnings from Broadway runs, not including subsidiary income, rose 250 percent in real terms [p. 155]. Writers also receive part of any subsidiary income from stock production, motion pictures sales, foreign rights, etc., all of which have increased substantially since the 1920s. The average payment to scenery designers rose 215 percent in real terms over the same period, while directors received 427 percent more. Those with the skills most needed by motion pictures and then by television reaped substantial gains in real income. On the other hand, real payments to the cast rose only 28 percent on a weekly basis over this period, although they benefited from longer-running shows and possibly less periods of unemployment.

Moore claimed, mostly on the basis of impressionistic data gathered in interviews, that the major constraint on Broadway production comes from a lack of high-quality scripts. Since motion pictures and television are also in need of quality writers, the proposition is reasonable and is consistent with the huge increase in payment going to dramatists. Thus it does appear that the inelastic supply of a major necessary factor, play scripts, was responsible for the low level of new productions put on each season.

This conclusion, Moore pointed out, implies that if more money is provided to the theater in the form of subsidies, the result is likely to be disappointing in terms of added new productions. It may be possible to divert some writers from the screen and from television to the theater but with the much larger resources of those mediums the added play scripts is likely to be small. The net result then of added funds for the theater would be to bid up the income of playwrights further, slightly decrease motion picture output, and slightly increase theater output.

Moore also surveyed Broadway audiences and found like Baumol & Bowen that the audience tends to be more affluent than the typical American or New Yorker. He found that the percentage of local theater-goers on expense accounts was less than 5 percent while about 12 percent of those from out-of-town were on expense accounts [p. 76].

About half of the cost of seeing a Broadway show was attributable to the cost of the tickets. Nearly three-quarters of the audience from New York area ate in a restaurant prior to the theater and then spent about as much on dinner including drinks as they did for their seats. The local audience on average spent about 50 minutes going home after the show. Single individuals spent on average about $22 for the evening while married individuals paid out about $31 [pp. 82–3].

Moore also collected data on the amount paid for tickets as well as their box-office price. He found some visitors to New York were charged as much as $29 for a $9.60 seat to a Friday night performance of a hit musical. He found that about 11 percent of the tickets sold during his survey were scalped. On this basis he estimated the total amount of scalped earnings above the legitimate ticket price at between $1.5 million and $3.5 million per year. The major sources of scalped tickets were ticket brokers which supplied over two-thirds of such illegal tickets. In all the illegal premium was likely to be about 5 percent of the total box-office receipts in a typical week [p. 88].

The 70 percent of the audience from the New York area [p. 71] tended to prefer serious drama, while those from out-of-town and those on expense accounts preferred comedies and musicals over dramas [p. 88]. If visitors to New York become a more important segment of the audience, the prospects for serious drama would be unfavorable.

Using the audience survey data, Moore estimated the income elasticity of demand for theater-going. On the basis of a linear demand function relating relative frequency of attendance to income, he found that the income elasticity was 1.14 at the mean and the regression explained 98 percent of the variance. When the relationship was run in logs, the income elasticity measured 1.03 and 98.6 percent of the variance was explained. Neither estimate was significantly different from one. Thus changes in income led to proportional changes in theater going.

Moore also looked at the relationship between income and expenditures on theater-going. He regressed the total cost of the evening, the cost of the evening per person, the cost of the tickets, and the cost of everything but tickets per person, on income and travel time one way, all in logs. Travel time was significantly related to costs of attending the theater as might be expected but not to the costs of the tickets. He found that a 1 percent rise in income would produce a 0.2 percent increase in the average price of tickets bought; a 0.35 percent increase in expenditures on other items per person, and a 0.41 percent increase in total outlays for the group as a whole [p. 166].

Income therefore seemed to be more closely related to attendance than to expenditures on theater-going. As people's incomes rise they go to the theater more often but they spend only slightly more per trip to the theater and little of that increase is spent on better tickets.

Moore also correlated the loss of frequency of attendance with travel time. The regression coefficient was -1.82, indicating a substantial affect of time commuting on theater-going [p. 173].

The audience survey was conducted in the spring of 1962 with ticket prices fixed. From that data, therefore, it was not possible to estimate the price elasticities of supply and demand. Moore consequently built a time series model to measure the impact of prices on attendance and on supply. His model was as follows:

(1) $A_i = f(Y_i, C_i, S_i)$;

(2) $S_i = g(A_i, P_i, M_i)$;

(3) $C_i = h(P_i, T_i, O_i)$.

Attendance in the ith period was A_i, Y was income, C was the cost of attending the theater, S was the number of shows (musicals and plays on Broadway), P was ticket prices, M was the dummy variable for sound motion pictures, T was transportation costs to the theater, and O was other costs of attending a Broadway show. Function (1) expressed demand by relating attendance to income, costs of going to the theater, and the number of different shows available to see. Function (2) expressed supply by relating the number of shows playing to attendance, ticket prices, and the length of time since sound motion pictures had been introduced. Function (3) expressed the relationship between the cost of attending the theater, ticket prices, travel costs, and other costs.

Moore assumed that average attendance per show tended to be constant and that the long-run equilibrium condition could be written: $A = \alpha S$. With this assumption there were four endogenous variables, A, S, P, and C, and four equations. In the model used, however, it was assumed that the market was not ever in long-run equilibrium and that prices tended to be a function of costs and a random element. This was justified on the grounds that prices were usually fixed long before the show opened and were likely, therefore, to be independent of demand—at least in the short run. Thus ticket prices were assumed to be exogenous.

The data used to estimate the coefficients of the model extend from 1928 to 1963 for the month of February. The 1927–8 season was the peak Broadway year in terms of both attendance and number of openings on Broadway. A permanent income variable was substituted for income and was computed using a distributed lag model. Since there was inadequate data to estimate equation (3) it was dropped from the model and P was substituted for C in equation (1).

Three approaches were tried to estimate the coefficients of the model. The first approach was simply to regress attendance on price, income, and the number of shows. This naive approach will tend to be biased if the number of shows is not an exogenous variable and does happen to be a function of attendance—the assumption made in the model. A two-stage-least-squares approach was also tried to eliminate this bias.

Two potentially relevant variables were left out of the model for lack of data; they were population and other expenses of attending the theater. *A priori*, it seemed reasonable that they would both have a positive trend with time and thus be closely correlated with income. Hence it seemed very likely that the coefficient of the income variable would reflect more than income and be biased. As a consequence, Moore substituted the cross-sectional income coefficient estimated from his audience survey into the demand equation.

Moore ran these three specifications of the model in logs and in the original values. The coefficients all had the appropriate sign and except for the price variable in the two-stage model with the income coefficient set at the cross-sectional level, all the coefficients were highly significant. Tables 1 and 2 give the demand and the supply elasticities with the elasticities for the linear models computed at the mean.

As can be seen from the two tables the magnitude of the elasticities are surprisingly consistent from specification to specification. Demand appears to be price inelastic with a coefficient around 0.5. This shows elasticity which expresses the relationship between the number of shows and attendance is approximately one. This indicated that a 1 percent increase in the number of shows increased attendance by 1 percent. Or to put it another way, the opening of another show did not affect average attendance at the other shows. This implies that the industry acts like a purely competitive one, with each firm free to enter without fear of cutting the business of rivals.

TABLE 1. ELASTICITIES OF DEMAND.

	Naive linear	Two-stage linear	Naive multiplicative	Two-stage multiplicative	Two-stage with income forced to cross-sectional multiplicative
Price elasticities	−0.482	−0.534	−0.453	−0.563	−0.643
Income elasticities	0.348	0.357	0.364	0.371	1.030[a]
Shows elasticities	0.917	0.962	0.973	1.075	1.153

[a] Income coefficient set at this level from audience survey data.
Source: Moore, Table D-2, p. 172.

TABLE 2. ELASTICITIES OF SUPPLY

	Naive linear	Two-stage linear	Naive multiplicative	Two-stage multiplicative
Price elasticity	0.516	0.489	0.445	0.426
Attendance elasticity	0.629	0.518	0.610	0.564

Source: Moore, Table D-3, p. 173.

Table 2 presents the elasticities of supply. They indicate that supply was both price and attendance inelastic. This is consistent with the argument made above that the major limiting factor for Broadway came from the supply side. An increase in price simply bids up the incomes paid to the necessary but scarce talents without increasing the number of shows proportionately.

Note that the price and attendance elasticities are both close to 0.5 and not significantly different from each other. This appears to be logical since a 1 percent increase in price holding attendance constant should increase revenues by 1 percent, and a 1 percent increase in attendance holding prices constant should do likewise. Thus the impact should be the same on the number of shows produced.

The audience survey data showed that in 1962 the cost of theater-going averaged $16.37 per person of which about half, $7.99, was spent on a ticket. Thus a 10 percent rise in ticket prices would have raised total costs by about 5 percent, and with the ticket price elasticity of about −0.5 would have decreased attendance by about 5 percent. Thus the cash-cost elasticity of demand would have been about −1.0 implying that theater-goers tended to spend a constant amount on attending Broadway shows. From the point of view of Broadway producers, however, demand was and probably continues to be inelastic, and thus higher prices will bring greater revenues. Since the industry appears to be competitive, there would seem to be little that the producers can do to take account of this fact without violating the anti-trust laws.

Moore pointed out that the dummy variable for the advent of sound motion pictures theoretically could affect both demand and supply. He argued that it probably had the most significant affect on supply. There was a higher correlation between the dummy and number of shows playing than between it and attendance. Moore noted that production costs tripled during the thirties and that ticket prices for straight shows increased in real terms every year, with the exception of 1932, from 1927 through 1935. If the advent of sound had affected demand primarily, ticket prices would have gone down rather than up.

As was pointed out above, the theater is not subject to appreciable productivity improvements and consequently as economic growth continues to lift wage rates in the economy it will continue to increase costs in the theater proportionately. If economic growth also increases the cost of other expenditures of attending the theater such as dining out, baby sitters, travel expenses, etc., the net result will be to have total cost rise in proportion to income. Thus while rising incomes will generate more theater-going, rising costs will decrease it. The net result will be little growth in attendance at Broadway shows. On the other hand, if costs grow somewhat slower than income, some growth in Broadway attendance can be expected.

SKRZYPCZAK

Skrzypczak investigated the factors affecting attendance at major symphony orchestras for the purpose of estimating whether there would be sufficient demand to support such an organization on Long Island. His investigation was not very sophisticated. No model of demand and/or supply was constructed. Neither price nor income were included among his variables.

His approach was simply to regress major symphony orchestra attendance on a number of variables. He found, not unsurprisingly, that the population of standard metropolitan statistical areas was highly correlated with attendance, explaining about 68 percent of the total variance for his twenty-three major symphonies [p. 171]. Adding various indexes of occupational distribution did not contribute significantly to increasing the explained variance. However, he found that adding the percent of adults with five or more years of college as another variable increased the proportion of explained variance to about 82 percent. The F ratio also increased slightly [p. 179].

Using income instead of education in his regression did not give as good results [p. 181]. He reported that a combined population, income, and education model was unsuccessful, probably because of the high intercorrelation between income and education [p. 180].

Skrzypczak added a quality variable in the form of expenditures on musicians' and conductors' salaries per performance. He reported that this added very slightly to the explained variance, but it reduced the F statistic. No standard errors of the regression coefficients were given for any of his variables. The significance of this variable seems to be marginal at best [p. 182]. He reported also trying the size of the auditorium, length of season, and number of performances per week without apparent success [p. 183].

This reduced form model with population, education, and his quality variable was then used to predict the size of audience for a Long Island symphony. His estimating equation was:

$$Y = -35.19 + .025X_1 + 3110.55X_2 + 2.08X_3$$

where X_1 was population, X_2 was percent of 16-year olds-and above with five or more years of college, and X_3 was dollars spent per performance for musicians and conductors [p. 185]. Unfortunately he made a mistake in decimal point in his education variable with the result that predicted home attendance should have been 103,700 instead of 180,400. As a result the predicted audience would rank the symphony in terms of home attendance, not eighth, but sixteenth. Given the closeness of the fine orchestras in New York City—a factor not taken into account in his model—it seems unlikely that a Long Island orchestra would even garner this many patrons.

STEADMAN

Steadman's paper attempted to provide a tool that would be useful to performing arts organization in attracting audiences. He developed a linear programming model to identify how a hypothetical performing arts organization on Long Island could maximize its audience for a given advertising budget.

He built his model on the findings of Baumol & Bowen that the individuals in an audience for performing arts are not a random sample of the public. As pointed out above, the audience is composed mainly of better educated, high-income individuals. The audience also tends to be white-collar and professional in composition. Thus Steadman attempted to maximize the advertising exposures to this type of audience rather than to the general public at large. His problem, as he put it, was: "Given an advertising budget of X dollars and a definition of the current performing arts audience, select from the available media serving the Long Island area those media which maximize the potential audience's exposure to the advertising message" [p. 204].

Of the seven potential advertising media—newspapers, magazines, radio, television, direct mail, poster, and transit—only newspapers and radio were used in the model because only for these media were there data on the reach and characteristics of the local audience. He suggested that such data should be gathered for the other media with extensive field research. Television was also eliminated because of its high cost in relation to a potential advertising budget for a performing arts audience [p. 214]. Direct mail was eliminated because the composition of the mailing list was unknown [p. 214]. Poster and billboard advertising, although cheap, was eliminated because of a lack of knowledge of its reach and audience characteristics [p. 214]. Magazines were not included because there were "few if any" with any exclusive impact on the Long Island area [p. 215].

Four newspapers were selected: *The New York Times*, *Newsday*, *The Long Island Press*, and the *Long Island Commercial Review*. *The New York Times* and *The Long Island Press* were published both daily and Sundays with sufficiently different characteristics that the daily editions were considered a separate media from the Sunday ones. Only *The New York Times* and *Newsday* were able to provide complete audience profiles.

The daily edition of the *Times* reached highly educated and high-income individuals. About 70 percent of the readers had incomes over $10,000 and 26 percent had incomes over $20,000, whereas only 25 percent of families in the New York metropolitan area had incomes over $10,000 and only 5 percent over $20,000. Some 47 percent of the readers had at least a college degree, whereas only 10 percent of the New York area public did [p. 216]. Thus the characteristics of the daily readers were very similar to those of the performing arts audience. Unfortunately the daily *Times* reached only 17 percent of the households in Nassau county, 7 percent in Suffolk, and 14 percent in Kings and Queens [p. 215]. The Sunday *Times* did better in terms of percent of the households reached, but its readers were not so exclusively high income, high education, and professional as the readers of the daily editions.

Newsday reached some 63 percent of the households in Nassau and 64 percent in Suffolk, but only 49 percent of its readers had family incomes over $10,000. About 12 percent of its readers had college degrees or better.

About half of the readers of *The Long Island Press* earned better than $10,000 a year while the newspaper reached some 30 percent of the families in Nassau and 19 percent in Suffolk counties. *The Long Island Commercial Review* concentrated on Long Island business and economy and included in its Thursday edition a section on the performing arts and cultural activities of the area. This paper had a daily circulation of over 8000 and was distributed to Long Island business offices and read by white-collar personnel.

Steadman selected two New York City radio stations—WOR and WQXR—for inclusion in his model because of the contrast in their reach and audience. Audience profiles and rates were available for four daily time intervals: 6 a.m. to 10 a.m.; 10 a.m. to 4 p.m.; 4 p.m. to 7 p.m. and 7 p.m. to midnight [p. 224]. The WQXR station had an audience profile closest to the performing arts one, especially in the morning hours and the evening hours. WOR, on the other hand, reached considerably more people—thirty times as many in the morning hours as WQXR but a considerably smaller proportion of its audience had a college degree or were professionals [pp. 226 and 227].

Steadman treated each time period as a separate media for purposes of analysis. This provided the model with fourteen different alternatives.

He defined the total number of exposures generated by an advertisement in medium *i* as:

$$E_i = g_i r_i N_i$$

where E was the total number of exposures, N was the number of times the advertising alternative is used per time period, r was the total circulation or reach of the alternative, and g was the qualifying constant of the *i*th advertising alternative to limit the total media circulation to include only the potential performing arts audience [p. 231].

To this equation he added two other constants, e and m to reflect the editorial content of the medium and the advertising effectiveness of it. These coefficients were then based on subjective judgments on whether the editorial content was conducive to performing arts advertising, whether free advertisements was likely in the form of favorable reviews, and whether radio advertising was more effective than newspaper ones.

This produced the following model:

$$\text{Maximize } E = \sum_{i=1}^{14} m_i e_i g_i r_i N_i$$

subject to the constraint of the advertising budget, B:

$$B \geq \sum_{i=1}^{14} C_i N_i$$

where C was the cost per advertisement. It was also required that:

$$N_i \geq 0$$

Finally the constraint was added that for each of the four daily newspapers $N_i = 6$ and for each Sunday paper $Ni = 1$ and for each radio station $N_i = 7$ [pp. 232 and 233].[7]

Steadman used a $2500 weekly advertising budget in his model. Using the data on audience profiles and the values of the other constants, three solutions were generated. The optimal solution for each week's schedule called for one advertisement in the *New*

---

[7] For *The Long Island Commercial Review* $N_6 = 5$.

York Times Sunday edition, six advertisements in each of two daily papers—*The New York Times* and the *Long Island Press*—one advertisement in the Sunday edition of the *Long Island Press*, and one advertisement on WOR between the 6 a.m. to 10 a.m. periods. This schedule was predicted to produce 3,609,290 exposures per week. Any other schedule would have produced less [p. 239].

The computer model generated coefficient sensitivity estimates in terms of the size the coefficient would have to reach to be included in the schedule. If the produce of the coefficients for WQXR had been about 7 percent higher the 10 a.m. to 4 p.m. and the 4 p.m. to 7 p.m. periods would have been included in the model. Since a number of the coefficients were established using subjective judgements, the inclusion of these time periods was promising. On the other hand, most of the other excluded media would have been excluded even with substantial changes in the size of their coefficients.

Steadman argued that this solution involved too much newspaper advertising with the possibility of considerable audience duplication. Therefore he ran the model again with the constraint that daily newspaper ads be limited to 12 per week. The result was to eliminate the advertisements in the daily Long Island Press and increase the number of advertisements over WOR during the 6 a.m. to 10 a.m. period from one to three. The result of this schedule would have resulted in 3,544,480 exposures per week, or about 2 percent less than the first schedule [p. 240).

The third solution generated by Steadman was obtained by eliminating the 6 a.m. to 10 a.m. WOR time period from the possibilities and keeping the constraint of not more than twelve advertisements in daily newspapers per week. The result was to replace the advertisements on WOR with seven advertisements per week on WQXR between 10 a.m. to 4 p.m. and six advertisements on WQXR between 4 p.m. to 7 p.m. The result would have produced 3,478,646 exposures or about 2 percent less than the second solution [p. 241]. The third solution would have generated the most free advertisements in the form of reviews. Steadman apparently believed that this solution was preferable to the other two solutions. He argued that it would minimize audience duplication and maximize the possibility of receiving discount advertising rates for multiple use of a media [p. 243].

The interesting aspect of Steadman's paper is that it presents a practical tool for the management of a performing arts organization in reaching its potential audience. Since most performing arts organizations are in desperate need of increasing their audience, the use of linear programming to allocate their advertising budget should be very helpful.

FURTHER RESEARCH

As indicated above the economic, scientific, and quantitative literature on the performing arts or the arts generally is meager. Few researchers have been active in the area, possibly because in terms of national income it is unimportant. More likely the lack of an objective function for arts organizations has held back research. The lack of an objective function for non-profit organizations generally has limited the applicability of traditional economic tools and this problem is especially acute in the performing arts.

What is the objective of the management of a symphony orchestra? Is it to maximize quality of playing, audience, revenues, variety of programs, prestige of symphony, length of season, pay for musicians, prestige of the board of directors, or what? Obviously no single objective function such as profit maximization will do. Clearly quality is important, so is length of season, so is variety of program, and most likely the prestige of the board of directors is important.

It may not be possible to specify a single objective function for all performing arts organizations. For the Broadway theater, profit maximization is a good assumption. For a chamber music quartet, profit maximization may also be a reasonable approximation of the correct objective function. But for an organization like the Metropolitan Opera such an assumption is obviously erroneous since if the Opera were designed to profit maximize, it would never do contemporary operas which are inevitably both costly and unpopular with the public. Thus an important problem that needs a solution in this area is to specify objective functions or types of functions that would provide meaningful insights into behavior of performing arts organizations.

Such a model might indicate whether the revenues can ever rise faster than costs. As suggested above it may be that any increase in revenues will induce a corresponding rise in costs. While this does not necessarily mean that additional revenues would not be beneficial it does imply that the performing arts "crisis" may not be as urgent as has been suggested.

The financial crisis of the performing arts stems, as all financial crises do, from costs exceeding revenues. Consequently research aimed to promote the performing arts can examine methods of holding down or reducing costs, raising box-office income, or increasing other financial support.

It was pointed out above that the performing arts are labor intensive and that increases in the wage rates must be reflected in higher costs. While this is generally true there is not an exact and fixed relationship. Even though it always will take four musicians three-quarters of an hour to play a 45-minute Bach quartet, other economic factors must be combined with the musicians to produce the concert. There must be a concert hall with seats; there need to be instruments, the musicians normally will have to travel to and from the auditorium and often to and from the locality. All of these factors are subject to productivity improvements that can reduce their costs.

Undoubtedly there have been such productivity improvements in the performing arts in the past. Baumol & Bowen found that costs for performing arts organizations moved up considerably more rapidly than did prices generally. In particular, expenditures per concert moved up at an average annual rate of 4.1 percent for the New York Philharmonic and 3.6 percent for the Cincinnati Symphony Orchestra between 1947 and 1964. During the same period they found that the Front Orchestra Price for the two orchestras moved up at an average annual rate of 3.7 and 2.5 percent [p. 272]. British figures indicated that ticket prices had moved up roughly with the cost of living while costs had tended to move up more rapidly [p. 265].

What is unclear from this data is whether the indicated growing gap between income and costs were filled by the reduced costs of other items or by increases in private and public philanthropy. For the Broadway theater Moore found that the tendency towards increased costs was offset by a trend towards longer running productions which lowered the average cost per performance.

Probably more significant for the health of the performing arts would be research designed to increase income of the performing arts. As mentioned above, good estimates of the elasticity of demand are needed. Such figures will show whether higher ticket prices would bring larger revenues. This research should include studies of the income and price elasticities for different symphony orchestras for the opera, the ballet, for chamber music groups, and so on.

Further study is needed on the price strategy of performing arts organizations. Moore and Baumol & Bowen commented on how prices are not changed to reflect market conditions as much as would appear to be profitable. For example, weekend Broadway performances are often sold out while weekday offerings have excess seats. A more appropriate pricing strategy would appear to be higher weekend prices so that average utilization of capacity was the same. The failure of Broadway managers to raise ticket prices for hit shows have been commented on and attributed to inappropriate state and Federal legislation but the law has recently been changed and sold-out shows continue in New York.

The Metropolitan Opera operated at 97 percent of capacity in the 1963–4 season [Baumol & Bowen, p. 238]. Undoubtedly many potential opera-goers were frustrated to find that all tickets were sold to a given performance. While the appropriate percentage utilization of capacity is unknown, it is clearly considerably less than 97 percent. Further research should be done on estimating the optimum capacity utilization level. In addition, more research is needed on why performing arts organizations believe that a sold-out house is the ideal situation rather than viewing such a result as potential lost revenue. It, of course, may be that individuals in the audience need the reassurance of a full house to appreciate the performance. Or, it may be that private philanthropy is dependent on the image created by full houses. Whatever the reason, more research should be done to discover it.

It is possible that the directors and major patrons of major symphony orchestras consider them as low cost (because of the potential tax deductions) methods of achieving prestige and public good will. In order for the directors to be in a position to control the orchestras, they must need large private gifts. In order for the orchestras to need large private gifts, ticket prices must be kept below market clearing levels, a practice which also has the benefit of appearing to be public spirited and of producing a large enthusiastic following. In addition, the directors and large givers inevitably have the most attractive seats or boxes in the house, which are most sought after but impossible to get by others. This provides additional prestige and is a possible source of pleasure.

Such a hypothesis comes back to the need for additional research on the objective function of performing arts organizations. Until such work is done it will be impossible to understand the behavior of such organizations.

Marketing and product strategies need to be developed for performing arts organizations. While artists will decry such steps as commercialization of the arts, it would be of great financial aid to know what the public wanted and what they would pay for. It may also be possible to develop methods of educating the public on contemporary works— which Baumol & Bowen found to reduce audiences [pp. 253–7].

Research in marketing strategies can be carried out in the same manner such research is carried out for producers of consumer products. Surveys can be taken. Sophisticated marketing and advertising strategies attempted.

It is possible that new or improved methods of soliciting private aid for the arts can be developed. For example, it has been suggested that art organizations solicit contingency contributions. That is, they request gifts on the basis that others will match the original gift. Such matching contributions may, it has been argued, stimulate others to give since each gift of a dollar will produce two or more dollars for the organization. Such a scheme needs study and experimentation.

Finally more research is needed on public aid for the arts. Both Moore and Baumol & Bowen devoted considerable space to the subject. They both discuss the rationale for public aid and in the main conclude that any such rationale must lie in social externalities from viewing a live performing arts performance. Neither are able to formulate well the source of such externalities.

From the point of view of a local government, aid to the arts may be important in bringing business or tourists to the area. Thus it may be financially beneficial to the community to spend tax money in this way rather than in, say, beautifying the community or buying more police protection.

Table 3 indicates that city support for the performing arts has increased substantially in the last 14 years. Of eight cities that spent nothing in 1959, seven of them were aiding the arts at the time of the 1973 survey. For the ten cities which both contributed to the performing arts and which had provided useable data for 1973, the average contribution had risen from $42,800 to $350,200, almost a ninefold increase.

Actually these figures understate the amount of public subsidies being provided to the performing arts by local governments. In many cases, city governments may provide little or no aid but county or regional governments may provide subsidies. In a few cases, school systems or public library systems, often separately incorporated public bodies, provide aid. Thus while the actual magnitude of public subsidies is unknown it is likely to be substantial.

TABLE 3. SUBSIDIES TO THE PERFORMING ARTS FOR SELECTED CITIES

City	Performing arts ($000)	
	1959	1973
New York City	96	1,709
Chicago	0	13,220
Los Angeles	0	299
Philadelphia	25	900
Detroit	0	29
Baltimore	120	298
Houston	28	253
Dallas	0	73
New Orleans	8	n.a.
Pittsburg	55	n.a.
San Antonio	2	n.a.
San Diego	0	173
Buffalo	57	62
Atlanta	19	126
Kansas City, NO	53	0
Newark	0	51
St. Paul	10	n.a.
Norfolk	2	32
Providence, RI	2	0
Richmond	0	39
Sacramento	26	22
Springfield, MS	0	0

Source: 1959 data from Moore, p. 115; 1972 data from survey taken by author.

There is obviously a large potential for research in this area. The actual magnitude of public subsidies needs to be established. The motivation and potential gain from subsidizing the arts should be measured.

In conclusion a great deal of work remains to be done on the performing arts. The objective function needs to be specified, demand estimated, ticket pricing explained, markets surveyed, private fund raising improved, and evidence developed on the gain to communities from having a symphony, an opera and a repertoire theater.

These studies will not in all cases necessarily require sophisticated research techniques. But they will require careful analysis. In some cases, they will require data gathering. The payoff, however, for the performing arts is likely to be substantial if this research is carried out. If it is not, the performing arts will continue to suffer as a declining handicraft industry in an increasingly mechanized world.

PART V

Urban Politics and Policy

10. *Public Policy-making in the Urban Setting*

IRA SHARKANSKY

This chapter deals with the formulation and delivery of public policy by officials of urban governments. Its task is complicated by the variety of participants. The urban setting provides the arena for much of what goes on in the United States today, and the participants range far beyond the traditional "local governments" of municipalities, counties, suburban towns and villages, school districts, and other special districts. Few units of the national or state governments count for much unless their work relates at least indirectly to the urban scene. Moreover, the "public sector" of established governments provides only some of the activities that have public significance in urban areas. The development of residential, commercial, and industrial patterns by private interests leads as well as follows the decisions of government officials. And there is much "quasi-governmental" activity involving profit-making and not-for-profit organizations working under contract with governmental bodies; these include the urban studies of the Rand Corporation and other consultants, subsidized projects in manpower development undertaken by business firms, and social service units funded by private contributions and the U.S. Office of Economic Opportunity.

It is necessary to recognize the potpourri of actors making publicly relevant decisions in the urban setting, at the same time that we identify the limited portion of this activity to be examined. We concentrate mostly on "local governments" and demonstrate below that they do most of the work in actually administering public services in urban areas. Yet no consideration of their activities is complete without some concern for the variety of other actors that supply them with financial resources, and share or compete with their formulation of public policies.

The complexity of government in urban areas reflects a process that has occurred throughout the public and private sectors of American life. Governments as well as individuals, business firms, and foundations have discovered the urban nature of our society. Indeed, the themes of this chapter follow from the urban nature of our society. It starts by documenting the urban-centered nature of contemporary governments in the United States, both in terms of local government activities and the increasing efforts of national and state governments to aid the local authorities. It then discusses the numerous actors, institutions, and other features said to influence urban policies, and finally considers what the plurality of influences means for the urban official, as well as for the analyst who would try to determine what makes government tick in the urban setting.

Urban Centered Government in the United States

The first problem in dealing with themes of urbanism is to define the key term. For many years the U.S. Bureau of the Census has considered "urban" to be those communities with at least 2500 residents. Settlements of this size might present an important change in

239

surroundings to a traveller caught in a "rural" area with fewer amenities than appear at the 2500 level. Even if that is true, however, the changes in social, economic, and political traits around 2500 population do not seem enough to warrant that standard in a consideration of contemporary urban government. In order to say something meaningful about the urban affairs that have attracted the attention of our public and private elites, we should deal with larger communities. The phenomena associated with "urbanism" seem to grow with increasing population. No single demarcation of "urban" would do justice to all the nuances we might wish (or allow us to use the results of studies that have considered "urban" communities of various sizes). Where the information permits, however, we concentrate on these communities having at least 500,000 population.

Symptoms of urban-centered government in the United States appear in the records of public finance. These show where our public dollars go, like a great scoreboard showing the allocation of resources to one or another social concern. Table 1 offers one estimate of the resources used for urban problems. It records the expenditures of municipal governments in the largest cities, as compared with expenditures for domestic programs by all other governments in the United States. Omitted are the expenditures of the national government for defense and international relations. Between 1960 and 1970–1, expenditures of the largest municipalities grew by a multiple of 3.07, while those of other domestic units grew by a multiple of 2.74. Most of the difference appeared in the years between 1966–7 and 1970–1; then the spending of large municipalities multiplied 1.86 times, while that of other domestic units increased by only 1.52 times.[1]

TABLE 1. GROWTH OF LARGE CITY EXPENDITURES RELATIVE TO SPENDING FOR OTHER DOMESTIC ACTIVITIES, 1960 TO 1970–1

	Total general expenditures cities of at least 500,000 population, in millions of dollars	Direct general expenditures of national, state, and all other local governments, minus national government spending for defense and international affairs, in millions of dollars
1970–1	15,435	204,751
1969–70	12,950	117,814
1968–9	11,237	163,191
1967–8	9,665	142,809
1966–7	8,311	134,359
1965–6	7,449	121,125
1964–5	6,864	110,939
. . .		
. . .		
1960	5,208	74,650

Sources: *City Government Finances in (1960 . . . 1970–1)*; *Government Finances in (1964–5 . . . 1970–1)*; and *Historical Statistics of Governmental Finances and Employment*, all published in Washington by the U.S. Bureau of the Census, 1961 through 1972.

Intergovernmental Support of the Largest Cities

Much of what passes for "municipal government" in the largest cities is actually the programs (and funds) of state and national governments. Increasingly, these superior levels of government use municipal authorities to administer their activities. Table 2 shows the

TABLE 2. LARGE CITIES' RECEIPT OF STATE AND NATIONAL
AIDS

Combined state and National aid as a percentage of city
expenditures

	Cities of at least 500,000 population	All other cities
1971–1	36.8%	21.7%
1964–5	24.0	18.1
	Per capita receipt of aid[a]	
1970–1	$175.40	$35.90
1964–5	58.20	18.90

[a] Of necessity, 1964–5 per capita calculations employ 1960 population figures.

Sources: *Government Finances in 1970–1 (and 1964–5)* (Washington: U.S. Bureau of the Census, 1972, 1966).

weight of inter-governmental assistance in city budgets. In the largest category of cities, 36.8 percent of the expenditures come initially from Washington and state capitals. For all other cities, the percentage received as aid is only 21.7. Here again is the concern of political elites for the largest urban areas. Since the most dramatic take-off of new federal social programs in the 1964–5 period, the largest cities' per capita receipts of intergovernmental aid have grown by 201 percent, while those of other cities have grown by only 90 percent.

There has been a growing federal role in local (and state) finance since 1961. Table 3 shows a continuous increase in federal aid as a percentage of state and local government

TABLE 3. FEDERAL AID
AS A PERCENTAGE OF
STATE AND LOCAL EX-
PENDITURES, 1961–73

	percent
1973	23.8
1972	21.3
1971	19.8
1970	18.3
1969	17.4
1968	18.2
1967	16.3
1966	15.6
1965	14.6
1964	14.6
1963	13.3
1962	13.2
1961	12.6

Sources: *Special Analyses: Budget of the United States Government Fiscal Year 1974* (Washington: U.S. Government Printing Office, 1973), p. 217.

expenditures from 12.6 in the last budget of the Eisenhower administration to 23.8 in 1973. For fiscal year 1974, the Nixon administration proposed a halt in growth that would bring federal contributions down to 21.3 percent of state and local expenditures. As this is being written, however, Watergate has complicated the President's relations with Congress, and the outcome of his proposal is not clear.

The President's budget tabulates a program-by-program record of federal-aid outlays in metropolitan areas. Although this data reaches further than cities having at least 500,000 population, it does identify the urban programs that receive the most federal support. The proposal for 1974 lists $31.4 billion in federal-aid outlays in metropolitan areas, with the biggest sums shown for public assistance ($5.4 billion), general revenue sharing ($4.2 billion), medical assistance ($3.2 billion), and highways ($2.6 billion). Seventy percent of the President's proposals for all federal aid to state and local governments are programmed for the metropolitan areas in 1974, whereas only 54.7 percent of federal aid went there in 1961.[2]

State governments also deserve credit for their awareness of urban affairs. Cities over 500,000 population received $1.2 billion from the national government during 1970–1, but $4.6 billion from the states. Admittedly, some unknown portion of the states' $4.6 billion came initially from Washington. Table 4 shows that the states, like the national government, are giving the greatest aids to the largest cities, and are increasing most the

TABLE 4. LARGE CITIES' RECEIPT OF STATE AIDS

State aid as a percentage of city expenditures

	Cities of at least 500,000 population	All other cities
1970–1	29.8%	17.0%
1964–5	20.9	14.3
Per capita receipt of aid [a]		
1970–1	$142.15	$28.10
1964–5	49.35	14.99

[a] Of necessity, 1964–5 per capita calculations employ 1960 population figures.

Sources: *Governmental Finances in* (*1970–1 and 1964–5*) (Washington: U.S. Bureau of the Census, 1972, 1966).

aids to those cities. From 1964–5 to 1970–1 state aids per capita to cities of over 500,000 population increased by 188 percent; per capita state aids to other cities increased by only 87 percent.

State governments are also changing their constitutions and statutes to permit local authorities more flexibility in raising their own revenues. Historically, localities have been limited to the tax on real property. This tax has suffered from sharp political hostility; from its failure to tap the economic resources of individuals who work and shop in the central city, but who reside in the suburbs; from its regressive rate structure;[3] and often from arbitrary and anachronistic assessments of property value. As of 1970, local governments in twenty-two states collected a sales tax, and localities in ten states collected an income tax.

Agencies of forty states pursue active programs to improve the administration of local property taxes. These typically involve systematic comparisons between market values as determined by actual sales and local property assessments. The sales-assessment ratios serve to equalize the distribution of those state aids that go to local governments on the basis of local property values, and to identify local areas that need additional attention from tax assessors. This can minimize tax competition between local governments, and keep assessments reasonably equivalent across the state for properties of similar value.

State governments also seem to be making greater direct expenditures in metropolitan areas. These take the form of state clinics and hospitals, parks, intraurban expressways, and urban branches of state universities. Most states also have a Department of Local Affairs. Twenty-six of these appeared during the 1965–9 period alone. Some departments integrate the distribution of state financial aids to local governments, and some offer sizable state supplements for such urban programs of the national government as public housing, mass transit, urban renewal, and manpower training.

Explanation of Urban-centered Governments

What accounts for this increase in the urban concern of American governments? Some explanations point to the general prominence of urban population and the resulting place of urban affairs on the public agenda. Others point to peculiarities of local boundaries and the revenue problems of local authorities to explain the special cases of increased national and state financial aids to large cities. The general explanations are summarized as follows:

(a) The increase in the metropolitan population of the United States from 96 million in 1950 to 139 million in 1970. Two decades ago, 63 percent of us lived in areas designated by the Bureau of the Census as "Standard Metropolitan Statistical Areas". In 1970 this percentage had increased to 69. Due to the advent of court-mandated legislative reapportionments in 1962, these increases in metropolitan populations produced even greater proportional increases in political representation during the 1960s.

(b) The strident demands of citizen groups, especially spokesmen of congested inner cities, seeking federal aid in the context of all the urban bads associated with the riots of the 1960s, and supported in their demands by the recommendations of several prestigious commissions.

(c) The commitment to national government initiates in urban policy began in the Kennedy and more so the Johnson Administrations, and continued during the Nixon Administration despite conflicts between occasionally reluctant White House and an aggressive Congress.

For each of these explanations, there is some difficulty in separating the causes and effects of increased urban awareness among political elites. In the case of reapportionment, for example, the string of decisions beginning with Baker *vs.* Carr in 1962 did increase the places for metropolitan representatives in the U.S. House of Representatives and both houses of state legislatures. Moreover, there is some evidence that legislative attention to certain metropolitan problems increased with the additional votes of those members.[4] Yet the Court's decisions themselves showed an increased awareness of urban problems, leading enough Justices to shift that institution from the position taken in 1946 that left apportionment in the hands of legislatures.[5] There is evidence from the Georgia legislature that even its heavily rural bias in the years before reapportionment did not prevent it from showing increasing attention to urban affairs. Once reapportionment came, the urban awareness increased further, but the tendency was there even before the push from the Supreme Court.[6] The demands coming from inner cities, the supporting recommendations of prestigious commissions, and the urban commitments of the Kennedy, Johnson, and Nixon Administrations do not represent only the activities and commitments of vocal or highly placed individuals. These activities and commitments themselves reflect magnitudes and discontents of urban populations, plus politicians' awareness of urban voters and the implications of urban problems for the entire society.

In order to account for the increases in national and state financial aids to metropolitan governments, it is necessary to focus on some special problems of local government boundaries, local fiscal options, and an earlier failure of reform movements that had operated within the metropolitan context.

LOCAL BOUNDARIES AND FINANCIAL CONSTRAINTS

Peculiarities of local government boundaries and local financial options serve to inhibit the public resources of communities that exist amidst private affluence.[7] The abundance of human and material resources in the metropolis should make its problems amenable to solution. There is lots of money in the cities, and lots of people with the skills needed to plan and implement social programs. The 1970 census reported the median income of white metropolitan area families to be $11,203, compared to $8881 for non-metropolitan white families.[8] As of 1960, the average educational attainment of metropolitan adults was 11.1 years, while that of non-metropolitan adults was only 9.5 years. The population growth of urban areas is another sign of their economic prosperity. Between 1960 and 1970 metropolitan areas increased by almost 20 million; "rural" areas, in contrast, showed an absolute decline of 167,000. Yet growth also presents difficulties for urban authorities. Many people come to the cities for the economic opportunities they promise. Urban prosperity attracts the untrained and unsuccessful who want better opportunities. For some newcomers, the cost to the city of providing them with services is substantially greater than the contribution of their skills to the city's economy. Urban slums represent the attractions of the city for the poor, plus the inability of many immigrants to be successful in the urban environment, and provide a stimulus that sends affluent families and business firms to the suburbs. Cities present an abundance of wealth that begets poverty even while it reproduces wealth, and a magnitude of resources that is not sufficient for local authorities to satisfy intense demands for public service.

The fractured nature of local government in urban areas is an important element in limiting the revenue available to local governments. Boundaries between neighboring cities, counties, suburban towns, school districts, and special districts divide an urban area into a surplus of jurisdictions. Often they compete with each other to keep taxes low. Some local jurisdiction have a greater tax base than required to support their services, so their levies can be low. Other jurisdictions have needs that surpass their resources. While they may raise taxes to the legal or political limits, there remains untapped resources in neighboring jurisdictions. One New Jersey school district had an assessed valuation of $5.5 million per pupil, and a neighboring district had only $33,000 per pupil.

State constitutions and statutes add to the problems of urban governments by limiting the kinds of taxes they can raise. Restrictions keep most localities to the regressive and unpopular tax on the real property that lies within their borders. The regressive nature of this tax restrains its contribution to local treasuries during periods of inflation; its unpopularity dampens the frequent increases that are needed to keep revenues up to increases in prices and service demands; restrictions to a tax on locally situated real property keep the cities from tapping much of the economic resources (e.g. the income and retail purchases of suburbanites) centered in the urban area.

A FRUSTRATED REFORM MOVEMENT

The first major response to the problem of surplus jurisdictions in metropolitan areas and the segregation of resources from needs came during the 1950s and 1960s, and sought to integrate the separate jurisdictions. There were several approaches to this goal:

1. municipal regulation of real estate developments in the rural fringe outside its borders;
2. development of metropolitan-wide districts;
3. annexation and city–city consolidation;
4. consolidation of the city with the urbanized county surrounding it; and
5. federation of several municipalities.

Few of these reform efforts were successful. Voters tended to be apathetic, and most established elites were hostile. Officials of local governments, political party chiefs, leaders of unions and the black community were accustomed to the existing structures in which they had come to power, and feared dilution of their political bases in any aggregation of diverse communities.[9]

Out of 47 referenda on metropolitan reorganization undertaken in 36 of the nation's 212 Standard Metropolitan Statistical Areas during 1946–68, only 18 produced favorable votes. Even this figure overstates the success of reform campaigns. It reports only those campaigns where reform forces were strong enough to put the issue on the ballot. In the largest metropolitan areas, few major reforms have been undertaken. Only four of the SMSAs with referenda for metropolitan reform (Buffalo, St. Louis, Seattle, and Cleveland) include a city with a 1960 population greater than 500,000. The failures outnumbered successes in those areas by a 2 to 1 margin, and the successes produced only minor changes. Most successes occurred in small-to-medium-sized cities in border states. Governmental change was easiest where the problems were moderate and the opposition to change correspondingly weak.

For a period during the 1960s, the more prominent movement in metropolitan areas created *more rather than fewer* jurisdictions. Between 1957 and 1967 the number of local governmental units other than school districts increased by 7579. This was largely a result of continued suburban development, but the growth also affected sentiments in the metropolitan core. The central city movements had several names: "decentralization", "neighborhood control", "community control", "control-sharing". Some arrangements would actually decentralize the power to make program decisions, and others would merely provide representation on a centralized policy-making body to program clients.[10]

Most of these efforts occurred in black ghettoes, but any effort to explain the move toward additional governments within central cities must take account of the earlier blossoming of suburban units. Spokesmen for inner-city decentralization justified their demands by reference to the suburbs. Ghetto leaders wanted for themselves the benefits of local autonomy.

With the failure of metropolitan interpretation to rationalize local government boundaries, the taxing and spending powers of state (and national) governments came to the fore. State and national governments collect taxes from throughout a metropolitan area regardless of municipal borders. Moreover, their levies on personal incomes are progressive, and help to keep revenue collections ahead of prices during inflation. Both state and national governments have increased their shares of local financing, and as we see in Table 2, they seem to be distributing these increases to local governments with the largest populations.

Revenue Sharing

The year 1972 saw a major new departure in the nature of federal aid. Revenue sharing began with grants of $2.6 billion to the states, with two-thirds earmarked for local governments. At this writing, total allocations to state and local governments under revenue sharing are scheduled to reach $30.2 billion over the 1972–7 period. The allotments to individual localities reflect various factors of the recipients, with revenue increasing along with the size of a community's population; the effort it shows in taxing locally available resources; and its poverty as reflected by income per capita. The requirement that two-thirds of a state's share go to local governments, plus the formula that rewards jurisdictions with large population and high tax effort should work to continue the recent increases in intergovernment aid going to the largest cities.

Revenue sharing differs most dramatically from traditional federal aids in its lack of "strings". The money goes to communities as a matter of right, without detailed applications. Recipients can spend money at their discretion, subject only to the following restrictions:

> Local governments must spend their allotments within certain "priority" areas: public safety, environmental protection (including sanitation), public transportation, health, recreation, libraries, social services for the poor and aged, financial administration, and "ordinary and necessary" capital expenditures.
> Discrimination on the basis of race, color, national origin, or sex is not permitted in any program financed with revenue-sharing funds.
> Funds may not be used to match federal funds provided under other grant programs.
> Construction workers paid with revenue-sharing funds must be paid at least the wage prevailing on similar construction activity in the locality.
> Recipient governments must publish plans and publicly account for the use of revenue-sharing funds.[11]

While the lack of detailed controls on revenue sharing appeals to local officials, this feature disturbs other actors in the local arena. Supporters of individual programs have no guarantee that the money will be spent on their favored projects. With the traditional grants-in-aid program supporters concentrated their efforts at the national level, and counted on state and local officials to carry out requirements in the federal statutes. The lack of program-specificity also poses a threat to the cities that originally welcomed the greater flexibility. Without support from program-oriented interest groups in Washington, the sums distributed under general revenue sharing may be especially vulnerable to the periodic efforts of the White House to dampen inflation by holding back on allotments of federal aid. The President's budget for 1974 would have 13.4 percent of federal aid to metropolitan areas in the form of general revenue sharing. Also in the budget, but cast into limbo during the year of Watergate, was a proposal for additional reform that would reduce allocations for certain grants-in-aid, and offer several "special revenue-sharing" programs that would allow state and local governments discretion in using federal money within broad program classifications. These proposals resulted in widespread opposition from the supporters of aided programs who saw their futures as battling in hundreds of local arenas to acquire the special revenue-sharing funds for the programs that had been guaranteed support under grants-in-aid.

The explanation of revenue sharing owes something to the traditional inclinations of Republicans now controlling the national executive branch, as well, perhaps, to some political needs of key Democratic legislators, plus some current problems in the nation's economy. Deteriorations in the international economic position of the United States and serious problems with domestic inflation and unemployment led the Republican Administration of Richard Nixon to become more active in national economic planning and control than it might prefer, with some of that planning directed toward reforms in federal aids for state and local governments. Nixon's efforts to decentralize the administration of federally supported programs via general and special revenue sharing reflect the calls for decentralization that we have heard from Republicans since the 1930s. Yet the change in policy represented by general revenue sharing could not come from the White House alone. It required the support of a Democratic Congress, and a change in heart of Chairman Wilbur Mills of the House Ways and Means Committee who earlier spoke strongly in opposition to revenue sharing. Mills' shift came early in the presidential campaign of 1972, when he may have been seeking some credit with local politicians and taxpayers for the Democratic candidate, who might have become himself! Whatever his reasons, Mills is known as a shrewd leader who is often responsible for the success or failure of major legislation in the revenue field.[12] Any explanation of revenue sharing must take account of his reasoning as well as the President's.

Continuity in Local Program Administration Amidst Increasing Intergovernmental Aid

While local governments have come to depend on increasing contributions of revenue from state and national governments, localities have retained major responsibilities as the ultimate administrators of domestic programs. As we see in Table 5, local officials have retained their share of the ultimate (direct) expenditures that provide services to the people despite all the expansions of new programs since 1960 and the growth in national and state funding. What this means, of course, is an increased—and *increasing*—separation of responsibility for raising revenue and making expenditures. Indeed, it is best to speak about "separations" of responsibility, reflecting the variety of national and state agencies that provide funds to a variety of local authorities. The recipients of intergovernmental aid are no more monolithic than the providers.

Two implications flow from this increasing separation of revenue and expenditure responsibility:

TABLE 5. NATIONAL, STATE AND LOCAL GOVERNMENTS'
SHARE OF DIRECT EXPENDITURES FOR DOMESTIC PROGRAMS,
1960 TO 1970–1[a]

	National percent	State percent	Local percent
1970–1	40.8	22.9	36.2
1969–70	40.5	22.6	36.9
1968–69	41.2	22.1	36.7
1967–8	41.5	22.3	36.2
1967 (1966–7)	42.1	21.7	36.2
1966 (1965–6)	42.1	20.9	37.0
1965 (1964–5)	42.2	21.0	36.8
1964 (1963–4)	42.1	21.3	36.6
1963 (1962–3)	41.9	21.5	36.5
1962	41.7	21.1	37.2
1961	41.0	21.6	37.3
1960	40.4	21.6	37.9

[a] Omitting federal expenditures for international relations and defense, as well as all intergovernmental expenditures of national and state government; yet the direct expenditures of state and local government come, in part, from intergovernmental revenues.

Sources: *Governmental Finances in 1970–1 (and 1969–70, 1968–9, 1967–8)* and *Historical Statistics of Governmental Finances and Employment*, all published in Washington by U.S. Bureau of the Census, 1969 through 1972.

1. Local officials spend much of their time in the pursuit of funds. This means negotiating with those national and state agencies that exercise discretionary control over the intergovernmental funds they have available. The mayor of Providence, Rhode Island, expressed some widely held sentiments in an address to a training Conference of the U.S. Civil Service Commission.

> I was off to Washington, New York or Philadelphia so many times during the early days of my administration that it took me nearly two weeks to meet a new secretary whom I had appointed to my staff. But I realized early that if I was to make my city the kind of place where people would want to live and raise their children, I was going to have to get federal dollars. I could not hope to raise locally the kind of money which was going to be necessary to undertake the massive effort which lay ahead. In fact, my career as a municipal administrator had been formulated by the Lees and Cavanaghs across the country who were putting their cities into the mainstream of political life by being effective disciples of the art of grantmanship. I became a student of their experiences, and of their lively encounters with the federal establishment, and with the programs which they had developed. Their long and tedious efforts had certainly had an affect upon the birth of creative federalism and I was not about to forego their broad experience. I had my own people, with and without me, attend conferences and seminars so that I could develop my own corps of specialists. We worked long and hard to satisfy regulations, federal officials and our own community. But for Providence it has worked very well.[13]

2. There is also a good deal of negotiating among the agencies of a local government receiving intergovernmental aid. The funds of numerous national and state agencies meet together in common local jurisdictions, where the process of combining the different program requirements leads inevitably to tradeoffs and compromises with the goals of individual donors and recipients. It is not possible to maximize the transportation criteria built into the federal highway programs at the same time that recipients also maximize the

relocation criteria of federal housing legislation or the environmental protection criteria of other federal programs. Efforts to maximize low and middle-income housing construction under programs from the U.S. Department of Housing and Urban Development run afoul of efforts to maximize racial integration in criteria of the U.S. Department of Health, Education, and Welfare; concerns for racial balance, neighborhood schools, and local opposition to the development of public housing outside the central core do not fit together into any neat package consistent with the guidelines from several Washington offices.

For the best explanation of revenue sharing, we might look no further than the weight of 35 years of program—specific grants-in-aids, now totalling over 400 separate programs. While the new principles of free money virtually uncontrolled from Washington found little enthusiasm among the supporters of those programs receiving money under existing grants, it was becoming increasingly clear that each grant program could not work as it alone was conceived. It was also clear that local governments—especially those in the largest metropolitan areas—had financial difficulties that could not be solved by the reformers who would integrate metropolitan governments. The result was general revenue sharing, mandating two-thirds of the annual sums to local governments, and including criteria of distribution (local tax effort, population, and per capita income) that would continue the recent trends of favoring large cities with severe financial problems. In this reform, we see a passing of the buck to local officials who will face conflicting program demands on their own. This is a significant change in the structure of intergovernmental relations. Whether it produces significant changes in the behavior of local officials or the policy benefits received by local citizens will have to await further time and later analyses.

Money in the Urban Policy System

This discussion of metropolitan finance brings us only part of the way toward an understanding of public policy-making in the urban setting. The dollars and cents provide a scoreboard for governmental growth, showing the prominence acquired by the largest city governments, and the support given to them by state and national governments. The record of expenditure and financial aid does not translate into any statements about the quality of public services coming from the largest cities. We have not dealt with the allocation of city budgets from one field of service to another. Nor have we considered the distribution of municipal resources among the various neighborhoods. Thus, we do not know about investments made for education, health, or transportation; nor to what extent municipal expenditures benefit residents of upper-, middle-, or lower-income classes. Within each field of service, we do not know if expenditures are allocated wisely among the various products or services to be purchased, and we do not know if the results of those expenditures satisfy the clients. We also remain in the dark about unintended consequences, i.e. those results from governmental actions that are not expected by the officials who design policies. By focusing on indicators of public finance we have learned some things of importance about the growth of urban awareness among the political elites of the United States. However, we must be careful lest the "veil of money" deceive us. The sheer levels of expenditures do not by themselves produce public services.

To understand the nature of urban policy-making more fully, we must look beyond the aggregates of money. To help in this quest, we can use a model of Urban Policy System. The model is an adaptation of political system models made popular by David Easton and others.[14] This version focuses our attention to the influences on—and the effects of—urban public policies; and it emphasizes the tenuous nature of relationships between policies announced and services actually delivered. The components of our model are: (1) an *environment* that both stimulates government officials and receives the products of their work; (2) *inputs* that carry stimuli from the environment to officials; (3) a *conversions process* that includes the formal structures and procedures of government, and transforms (converts) inputs to policy statements; (4) the *policies* that represent the formal goals, intentions, or statements of government officials; (5) the *performance* of the policy as it is shaped by numerous competitive and complementary stimuli from policy and the environment; and (6) *feedback* that transmits the policies and performances of one period—as they are shaped by interacting with the environment—back to the conversions process as the inputs of a later time.

"Policy" represents actions taken by government officials. As indicated by the model, however, "policy" is distinct from "service performance". "Policy" represents current actions that are subject to the control of officials, and undertaken at least partly with an eye toward affecting the quantity or quality of public services. Public officials cannot directly control the learning of schoolchildren or the wellbeing of welfare clients. They can only aim at these service targets by policy decisions that define such elements as expenditures, salary levels, employees' workloads, the substance of programs, and the rules and regulations that govern the treatment of clients. Of course, not all of these policies are subject to the free will of government authorities. Expenditures depend partly on economic resources and the tolerance for taxation that exists in the political environment, plus constitutional and statutory controls that affect the conversions process. Conceptions of policies must be made specific according to the kinds of services at issue. For elementary and secondary education, policies about the teacher–pupil ratio, the education required of teachers, and teacher salaries will supplement expenditures for education. In the welfare field, policies include the professional training required of social workers, their salaries, workload, the discretion permitted them in dealing with clients, and the maximum and minimum grants that are authorized.

Notions about "performance" also vary with the kind of service at issue. There are different aspects of each service, and each of the important aspects deserves some recognition in any assessment of performance. Elementary and secondary education claims to impart the proverbial skills of reading, writing, and arithmetic; substantive knowledge in a wide range of academic fields; technical skills under the headings of vocational training, automobile driving, and human reproduction; plus social amenities and some measure of patriotism. The welfare field also has diverse goals: for various programs they include material sustenance employment ambition and skills, and the performance can be measured by the *number of service units* provided in relation to the likely clientele group; by the *rate* at which a program is performed; by *changes in the traits of clients* as a result of a program; by the *frequency with which a population chooses to use* a program; by the *kinds of people who are served* by a program; or by the *continued existence of conditions* that a program is designed to control.

It is necessary to portray "policy" and "performance" as two separate categories of the Urban Policy System because the policies of governments do not always produce the kind of service performance that is sought. Different policies may work at cross purposes. Because of conflicting demands from the environment, officials may water down their intentions and pursue policies that are so weakened by compromise that they cannot accomplish their intentions. At times, the social or economic environments that are the targets of policies are more resistant than first believed. The problems of lower-income families in urban slums have proved "intractable" in the face of certain policies that were thought capable of dealing with them. Some health policies have proved insufficient to stop the spread of certain diseases.

Much of the political science that is written about the cities adds at least indirectly to an understanding of the policy system. The reams of literature about community power remind us that local government decisions may be the work of officials who occupy formal positions in government, or merely those officials' ratification of decisions formulated by influential persons outside of government. Furthermore, officials and private citizens can exercise policy-relevant power by using their authority and influence to keep decisions from being made (i.e. non-decisions) and thereby let actions in the private sector continue unchallenged by any public policies. Studies of various groups in local electorates make us sensitive to income, education, occupation, ethnicity, and race as determinants of individuals' feelings about policy issues, and the likelihood of their inputs to local policy. Additional research about behaviors of mayors, city managers, councilmen, and administrators help explain the workings of the urban conversions process. Increasingly, political scientists ask directly about the significance of political behaviors for the nature of policies offered by local governments.[15] Their studies describe the range of behaviors to be expected from various participants in urban policy-making. For certain cities that have been made the subject of close investigations, it may be possible to judge the frequencies of various behaviors, and how different participants (e.g. managers and council members) will probably interact on certain issues.[16]

The model of the urban-policy system does not define a good policy. Much of the research displays an implicit assumption that policy performance improves with the more (or less) of some objective indicator measured in a city. Yet we are already alert to the problems of translating money aggregates into performance satisfaction. Other research warns us that "objective" measures of performance do not always produce client approval.[17] One study found that popular satisfaction with parks and playgrounds showed little relationship to the incidence of facilities; and satisfaction with police services showed little relationship to the number of police personnel or the crime rate.[18] Edward Banfield's widely known argument is that residents of the Unheavenly City are angrier even while living amidst conditions that are better than in the past.[19]

Problems of Measurement and Analysis

Beyond the problem of determining good policies or performance, there is also the problem of measuring the characteristics of the urban scene that are actual products of public policy. We have already noted the large role of the private sector in urban affairs. Much of what stands as attractive (or unattractive) features of the city reflect the land-use decisions of private individuals and business firms. In looking at what seems to occur in the classroom of the public school, we find that much of children's learning reflects their parents' and friends' attitudes toward education, and the availability of intellectual stimuli outside of school.[20] As one urban specialist writes:

> To what extent are social indicators also indicators of the quality of government? . . . The newer urban studies attempt to assess performance throughout the urban environment: the natural environment, the spatial environment, the transportation-utilities environment, the household-shelter environment, and the workplace environment. . . .
> As the number and sophistication of urban indicators grow, the uneasiness of the policy analyst grows also. To study the activities and effectiveness of government bureaucracies has a satisfying concreteness, yet it generates the feeling that all the spending and activity may be but sound and fury.[21]

There are studies that make serious efforts to separate out the effects of governmental activities from other determinants of urban society.[22] Even then, however, it is another difficult step to sort out the effects of local officials' actions from those mandated or supported by national and state authorities. For much of what affects the goods and bads of urban living we must look to a college of public and private decisions.

Determinants of Local Spending: The Systems Model at Work

Despite the necessary caveats about the imperfect linkages between measures of local government spending and the performance of public services in urban areas, it is in the area of spending that we have the most systematic information about the urban-policy system. Some findings fit into patterns that advance our general understanding of policy-making in the urban setting, but others fit no apparent pattern. There is much "adhockery" in the explanations (i.e. speculation about why certain measures of the environment, inputs, or conversions process relate to certain measures of expenditures).[23] The variety of studies, with different definitions used in measuring expenditures and their determinants, and different statistical techniques require the reader to use discretion in his interpretations. Table 6 summarizes the direction of statistical findings for several determinants. City spending per capita tends to be high where there is generally *high income* among local residents, a *manufacturing base* to the local economy, a *low incidence of owner-occupied homes*, a *high incidence of ethnics* in the population, where the state government leaves a *high proportion of service responsibilities in the hands of local governments*, where *intergovernmental aids are high*, and where *state debt and expenditure limits are unrestrictive*.[24] It should be noted, however, that individual studies have found variations from these patterns with respect to spending in different fields of service.

One finding does emerge sharply from the statistical comparison of many cities' expenditure patterns. Cities, like other governments in the United States (and elsewhere in many countries of the world), budget incrementally. Expenditures tend to move upward in relatively small additions to the base of previous and current expenditure. This finding is evident in studies of spending aggregates: measures of spending at some point in the distant past show significant relationships with current spending.[25] Incrementalism also appears in studies of officials' decision-making techniques. Bureaucrats, mayors, city managers, and council members usually focus their attention on the difference between the pending request and the base of current expenditures, and keep their decisions for the coming period close to the current base. Budget procedures in many cities require explicit justifications for any departures from the current levels. Furthermore, each actor in the process helps to enforce incrementalism by cutting the most out of those recommendations that ask for the greatest increases.[26]

Aside from incrementalism, the finding of most general significance that emerges from the studies of spending is the weakness of most other determinants. Many entries in

TABLE 6. SUMMARY OF RELATIONS BETWEEN SOCIO-ECONOMIC VARIABLES AND MUNICIPAL SPENDING LEVELS[a]

Variable	Relation with municipal spending	Variable	Relation with municipal spending
Income		State-local centralization	
High	+	State responsibilities greater	−
Low	−	Local responsibilities greater	+
Economic base		Intergovernmental aid	
Manufacturing	+	High	+
Other	−	Low	−
Density		State debt and expenditure limits	
High	?	Restrictive	−
Low	?	Unrestrictive	+
Growth rate		Previous expenditures	
High	?	High	+
Low	?	Low	−
Owner occupancy		Degree of government reformism	
High	−	High	?
Low	+	Low	?
Ethnic character		Participation in local politics	
Heavy	+	High	?
Nonethnic	−	Low	?
Metropolitan type		Party competition	
Central city	+	High	?
Outside central city	−	Low	?

[a] A plus sign indicates a relationship generally identified as positive. A minus sign indicates a relationship generally identified as negative. A query indicates a variable about which findings are either incomplete or mixed.

Source: Robert L. Lineberry and Ira Sharkansky, *Urban Politics and Public Policy* (New York: Harpers, 1971), pp. 219, 223.

Table 6 are marked with a "?" signifying incomplete or mixed findings. Other findings are weak in strength. They may pass minimal tests for statistical significance, but generally account for less than two-thirds the city-to-city variance in the measures of spending.[27] Where we have findings about one determinant of spending going back many years (relationships between income per capita and the combined spending per capita of state and local governments), the weight of the determinant has declined considerably over the time series. In 1903 income per capital accounted for some 85 percent of the variance in government spending per capita. By 1964–5 income per capita accounted for only 31 percent of the variance in spending.[28] Explanations for this decline point to increasing revenue options of state and local government in recent years, with taxes on personal and corporate incomes and retail sales allowing the lower-income jurisdictions to extract more revenues from their own economies than the simple tax on real property that prevailed at the beginning of the century. Also, federal aids—many of them explicit efforts to redistribute resources from "have" to "have not" states—have increased the funds available to the officials of lower-income jurisdictions. The findings of incrementalism are generally strong (accounting for upwards of 80 percent of the variance in some cases), but even they include deviant cases of sharp upward spending increases in certain jurisdictions for certain activities. And we must remember that the bias against the great spurts of spending have not stabilized city expenditures. Between 1960 and 1970–1 per capita expenditures in cities over 500,000 population increased by 176 percent, and by 102 percent after accounting for inflation.

What can we learn from the departures from incrementalism, and the weakness of other determinants of local government spending? One interpretation looks to the complexity of the urban-policy system. With many variables having some impact on policy, there is no one of them capable of dominating the system. Empirical analysis finds the system is just what its theoretical authors suggest: a simplified model of reality with separate cells for each of environment, inputs, conversions process, policy, and performance, but with each of these categories containing numerous elements that interact among themselves and with components from the other cells to have some influence on policy and performance.

Another interpretation of the diverse and often weak influences on spending emphasizes their implications for policy-makers. As scholars have not succeeded in identifying traits that provide a full explanation of urban policy, policy-makers seem to have significant freedom in making their decisions. As far as we know, there is nothing about the economy, previous decisions, the magnitude of state or federal aids, the size or nature of the local population that has such power over local policy-makers as to fix their decisions. Ideologues, apologists, or frustrated local officials can point to certain features of the environment as predetermining the activities of local government; yet the studies of local spending find no strong evidence to support their case. It is still legitimate for local officials to strive to overcome environmental conditions that may "generally" (but by no means "always") shape local policies or performance; and local citizens can still hold their officials responsible for policies that are—or are not—implemented.

Notes

1. These calculations show a conservative estimate of the urban centeredness of American governments. They omit the "direct" expenditures of national and state governments (i.e. those not funneled to local units through intergovernmental aids) plus the spending of other local governments (e.g. school districts, county governments, and special districts) that are made within the boundaries of cities having at least 500,000 residents.
2. *Special Analyses: Budget of the United States Government, Fiscal Year 1974* (Washington: U.S. Government Printing Office, 1973), p. 219.
3. Which prevents the local property tax from operating like the state and national progressive income taxes, i.e. increasing in productivity faster than inflation as the inflation moves individuals into brackets where they pay a higher percentage of their income as taxes.
4. See H. George Frederickson and Yong Hyo Cho, "Legislative reapportionment and public policy in the American states", a paper given at the 1970 meeting of the American Political Science Association, Los Angeles; and *Reapportionment in Georgia* (Institute of Government, The University of Georgia, Athens, Georgia, 1970).
5. In Colegrove *vs.* Green.
6. See my "Legislative reapportionment in Georgia: changes in voting patterns and their policy implications", in *Reapportionment in Georgia*.
7. This section relies on Robert L. Lineberry and Ira Sharkansky, *Urban Politics and Public Policy* (New York: Harper, 1971), Chapter 2.
8. These figures are for non-farm, non-metro whites; for Negroes, even sharper differences prevail: $7140 metro families and $4605 non-metro, non-farm families. Among both white and Negroes, the lowest median family incomes appear for non-metro farm families: $6819 for whites and $3106 for Negroes. The figures come from the *Statistical Abstract of the United States*, 1972 (Washington: U.S. Government Printing Office, 1973), p. 323.
9. See Robert L. Lineberry, "Reforming metropolitan government: requiem or reality?" *Georgetown Law Journal*, 58 (May 1970).
10. See, for example, Milton Kotler, *Neighborhood Government: The Local Foundations of Political Life* (Indianopolis: Bobbs-Merrill, 1969), and Alan A. Altshuler, *Community Control: The Black Demand for Participation in Large American Cities* (New York: Pegasus, 1970).

11. *The Budget of the United States Government, Fiscal Year 1974* (Washington: U.S. Government Printing Office, 1973), p. 163.
12. See John F. Manley, *The Politics of Finance: The House Committee on Ways and Means* (Boston: Little, Brown, 1970).
13. Douglas Fox, ed., *The New Urban Politics: Cities and the Federal Government* (Pacific Palisades, Calif: Goodyear, 1972), p. 91.
14. See David Easton, *A Framework for Political Analysis* (Englewood Cliffs: Prentice Hall, 1965).
15. See, for example, John P. Crecine, *Governmental Problem-solving: A Computer Simulation of Municipal Budgeting* (Chicago: Rand McNally, 1969); Robert Eyestone, *The Threads of Public Policy: A Study in Policy Leadership* (Indianapolis: Bobbs-Merrill, 1971); Ronald O. Loveridge, *City Managers in Legislative Politics* (Indianapolis: Bobbs-Merrill, 1971); and Wallace S. Sayre and Herbert Kaufman, *Governing New York City: Politics in the Metropolis* (New York: Norton, 1965).
16. For summaries of these literatures, see Lineberry and Sharkansky, *op. cit.*, especially Chapters 3 and 5.
17. See Robert C. Fried, "Comparative urban performance", in Fred I. Greenstein and Nelson W. Polsby, eds., *The Empirical Study of Politics and Policy-making*, Vol. 8 (Mass.: Addison-Wesley, 1974).
18. Howard Schuman and Barry Gruenberg, "Dissatisfaction with city services: is race an important factor?", in Harlan Hahn, ed., *People and Politics in Urban Society* (Beverly Hills: Sage, 1972), as cited in Fried.
19 Edward C Banfield, *The Unheavenly City*, (Boston: Little, Brown, 1970).
20. See, for example, James S. Coleman *et al.*, *Equality of Educational Opportunity* (Washington: U.S. Government Printing Office, 1966).
21. Fried, *op. cit.*
22. Coleman, *op. cit.*
23. Fried, *op. cit.*
24. For interpretations of these findings, see Lineberry and Sharkansky, *op. cit.*, pp. 218ff.
25. See my *Routines of Politics* (New York: Van Nostrand Reinhold, 1970), especially Chapter 3; and Bernard Brown, "Municipal finances and annexation: a case study of post-war Houston", *Social Science Quarterly*, **48** (Dec. 1967).
26. Crecine: Also my *Routines*.
27. Fried, *op. cit.*
28. Alan K. Campbell and Seymour Sacks, *Metropolitan America: Fiscal Patterns and Governmental Systems* (New York: The Free Press, 1967), especially p. 57.

11. Quantifying Conflict Resolution with Applications to Urban and International Problems

THOMAS L. SAATY

1. Introduction

In an age when conflicts, large and small, regional and urban, domestic and international, are the mode of the day, an increasing number of individuals, groups, and organizations are undertaking the study of conflicts. At the rate their understanding is going, none of us may be around to see its fruits. Mathematicians have also been in on the subject, and they have a few interesting things to say. Unlike most scientific disciplines, no one seems to have a monopoly on explaining human behavior, which gives rise to conflict. The psychologists and the social workers cannot do it—neither the anthropologists nor the historians, and the scientists seem out-of-it. But each school has an interesting angle to tell. Probably, if all the theories disappeared, we would be just as badly off—or maybe a little better—because these parties themselves would not be around to have conflict between their disciplines.

At every plateau of "human progress" there are more reasons for people to rebel and take up fights. Maybe the average man's lot is better than it was 50 years ago, but there is little reason to be optimistic. A major sign of progress in the world is a rising standard of living, but World War II occurred between countries with the highest standards of living—and today, the richest nations are constantly preparing for war. The presence of nuclear weapons has not been a deterrent for wars. No one who counts the wars which occurred since Hiroshima would believe in the deterrent value of nuclear weapons except perhaps to deter nuclear wars. Finally, our hope may be pinned on the United Nations, on improved communications or on the shrinking world contracted by the jet plane—but none of these has withstood the test either.

The pessimist sees possible conflicts about dense population and shortage of food, demand for energy and limited resources and environmental pollution looming over the horizon. He sees no lack of opportunity for conflicts.

The optimists are hopeful regarding the increased awareness of people about these problems and the willingness of groups and nations to create organizations to cope with international problems. Examples of such efforts have been the special United Nations food and health organizations and some successful disarmament agreements.

Multinational corporations, global econometric modeling, cultural cooperation, joint economic projects and cooperative undertakings including control of environmental pollution are helping to reduce divergent multiple interests to manageable proportions in the business of living together.

Within each country of the world there is greater awareness of the need for individual freedom concomitant with a constant effort to improve and democratize legal processes.

257

However, we still have a long way to go to learn to survive through cooperation coupled with successful bargaining processes.

Two journals mostly dedicated to quantitative work in conflict resolution are the *Journal of Conflict Resolution* at Yale University and the *Peace Science Journal* at the University of Pennsylvania. There are also a number of research organizations concerned with the study of peace and the analysis of armament and conflicts. Among them are The International Peace Science Society which publishes Peace Science, University of Pensylvania; The International Institute for Strategic Studies, London, with many publications appearing regularly and periodically and The Stockholm International Peace Research (SIPRI), with its *Yearbook of World Armaments and Disarmament*—as well as other publications. The U.S. Arms Control and Disarmament Agency in Washington is one of the best known and most active institutions working for peace and arms control. It is also involved in negotiations on arms control.

Conflicts will probably always be there, but men as well as nations must learn to deal with them effectively because of their escalating number due to increased interdependence of the world community. There should be ground rules for negotiation, the possibility of arbitration, a respect for law and the presence of adequate means of control.

The methods of conflict resolution range from one extreme: outright giving in to the opponent's wishes, to the other extreme: the use of force and violence in a pursuit adequately described by the adage, "might makes right". In between these extremes there is the possibility of letting time obviate the necessity of a solution such as between people whose grievance cannot be solved without creating an equal grievance to someone else. There is also the possibility of arbitration by a disinterested party who would attempt to understand the issues as viewed by both sides and then make a decision. Another way along these lines is to obtain a vote on the issue from a number of people.

The most desirable and time-honored method of resolving conflicts is through negotiation and bargaining in which concessions are made to diminish basic differences. Usually each party has threats which, if implemented, would produce less desirable outcome (perhaps to all concerned) than would result from making concessions in negotiation. It is this combination of threats and concessions which one seeks to stabilize through negotiation. One may assume that by accepting to negotiate, the parties see a more desirable outcome than would be obtained through protracted conflict.

It is my purpose here, with the space limitations allowed, to write about a few aspects of conflict and control which are amenable to mild forms of quantification. Complex conflict studies can be analyzed very successfully in the framework of these new methods of conflict resolution. Because much of the work has been done on international conflicts, it is also useful to illustrate the methodology through some examples from international conflicts. We include a detailed and lengthy application to an urban conflict situation and also discuss a method for conflict resolution which allows one to assign priorities in spite of the incompatible goals of the participants, and apply this to another urban problem.

2. Remarks on International Conflicts and Arms Control

In the gamut of international relations today, there is a great desire on the part of many nations to improve the atmosphere by averting hostile action in the resolution of conflicts. The intensification of the search for peaceful methods in this generation is a consequence of the presence of nuclear weapons in the hands of several nations. It is feared that each hostile step in a conflict becomes an inevitable consequence of the one that went before, and that at the end of such inexorable escalation lies general annihilation. Therefore, our efforts to avoid belligerent confrontations between nations have an urgency. Indeed, almost all situations today are approaching critical mass, so that finding resolutions to conflicts has become vitally important in all areas.

It should be emphasized here that, historically, the development of arsenals of nuclear weapons has been a result of suspicions between nations. These suspicions have been aroused by the methods used to further national interests. Some governments, which tend to rule more through power than through persuasion, eventually become a nuisance to their own people (an internal matter) or to other nations (an international concern). Therefore, major weapons cannot be given up without first diminishing the causes of suspicion. To the extent that nations have improved relations with other nations and feel that their ambitions are not in conflict and that their differences can be settled by negotiation and compromise, they might be willing to limit their power holding. However, nations do not have precise means for acquiring weapons to deter aggression. In recent years, to deter an aggressor has meant building power to flatten his country several times over. It is clear that knowledge of the utility of weapons provides a rational means for assessing the amount needed for various contingencies and for deciding whether it is possible and safe to negotiate tradeoffs for disarmament purposes. The upshot of negotiations may be to reduce the factor of destroying the other side from 10 times over to 3 times over. Two significant questions are: how much power does a country need to defend itself, to deter other countries' aggressive actions and to maintain its prestige in the world? What means have we to convince other nations to give up a part of their might as we also reduce ours? The amount of resources the world wastes each year on armament is measured in hundreds of billions of dollars ($300+ billion in 1977). This huge sum spent on an unproductive, potentially destructive activity could well be used in a rational world to lift the majority of the world population out of starvation.

Wiesner[25] has pointed out that very few of the world's leaders and citizens regard disarmament as realizable; therefore, most are unwilling to risk a loss of national freedom and initiative to explore the untried routes needed to achieve it. This is why it is very important to mathematically analyze the situation and demonstrate the practicality of disarmament.

3. The Role of Quantitative Models

It is well known that quantification in the social sciences depends on one's ability to form models which inherently do not depend on the absolute magnitude of numbers, but rather on their order, i.e. ordinal instead of cardinal utilities. Consequently, models are oriented towards deciding whether a given property, e.g. stability, holds or does not hold, rather than on the numerical magnitude of results.

Four major areas of research present themselves:

1. those concerned with conflicts, why they occur, and why they escalate;
2. those concerned with stability (the balance of power and with weapons, their utility and effectiveness in securing defense and offense);

3. those concerned with negotiating to settle conflict problems, control the use of force; and, finally;

4. those concerned with inspection and verification to ensure enforcement.

Generally, there are two types of mathematical analyses of problems—tactical or local (microscopic) and strategic or global (macroscopic). We are interested in giving the reader examples of global models to some problems. The object is to indicate variety and scope. Some of the ideas represented here are rather recent, and the research leading to them was not designed to solve the problem of conflict in a few years. However, it is expected that such lines of thinking will help point to new methods and directions to pursue in thinking of solutions. They also provide us with tools to articulate our basic problems and some of their finer components.

Because nations are in some ways like individuals, having different utility scales for evaluating their objectives and projecting them into the world, and because the pursuit of the fulfilment of these objectives may lead to alliances with some nations and conflicts with other nations, the need to come together and negotiate, to "compare utilities", stating and interpreting objectives and policies, and making compromises to reach agreement is essential. How each individual or each nation views its objectives and its strategies and how it works to attain these objectives with the ambition of high utility returns needs to be understood.

Problems concerned with the resolution of conflicts between different interests with an aim of doing the best possible for each player over the set of available strategies by also considering the alternatives available to the opponents is a concern of the mathematical theory of games. Of course, the problem here is different from that of maximizing a single utility objective subject to constraints which is the forte of classical optimization techniques.

Recent attempts have been made in game theory to formalize a negotiation situation together with optimum bargaining procedures. These methods take into consideration not only the difference in utility scales but also that each side may not know exactly the utility scale used by the opposite side, but has only an estimate of the probability that it may be one of several known and possible alternatives.

Equilibrium is a central concept in the analysis of conflict between several parties. A stable equilibrium may or may not be a desirable objective. Being inevitably caught between two evils is an undesirable stable equilibrium. On the other hand, instability may be a desirable way out of long-established and perhaps non-progressive methods. In a multi-party conflict, stability means that none of the parties would find it profitable to change from this strategy to any other while the remaining participants adhere to this strategy. John Nash has proved that every n-person game with a finite number of strategies has a stable equilibrium in mixed strategies. Pure stable equilibrium strategies do not always exist. A game theoretic approach to conflicts can increase the understanding of the parties as to the possible outcome of their insisting on a course of action opposed by the other players.

The principle of rationality on which the analysis of conflicts in the context of game theory is based requires that each player have a consistently chosen set of objectives and that he choose his strategy consistently with the expectation that the other players are each selecting their best replies to his own strategy. He should not expect them to give him concessions that were he in their position he would not give. A main contribution of the systematic approach of game theory is to make one aware of what are intelligent expectations regarding other peoples' reactions to one's own policy.

Games may be classified in terms of interests into identical, opposite and mixed interests. In the former, each player expects exactly the same return as any other player for a particular choice of strategy by each one. Rational behavior should guide them to a choice of strategies that have the greatest payoff. Such behavior involves cooperation. Not many real-life situations are of this kind. The players' interests may be exactly opposed. An extreme example of this are zero-sum two-person games (where the winnings of one player are the losses of the other player) noted applications of which are made to parlor games and to wars where the players are only interested in victory.

Games with mixed interests more closely typify social situations. Here the interests may be nearly the same for some strategies and nearly opposite for other strategies—and still for others, the interests are in-between. Such games can be both cooperative and non-cooperative. One must specify the conditions for rational players to play cooperatively or without cooperation, i.e. to point out strategies that are cooperative and those that are not.

In pursuing their best interests, both players, with reason for suspicion and mistrust of the opponent, start out reasoning from cooperation that is best for both, to non-cooperation that leads to a harmful outcome to both. Thus, it often happens that rational behavior leads the players to a non-cooperative solution, resulting in double-dealing because of mounting suspicion. Here, the social situation itself (rather than the players individually) is irrational. The players may need to enter into binding and enforceable agreements. Such agreements can be in the form of externally imposed arbitration with penalties—or what is equivalent, they may be incorporated into the payoffs as violation penalties which reduce the net payoff.

A major contribution of game theory is simply the highlighting of the fact that mixed interests games lead to harmful non-cooperation unless the players enter into binding agreements.

4. An Application to Urban Conflict[2]

As we have already mentioned, John Nash, in search of the concept of a solution for games, advanced the notion of an equilibrium or stable payoff. An equilibrium payoff is a payoff whereby if all players adhere to the strategies leading to this payoff, but one of them tries another strategy, he cannot improve his own payoff. This definition is both realistic and sophisticated. Many real-life problems have a political origin and are difficult to view as mixed strategy games because the rules change from play to play. One may seek a pure strategy solution in the hope of finding one. Occasionally, there is an impasse at a low payoff to all players which can only (if at all) be broken by embedding a negotiation problem in a larger one with a larger number of alternatives. The hope is to convince the parties that compromise on the present issue by one party would entail some kind of commitment to compromise on a future issue by the other party (or parties). There is an elementary, rather simple-minded way of testing for pure Nash equilibrium. Let us examine the procedure in the context of an application.

The following is an example of an application to an urban conflict. It was done in collaboration with Henry Bain and Nigel Howard and appeared in the *Journal of Conflict Resolution*, Vol. 15, No. 2. We will work this example out in detail.

Perhaps one of the greatest needs in dealing with social and political conflict is to develop methods that spell out and analyze in detail who the participants in a conflict are, what their options are, and how they are expected to act given their own set of preferences. In general, we need to sort out the various ramifications of the problem in a systematic manner. This process of rigorization is not so much a contraction or a simplification of the problem as it is a clarification of the ideas and issues involved. By requiring that one examine, at least in theory, all the possible outcomes, the process expedites convergence on the relevant outcomes. In assigning preferences to the parties, one needs to consult the parties themselves. If they prove unwilling to divulge their preferences (for parties in a negotiation would seldom want their opponent to know how they intend to act under various alternatives), the analysts advising a decision-maker must make the best use of available information and special talent to surmise the other parties' preferences. Central to the analysis is the identification of outcomes that would be stable and hence merit attention.

It would be advantageous to repeat the analysis if necessary after each negotiation session, using whatever additional information is obtained to check for stability, thereby developing arguments in favor of promising decisions for compromise. This general procedure is illustrated here in the context of a particular community problem. The same approach has been applied to a number of other domestic and international conflicts. On occasion (although not in the example given here), the analysis has revealed possible "dramatically different" solutions other than those reached in actual negotiation when some of the parties "tired" of their role and withdrew from negotiation before using their powers of sanctions against and of cooperation with their opponents.

(a) THE ANALYSIS OF OPTIONS TECHNIQUE

We illustrate here an approach to conflict problems based on the so-called Analysis of Options (Howard, 1968, 1969, 1971; Management Science Center, 1969) initially developed and used for problems of arms control under the auspices of the United States Arms Control and Disarmament Agency (Saaty, 1964, 1968). This method is designed to take the knowledge, arguments, and insights of informed experts or participants in a particular conflict problem and build them into a game-theoretic model. The subsequent analysis of the model is based on the theory of metagames (Howard, 1968, 1971). The method does not require the data used to be built into the model in a quantitative form. In this study, for example, the data used are non-quantitative knowledge and insights supplied by Bain from his many years' experience with the problem.

The following is a descriptive outline of the formal Analysis of Options technique.

> Because it is futile to attempt the resolution of a conflict problem without knowing what each party considers an acceptable solution, each participant's preferences among the several possible outcomes must be known. Often an outcome may be described by listing the actions (called options) available to each party and stating whether that party takes or does not take the action for the outcome being considered. If necessary, each option can be subdivided.

In a nutshell, this is what we do below to test the stability of the outcomes by using informed judgment on the preferences of each of the parties.

Stability is perhaps the most central concept in the theory of n-person games. An outcome is potentially stable for a particular player (participant) if any action he might take to improve his position can be responded to by a sanction wielded by the other players, so that, whatever the particular player does, he will be in a position not preferred by him to the initial outcome. A potentially stable outcome will be actually stable for a player if he finds it credible that such a sanction would be applied if he moved to a preferred position. Finally, an outcome as a whole is stable if and only if it is stable for each individual player.

Using this definition of stability, the analyst first lists the options available to each player as described above. Then he selects what appears to be a stable outcome and examines it from the viewpoint of each player to decide if it is stable for him. The analyst lists all unilateral changes this player can make and decides if each change tends to a preferred outcome. If there exist any which would lead the player to a preferred outcome, the analyst examines all possible sanctions the other players could use against the option to decide if the option-sanction combination does yield only "not-preferred" outcomes. Because it is unnecessary to examine all possible outcomes, a considerable economy is effected in the number of assumptions which must be made to arrive at a conclusion regarding stability.

An outcome can also be examined from the viewpoint of coalitions of individual parties. A coalition (i.e. a particular subset of parties) is defined as preferring one outcome to another if, and only if, each coalition member has that preference. The definition is designed to enable us to examine how groups of players can reach jointly preferred outcomes by joint action.

If the analysis of these options does not lead to an outcome that is acceptable to all the parties, the same problem, with a larger number of options, may be examined to see if concessions could be made by one party to the opposing party in order to reach a compromise. For conflicts which arise in the field of planning, these additional concession-options may require action at a future date. If one party seeks action for a development in the not too distant future and objects to an option the remaining parties want in the conflict under analysis, then these parties might attempt to get a concession from the first party by offering action on the future development where interests are better served, thereby enlarging the scope of the game.

(b) THE SUBWAY–HIGHWAY DEBATE IN WASHINGTON, DC, JULY 1969

In July 1969, when this study was undertaken, the District of Columbia had been plagued with delays in its construction of transportation routes believed essential for its future growth and for the health of the community. A number of parties were involved in a difficult and stubborn debate. Little action had come of this debate, and it seemed likely that even if action did materialize in the future based on decisions made in 1969, that action would be diluted by inflation and rising costs. We have written the following brief description of the study as a play scenario, using the present tense. The scene is the District of Columbia in July 1969 as it debates and delays the construction of a subway system, a system of highways, and a bridge across the Potomac River.

The initial impasse

A major impediment to progress on the highway–subway construction in the District is lack of agreement on a compromise between the several parties involved. Funds to start subway construction ($18.7 million to be matched by $37.4 million of federal money) have been tentatively dropped from the supplemental appropriation bill which recently came before the House and Senate appropriations committees. The intent of the committees has been that the District government (represented by the Mayor and the City Council

Chairman) include in its plans a merger of the city's 24.5-mile, $500-million prospective freeways into the national system by the building of the Three Sisters Bridge to Interstate 95 in Virginia and the North Central Freeway to Interstate 70S in Maryland, or alternative routes. House members generally favor the subway, but some of them (e.g. Representatives Joel T. Broyhill and William H. Natcher) have backed Secretary John A. Volpe in his effort to get a freeway–subway agreement from the District government which would respond to suburban commuters' desire for easier access to the District. Thus, those congressmen who want to see the subway started have not been able to beat the "package" group even though Secretary Volpe has not insisted on the connections to Maryland and Virginia.

The District government must also consider the desire of many residents who oppose major freeway construction in general and particularly the routes through inner-city residential areas.

Another important group who oppose highway and bridge construction are the conservationists. This is a group of middle-class, primarily suburban dwellers who object to turning parkland into highways. Some of them live in areas where the highways would pass, perhaps exercising an unfavorable effect on the neighborhood. Thus they propose highway constraints.

Analysis of options in the debate

First the major construction projects involved in the dispute were listed, as below:

3 Sisters (3S) Bridge
North Central (NC) Freeway
Subway
Air Rights Housing on NC Freeway
Potomac River Freeway
Center Leg Freeway
South Leg Freeway
Industrial Highway
East Leg Freeway
North Leg Freeway

Next the parties (interest groups) involved in the dispute were identified as below. Each category is, of course, an abstraction; there would be people in each who do not behave or think as we have characterized here, nor do they evaluate alternatives in a monolithic way.

PORS Public Officials for Roads (backed by certain Congressmen interested in highway construction)
ICRS Inner-City Residents
CONS Conservationist Interests
DBIS Downtown Business Interests
SCIS Suburban Commuter Interests

From a theoretical viewpoint, we can isolate a group containing diverse interests as a "player" if we can describe the group as having "preferences" between alternatives in the following operational sense. "X prefers A to B" means simply that if the choice between A and B depended solely on X (however, the members of X came to agreement among themselves), that choice would be A. The above parties were regarded or known to have the preferences indicated in Table 1.

TABLE 1. PREFERENCES OF PARTIES

	PORS	DBIS	SCIS	ICRS	CONS
3S Bridge	1[a]	1	1		0
NC Freeway	1	1	1	0	0
Subway		1	1	1	1
Air Rights Housing				1	
Potomac Highway	1	1	1		0
Center Leg	1	1	1		
South Leg	0	1	1		0
Industrial Highway	1	1		0	
East Leg	1	1	1	0	0
North Leg	1	0	1		0

[a] "1" means favorable. "0" means unfavorable. A blank means indifferent or neutral.

Some pilot studies analyzing compromises on these ten alternatives by the five parties (players) revealed that several things had already become clear in the earlier stages of the Washington controversy. It was apparent that air rights housing was not a sufficient inducement to secure ICRS's endorsement of the NC freeway. The analysis also Revealed possible instabilities in a PORS–DBIS coalition because each of the parties was opposed to a freeway element backed by the other. However, it seemed that this potential conflict between PORS and DBIS was of subsidiary importance compared to the main issue—the general subway–freeway controversy.

Our final decision as to how to deal with this main issue involved dividing the players into two types—those which could be seen as making "political" decisions (i.e. as being willing to shift their preferences in order to make a "deal" etc.), such as PORS, ICRS, and, CONS, and those which exercised relatively constant pressure on PORS in favor of their interests, such as SCIS and DBIS. Of course, different departments of the government, such as Congress, the Administration, and even the Bureau of Roads, were all applying pressure on PORS in support of one or the other of the parties involved. The classification of the parties as "constant pressure" or "political decision" types influencing PORS's decision is a useful device for understanding where there is positive continuing pressure for action (through Congress and city government factions whose members voted on fund allocation) and where some parties' power is a reaction to actions by others. We regarded other players as participating in the controversy by exercising pressure on the three "political" parties—PORS, ICRS and CONS—which were taken as our final set of "players".

The next step was to assign options to the players. However, the construction options (for simplicity and without loss of realism, as careful study of the preferences revealed) could be reduced to three major options on which compromise seemed possible: the bridge, the major highway, and the subway. Thus the parties were regarded as having the choice of being for or against three key projects: the 3S Bridge, the NC Freeway (possibly with Air Rights Housing), and the Subway. In addition, it was seen that the ICRS could possibly exercise an "extreme" sanction (civil disturbances) if the freeway were built. The CONS were also given a possible "extreme" sanction againt the bridge—going into litigation. Exercise of these sanctions (disturbances in response to the bridge, litigation against the freeway) was regarded as possible but unlikely.

The players and options used in the analysis are shown in Table 2, also illustrated are two possible outcomes. In Table 2 (and in Tables 3–5) "1" means the option is said to be taken, or pressure is exercised for it; "0" means the option is said to be not taken, or pressure exercised against it. A column of 0s and 1s represents a preference outcome obtained in the analysis by assigning 1 or 0 to each option for each party. An outcome could become a set of possible outcomes if one or more options were assigned a value indicated by a "—", a symbol which means the option may or may not be taken. For example, in the set of all situations in which PORS is for the bridge and against the subway and ICRS is for the bridge, the remaining options are assigned "—". There are 2^{11} possible outcomes;[*] each of these is merely a logical possibility to be considered regardless of the preference patterns mentioned earlier. A party could be advised to change its preference on some options, if it is discovered that by doing so it could obtain cooperation from another party and win the case by a compromise outcome (instead of losing the case by insisting on all its preferences).

TABLE 2. OPTIONS USED IN TWO POSSIBLE OUTCOMES

| Players | Options | Examples of possible outcomes | |
		A	B
PORS	1. 3S Bridge	1	1
	2. NC Freeway	1	1
	3. Subway	1	1
ICRS	4. 3S Bridge	1	1
	5. NC Freeway	1	0
	6. Subway	1	1
	7. Disturbances	0	0
CONS	8. 3S Bridge	0	0
	9. NC Freeway	0	0
	10. Subway	1	1
	11. Litigate	1	0

Note that although a party may not have all its preferences repeated from Table 1 in the assignment of values to its options in the outcome being considered, nevertheless it may prefer that outcome to other outcomes, according to information available on its preferences among a combination of options (see Section 4(c) for a discussion of these). Thus, outcome B, Table 2, is one in which PORS is for the bridge, the freeway, and the subway. ICRS and CONS are for the subway and against the freeway, but ICRS has made a deal with PORS to accept the bridge. There are no disturbances or litigations.

* One should not be dismayed at the large number of possible ways of filling in the columns. The number of possibilities should be organized into 5 to 9 groups of vectors. Research has shown that people can deal with only 5 to 9 bits of information (see Chapter 6, *Solving Problems in the R and D Game*, ed. by D. Allison, or "The magic number seven, plus or minus two" by George A. Miller, *Psych. Review*, vol. 63, Mar. 1956).

It can be seen that each possible column of 1s and 0s represents an alignment of players which, we further assume, will result in a particular construction "package", perhaps accompanied by disturbances and/or litigation. Specifically, we assume the "rule" that a project will actually be built only if PORS and at least one other player are for it. Thus, for example, outcome A would result in a "bridge–freeway–subway" package litigated against by CONS.

As a first step in the analysis of the problem we investigate the stability of a proposed outcome *p* as a solution to the problem. We call such an outcome for the purpose of the analysis the status quo, or starting, position. By using available information on each player, we ask whether this player prefers another outcome *r* to outcome *p*, and given the other players' choices, whether he is able to move to *r* from *p* by changing some of the values on his options. We then need to determine if a player can be deterred from moving to *r* by fear of certain reactions (or sanctions) which others can make by changing some of the values on their options so that the player no longer prefers the resulting outcome to outcome *p*. For a reaction on the part of the others to be called a sanction, it must be true that if the reaction occurred, the player could not, whatever he did to change the values on his own options, return to position *p*—the position from which he started. However, given that a sanction exists, we cannot say that the player will, in fact, be deterred by it. He will be deterred only if to him the sanction is "credible", i.e. if he believes it would be invoked if he made the contemplated move. If each player and each coalition of players is either unable to move to a preferred position or is deterred by fear of the others' reactions, the outcome will be stable. Otherwise, it will be unstable and not a negotiable compromise.

The above procedure is illustrated in Tables 3–5 which show the exact assumptions made. The first outcome investigated for stability was the initial impasse taken as the status quo—no projects under construction due to veto to the subway by PORS and opposition to highways by the other players. In Table 3, sections A–E analyze the stability of this outcome from the viewpoints of each player and of two coalitions of players. It turned out that the initial impasse had a great deal of stability making it a dangerous "trap" into which the players might fall due to lack of agreement.

In Table 3, sections A–C show explicitly that no player can improve on the impasse situation by himself. The rule is, as we have said, that support from PORS plus at least one other player is necessary for any project to be undertaken. Thus Section A, for example, shows the impasse to be stable against moves by PORS alone because the column to the right shows that anything PORS can do given the others' fixed choices is "not preferred" to the impasse. To test the assumption that an outcome is not preferred, we try filling in the "—" spaces with the best possible values (0 or 1) for the player being considered. These values are shown in parentheses beside the "—" spaces. Sections B and C show that the impasse is stable for the other players, too. Thus we need not list all other possible outcomes ($2^{11}-1$) in the preferred and not-preferred columns, for each player to decide the stability of the impasse.

Coalition preferences are defined by the rule that the coalition will prefer an outcome to the status quo if all coalition members prefer it and will not prefer it if any coalition member does not prefer it. Table 3, sections D and E, thus show two possible ways out of the impasse—a coalition of PORS and either ICRS or CONS.

In this and Tables 4 and 5 an arrow to the left shows the direction of movement from the status quo by the indicated party. This is sometimes followed by arrows to the right indicating possible sanctions by the opponents, moving the situation to an outcome not

TABLE 3. STABILITY OF THE CURRENT IMPASSE[a]

	A PORS			B ICRS			C CONS			D PORS–ICRS coalition			E PORS–CONS coalition		
	Preferred	Status quo	Not preferred	Preferred	Status quo	Not preferred	Preferred	Status quo	Not preferred	Preferred	Status quo	Not preferred	Preferred	Status quo	Not preferred
PORS: 3S		1	—(1)		1	1		1	1	1	1	1	0	1	
NC		1	—(1)		1	1		1	1	0	1	0	1	1	
Subway		0	—(0)		0	0		0	0	1	0	1	1	0	
ICRS: 3S		0	0		0	—(0)		0	0	1	0			0	
NC		0	0		0	—(0)		0	0	0	0			0	
Subway		1	1		1	—(1)		1	1	1	1			1	
Disturbances		0	0		0	—(0)		0	0	0	0		0		1
CONS: 3S		0	0		0	0		0	(0)	0	0	0	0	0	
NC		0	0		0	0		0	(0)	0	0	0	1	0	
Subway		1	1		1	1		1	(1)	1	1	1	0	1	
Litigate		0	0		0	0		0	(0)	0	0	0	0	0	

[a] In Section A, PORS's preferences show it cannot unilaterally improve on the present impasse. Also ICRS (in Section B) and CONS (in Section C) cannot unilaterally improve on the present impasse. In Section D, the PORS–ICRS coalition preferences show a possible improvement for both these players—a deal in which ICRS accepts bridge in any return for subway. Section E illustrates, as an alternative to Section D, that the PORS–CONS coalition also has a joint improvement—the subway-freeway deal. Countering this deal is the possible threat of disturbances from ICRS.

TABLE 4. STABILITY OF THE PORS–ICRS AND PORS–CONS COALITIONS[a]

| | PORS–ICRS coalition | | | | | | PORS–CONS coalition | | | | | | | | |
| | A from PORS | | | B from ICRS | | | C from CONS | | | D from CONS | | | E from PORS and ICRS | | |
	Pre-ferred	Status quo	Not pre-ferred	Pre-ferred	Status quo	Not pre-ferred	Pre-ferred	Status quo	Not pre-ferred	Pre-ferred	Status quo	Not pre-ferred	Pre-ferred	Status quo	Not pre-ferred
PORS: 3S	1	1	−(1)		1	1	1	1	−1	0	0	−1	1	0	—
NC	0	0	−(1)		0	0	0	0	−1	1	1	—	0	1	—
Subway	1	1	−(0)		1	1	1	1	0−	1	1	0−	1	1	—
ICRS: 3S	1	1	1	1	1	−(0)	1	1	−1	0	0	−1	1	0	−1
NC	0	0	0	0	0	−(0)	0	0	−1	0	0	—	0	0	—
Subway	1	1	1	1	1	−(1)	1	1	—	1	1	—	1	1	—
Disturbances	0	0	0	0	0	−(0)	0	0	—	0	0	—	0	0	—
CONS: 3S	0	0	0	0	0	0	0	0	—	0	0	—	0	0	—
NC	0	0	0	0	0	0	0	1	—	0	1	—	1	1	—
Subway	1	1	1	1	1	1	1	1	—	1	1	—	1	1	—
Litigate	0	0	0	←	0	0	←	0−	←	←	0−	←←	←	0	←

[a] Section A illustrates the stability of the subway–bridge package for PORS, assuming that PORS finds the subway acceptable if the bridge is built. Section B illustrates the stability of the subway–bridge package for ICRS, assuming that ICRS finds the bridge acceptable if accompanied by just a subway. In Section C to counter the subway–bridge deal CONS may prefer to move to litigation, but as deterrence PORS can threaten to not build the subway. The possible threat by PORS of bridge and freeway but not subway, involves ICRS cooperation in approving the freeway and is therefore not credible. Section D illustrates the improvement for and sanctions against CONS given the PORS–CONS coalition's deal of subway–freeway. Section E shows that to deter the POR—ICRS coalition from upsetting the PORS–CONS deal, CONS's sanction of litigation must be credible to PORS.

preferred to the status quo by the party indicated. In section D, note that the column on the left—the preferred outcome or "improvement" for PORS and ICRS—can be reached by the action of PORS and ICRS, assuming no change in the choices of CONS. ICRS backs the bridge and PORS ceases to back the freeway but backs the subway. In Section E, the PORS–CONS coalition reaches an improvement by PORS ceasing to back the bridge and accepting the subway, while CONS accepts the freeway. In each case, however, there is a reaction to be feared from the excluded player. Against the PORS–ICRS coalition, CONS can litigate—a possible deterrent for PORS. Against the PORS–CONS coalition, ICRS can start disturbances.

The ICRS–CONS coalition, though it has considerable interests in common, can achieve nothing without PORS because of the "rule" that PORS's support is required for any project. Finally, the coalition of all three players cannot move to an improvement, because the impasse is assumed preferred by ICRS to any deal including the freeway (or by CONS to any deal including the bridge), and because the subway alone, although preferred by the others to the impasse, is assumed not preferred by PORS.

To investigate further the two possible compromises leading out of the impasse, we investigate their stability directly. In Table 4, sections A–C, we consider the deal between PORS and ICRS from the viewpoint of each of the three players, and find that it is stable for PORS and ICRS. CONS might prefer to litigate (section C) but the litigation could be countered by the threat of discontinuation of the subway project. If credible, this threat is assumed to be sufficient. Finally, no coalition can find a joint improvement, so this outcome is stable against coalitions of players.

Next, we investigate the stability of the coalition between PORS and CONS in which the subway–freeway deal is developed. Table 4, section D, shows two threats which might deter CONS from defecting from its deal with PORS and blocking the freeway. The first is that PORS might withdraw its support for the subway. The second is the threat of a bridge, which is highly credible since for CONS to defect from its deal with PORS might well lead to a PORS–ICRS coalition involving the bridge.

The subway–freeway deal also appears stable individually for PORS and ICRS. It is less stable, however, against a PORS and ICRS coalition which, as shown in section E, can move to a preferred outcome essentially by setting up the subway–bridge deal we have discussed above. This is countered by the threat of litigation by CONS which is a possible deterrent for PORS.

In Table 5, sections A and B, we investigate the stability of a solution in which PORS gets both bridge and freeway, necessarily with the cooperation of ICRS or CONS, respectively. On the assumption that both ICRS and CONS would prefer nothing at all, which is the present impasse, to the full bridge–freeway–subway deal, this is shown to be quite unstable against an ICRS–CONS coalition. Section A shows the status quo package arrived at via a deal with ICRS; section B shows it resulting from a deal with CONS. Note that in both tables the "—" spaces in the preferred columns tell us that no possible reaction by PORS could deter the ICRS–CONS coalition from moving to the indicated improvement.

Finally, in Table 5, section C, we analyze the stability of the subway-alone solution. It appears unstable against PORS who would prefer not to build a subway if they get nothing else. The only sanction (ICRS disturbances) seems unlikely as a reaction to the PORS subway veto.

TABLE 5. INSTABILITY OF THREE ADDITIONAL SOLUTIONS[a]

	A ICRS–CONS coalition			B ICRS–CONS coalition			C PORS		
	Preferred	Status quo	Not preferred	Preferred	Status quo	Not preferred	Preferred	Status quo	Not preferred
PORS: 3S	—	1	—	—	1	—	—	0	—
NC	—	1	—	—	1	—	—	0	—
Subway	—	1	—	—	1	—	00	1	—
ICRS: 3S	0	1	—	0	0	—	—	0	—
NC	0	1	—	0	0	—	0	0	—
Subway	1	1	—	1	1	—	—	1	—
Disturbances	0	0	—	0	0	—	00	0	1
CONS: 3S	0	0	—	0	1	—	0	0	—
NC	0	0	—	0	1	—	0	0	—
Subway	1	1	—	1	1	—	—	1	—
Litigate	—	0	—	—	0	—	0	0	—

[a] Section A illustrates the instability of the full list against the ICRS–CONS coalition—when ICRS approves the full list, and Section B shows this instability when CONS approves the list. In Section C, if a subway alone is planned, PORS will veto it unless they fear ICRS disturbances.

(c) CONCLUSIONS FROM THE ANALYSIS

The above situation represents a type of game equilibrium which is often dangerous and destructive. This is the so-called "conflict point" at which a player deliberately acts against the others' interests in order to induce them to accept a compromise he prefers. Examples are a stalemate between a buyer and a seller and the prolongation of a war which both sides would prefer to settle (e.g. Vietnam). In the present case, the PORS will not allow building the subway mainly because a subway is desired by the others. Meanwhile, the others, if they cannot have a subway, will not accept construction of the highways desired by the officials. Historically, each side has tended to block the proposal of the other for fear that construction of subways would show that some freeways (e.g. the Three Sisters Bridge) are not needed, or vice versa.

Various compromises are possible. Starting from the present impasse, the first problem is that if a compromise package is to be worked out with PORS, the two players, ICRS and CONS, are in conflict over what the package should be. We found the most stable compromise to be the subway–bridge deal (no freeway) but this compromise is favored by ICRS rather than by CONS.

From our information on the participants' preferences, this solution could plausibly be brought about by a coalition between PORS and ICRS. The threat to this coalition would be the possibility of litigation against the Three Sisters Bridge by CONS (the excluded player). This would affect PORS (who would lose their bridge if the litigation succeeded) rather than ICRS (who would not lose their subway). Thus, the threat might break up the coalition. Nevertheless, this seems the most stable compromise possible.

Another possibility, however, is that a PORS–CONS coalition might form to obtain the compromise preferred by CONS. CONS would accept the construction of the freeway in return for that of the subway. This would be preferred by CONS to the bridge–subway deal, but not by ICRS; indeed, ICRS would prefer nothing (the present impasse). Thus, this solution is not preferred by all three players to the present impasse—only by PORS and CONS. The threat against it would be disturbances (riots, etc.), and refusal to sell land for freeways by ICRS. PORS, in any case, would prefer a successful coalition with ICRS (involving the subway–bridge package) to the freeway–bridge package, mainly because the bridge has become a symbol in a nationwide contention between pro-highway and anti-highway forces.

So far it seems that the conflict is between CONS (white middle class) and ICRS (poor and mainly black), each competing for a favorable deal from PORS. In fact, this is deceptive. ICRS and CONS are only in conflict because PORS insists on a "price" for building the subway, and the players, ICRS and CONS, though they agree on a subway, have disagreements on the price. The main disagreement in preferences we find to be between PORS on the one hand (for highways) and ICRS and CONS (mainly against highways and for a subway). This appears if we look at the best compromise for PORS (3S Bridge–NC Freeway–subway). This is unstable against an ICRS–CONS coalition, which prefers nothing at all to such a package, and can (on our assumptions) obtain it. It appears again if we observe that the subway-alone solution is the most preferred solution by both ICRS and CONS. To obtain it, however, they would have to deter PORS from vetoing the subway—an action PORS would no doubt prefer to take if the subway came alone. PORS could be deterred by the threat of disturbances from ICRS, but these are perhaps unlikely to result simply from the non-construction of a subway.

To sum up, to move from the present impasse, one of the two players, ICRS or CONS, must be "bought", i.e. they must accept a package deal including some highways, and the price for their acceptance is a subway. In fact, any compromise requires: (1) a subway; (2) the player (ICRS or CONS) "bought" by the subway must prefer the compromise package to nothing at all (i.e. to the present impasse); and (3) if CONS is the player who is "bought", the package must not be likely to evoke disturbances by ICRS.

Of all the compromises investigated, the subway–bridge package seems the most likely to be stable and acceptable. In addition, it is the only compromise possibly preferred by all three players to the present impasse, though this would cease to be so if CONS went into opposition and started to litigate.

(d) EPILOGUE

Congressman Natcher's office in 1971 sent us the *Congressional Record*, May 11, 1971 (pp. H 3755–73) and May 20, 1971 (p. H 4199) to summarize the status of the project 2 years after our 1969 analysis. The impasse is so stable that attempts to get out of it have resulted in grave problems which have led back into it. The city has not agreed to plans to build the freeways; inner-city residents do not want to sell their houses and move out for this purpose.

Work under way on the Three Sisters Bridge (by a 1968 Congressional Act) with a $1 million contract for constructing the piers was halted on August 8, 1970, by Judge John J. Sirica. The grounds were that the present design is so different from that proposed and debated in 1964 that the public should have an opportunity to present their views on the project as presently planned. The Design Hearing was completed on December 16, 1970, after hearing 130 witnesses. The decision was to build an 81-foot model first. The foes of the bridge planned to use the hearing to press their campaign to kill the controversial project. While work on the project was stopped the contractor was to receive $500 a day and $30,000 a month.

Recall that city officials had deleted the bridge and other controversial freeway segments from master plans in late 1968. This resulted in a refusal by the House District Appropriations Subcommittee (Natcher as Chairman) to release subway building funds until the city built roads ordered by Congress. However, excavations of stations and tunnels were begun under the Transportation Act of 1969 and now dot the District.

Delay on the bridge has given ammunition to pro-freeway Congressmen and they have held up appropriations for continued construction of the area subway. The cost of this 98-mile "balanced transportation system" project of highways, subways, and bridge initially (in 1955) estimated at $2.5 billion has recently pushed up to $2.9 billion, and the Washington papers have said that Maryland's Governor, Marvin Mandell, has estimated its costs at $4 billion when completed—hopefully in 1980. Both Maryland and Virginia had hoped to connect some of their interstate highways with those planned for the District. They were also willing to share in the subway costs because it extended into their two states. With the impasse, their contributions will have to be increased because of rising costs. Congressman Natcher pointed out that this is the most expensive public works project in the history of the United States and the world—exceeding by far the costs of the High Aswan Dam, any single public works project undertaken by the Tennessee Valley Authority or by NASA and the Manhattan project during World War II. (There have been eighty-two studies of the District transportation projects at a cost of $20 million.)

In January 1971 the Secretary of Transportation, John A. Volpe, said that he would release $68 million in matching federal funds immediately even though the District's share of subway costs, totaling $34.2 million, remained frozen in the House Appropriations Committee. Later it turned out he could not. The administration, including the President, has been trying hard to get the variety of construction going by exercising diplomacy with Congress and with the city administration and by fighting the Three Sisters Bridge halt. The situation is still deadlocked—back to the original impasse!

(e) GENERAL IMPLICATIONS

Our analysis shows that, given the equal credibility of each party's sanctions, and a possible willingness of each to accept the pain of these sanctions, there are strong structural reasons in the bargaining situation which lead one to expect an impasse. However, pressures for a decision arise from the necessity to proceed with subway financing in this Congress if it is to be any Congress.

In a constructive vein, we should perhaps strive not for an immediate package deal, but for a "sequential" package which would meet the needs of two of the parties by building the subway without hurting PORS. However, recognizing that this will destroy some of PORS's bargaining power, it would be incumbent on the other parties to realistically reconsider their preferences in the light of PORS's interests for the next step in the sequence of bargaining.

In sum, while our conclusions regarding this problem might be obvious to a reader of the Washington newspapers, the analysis has, in fact, clarified the relations of these parties and the feasibility of some possible compromises, in a way that is not explicitly apparent to most observers. Furthermore, if this kind of analysis were introduced at an earlier stage of the controversy before prolonged debates had so sharpened the issues, it might have helped the parties to arrive at a compromise before the situation reached such a parlous state as we find ourselves in today.

The Analysis of Options Technique has been used recently as a framework for a logical, thorough discussion of what stabilities exist in an ongoing political crisis. Once the participants became familiar with the procedure, they took over the assignment of preferences and were able to draw conclusions which it was felt probably would not have been drawn had the problem not been examined within such a broad and thorough context. The fact that the approach does not use quantitative payoffs makes it a very convenient device for translating some useful mathematical ideas from the theory of games to some complex real-life problems. In about ten applications under varying circumstances, in which the participants ranged from decision-makers to advisors, one never heard the usual complaint about distorting reality (a complicated social problem) to fit a model. Nevertheless, considerable work remains to be done to make facile use of the model, among a variety of typical problems, available to all interested people.

5. Power Index in Negotiation[7]

In many bargaining situations, the players may form coalitions in various ways. The ability of each player to enter into a winning coalition is in some sense a measure of his strength. For example, one player might be so strong that any coalition formed against him must lose. One way of measuring this, however, is through the Shapley value.

First, let us consider the following negotiation game:

1. There are 5 players called small (S).
2. There are 2 players called big (B).
3. The following coalitions formed among these players win the game:

    (a) 2B players and at least 1S player,
    (b) 1B player and at least 3S players,
    (c) 5S players.

The game follows the following cycle:

Step 0. The seven players negotiate among themselves until a winning coalition can be formed with each member of the coalition in agreement with respect to his share of the prize.

Step 1. The coalition is registered. Ten-minute timer is started.

Step 2. The players, which are not members of the registered coalition, try to break up the coalition by offering more attractive coalitions to the members of the registered coalition. All the players can negotiate during this step to protect their positions or to try to improve them.

There are two possible results of this step:

(a) The registered coalition stands for 10 minutes. In this case the game is over and the prize is divided as agreed.

(b) The coalition is broken and a new one is formed. The game is then continued from step 1. The value of this game to each of the players may be computed in a number of ways. A simple way to perform the analysis is to look on the game as a "Voting Game" and then to compute the Power Index (P.I.) of each player assuming that the value of the game to each player is proportional to his P.I.

In order to compute the P.I. of a player we must consider all orderings of the players and then the number of times a player casts the Pivotal vote divided by the total number of orderings will be his P.I. From the symmetry of the game, the 5 small players have the same P.I. as do the 2 big players. Thus there are effectively only

$$21 = \left(\frac{7!}{2!\,5!}\right) \text{orderings}$$

of the B and S players (each standing for 5! 2! equivalents). We can thus enumerate these orderings and compute PI(S) and PI(B). The pivotal voter in each case is parenthesized.

ØRDER (pivotal voter in parentheses)	PIVØTAL by an S	VØTE by a B	
BB(S)SSSS	×		Partial totals:
BS(B)SSSS		×	7 pivotal votes cast by S players.
BSS(B)SSS		×	
BSS(S)BSS	×		4 pivotal votes cast by B players.
BSS(S)SBS	×		
BSS(S)SSB	×		
SB(B)SSSS		×	
SBS(B)SSS		×	
SBS(S)BSS	×		
SBS(S)SBS	×		
SBS(S)SSB	×		11 types of orders considered to here

Thomas L. Saaty

ORDER	PIVOTAL by S	VOTE by B	(Pivotal voter is parenthesized in each ordering)
SSB(B)SSS		×	
SSB(S)BSS	×		
SSB(S)SBS	×		
SSB(S)SSB	×		(Note the predominance of 1B–3S type coalitions.)
SSS(B))BSS		×	
SSS(B)SBS		×	
SSS(B)SSB		×	
SSSS(B)BS		×	
SSSS(B)SB		×	
SSSS(S)BB	×		
Totals this page	4	6	
Totals previous page	7	4	
Totals	11	10	

Thus

$$PI(S) = \frac{1}{5}\left(\frac{11}{21}\right) = \frac{2.2}{21}$$

(there are 5 equivalent S players)

and

$$PI(B) = \frac{1}{2}\left(\frac{10}{21}\right) = \frac{5}{21}$$

(there are 2 equivalent B players).

Finally, if one played such a game with a $27 payoff, for example, the value of the game to a B-player would be

$$\frac{5}{21}(27) \cong \$6.43$$

and the value of the game to an S-player would be

$$\frac{2.2}{21}(27) \cong \$2.83.$$

Shapley has studied the measurement of power (and obtains the same answer for the above game) advancing a very useful notion of solution for an *n*-person game. To develop the ideas we need some definitions.

A characteristic function *v* assigns a value $v(C)$ to every coalition *C*. A coalition is a subset of the set *n* of all players. A characteristic function is assumed to satisfy the following conditions:

(A) $v(O) = 0$ [O is the empty set],

(B) *superadditivity:*

$$\text{for } C_1 \cap C_2 = O \qquad v(C_1 \cup C_2) \geq v(C_1) + v(C_2).$$

The Shapley value is an *a priori* assessment of the chances of a player in a characteristic function game. It is based on a system of axioms, e.g. (1) efficiency, (2) symmetry, (3) additivity.

The Shapley value can be described as an average over the player's marginal contribution $v(c) - v(C - (i))$ to a coalition C with $i \in C$.

For characteristic functions with a small number of players a simple tabular method can be used in order to compute the Shapley value.

Determination of the number of sequences such that player i contributes to a fixed coalition C with $i \in C$. Such sequences have the following structure:

$$\ldots . i \ldots$$

$|C|$ is the number of players in C,
$(|C| - 1)!$ is the number of such sequences,
L_i denotes the set of all C with $i \in C$.

$$\underbrace{|C| - 1}_{\text{players before } i} \quad n - |C|}_{\text{players after } i}$$

The formula for the Shapley-value to player i is given by:

$$S_i = \sum_{C \varepsilon L_i} \frac{(|C| - 1)! \, (n - |C|)!}{n!} \, [v(C) - v(C - (i))].$$

TABLE 6. COMPUTATIONAL TABLE FOR THE SEVEN-PERSON DEMONSTRATION GAME DUE TO R. SELTEN

Coalition type (no. of big, no. of small)	Number of coalitions with Player I	$\dfrac{(\lvert C\rvert - 1)!(n - \lvert C\rvert)!}{n!}$	$v(C) - v(C - (i))$	$S_1 = S_2$ (product of 3 columns)
(2,1)	5	$\frac{1}{105}$	27	$\frac{135}{105}$
(2,2)	10	$\frac{1}{140}$	27	$\frac{270}{140}$
(2,3)			0	0
(2,4)			0	0
(2,5)				0
(1,3)	10	$\frac{1}{140}$	27	$\frac{270}{140}$
(1,4)	5	$\frac{1}{105}$	27	$\frac{135}{105}$
(1,5)			0	0
(0,5)			0	0

$$S_1 = S_2 = 6\tfrac{3}{7} \approx 6.43,$$

$$S_3 = S_4 = S_5 = S_6 = S_7 = \frac{27 - 2 \times 6.43}{5} = 2\tfrac{29}{35} \approx 2.83.$$

6. Cooperative Solutions to n-person Games[22]

H. Scarf has proved the existence of cooperative solutions for a certain important class of games. Consider an n-person game in which the first player has a set of possible strategies X^1, the second player X^2, etc. A typical strategy for player i will be denoted by a lower case x^i, an arbitrary element of the set X^i. We shall make only the following assumption about these strategies:

1. Each X^i is assumed to be a closed bounded convex set in a finite-dimensional Euclidean space.

The significant aspect of this assumption is the requirement that each strategy-set be convex; the remaining qualifications are technical and in particular the assumption that each strategy set be contained in a finite-dimensional Euclidean space can be relaxed.

The ith player is assumed to have a utility function $u_i(x)$ describing his preferences in the sense that, given an arbitrary pair of states x and x', he will prefer the outcome with the higher utility.

The preferences are assumed to satisfy:

2a. Each $u_i(x)$ is a continuous function of x.
2b. The utility functions $u_i(x)$ are quasi-concave.

In other words if x and x' are two possible states, and α is between 0 and 1, then

$$u_i(\alpha x + (1 - \alpha)x') \geq \min[u_i(x), u_i(x')].$$

Then the following theorem is proved.

Theorem. *In an* n-*person game satisfying 1 and 2, there will be at least one joint strategy choice* $x^1, \ldots, x^n$, *which is in equilibrium in the sense that no coalition has an alternative strategy which guarantees higher utility levels for all of its members, independently of the actions of the complementary coalition.*

Scarf points out that this solution concept has both merits and defects. On the positive side, the above theorem implies that the concept can be applied successfully to a large class of easily recognizable games. (Regardless of its other characteristics, a method of solution is of little value if the corresponding set of outcomes is empty for most games.) In addition, the solution is cooperative in nature, permitting coalitions to act collectively in ways consistent with their perceived interests. For example, these solutions have the property, generally not possessed by Nash equilibrium points and other non-cooperative solutions, that there is no alternative strategy choice that will improve all of the players' utility levels simultaneously. And this cooperative aspect is achieved in a purely ordinal framework, so that none of the obscure assumptions of transferable and comparable utility, which have characterized so much of game theory, are required.

The major drawback to the solution is in its excessively conservative treatment of threats. A coalition S, in attempting to obtain an improved position for all of its members, must confront the entire range of strategic possibilities open to the players not in S, including those which lead to disastrous consequences for the complementary coalition and would in all probability not be undertaken. This inability to discriminate among counter-responses reduces the opportunities of a coalition to object to the status quo, and results in the inclusion of more outcomes in the solution than might seem reasonable.

In order to overcome this problem, the responses of the complementary coalition would have to be restricted by considerations of plausibility. There is no way known for doing this within the general framework discussed here. It is perhaps best to err in the direction of including more rather than fewer outcomes in the solution, and then applying *ad hoc* criteria to any specific example in order to obtain a further reduction.

7. Inspection and Verification[22]

The following example has its origins in international inspection and verification systems for weapon-limitation purposes. However, it applies to inspection of production facilities with regard to environmental pollution or even to the sanitary conditions in a food-processing plant.

Under an arms control or disarmament agreement, inspection and verification take the form of a complex set of rules which define the options available to the inspector and which are designed to circumscribe counteractions available to the inspected party. Depending on the nature of the agreement and the type of activity to be controlled, the actions available to the inspector must be designed to provide a maximum amount of reliable information with a minimum amount of intrusion. To achieve this the inspector may have to make use of sampling procedures which can produce reliable inferences from partial inspection of the total statistical population involved. For each inspection or verification procedure adopted by the inspector, the inspected party can adopt counter-measures designed to thwart or evade the purposes of the inspector. Arms control and disarmament agreements, therefore, produce complex situations to which traditional statistical theory has not been applied.

Maschler has treated the interesting case in which the violator considers the violation important enough to be conducted when he is sure that it is not inspected, but the inspection has some deterrent power and the violator will refrain if he is sure that inspection will follow. This is the most complicated case, because it leads to a non-constant-sum game.

A complete solution to this problem is provided where the best way of using the r inspections is given. It is proved that if the inspector uses this recommended strategy, and if the violator acts rationally (i.e. to maximize his own payoff) then the violator's payoff (in utility units) will essentially be his minimum possible payoff (i.e. that payoff which he can always guarantee for himself) and the inspector's payoff will be his maximum possible payoff.

Verbally stated—the inspector's best strategy is *to announce in advance* that he is going to act essentially in a way which is strictly opposing to the interests of the violator (i.e. he should announce that he will play essentially a minimax strategy based on the payoff matrix of the violator), but that he will modify slightly his strategy so that it will be most advantageous for the violator to keep to the wait-until-all-the-available-inspections-have-been-used-up-and-then-conduct-a-violation-if-there-are-any-events-left strategy.

It may seem surprising that the inspector should announce his *mixed* strategy in advance (i.e. that the inspector announces what his probabilities of inspecting an event at each stage will be, given that such and such combinations of the various signals occur. The following is a simple example to show that sometimes it is even advantageous to announce a pure strategy.

Consider two players, each having two available pure strategies called "1" and "2". Suppose that if both use the same strategy then each obtains $100 whereas if they use opposing strategies each looses $100. We illustrate this as follows:

	1		2	
1	100,	100	−100,	−100
2	−100,	−100	100,	100

It is assumed that, as far as the inspector is concerned, the main purpose of the treaty is that it be obeyed. In other words: the inspector would prefer that the terms are kept, over a situation in which a violation occurs and it is inspected. Needless to say that *if* a violation should occur—the inspector prefers that it be inspected.

What is the best way of using the *r* available inspections, taking into account the information obtained from the various detectors? The answer depends on the advantages that the violator expects to obtain from conducting a violation. If a violation is extremely important to him so that he will violate even in the face of a sure inspection, then a violation must occur and the only task the inspector has is to increase his probability of inspecting.

Taking the other extreme case in which the violator himself prefers not to conduct a violation even if he is sure that such a violation is not inspected we note that no violation will occur and no inspection is necessary. In this case all inspection procedures will yield the same payoff.

In this case it is advantageous for each player to announce his pure strategy in advance. This is a case where the interests of the players are completely parallel. In the inspector's game the interests are neither completely parallel nor are they completely opposing and it is advantageous for each player to announce only his mixed strategy in advance. (It is not difficult to give examples of other games in which it is *not* advantageous to one player or to both players to announce even a mixed strategy.) Fortunately for the inspector, he can be the first player who announces his mixed strategy. If the violator were to announce a strategy, this would make it a different game.

Every mathematical model of a real situation necessarily makes simplifying assumptions. These assumptions are clearly stated in the papers cited and their merits and demerits are discussed. Here are some merits for this model:

1. The results are quite general and can be used also for treaties other than test-ban treaties.

2. The author succeeds in combining outcomes provided by various detectors working dependently or independently.

3. The fact that the method works for a wide class of situations gives rise to the hope that it can be applied to more complicated situations.

4. Even though the game is not constant-sum, and there are no convincing theories to treat such games, in this particular case a solution is given which is mathematically as sound as the minimax solution recommended by constant-sum games. Some weaknesses of this model are:

1. The optimal strategy for the inspector depends on the estimate of how important it is for the violator to violate. Utility theory shows how to measure this factor, but, in general, the violator will not furnish the information. The results are therefore reliable only if the intelligence service has enough reliable information concerning this factor.

2. It has been assumed that natural events as well as violations cause the detectors to produce signals with given *fixed* probabilities. This may not be the case, especially in test-ban treaties. Various detonations (natural and intentional) are possible as well as various kinds of tests, and therefore the division of events into two groups, "violations" and "natural events", may not be the best thing to do. The author expresses the belief that his method will work in a more general context, and that those authorities who possess more technical information will be able to construct similar and better models.

3. The model assumes only one possible violation during the *n* events. If *n* is small enough—say the number of expected events during a year—perhaps it is reasonable to assume that the violator will not benefit much and the inspector will not lose much if more than one violation takes place. This may or may not be the case.

4. The real-life case of test-ban treaties is not a one-shot game. It is a sequence of games

of the above type with varying degrees of utility (it makes a difference if a violation occurs tomorrow or after 100 years). The utilities for conducting several violations cannot be simply the sum of the utilities for each single violation. Moreover, one has to take into account future discoveries as well as changes in the political atmosphere. This general situation requires extensive study which is quite involved, if not insurmountable. Altogether, if n is small enough—it is not a bad approximation to treat each game separately as is the case in the research on this model.

5. Of course, different types of treaties give rise to different games. For example, specifying r inspections within a year instead of in each set of n events can be treated in similar fashion if one knows the probability distribution of the various earthquakes in different locations. The calculations in this case have to be worked out. It is not clear *a priori* that the same type of optimal strategy will work.

8. Resolving the Priority Conflict Problem[21]

As a final example, we consider a problem involving the allocation of a scarce resource—in this case, electricity—to users, each of which believes that he is entitled to as much as he needs. The conflict is in the distinct (and incompatible) priorities which these users assign. The decision-maker must come up with a defensible uniform prioritization with which to determine allocations.

In developing voluntary and mandatory power-allocation strategies, the utility is confronted with the problem of determining priorities of classes of end use. A power-allocation model has been developed to establish a means of prioritizing electric power demands.

The purpose of the model is to provide a quantitative measure of the impact of each electricity-consuming activity on different goals and also to derive an overall measure of the importance of the activity for all goals. For example, preliminary work on the model focused on national goals such as improving the economy, environment, health, education, and national security. The activities for which priorities were needed were groups of industries classified as presented by the Standard Industrial Classification Code.

There are various approaches to prioritization. Although all such schemes are based on data derived in the form of judgments and then analyzed according to some criterion to develop the desired priorities, our comparison shows that the mathematical model described here has sophisticated refinements and enables us to approach the subject with better understanding of the judgmental process involved in priority assignment.

Since it is difficult to present the full analysis of the electrical allocation problem, as it requires considerable space, what we have done here is to present a brief description of the methodology.

The model involves the use of hierarchies of sets. The elements of each level comprise the goals of the immediately lower level. The elements of the lower level are ranked according to their impact on each element of the next higher level. The results are then appropriately weighted and combined with input–output data; then they are used as components of a linear programming allocation model.

The question of how to define the hierarchy of activities and goals requires careful study for each problem. Many discussions and meetings with interested people were held to define and review the hierarchy used in the study. How to elicit numerical comparisons from individuals providing the judgments is also a delicate task that requires considerable

Thomas L. Saaty

deliberation and discussion. A preliminary study is required to determine those properties of the activities to be taken into consideration which have bearing on the goals. For example, in the case of pollution the amounts of pollutants released by each activity, and its impact on the environment, give a basis for ranking their relative importance in the pollution-goal matrix. One needs to understand carefully the extent to which activity has any of these properties and then set out to compare the activities numerically.

Our priority system requires judgments to be supplied by questioning personnel expert in the uses of electricity and knowledgeable about the contribution of consuming activities to national goals. These judgments indicate the relative importance of one activity over another for each of the several goals being considered based on a numerical scale from 1 to 9.

In constructing a scale of importance, one customarily asks a decision-maker to state (a) which of two activities, in his opinion, is more important, and (b) his perception of this intensity of difference in importance, expressed as a rank number on an ordered category scale.[62, 65] Importance here is an indication of the direct effects of the activities on the goals. The indirect effects are considered later using input–output relations.

As a preliminary step towards the construction of an intensity scale of importance for activities, we have broken down the categories as in Table M.

TABLE 7

Intensity of importance	Definition	Explanation
1	Equal importance	Two activities contribute equally to the objective
3	Importance of one over another	There is judgment favoring one activity over another but is not conclusive
5	Essential or strong importance	Good judgment and logical criteria show that one is more important
7	Demonstrated importance	Conclusive judgment as to the importance of one activity over another
9	Absolute importance	The judgment in favor of one activity over another is of the highest possible order of affirmation

Note that we have included an intensity of 9 to denote the absolute conclusiveness of judgment favoring the dominance of one activity over another. Numbers between the ones given above are allowed to show shades of importance between two given categories.

In constructing the matrix of judgments, we observe that if activity A is assigned the value 6 when compared with B, then B is usually assigned the value $1/6$ when compared with A. For each goal a matrix is generated by comparing the activities in pairs. Thus, each matrix has unit entries on the diagonal whereas symmetrically located elements off the diagonal are reciprocals of each other. Note that we are not dealing with a win–lose situation, but rather with relative magnitude or relative strength. Generally, this precludes the use of zeros, unless of course two activities cannot be compared directly. However, the two activities could inherit a relationship other than zero through intermediate activities. Our problem is analogous to comparison of star brightness or the cost of an object. One star (object) may be several times brighter (more expensive) than another and hence the other has the reciprocal brightness (cost) relative to the first. Each star (object) compared with itself must have unit value; similarly for activities. Thus, we do not use negative numbers but reciprocals. Note that people may not judge with numerical consistency and may not assign the exact reciprocal.

We do not insist that judgments be internally consistent (although we examine consistency) and hence they need not be transitive, i.e. if A is preferred to B and B to C, A need not be preferred to C, a common occurrence in human judgments.

One uses the resulting matrix of pairwise comparisons to determine the relative weights of the activities. This turns out to be an eigenvalue problem in which one solves for the largest eigenvalue (a unique value for this type of matrix[21]) and normalizes its corresponding eigenvector (which is also unique if the matrix is irreducible). The eigenvector is a priority vector of activities with respect to a particular goal. The normalized eigenvectors of the activities corresponding to the goals form a matrix. This matrix is multiplied by the corresponding normalized eigenvector of the matrix of goals, yielding the final overall priority vector.

Once these relative weights are obtained, they are used as coefficients in an objective function of a linear program whose corresponding variables, give the level of output (in dollars) of the activities after the allocation of electrical energy. The constraints of this linear program require that the sum of the allocated energy lies within a postulated available amount. In this phase, we will have the occasion to use total electric energy coefficients signifying the amount of electric energy required to bring a single dollar of output to final users, in order to convert dollar figures to energy figures. In addition, equations representing the interdependence of activities must be incorporated in order to prevent bottlenecks. These equations may be formulated using input–output coefficients. The result of the linear program is the total level of output (in dollars) of every industry after the allocation, and this may be converted to appropriate energy figures.

9. Conclusion

A main goal of human society today might be described as making it more and more possible for individuals and nations to pursue their goals as freely as possible. This is a natural corollary of freedom and democratization. However, it carries with it the penalty of increasing conflicts. As the problems increase in difficulty and complexity, we shall be increasingly dependent on sophisticated and efficient techniques for the resolution of conflicts. Undoubtedly, part of the solution will involve a much greater willingness to compromise.

References

1. Aumann, R. J. and Maschler, M. "Game theoretic aspects of gradual disarmament." In *Development of Utility Theory for Arms Control and Disarmament*, Contract No. ACDA/ST-80 with *Mathematica*, Princeton, New Jersey, 1966.
2. Bain, H., Howard, N., and Saaty, T. L. "Using the analysis of options technique to analyze a community conflict." *Journal of Conflict Resolution*, **15**, No. 2.
3. Harsanyi, J. "Game theory and the analysis of international conflicts." *The Australian Journal of Politics and History*, Dec. 1965.
4. Howard, N. *The Theory of Metagames*, Doctoral Thesis, University of London, 1968.

5. Howard, N. "Metagame analysis of Vietnam policy." *Peace Research Society: Papers* (*International*), **10**, 1968. Also in W. Isard (ed.), *Vietnam: Some Issues and Alternatives*, Schenkman, Mass., 1969.
6. Howard, N. *Games, Metagames and Rationality*, M.I.T. Press, Mass., 1971.
7. Luce, R. Duncan and Raiffa, Howard. *Games and Decisions*, John Wiley & Sons, Inc., New York, Second Printing 1958.
8. Management Science Center, University of Pennsylvania, *The Analysis of Options: a computer aided method of analyzing political problems*, Vol. 2, of Report ACDA/ST-49, prepared for the United States Arms Control and Disarmament Agency, 1969.
9. McGuire, Martin C. *Secrecy and the Arms Race*, Howard University Press, 1965.
10. McKinsey, J. C. C. *Introduction to the Theory of Games*, McGraw-Hill Book Co., New York, 1952.
11. Nash, John. "Non-cooperative games." *Annals of Maths*, **54**, No. 2 (Sept. 1951).
12. Rapoport, A. *Fights, Games and Debates*, University of Michigan Press, Ann Arbor, 1960.
13. Rapoport, A. *Two-Person Game Theory: The Essential Ideas*, The University of Michigan Press, Ann Arbor, 1966.
14. Rapoport, A. *N-Person Games*, The University of Michigan Press, Ann Arbor, 1970.
15. Richardson, L. F. *Statistics of Deadly Quarrels*, Chicago, Quadrangle Books, 1960.
16. Richardson, L. F. *Arms and Insecurity*, Pittsburgh, Boxwood Press, 1960.
17. Saaty, Thomas L. *Mathematical Methods of Operations Research*, McGraw-Hill, 1959.
18. Saaty, Thomas L. "A model for the control of arms." *Operations Research*, **12**, 586–609 (July–Aug. 1964).
19. Saaty, Thomas L. *Mathematical Models of Arms Control and Disarmament*, John Wiley, 1968.
20. Saaty, Thomas L. and Long, P. J. *Mathematical Foundation of the Stability of Deterrence*, The Arms Control and Disarmament Agency, Jan. 1968.
21. Saaty, Thomas L. *An Eigenvalue Method for Prioritization and Planning*, in publication 1974.
22. Several reports for the Arms Control and Disarmament Agency by Contractors notably by the University of Pennsylvania ACDA/ST-64, 94, 127, 149, 1964–9 (all concerned with escalation of conflicts) and by *Mathematica*, ACDA/ST-3, 37, 80, 116, 143, 1962–8 (ST 3 and 37 are concerned with inspection and verification, the others with negotiations).
23. Schelling, T. C. *The Strategy of Conflict*, Harvard University Press, Cambridge, 1960.
24. von Neumann, John and Morgenstern, Oskar. *Theory of Games and Economic Behavior*, Princeton University Press, Princeton, New Jersey, 1944.
25. Wiesner, Jerome B. "A strategy for arms control." *Saturday Review*, **50**, 17–20 (Mar. 1967).
26. Williams, J. D. *The Compleat Strategyst*, McGraw-Hill Book Co., New York, 1954.

About the Authors

SAMUEL J. BERNSTEIN

Dr Bernstein is a University professor and chairman of the Department of Public Administration, Baruch College of The City of New York. Formerly he was consultant to the Executive Office of the President, Washington, DC on social and economic model building; the Department of Transportation Planning of The Polytechnic Institute of New York and assistant professor of Political Science at Yeshiva University, and the University of Rochester. Dr Bernstein has published in various journals including *Traffic Quarterly*, the *Journal of Socio-Economic Planning Sciences*, *Policy Sciences*, the *Western Political Quarterly*, and *Polity*. He is editor and author of *Computers in Public Administration*.

Dr Bernstein has an extensive background in the social sciences and the methodologies of quantitative social research with particular emphasis on policy studies.

W. GILES MELLON

Dr Mellon is Professor of Business Administration and Area Chairman for Finance at the Graduate School of Business Administration of Rutgers University. A Princeton Ph.D. in Economics and a former member of the Princeton Economics faculty, Dr. Mellon was, prior to joining the Rutgers faculty, a second vice-president and the Financial Economist of the Chase Manhattan Bank. Dr. Mellon is the author of numerous publications in the areas of economics, banking, and public policy and is currently an Economic Consultant to the Irving Trust Company.

JULIUS SURKIS

Dr. Surkis is an Associate Professor in the Graduate School of Business Administration at Rutgers University. He was an Assistant Professor in the Industrial and Management Engineering Department at Columbia University prior to his present position. He holds a Ph.D. in Operations Research from the Polytechnic Institute of Brooklyn, an M.S. in Operations Research from Stevens Institute of Technology, another M.S. in Civil Engineering from Michigan State University, and a B.S. in Civil Engineering from Robert College, Istanbul, Turkey. Some of his research interests are: modeling of social systems—urban emergency systems, health care delivery systems; optimization theory; statistical simulation techniques. He is active as a consultant to industry in the areas of simulation, design of production and inventory control systems. Prior to his academic career, Dr. Surkis had 10 years of full-time industry experience, the last of which was as manager of Management Science Technology, UNIVAC, Division of Sperry Rand Corporation.

JOHN H. HERDER

Dr. Herder, a former college president and corporate executive, heads Herder Associates, Inc., Hamden, Connecticut, a management consulting organization specializing in human resource development and organization problems. Dr. Herder has conducted organization studies of more than a dozen police departments in the New England area, including New Haven, Connecticut, Springfield and Amherst, Massachusetts. He lives with his family in North Haven, Connecticut.

ISRAEL PRESSMAN

Dr. Pressman is an assistant Professor of Statistics at the Baruch College of the City University of New York teaching courses in Statistics and Operations Research. Previously he was an Assistant Professor of Operations and Research at the Polytechnic Institute of Brooklyn.

Dr. Pressman has served as a consultant to the American Telephone and Telegraph Company, the New York Police Department, the Advanced Computer Techniques Corporation and Applied Urban Systems, Inc., working on problems of Mathematical Economics, Operations Research, Statistical Analyses, and Educational Evaluations. He has also presented seminars and lectures on Linear Programming, Mathematical Economics, and Statistical Methods and Techniques.

He has published several articles on the Theory of the Firm, Peak Load Pricing, Crime, Computer-Assisted Instruction, and Planning Urban Health Facilities. He has recently submitted articles relating to Inventory Theory, Design Theory, and Evaluating Community Educational Programs.

JAMES McPARTLAND

Dr. James McPartland is Co-Director of the Center for Social Organization of Schools at Johns Hopkins University and Associate Professor of Social Relations. He is a co-author of the well-known national studies of education, *Equality of Educational Opportunity* (the Coleman Report) and *Racial Isolation in the Public Schools* and has published several monographs and articles in the field of sociology of education. Related to the topic of the present chapter, he assisted the Maryland State Department of Education in designing a state-wide school assessment and accountability program to assist the work of local educational planners.

EDMUND J. CANTILLI

Dr. Cantilli, Associate Professor of Transportation Planning and Engineering at the Polytechnic Institute of New York, is a graduate of Columbia, Yale, and the Polytechnic. After many years with the Port of New York Authority as a planner and engineer, he joined the faculty of the Polytechnic in 1969. He has taught and teaches many courses in transportation and urban planning, including traffic engineering, urban planning, urban geography, land-use planning, transportation safety, and environmental aspects of planning. He is a fellow of the American Society of Civil Engineers and the Institute of Traffic Engineers, and a full member of the American Institute of Planners, the American Society of Planning Officials, the American Society of Safety Engineers, and other national and international organizations. He is a professional engineer and a professional planner.

IRA SHARKANSKY

Ira Sharkansky is a Professor of Political Science at the Hebrew University of Jerusalem and the University of Wisconsin-Madison. His fields of interest are public administration, policy analysis, state politics, and urban affairs. Among his books are *Urban Politics and Public Policy* (with Robert L. Lineberry); *Public Administration: Policy-making in Government Agencies*: and *The United States: A Study of a Developing Country*.

THOMAS L. SAATY

Dr. Saaty is professor and chairman of the Department of Operations Research at the University of Pennsylvania. Among his many (outstanding) books are *Mathematical Methods in Operations Research* (1959) translated into Russian and Japanese and *Elements of Queuing Theory with Applications* (1969), translated into Russian, Spanish, and German. In addition he has authored and/or edited ten additional books in the area of applied mathematics. His articles, which number more than 100, have appeared in a variety of scholarly journals. Dr. Saaty's contributions to mathematical applications in the physical, biological and social sciences are of singular importance.

JEROME ROTHENBERG

Professor Rothenberg is Professor of Economics at the Masschusetts Institute of Technology. He has authored seven books in the areas of public sector economics, urban economics, housing utility theory, and welfare economics. In addition to his outstanding scholarly work Professor Rothenberg has been consultant to the Bendix Corporation, Rand Corporation, HUD, DOT, among others. During 1973–4 he was an Academic Visitor in London School of Economics.

ELCHANAN COHN

Professor Cohn is currently Professor of Economics at the College of Business Administration, University of South Carolina. A graduate of the University of Minnesota (BA, MA) and Iowa State University (Ph.D.), he taught at the Pennsylvania State University from 1968 to 1974. He is the author of four books: *The Economics of Education* (Ballinger, 1975; originally published by Heath, 1972), *Public Expenditure Analysis* (Heath, 1972), *Economics of State Aid to Education* (Heath, 1974), and *Input–Output Analysis in Public Education* (Ballinger, 1975). Author or co-author of several research monographs, he has published widely in professional journals in economics, business, and education. During 1968 through 1970 he participated in a project at Penn State which attempted to evaluate the success of the Concentrated Employment Program in Columbus, Ohio. He has served as a consultant to the South Carolina Commission on Higher Education and other private organizations.

C. GLYN WILLIAMS

Professor Williams is a Professor of Economics at the University of South Carolina. A graduate of the University of Wales (B.A.), Manchester University (M.A.), and the University of Virginia (Ph.D.), he has taught at the University of Alberta (Edmonton), Indiana University, and Boston College. He is the author of *Labor Economics* (Wiley, 1970). He has authored or co-authored research monographs in labor economics on the impact of technological change on Canadian railroad employment, on the changing structures of the labor force over time, and wage and price analysis. Among other duties he is currently supervising a project to investigate the feasibility of constructing a data bank for the evaluation of capital expenditure proposals by hospitals participating in a cost-savings reimbursement program sponsored by the Social Security Administration.

RICHARD M. WALLACE

Dr. Wallace is currently a Ph.D. student in Economics at the College of Business Administration, University of South Carolina, where he is also serving as the Assistant to the Director of the Center for Studies in Human Capital, Bureau of Business and Economic Research. He holds the A.B. degree in History from the University of South Carolina.

JANET C. HUNT

Dr. Hunt is currently a Ph.D. student in economics at the College of Business Administration, University of South Carolina. She holds the B.S. degree in marketing and economics from the University of South Carolina.

THOMAS GALE MOORE

Dr. Thomas G. Moore is a Senior Fellow at the Hoover Institution at Stanford University. Formerly he was Professor of Economics at Michigan State University, a position he held since 1969. He received his B.A. from the George Washington University, and his M.A. and Ph.D. degrees in Economics from the University of Chicago. From 1960 to 1961, he was a foreign research analyst for the Chase Manhattan Bank, and from 1961 to 1965 an Assistant Professor at the Carnegie Institute of Technology. In 1965 Professor Moore became an Associate Professor at Michigan State University, and served as a Senior Staff Economist of the Council of Economic Advisors from 1968 to 1970. Professor Moore has served as a consultant to various private and governmental bodies, and is the author of numerous books and articles, including *The Economics of the American Theater*.

Author Index

Albin, P. S.   51
Allen, David   169
Allerand, M. E.   55, 57
Allison, Graham   266
Alonso, Walter   70
Alper, Benedict Soloman   177
Altman, S.   179

Bain, Henry   261, 262
Banfield, Edward   37, 57, 251
Barth, P. S.   51, 57
Batty, Joseph   5, 9
Baumol, William J.   220, 221, 222, 223, 224, 229, 232, 233, 234
Bell, Colin E.   169, 171
Beltrami, E.   179, 181, 183
Berlin, Moses   155
Bernstein, Samuel J.   3, 5, 25, 26, 151
Bernstein, A. Isaac   25
Betz, J. M.   182
Blum, Edward   152, 153, 168
Blumberg, Donald F.   5, 21, 22
Bodin, Larry   183
Bonini, Charles P.   130
Bowen, William G.   220, 221, 222, 223, 224, 229, 232, 233, 234
Bradford, David R.   4
Brehm, C. T.   51
Brown, G. F.   54
Broyhill, Joel T.   264
Burtt, E.   42

Cain, John   51, 53
Cantilli, Edmund J.   97, 107
Carter, G. M.   159, 160, 161, 169
Chaiken, J. M.   157, 161, 169
Charnes, A.   190, 191
Clark, R. M.   175, 177, 183
Clarke, G.   183
Cohn, Elchanan   37, 55, 56
Coyle, John W.   168
Crecine, John P.   9
Cripps, Jeremy H.   5, 9
Crowther, R. F.   195, 211
Cyert, R. M.   130

Danzig, George   183
Davidson, R. H.   56
Deems, John M.   164, 171, 182
DeLeeuw, Frank   72

Dernburg, T.   51
Doeringer, P. B.   44, 46
Dosser, Douglass G.   198

Easton, David   250
Edwards, F. E.   37, 46

Fechter, A.   53, 56
Feldstein, M. S.   55, 56
Ferber, Roman   25
Fitzsimmon, James Albert   165, 166
Flagle, C. D.   129
Foot, Paul   5, 9
Forrester, J. W.   4, 21, 27, 130, 139
Fox, Karl A.   40, 42
Friedlander, S. L.   51, 52
Fuchs, V. R.   47

Gibson, Geoffrey   164
Gilman, H. J.   51
Ginn, J. Royce   10
Goldner, William   4, 8, 9, 41
Goldstein, J. H.   53
Goodman, Y. F. B.   42
Gramm, W. L.   44
Graybill, Franklin A.   9
Greco, J. R.   175, 184
Gronau, R.   44
Guild, R. D.   154

Handelman, Sigmund   3
Harrington, Donald   177
Harrison, B.   44, 46, 50, 51
Hawkins, A. F.   103
Heckman, Y.   44
Hemmens, G. C.   3
Herder, John H.   189
Hill, G. J.   103
Hirsch, W. Z.   172, 173
Hisserich, John C.   163, 164, 171
Hoey, Jan Morris   168
Hogg, J. M.   155, 156
Holt, C. C.   44
Howard, Nigel   261, 262
Hudson, J. F.   182
Hunt, Janet C.   37

Ignall, E.   161, 162, 169, 180, 181

Subject Index

Subject Index